THE PENGUIN CLASSICS

FOUNDER EDITOR (1944–64): E. V. RIEU

PRESENT EDITORS:
Betty Radice and Robert Baldick

JOHANN WOLFGANG GOETHE was born in Frankfort-on-Main in 1749. He studied at Leipzig, where he showed interest in the occult, and at Strassburg, where Herder introduced him to Shakespeare's works and to folk poetry. He produced some essays and lyrical verse, and at twenty-four wrote *Goetz von Berlichingen*, a play which brought him national fame and established him in the current *Sturm und Drang* movement. *Werther*, a tragic romance, was an even greater success.

Goethe began work on *Faust*, and *Egmont*, another tragedy, before being invited to join the government of Weimar. His interest in the classical world led him to leave suddenly for Italy in 1768, and the *Italian Journey* recounts his travels there. *Iphigenie auf Tauris* and *Torquato Tasso*, classical dramas, were begun at this time.

Returning to Weimar, Goethe started the second part of *Faust*, encouraged by Schiller. During this late period he finished his series of *Wilhelm Meister* books and wrote many other works, including *The Oriental Divan*. He also directed the State Theatre and worked on scientific theories in evolutionary botany, anatomy, and colour.

Goethe was married in 1806. He finished *Faust* before he died in 1832.

W. H. AUDEN was born in 1907 and went to Oxford University, where he became Professor of Poetry from 1956 to 1960. After the publication of his *Poems* in 1930, he became the acknowledged leader of the 'thirties poets'. His poetic output is prolific, and he has also written verse plays in collaboration with Christopher Isherwood, with whom he visited China. He has also lived in Berlin. In 1946 he became a U.S. citizen.

ELIZABETH MAYER was born in Mecklenburg in 1884 and emigrated to the U.S. in 1936. In collaboration with Louise Bogan she has translated *Werther* and *Elective Affinities*.

J. W. GOETHE

ITALIAN JOURNEY
[1786-1788]

TRANSLATED BY W. H. AUDEN AND
ELIZABETH MAYER

PENGUIN BOOKS

Penguin Books Ltd, Harmondsworth, Middlesex, England
Penguin Books Australia Ltd, Ringwood, Victoria, Australia

—

This translation first published by Collins 1962
Published in Penguin Classics 1970
Copyright © Wm. Collins, Sons & Co. Ltd, 1962

—

Made and printed in Great Britain
by Hazell Watson & Viney Ltd,
Aylesbury, Bucks
Set in Linotype Juliana

Quotations from Goethe's letters in the
Introduction are reprinted from Letters from Goethe,
translated by Dr M. Herzfeld and C. A. M. Sym,
by permission of the Edinburgh University Press

CONTENTS

INTRODUCTION *by W. H. Auden and Elizabeth Mayer* 7

ITALIAN JOURNEY

PART ONE

From Carlsbad to the Brenner, *September 1786* 23
From the Brenner to Verona, *September 1786* 36
From Verona to Venice, *September 1786* 52
Venice, *October 1786* 74
From Ferrara to Rome, *October 1786* 105
Rome, *First Roman Visit, October 1786–February 1787* 128

PART TWO

Naples, *February–March 1787* 179
Sicily, *March–May 1787* 223
Naples, *May–June 1787* 309

PART THREE

Rome, *Second Roman Visit, June 1787–April 1788* 343
June 1787 345
July 1787 358
August 1787 373
September 1787 383
October 1787 397
November 1787 415
December 1787 425
January 1788 440
February 1788 471
March 1788 478
April 1788 487

INDEX 499

INTRODUCTION

EVERYBODY knows that the thrones of European Literature are occupied by the triumvirate referred to in *Finnegans Wake* as Daunty, Gouty and Shopkeeper, but to most English-speaking readers the second is merely a name. German is a more difficult language to learn to read than Italian, and whereas Shakespeare, apparently, translates very well into German, Goethe is peculiarly resistant to translation into English; Hölderlin and Rilke, for example, come through much better. From a translation of *Faust*, any reader can see that Goethe must have been extraordinarily intelligent, but he will probably get the impression that he was too intellectual, too lacking in passion, because no translation can give a proper idea of Goethe's amazing command of every style of poetry, from the coarse to the witty to the lyrical to the sublime.

The reader, on the other hand, who does know some German and is beginning to take an interest in Goethe comes up against a cultural barrier, the humourless idolization of Goethe by German professors and critics who treat every word he ever uttered as Holy Writ. Even if it were in our cultural tradition to revere our great writers in this way, it would be much more difficult for us to idolize Shakespeare the man because we know nothing about him, whereas Goethe was essentially an autobiographical writer, whose life is the most documented of anyone who ever lived; compared with Goethe, even Dr Johnson is a shadowy figure.

For those whose ignorance of German cuts them off from Goethe's poetry and who have an instinctive prejudice against professional sages, his *Italian Journey* may well be the best book of his to start on. To begin with, there are hundreds and thousands of Englishmen and Americans who have made an Italian journey of their own and, to many of them, their encounter with Italy, its landscape, its people, its art, has been as important an experience as it was to Goethe, so that the subject-matter of the book will interest them, irrespective of its author, and they will enjoy comparing the post-Second World War Italy they know with the pre-French-Revolution Italy which Goethe saw. (Speaking for myself, I am amazed at their similarity. Is there any other country in Europe where the character of the people seems to have been so little affected by political and technological change?)

Goethe did not go to Italy as a journalist in search of newsworthy stories, but some of the best passages in *Italian Journey* owe as much to journalistic good luck as they do to literary talent. While sketching a ruined fort in Malcesine he is nearly arrested as an Austrian spy; Vesuvius obliges with a major eruption during his stay in Naples; sailing back from Sicily, the boat he has taken is kind enough to get itself nearly shipwrecked on Capri; eccentric and comic characters cross his path, like the Neapolitan Princess with the outrageous tongue, the choleric Governor of Messina, or Miss Hart, the future Lady Hamilton, who seems – God forgive her! – to have invented the Modern Dance; a chance remark overheard leads to his meeting with the humble relatives of Cagliostro, the most famous international swindler of the time. Goethe is not usually thought of as a funny man, but his descriptions of such events reveal a real comic gift and, even more surprisingly, perhaps, they show how ready he was to see himself in a comic light.

To write a successful travel book, one must have an observant eye and a gift for description. Goethe held definite views about how things should be described, which are summed up in a letter he wrote in 1816 about a young writer who had consulted him.

Up till now he has limited himself to subjective modern poetry, so self-concerned and self-absorbed. He does very well with anything confined to inner experience, feeling, disposition and reflections on these; and he will deal successfully with any theme where they are treated. But he has not yet developed his powers in connexion with anything really objective. Like all young men, nowadays, he rather fights shy of reality, although everything imaginative must be based on reality, just as every ideal must come back to it. The theme I set this young man was to describe Hamburg as if he had just returned to it. The thread of ideas he followed from the start was the sentimental one of his mother, his friends, their love, patience and help.

The Elbe remained a stream of silver, the anchorage and the town counted for nothing, he did not even mention the swarming crowds – one might as easily have been visiting Naumburg or Merseburg. I told him this quite candidly; he could do something really good, if he could give a panorama of a great northern city as well as his feelings for his home and family.

Goethe's own practice is peculiar and reminds me in a strange way of the a-literature of some contemporary French novelists. The traditional method of description tries to unite the sensory perception of objects with the subjective feelings they arouse by means of a simile or a metaphorical image. This Goethe very rarely does. On the contrary, he deliberately keeps the sensory and the emotional apart. He makes enormous efforts, piling qualifying adjective on qualifying adjective, to say exactly what shape and colour an object is, and precisely where it stands in spatial relation to other objects, but, in contrast to this precision, the adjectives he employs to express his emotional reactions are almost always vague and banal – words like *beautiful, important, valuable* occur over and over again.

The difficulty about this procedure is that, by its nature, language is too abstract a medium. No verbal description, however careful, can describe a unique object; at best, it describes objects of a certain class. The only media for showing an object in its concrete uniqueness are the visual arts and photography. Goethe, of course, knew this, and said so.

We ought to talk less and draw more. I, personally, should like to renounce speech altogether and, like organic nature, communicate everything I have to say in sketches.

He also knew, of course, that this was an exaggeration. There are certain characteristics of things which are every bit as 'objective' as their visual appearance and with which only language can deal. A drawing can show what something is at a moment, but it cannot show us how it came to be that way or what will happen to it next; this only language can do. What gives Goethe's descriptions their value is not his 'word-painting' – he cannot make us 'see' a landscape or a building as D. H. Lawrence, for example, can – but his passionate interest in historical development – more than most writers he makes us aware of *why* things have come to be as they are. He always refused to separate the beautiful from the necessary, for he was convinced that one cannot really appreciate the beauty of anything without understanding what made it possible and how it came into being. To Goethe, a man who looks at a beautiful cloud without knowing, or wishing to know, any meteorology, at a landscape without knowing any geology, at a plant without studying its structure and way of growth, at the human body without studying anatomy, is imprisoning himself in that aesthetic subjectivity which he deplored as the besetting sin of the writers of his time.

Goethe is more successful at describing works of nature than he is at describing works of art. Indeed, the reader sometimes finds himself wishing he had more often practised what he preached when he said : 'Art exists to be seen, not to be talked about, except, perhaps, in its presence.' One reason for this is, of course, that Goethe knew a lot about natural history and very little about art history. Another may be that the two kinds of history are different. Natural history, like social and political history, is continuous; there is no moment when nothing is happening. But the history of art is discontinuous; the art historian can show the influences and circumstances which made it possible and likely that a certain painter should paint in a certain way, *if he chooses to paint*, but he cannot explain why he paints a picture instead of not painting one. A work of nature and a great work of art both give us, as Goethe said, a sense of necessity, but whereas the necessity of nature is a *must*, that of art is an *ought*.

When, thirty years later, the first part of *Italian Journey* was published, the German artistic colony in Rome was outraged. Those whom he had not mentioned were offended, and the works he had failed to see and the judgements he passed on those he did made them say that he must have gone through Italy with his eyes shut.

This was unfair. Like everybody's, Goethe's taste had its limitations, owing in part to his temperament and in part to the age in which he lived. It seems that the Giotto frescoes in the Arena Chapel were not on view when he was in Padua, and we know that he tried to see them, but he deliberately refused to visit the

Two Churches in Assisi. For Goethe there was no painting or sculpture between Classical antiquity and Mantegna.

Yet, when one considers how little painting and sculpture and architecture Goethe had seen before he came to Italy, one is astounded at his open-mindedness. Though Palladio, for example, is his ideal modern architect, he shows far more appreciation of Baroque than one would have expected, more indeed than most of his successors in the nineteenth century. He started out with a strong prejudice against Christian themes as subjects for paintings and overcame it. Though to him the Apollo Belvedere was the finest achievement in Greek art, he learned to admire works of the archaic period like Paestum, and though he professes to be shocked by the grotesque villa of the Prince of Pallagonia, the zest with which he describes it betrays his fascination. And, in any case, Goethe made no claim to be writing a guide to Italian art; he tells us what he looked at and liked, he makes no claim that his judgements are absolute, and though he may, in our view, have overpraised some pictures, I do not think that he condemned any which seem to us really good.

One reason why we enjoy reading travel books is that a journey is one of the archetypal symbols. It is impossible to take a train or an aeroplane without having a fantasy of oneself as a Quest Hero setting off in search of an enchanted princess or the Waters of Life. And then, some journeys – Goethe's was one – really are quests.

Italian Journey is not only a description of places, persons and things, but also a psychological document of the first importance dealing with a life crisis which, in various degrees of intensity, we all experience somewhere between the ages of thirty-five and forty-five.

The first crisis in Goethe's life had occurred in 1775 when he was twenty-six and already famous as the author of *Götz von Berlichingen* and *Werther*. One might say, though it is a gross oversimplification, that the *Sturm und Drang* literary movement of which Goethe was then regarded as the leader stood for spontaneity of emotion as against convention and decorum, Shakespeare and Ossian as against Racine and Corneille, the warm heart as against the cool reason. Such a movement has often arisen in history and the consequences have almost always been the same; those who embrace it produce some remarkable work at an early age but then peter out if they do not, as they often do, take to drink or shoot themselves. An art which pits Nature against Art is bound to be self-defeating. What Kierkegaard called the aesthetic religion which puts all its faith in the mood of the immediate moment leads, first, to the 'cultivation of one's hysteria with delight and terror', as Baudelaire put it, and, ultimately, to despair, and it brought Goethe to the brink of disaster. 'I am falling', he wrote in April of 1775, 'from one confusion to another.' His father suggested a trip to Italy, but he did not go. At the beginning of November he was in Heidelberg; the young Grand Duke of Weimar was passing through in his coach and invited Goethe to go with him; without a moment's hesitation, Goethe jumped in and was whisked away.

One would not have expected a young poet, who was well enough off to do as he liked, to choose to become a civil servant at a small court when he could have chosen to go to Italy. That Goethe did so is proof of his amazing instinct, which he was to show all through his life, for taking the leap in the right direction. In the state he was in, what could rescue him from a meaningless existence was not freedom but a curtailment of freedom, that is to say, the curb upon his subjective emotions which would come from being responsible for people and things other than himself, and this was precisely what Weimar offered. With the exception of the Grand Duke and Duchess, who were only eighteen, Goethe was the youngest person at court, yet, a year later, he became a Privy Councillor and, in the course of the next ten years, found himself at one time and another responsible for the mines, the War Department, and the Finances of the Duchy. In addition to these duties and as a further defence against subjectivity, he began to study science seriously, and in March 1784 he made an important discovery: he was able to show that the intermaxillary bone existed in man as well as in the other mammals.

These first eleven years in Weimar were also the period of his platonic affair, conducted largely by notes and letters, with Charlotte von Stein, a rather plain married woman with three children and eleven years older than he. Again it seems strange that a man in his twenties and thirties should have been satisfied with such a 'spiritual', uncarnal relationship; yet again, perhaps, it shows the soundness of Goethe's instinct. While, as a Privy Councillor, he was ready to take impersonal responsibility, he was not yet ready to take emotional responsibility for another person; what he needed at the time was emotional security without responsibility, and that is obtainable only in a platonic relationship, as to a mother or an older sister.

To an outsider, Goethe's life in 1786 must have looked enviable. He held an important position; he was admired and loved. Yet, in fact, he was on the verge of a breakdown. The stability which Weimar had given him was threatening to become a prison. Though it had enabled him to put *Werther* behind him, it had failed to give him any hints as to what kind of thing he should be writing instead, for, while he had come to Weimar to get away from *Werther*, it was as its author that Weimar had welcomed and still regarded him. His official life had had its remedial effect, but as public affairs were not his vocation, his duties were becoming senseless tasks which exhausted his energies without stimulating his imagination. His greatest gains had been in his scientific studies, yet here again Goethe was not a scientist by vocation but a poet; scientific knowledge was essential to the kind of poetry he wanted to write, but, so long as he remained in Weimar, his scientific researches and his poetry remained two separate activities without real influence upon each other. As for his Weimar friends, he was beginning – this is one of the misfortunes of genius – to outgrow them. Herder, to whom, since he was a young student in Strassburg, he had owed so much, had nothing more to teach him and, probably, Herder's schoolmaster temperament which liked to keep disciples was beginning to irk him. So far as Charlotte was concerned, Goethe seems to have been, like Yeats, a man in whom the need for physical sexual relations became imperative only relatively late in life; by 1786 it had.

When the idea of escaping from Weimar to Italy first occurred to him we shall never know. He tells us that the longing for 'classic soil' had become so great that he dared not read the classics because they upset him too much, but his actual decision to go may have been taken at the very last moment. On 28 August, he celebrated his thirty-seventh birthday in Carlsbad, where a number of the court were taking the waters. Two or three days later all the party except Goethe and the Grand Duke returned to Weimar under the impression that Goethe was going on a short geological excursion into the mountains. After they had gone, Goethe asked the Duke for leave of absence and, at three in the morning on 3 September, jumped into a coach with no servant and hardly any luggage, assumed the name of Möller, and bolted. He does not appear to have been very explicit about his plans even to his sovereign, for the Duke cannot have received his letter, dated 2 September, until after he had left.

Forgive me for being rather vague about my travels and absence when I took leave of you; even now I do not quite know what will happen to me.

You are happy, you are moving towards an aim you wished and chose for yourself. Your domestic affairs are in good order and in a good way, and I know you will permit me now to think of myself. In fact, you have often urged me to do so. I am certainly not indispensable at this moment; and as for the special affairs entrusted to me, I have left them so that they can run on for a while quite comfortably without me. Indeed, I might even die without there being any great shock. I say nothing of how favourable these circumstances are at present and simply ask you for an indefinite leave of absence. The baths these two years have done a great deal for my health and I hope the greatest good for the elasticity of my mind, too, if it can be left to itself for a while to enjoy seeing the wide world.

My first four volumes are complete at last. Herder has been a tireless and faithful helper; now I need to be at leisure and in the mood for the last four. I have undertaken it all rather lightly, and I am only now beginning to see what is to be done if it is not to become a mess. All this and much else impels me to lose myself in places where I am totally unknown. I am going to travel quite alone, under another name, and I have great hopes of this venture, odd as it seems. But please don't let anyone notice that I shall be away for some time. Everyone working with or under me, everyone that has to do with me, expects me from one week to the next, and I want to leave it like that and, although absent, to be as effective as someone expected at any moment . . .

The only person Goethe knew in Rome, and by correspondence only, was the German painter Tischbein. Through him Goethe was introduced to the German artistic colony, and, though he keeps telling Weimar how lonely he is, it is clear that he was soon leading quite an active social life. But in Rome he was free, as in Weimar he had not been, to choose his own company, and his anonymity, though it did not remain a secret for long, seems to have been respected. Whether by his own choice or because Italians were difficult to get to know, he stuck pretty closely to his fellow countrymen. Whereas in Weimar most of his friends had been older than he was, those of whom he saw most in Rome, with the exception of Angelica Kauffmann, were all younger When Goethe was thirty-seven, Tischbein was thirty-five, Kayser, Kniep and Schütz thirty-one, Moritz twenty-nine, Lipps twenty-eight, Meyer twenty-six and Bury twenty-three. Only one of them, Moritz, was a writer and an intellectual, not one of them was a poet or a clergyman, and, again with the exception of Angelica, they were all poorer than he. For Goethe at this period in his life, such a company had many advantages. Before he came to Italy he had seen very little original architecture, sculpture and painting, Classical or Renaissance, and he had the common sense to realize that before he could understand and appreciate it properly, his eye would have to be educated. He also wanted to learn to draw, not so much for its own sake – he never fancied that he might become a serious artist – as for the discipline; drawing was the best way to train his mind to pay attention to the external world. To train his eye, to learn to draw, he needed the help of professional artists, which most of his Roman friends were. Secondly, if he were to develop as a poet, the best companionship for him at this point, failing a real literary equal like Schiller, was an unliterary one or, at least, a company whose literary judgements he did not have to take seriously. They all knew, of course, that he was a famous poet and Angelica was a sympathetic feminine audience, but they did not pretend to be expert judges of poetry, and if they objected to anything, he could disregard their criticisms in a way that he still found it difficult to ignore the criticisms which came from Weimar. He acknowledged a debt to Moritz's prosodical theories, but otherwise the fresh stimuli to his imagination came, not from conversations or reading, but from watching the behaviour of Italians and living in the midst of Italian nature, the climate, shapes and colours of which were so utterly different from the northern nature he had known hitherto. How necessary it was for Goethe to remove himself from the literary atmosphere of Weimar can be guessed from his letters about his new versions of *Iphigenie* and *Egmont*, for it is clear that Weimar preferred the old versions and did not care for his new classical manner.

Lastly, an artistic, somewhat bohemian, foreign colony in a great city gave him a freedom in his personal life which would have been out of the question at a provincial German court. As he gives us only his side of the correspondence, we have to infer what the reactions of Weimar were to his whole Italian venture. It seems fairly clear that they were hurt, suspicious, disapproving and jealous. If the reader sometimes becomes impatient with Goethe's endless reiterations of how hard he is *working*, what a lot of *good* Italy is doing him, he must remember that Goethe is trying to placate his friends for being obviously so radiantly happy without them. One of the reasons why his account of his time in Rome, particularly of his second stay, is less interesting than the rest of *Italian Journey* is that one feels that much is happening to Goethe which is of great importance to him, but which he declines to tell. There is no reason to suppose that Goethe's life in Rome was anything like Byron's in Venice, but it is impossible to believe that it was quite so respectable, or so exclusively devoted to higher things as, in his letters home, for obvious reasons, he makes it sound. The difference between the over-refined, delicate, almost neurasthenic face of the pre-Italian portraits and the masculine, self-assured face in the portraits executed after his return is very striking; the latter is that of a man who has known sexual satisfaction.

If Goethe did not tell everything, what he did tell was true enough. He did work very hard and Italy did do him a lot of good. Any writer will find *Italian Journey* fascinating for what Goethe says about his own methods of working. He would compose with extraordinary rapidity and in his head – if he did not write it down at once, he often forgot it – and under any circumstances: there cannot be many poets who have been able to write while suffering from seasickness. His chief difficulty, partly out of a temperamental impatience and partly because he kept having so many ideas and was interested in so many things, was in finishing a work. He starts rewriting *Iphigenie auf Tauris* and becomes distracted by the thought of another play, *Iphigenie in Delphi*; he is walking in the Public Gardens of Palermo, planning a new play about Nausicaa, when suddenly he is struck by an idea about the Primal Plant, and Botany chases away the Muse.

And he has so many unfinished pieces. When at last he finishes *Iphigenie*, begun in 1779, there is *Egmont* waiting, begun in 1775. He finishes *Egmont*, and there are two old *Singspiele* to rewrite. These done with, he takes out the yellowed manuscript of *Faust*, which is eighteen years old, and adds a scene or two, and he departs from Rome with the nine-year-old *Tasso* to rework while travelling. And he does all this in the midst of social life, sightseeing, collecting coins, gems, minerals, plaster casts, taking drawing lessons, attending lectures on perspective and making botanical experiments. If to read about such energy is rather exhausting, to read about a man who is so enjoying himself is enormous fun.

We have tried to produce a translation, not a crib. A crib is like a pair of spectacles for the weaksighted; a translation is like a book in Braille for the blind. A translator, that is to say, has to assume that his readers cannot and never will be able to read the original. This, in its turn, implies that they are not specialists in his author. On the one hand, they probably know very little about him; on the other, their appetite for scholarly footnotes is probably small.

The translator's most difficult problem is not *what* his author says but his tone of voice. How is a man who thought and wrote in German to think and write in English and yet remain a unique personality called Goethe? To offer a translation to the public is to claim that one does know how Goethe would have written had English been his native tongue, to claim, in fact, that one has mediumistic gifts, and, as we all know, mediums are often rather shady characters.

The circumstances under which *Italian Journey* was written, put together and published present a special problem. Most of its contents are based upon letters and a journal written at the time, but it was not until twenty-five years later that Goethe set to work to make a book out of them, and the third part was not published until he was almost eighty. A compilation of this kind involves editing, and it must be admitted that, as an editor, Goethe did not do a very good job. If a man writes two letters at the same time to two different people, it is only to be expected that he will repeat himself a little, and if at the end of an exciting and exhausting day he hurriedly jots down the events in his journal, it is natural enough if there is some disorder in his narrative – what should have come first comes as an afterthought, etc. – but if he decides to make a book out of such material, one has a right to expect him to cut out what is repetitious, to rearrange what is chaotic and clarify what is obscure.

Even in the first two parts of *Italian Journey*, there are places where Goethe has been careless. For instance, he presents his visit to Cagliostro's relatives as a passage from his journal, dated 13 and 14 April 1787. But suddenly, without warning, the reader finds him referring to events which did not take place until 1789. What Goethe has actually done is to print, not his original journal, but a talk about Cagliostro based on it which he gave to Weimar in 1792.

As for Part Three, one can only conclude that Goethe handed the material over to his secretary without rereading it and that the secretary was too overawed by the great man to suggest any corrections.

We have seen fit to do some editing ourselves. One previous English translator, an Anglican clergyman, omitted all favourable references made by Goethe to the Roman Catholic Church; we have confined ourselves to stylistic matters. We have cut some passages which seemed to us unduly repetitious and some allusions to things which were known to his correspondents but would be unintelligible to a reader without a lengthy note, and, here and there, we have transposed sentences to a more logical position. We have also omitted the whole article *Concerning the Pictorial Imitation of the Beautiful*. Our official excuse is that the ideas in it are not all Goethe's but chiefly Moritz's; our real reason is that it is verbose rubbish and sounds like a parody of 'deep' German prose.

To those who regard such tinkering as sacrilege, we can only cite the authority of the Master himself.

If the translator has really understood his author, he will be able to evoke in his own mind not only what the author has done, but also what he wanted and ought to have done. That at least is the line I have always taken in translation, though I make no claim that it is justifiable. [To *Streckfuss, 1827*]

W. H. AUDEN · ELIZABETH MAYER

ITALIAN JOURNEY

Et in Arcadia ego

PART ONE

FROM CARLSBAD TO THE BRENNER

I SLIPPED out of Carlsbad at three in the morning; otherwise, I would not have been allowed to leave. Perhaps my friends, who had so kindly celebrated my birthday on 28 August, had thereby acquired the right to detain me, but I could wait no longer. I packed a single portmanteau and a valise, jumped into the mail-coach, and arrived in Zwota at 7.30. The morning was misty, calm and beautiful, and this seemed a good omen. The upper clouds were like streaked wool, the lower heavy. After such a wretched summer, I looked forward to enjoying a fine autumn. At noon I arrived in Eger. The sun was hot, and it occurred to me that this place lay on the same latitude as my native town. I felt very happy to be taking my midday meal under a cloudless sky on the fiftieth parallel.

On entering Bavaria, the first thing one sees is the monastery of Waldsassen. The clerics who own this valuable property have been wiser than most people. It lies in a saucer- or basin-like hollow amid beautiful meadows and surrounded on all sides by fertile, gently rolling hills. The monastery owns property all over the countryside. The soil is a decomposed clayey slate. The quartz which is found in this type of rock formation does not decompose or erode, and it makes the soil loose and fertile. The land rises steadily all the way to Tirschenreuth, and the streams flow towards the Eger and the Elbe. After Tirschenreuth, the land falls to the south and the streams run towards the Danube. I find I can quickly get a topographical idea of a region by looking at even the smallest stream and noting in which direction it flows and which drainage basin it belongs to. Even in a region which one cannot overlook as a whole, one can obtain in this way a mental picture of the relation between the mountains and the valleys.

Before reaching Tirschenreuth, we struck a first-class high road of granitic sand. This decomposed granite is a mixture of feldspar and argillaceous earth which provide both a firm foundation and a solid binding, so that the road is as smooth as a threshing floor, all the more desirable because the region through which it runs is flat and marshy. The gradient was now downhill and we made rapid progress, a pleasant contrast after the snail's pace of travel in Bohemia (I enclose a list of the places at which we stopped). By ten o'clock next morning we reached Regensburg, having covered a hundred and four miles in thirty-one hours. Dawn found us between Schwandorf and Regenstauf, and I noticed that the soil had already changed for the better. It was no longer debris washed down from the mountains, but mixed alluvial earth. In primeval times tides from the Danube area must have passed up the Regen and invaded all the valleys which now discharge their waters into that basin. This invasion formed the polders upon which agriculture depends. This holds good for all river valleys, large or small, and by noting their presence or absence, any observer can discover at a glance whether the soil is fit for cultivation.

Regensburg has a beautiful situation. The lie of the land was bound to invite the founding of a town, and its spiritual lords have shown good judgement. They own all the fields around, and in the town itself church stands by church and convent by convent. The Danube reminds me of the Main. The river and the bridges at Frankfurt are a finer sight, but the Stadt-am-Hof on the far bank of the Danube looks very impressive.

The first thing I did was to visit the Jesuit College, where the students were performing their annual play. I saw the end of an opera and the beginning of a tragedy. The acting was no worse than that of any other group of inexperienced amateurs, and their costumes were beautiful indeed, almost too magnificent. Their performance reminded me once again of the worldly wisdom of the Jesuits. They rejected nothing which might produce an effect, and they knew how to use it with love and care. Their wisdom was no coldly impersonal calculation; they did everything with a gusto, a sympathy and personal pleasure in the doing, such as living itself gives. This great order had organ-builders, wood-carvers and gilders among its members, so it must also have

included some who, by temperament and talent, devoted themselves to the theatre. Just as they knew how to build churches of
imposing splendour, these wise men made use of the world of the
senses to create a respectable drama.

I am writing this on the forty-ninth parallel. The morning was
cool, and though, here too, people complain of the cold, damp
summer, a glorious day unfolded. Thanks to the presence of the
great river, the air is extraordinarily mild. The fruit, however, is
not particularly good. I ate some nice pears, but I am longing for
grapes and figs.

I keep thinking about the character and the activities of the
Jesuits. The grandeur and perfect design of their churches and
other buildings command universal awe and admiration. For ornament, they used gold, silver and jewels in profusion to dazzle
beggars of all ranks, with, now and then, a touch of vulgarity
to attract the masses. Roman Catholicism has always shown this
genius, but I have never seen it done with such intelligence, skill
and consistency as by the Jesuits. Unlike the other religious
orders, they broke away from the old conventions of worship
and, in compliance with the spirit of the times, refreshed it with
pomp and splendour.

A peculiar mineral is found here, which is worked up into
specimens for collectors. It looks like a sort of puddingstone, but
it must be older, primary or even porphyritic. It is greenish in
colour, porous, mixed with quartz, and embedded in it are large
pieces of solid jasper in which again small round specks of breccia
may be seen. I saw one very tempting specimen, but it was too
heavy, and I have vowed not to burden myself with stones on
this journey.

Munich, 6 September

I left Regensburg at 12.30 p.m. From Abach, where the Danube
dashes against the cliffs, to Saale the countryside is beautiful. The
limestone is of the same kind as that round Osterode in the Harz
Mountains – compact but porous.

I arrived here at six in the morning. After looking around for
twelve hours, I have little to remark. In the picture gallery I felt

rather lost; my eyes have not yet reaccustomed themselves to looking at paintings. But I saw some excellent things. The sketches by Rubens from the Luxembourg Gallery, for instance, delighted me. There was one precious and curious object, a miniature model of the Trajan column – the ground was lapis lazuli, the figures were gilt. A fine piece of craftsmanship and pleasant to look at.

In the Hall of Classical Antiquities I became acutely aware that my eyes have not been trained to appreciate such things. For this reason I felt I should be wasting my time if I stayed there long. There was little that appealed to me, though I cannot say why. A Drusus attracted my attention, there were two Antonines and a few other pieces which I liked. On the whole, the arrangement is none too happy. The intention behind it was obviously good, but the Hall, or rather the large vaulted room, would have looked better if it had been kept cleaner and in better repair. In the Museum of Natural History I found beautiful minerals from the Tirol. I was already familiar with these and even own some specimens myself.

I met an old woman selling figs, the first I have ever tasted. They were delicious. But although Munich lies on the forty-eighth parallel, on the whole the fruit here is not particularly good. Everyone is complaining about the cold, wet weather. Before reaching Munich, I ran into a fog which was almost rain, and all day long a cold wind has been blowing from the mountains of the Tirol. When I looked towards them from the tower, they were hidden in clouds and the whole sky was overcast. Forgive me for talking so much about wind and weather: the land traveller is almost as dependent upon them as the mariner. It would be a shame if my autumn in foreign lands should turn out to be as unpropitious as my summer at home has been.

I am on my way to Innsbruck. How much I fail to notice to right and left because of the goal by which I have been so long obsessed that it has almost gone stale in my mind !

Mittenwald, 7 September. Evening

My guardian angel, it seems, says Amen to my Credo, and I am grateful to him for having guided me to this place on such a perfect day. My last postilion exclaimed with joy that it was the first of the whole summer. I cherish a secret superstition that the fine weather will continue.

My friends must forgive me for talking again about temperature and clouds. By the time I left Munich at five, the sky had cleared. The clouds were still massed over the mountains of the Tirol and their lower layers were motionless. The road keeps to the high ground over hills of alluvial gravel from which one can see the Isar flowing below. The tidal action of the primeval ocean is easy to grasp. In many a pile of granite rubble I found cousins of the specimens in my collection which Knebel gave me. The mist which rose from the river and the meadows persisted for a time but finally dispersed. Between the gravel hills, which you must picture as stretching far and wide, hour after hour, the soil is fertile and similar to that of the Regen valley. We came back again to the Isar at a point where the hills end in a bluff some one hundred and fifty feet high. When I got to Wolfrathshausen, I had reached the forty-eighth parallel. The sun was blazing fiercely. No one believes the fine weather will last; they all grumble because the weather of the declining year has been so bad and lament that the Good God does nothing about it.

As the mountains slowly drew nearer, a new world opened before me. The situation of Benediktbeuren is surprising and enchanting. The abbey, a long, sprawling white building, stands on a fertile plain beyond which rises a high, rocky ridge. The road climbs to the Kochelsee and then still higher into the mountains until it reaches the Walchensee. There I saw my first snow-capped peaks, and when I expressed my surprise at being already so close to the snow line, I was told that only yesterday there had been a thunderstorm followed by snow. People here interpret these meteorological events as a promise of better weather, and from the early snows they anticipate a change in temperature. All the surrounding cliffs are of limestone – the oldest formation

which contains no fossils. These limestone mountains stretch
in an immense, unbroken chain from Dalmatia to Mount St
Gotthard and beyond. Hacquet has travelled over much of it. It
leans against the primal mountain range which is rich in quartz
and clay.

I reached Walchensee at half past four, having met with a
pleasant adventure an hour or so before. A harp player who had
been walking ahead of us with his eleven-year-old daughter
begged me to let her ride with me in the coach. He himself
walked on, carrying his instrument. I let her sit by my side, and
she placed a large new bandbox carefully at her feet. She was a
pretty young creature who had already seen a good deal of the
world. With her mother, she had made a pilgrimage on foot to
Maria-Einsiedeln, and both of them had been planning a longer
pilgrimage to S. Jago de Compostela. But her mother had been
carried away by death before she could fulfil her vow. One could
never, she told me, do too much in veneration of the Mother of
God. After a great fire in which a whole house had been burned
to the ground, she had seen with her own eyes that the picture of
Our Lady in the niche over the door had remained undamaged
and the glass as well. This was certainly a true miracle. She
always travelled on foot, and on her last journey she had played in
Munich before the Elector. All in all, she had performed before
twenty-one royal personages. She had large brown eyes, an obstinate forehead, which she sometimes screwed up, and I found
her quite good company. When she talked, she was natural and
agreeable, especially when she laughed out loud like a child, but
when she was silent, wishing, evidently, to look important, she
pouted her upper lip, which gave her face an unpleasant expression. I talked with her on many topics; she was familiar with
them all and observant of everything about her. Once, for instance, she asked me the name of a tree. It was a beautiful tall
maple, the first I had seen on my journey. She had noticed it
immediately and was delighted when more and more of them
appeared and she was able to recognize them. She told me she
was on her way to the fair in Bolzano and assumed I was going
there too. Should we meet there, I must buy her a fairing. This
I promised to do. She was also going to wear her new bonnet

which she had had made to order in Munich and paid for out of her earnings. She would show it to me in advance. At which she opened her bandbox and I had to share her admiration for the richly embroidered, gaily beribboned headdress.

We shared another cheerful prospect as well : she assured me we would have fair weather, because she carried a barometer with her – her harp. When the treble string went sharp it was a sign of good weather, and this had happened today. I accepted the good omen and we parted gaily, hoping to meet again soon.

On the Brenner Pass, 8 September. Evening

Led, or rather driven, I reached at last as quiet a resting place as I could have hoped for. It has been one of those days which I shall remember with joy for many years. I left Mittenwald at six. A bitter wind had cleared the sky completely. It was as cold as one only expects it to be in February, but, in the radiance of the rising sun, the dark pine-grown foothills, the grey limestone cliffs between them and the snow-capped peaks in the background against a deep-blue sky were a rare and ever-changing vision.

Near Scharnitz one enters the Tirol. At the frontier the valley is closed in by a rock wall which joins the mountains on both sides. On one side the cliff is fortified, on the other it rises perpendicularly. It is a fine sight. After Seefeld the road becomes more and more interesting. From Benediktbeuren on, it had been climbing steadily from one height to another and all the streams ran towards the basin of the Isar, but now I looked down from a ridge into the valley of the Inn and saw Inzing lying below me. The sun was high in the heavens and shone so hotly that I had to take off some of my outer garments. Because of the ever-varying temperature, I have to make several changes of clothing during the course of the day.

Near Zirl we began to descend into the Inn valley. The landscape is of an indescribable beauty, which was enhanced by a sunny haze. The postilion hurried faster than I wished; he had not yet heard Mass and was devoutly eager to hear it in Innsbruck because it was the Feast of the Virgin's Nativity, so we rattled downhill beside the Inn and past St Martin's Wall, a huge, sheer

limestone crag. I would have trusted myself to reach the spot
where the Emperor Maximilian is said to have lost his way and
to have come down safely without the help of an angel, though I
must admit it would have been a reckless thing to do.

Innsbruck is superbly situated in a wide fertile valley between
high cliffs and mountain ranges. My first thought was to make a
stop there, but I felt too restless. I amused myself for a little by
talking to the innkeeper's son, who was 'Söller' * in person. It is
curious how I keep meeting my characters one after the other.

Everything has been made clean and tidy for the Feast of the
Virgin's Nativity. Healthy, prosperous-looking people are making
a pilgrimage to Wilten, a shrine an hour's walk from the town
in the direction of the mountains. At two o'clock when my coach
rolled through the gay and colourful crowd, the procession was
in full swing.

After Innsbruck the landscape becomes increasingly beautiful.
On the smoothest of roads we ascended a gorge which discharges
its waters into the Inn and offers the eye a great variety of scenery.
The road skirts the steepest rock and in places is even hewn out
of it. On the other side one could see gentle cultivated slopes.
Villages, large and small houses, chalets, all of them whitewashed, lay scattered among fields and hedges over a high, wide
slope. Soon the whole scene changed: the arable land became
pasture and then the pasture, too, fell away into a precipitous
chasm.

I have gained some ideas for my cosmological theories, but
none of them is entirely new or surprising. I have also kept
dreaming of the model I have talked about for so long, with
which I should like to demonstrate all the things which are
running through my head but which I cannot make others see in
nature.

It grew darker and darker; individual objects faded out and the
masses became ever larger and more majestic. Finally everything
moved before my eyes like some mysterious dream picture and all
of a sudden I saw the lofty snow peaks again, lit up by the moon.

---

* *Söller*. Character in Goethe's comedy *The Accomplices* (*Die Mit-
schuldigen*), 1768.

Now I am waiting for dawn to light up this cleft in which I am wedged on the dividing line between north and south.

Let me add some more remarks about the weather, which is treating me so kindly, perhaps because I pay it so much attention. On the plains, one accepts good or bad weather as an already established fact, but in the mountains one is present at its creation. I have often witnessed this as I travelled, walked, hunted or spent days or nights among cliffs in the mountain forests, and a fanciful idea has taken hold of my mind which is as difficult to shake off as all such fancies are. I seem to see its truth confirmed everywhere, so I am going to talk about it. It is my habit, as you know, to keep trying the patience of my friends.

When we look at mountains, whether from far or near, and see their summits, now glittering in sunshine, now shrouded in mists or wreathed in storm-tossed clouds, now lashed by rain or covered with snow, we attribute all these phenomena to the atmosphere, because all its movements and changes are visible to the eye. To the eye, on the other hand, shapes of the mountains always remain immobile; and because they seem rigid, inactive and at rest, we believe them to be dead. But for a long time I have felt convinced that most manifest atmospheric changes are really due to their imperceptible and secret influence. I believe, that is to say, that, by and large, the gravitational force exerted by the earth's mass, especially by its projections, is not constant and equal but, whether from internal necessity or external accident, is like a pulse, now increasing, now decreasing. Our means for measuring this oscillation may be too limited and crude, but sensitive reactions of the atmosphere to it are enough to give us sure information about these imperceptible forces. When the gravitational pull of the mountains decreases even slightly, this is immediately indicated by the diminished weight and elasticity of the air. The atmosphere can no longer retain the moisture mechanically or chemically diffused through it; the clouds descend, rain falls heavily, and shower clouds move down into the plain. But when their gravitational pull increases, the elasticity of the air is restored and two significant phenomena follow. First the mountains gather round their summits enormous cloud masses, holding them firmly and immovably above themselves like second summits. Then, through an inner struggle of electrical forces, these clouds descend as thunderstorms, fog or rain. The elastic air is now able to absorb more moisture and dissolve the remaining clouds. I saw quite distinctly the absorption of one such cloud. It clung to the steepest summit, tinted by the afterglow of the setting sun. Slowly, slowly, its edges detached themselves, some fleecy bits were drawn off, lifted high up, and then vanished. Little by little the whole mass disappeared before my eyes, as if it were being spun off from a distaff by an invisible hand.

If my friends smile at the peripatetic meteorologist and his strange theories, I shall probably make them laugh out loud with a few further reflections. Having taken this journey in order to escape the inclemencies I had suffered on the fifty-first parallel, I had hoped, I must confess, to enter a true Goshen on the forty-eighth. I found myself disappointed, as I should have known beforehand, because latitude by itself does not make a climate but mountain ranges do, especially those which cross countries from east to west. From the great atmospheric changes which are continually going on there, the northern countries suffer most. Thus it seems that the weather last summer in all the northern lands was determined by this great Alpine chain from which I am now writing. Here it has rained without stopping for the last months, and winds from the south-west and south-east have blown the rain northward. The weather in Italy is reported to have been fine and, indeed, almost too dry.

Now a few words about the plant life, which is also greatly influenced by climate, altitude and moisture. So far I have seen no marked change, but a certain improvement is observable. In the valley, before reaching Innsbruck, I frequently saw apples and pears on the trees. Peaches and grapes are brought here from Italy or, rather, South Tirol. Around Innsbruck much maize is grown as well as buckwheat. On the way up the Brenner Pass I saw the first larch trees and near Schönberg the first pine. I wonder if the harper's daughter would have asked me their names too.

As for the plants, I am very conscious of how much I have still to learn. Until I reached Munich I was only aware of seeing familiar ones. But then my hasty travelling day and night did not lend itself to careful observations, even though I carried my Linnaeus with me and had his terminology firmly stamped on my mind. (When shall I find the time and the peace for analysis which, if I know anything about myself, will, in any case, never become my forte?) I keep a sharp lookout for general characteristics; when I saw my first gentian by the Walchensee, it struck me that it has always been in the vicinity of water that I have found new plants.

My attention was drawn to the obvious influence of high altitude. I not only saw new plants but also familiar ones with a different kind of growth. In the low-lying regions, branches and stems were strong and fleshy and leaves broad, but up here in the mountains, branches and stems became more delicate, buds were spaced at wider intervals and the leaves were lanceolate in shape. I observed this in a willow and in a gentian, which convinced me that it was not a question of different species. Near the Walchensee, the rushes I saw were also taller and thinner than those of the plain.

The limestone Alps through which I have been travelling so far have a grey colour and beautiful irregular shapes, even though the rock is divided into level strata and ridges. But since bent strata also occur and the rock does not weather equally everywhere, the cliffs and peaks assume bizarre shapes. This formation continues up the Brenner to a considerable altitude. In the neighbourhood of the Upper Lake, I came across a modification of it. Against a dark-green and dark-grey mica schist, strongly veined with quartz, there leaned a white solid limestone which towered glimmering above its screes, a huge, deeply fissured mass. Further up, I found mica schist again, though it seemed of a softer texture than that lower down. Higher still, appeared a special type of gneiss or, rather, a kind of granite approximating to gneiss, such as one finds in the district of Elbogen. Up here, opposite the Inn, the cliff is mica schist. The streams which flow from these mountains deposit nothing except this rock and grey limestone.

The granite massif upon which all this leans cannot be far away. My map shows that we are on the slope of the Great Brenner proper where all the streams of the surrounding region have their sources.

My impression of the outward appearance of the people is as follows: they look brave, straightforward and, in their physique, very much alike. They have large, dark eyes; the eyebrows of the women are dark and finely traced, whereas those of the men are fair and bushy. The green hats worn by the men add a gay note to the grey rocks; these are decorated with ribbons or wide fringed taffeta sashes pinned on with great elegance. Everyone wears a flower or a feather in his hat as well. The women, on the other hand, disfigure themselves by wearing very large caps of shaggy white cotton which look like monstrous men's nightcaps. They look all the odder because everywhere except in this region the women wear the same becoming hats as the men.

I frequently had occasion to observe that the people here attach great value to peacock feathers and, indeed, to any brightly coloured feather. A person who intends to travel in these mountains should carry some with him, for such a feather, given at the right moment, will serve as the most welcome gratuity.

As I collect, sort and sew these pages together in order to give my friends a brief review of my adventures up to the present moment and at the same time relieve my mind of all I have experienced and thought, I look with alarm at some of the packages of manuscript which I have brought with me. Still, are they not, I say to myself, my travelling companions, and may they not have a great influence on my future?

I took all my writings with me to Carlsbad in order to prepare the definitive edition which Göschen is going to publish. Of those which had never been printed, I already possessed copies beautifully written by the practised hand of my secretary Vogel, who also came to Carlsbad with me. Thanks to his help and Herder's loyal cooperation, I had been able to send the first four volumes to the publisher and was intending to send the last four. Some of their contents were only outlines of works and even fragments, because, to tell the truth, my naughty habit of beginning works, then losing interest and laying them aside, had grown worse with the years and all the other things I had to do.

Since I had these with me, I gladly yielded to the request of the intellectual circle in Carlsbad, and read aloud to them everything they had not yet seen. Whenever I did, there were bitter complaints about the unfinished pieces which they wished were longer.

Most of my birthday presents were poems about my projected but unfinished works in which their authors complained of my habits of composition. One bore the distinguished title of 'The Birds'. A deputation of these gay creatures sent to the 'True Friend'* besought him earnestly to found and furnish forthwith the kingdom he had promised them for so long. The allusions to my other fragmentary pieces were no less intelligent and amiable, so that they suddenly came to life again for me, and I told my friends about other projects I had, and outlined them in detail. This gave rise to more insistent requests and played into Herder's hand, who tried to persuade me to take all my manuscripts with me and, above all, to reconsider *Iphigenie* with the attention it deserved. In its present form it is rather a sketch than a finished play. It is written in a poetic prose which occasionally falls into iambics and even other syllabic metres. I realize that, unless it is read with great skill, so that the blemishes are artfully concealed, this is detrimental to the effect of the play.

Herder urged all this very seriously. I had concealed from him my plans to extend my journey. He believed it was to be merely another mountain excursion, and as he has always ridiculed my passion for mineralogy and geology, he suggested that it would be much better if, instead of tapping dead rocks with a hammer, I were to use my tools for literary work. I promised to try, but so far it has been impossible. Now, however, I have extracted *Iphigenie* from a bundle of manuscripts and shall carry her with me as my travelling companion in a warm and beautiful country. The days are long, nothing distracts my thoughts and the glories of the scenery do not stifle my poetic imagination: on the contrary, favoured by motion and the open air, they excite it.

---

*Truefriend (Treufreund). Character in Goethe's comedy *The Birds*, (*Die Vögel*) modelled on Aristophanes, 1780.

FROM THE BRENNER TO VERONA

AFTER fifty crowded lively hours I arrived here at eight o'clock last night, went early to bed and am now once more in a condition to continue with my narrative. On the evening of the ninth, after finishing the first instalment of my diary, I thought I would try to make a drawing of the inn, a post-house on the Brenner, but I was unsuccessful. I failed to catch the character of the place and returned indoors in somewhat of an ill-humour. The innkeeper asked me if I would not like to start on my way at once because the moon would soon be rising and the road was excellent. I knew that he wanted the horses back early next morning to bring in the second hay crop, so that this advice was not disinterested, but, since it corresponded with my heart's desire, I accepted it with alacrity. The sun came out again, the air was balmy: I packed and at seven o'clock I set off. The clouds had dispersed and the evening became very beautiful.

The postilion fell asleep and the horses trotted downhill at great speed along a road they knew. Whenever they came to a level stretch they slowed down. Then the driver would wake up and goad them on again. Very soon we came to the Adige, rushing along between high cliffs. The moon rose and lit up the gigantic masses of the mountains. Some watermills, standing above the foaming river among age-old pines, looked exactly like a painting by Everdingen.

When I reached Vipiteno at nine o'clock, it soon became obvious that they wanted me to leave at once. We reached Mezzaselva on the stroke of midnight. Everyone except the new postilion was fast asleep. On we went to Bressanone, where again I was, so to speak, abducted, so that I arrived in Colma as dawn was breaking. The postilions tore along the road so fast that it took my breath away, but in spite of my regret at travelling in such haste and by night through this lovely country, deep down inside I was happy that a propitious wind was behind me, hurrying me on towards my goal. At dawn I saw the first hillside vineyards. We met a woman selling pears and peaches.

On we drove. I reached Trinità at seven and was immediately carried off again. For a while we travelled north and at last I saw Bolzano, bathed in sunshine and surrounded by steep mountains which are cultivated up to a considerable height.

The valley is open to the south and sheltered on the north by the mountains of the Tirol. A balmy air pervaded the whole region. Here the Adige turns south again. The foothills are covered with vineyards. The vines are trained on long, low trellises and the purple grapes hang gracefully from the roof and ripen in the warmth of the soil so close beneath them. Even on the valley bottom, which is mostly meadowland, vines are grown on similar trellises, which are placed closely together in rows, between which maize is planted. This thrusts out higher and higher stalks: many I saw were ten feet high. The fibrous male flowers had not yet been cut off, for this is not done until some time after fertilization has taken place.

The sun was shining brightly when I arrived in Bolzano. I was glad to see the faces of so many merchants at once. They had an air about them of purpose and well-being. Women sat in the square, displaying their fruit in round, flat-bottomed baskets more than four feet in diameter. The peaches and pears were placed side by side to avoid bruising. I suddenly remembered a quatrain I had seen inscribed on the window of the inn at Regensburg:

> *Comme les pêches et les melons*
> *Sont pour la bouche d'un baron,*
> *Ainsi les verges et les bâtons*
> *Sont pour les fous, dit Salomon.*

Evidently this was written by a northern baron, but one can be equally sure that, if he had visited these parts, he would have changed his mind.

In the Bolzano market there is a lively traffic in silk; traders also bring cloth there and all the leather they can procure in the

mountain districts. Many merchants, however, come mainly to
collect money, take orders and give new credits. I should much
have liked to inspect all the various products offered for sale, but
my heart's desire will not let me rest, and I am as impatient as
ever to leave at once.

I console myself with the thought that, in our statistically
minded times, all this has probably already been printed in books
which one can consult if need arise. At present I am preoccupied
with sense-impressions to which no book or picture can do justice.
The truth is that, in putting my powers of observation to the test,
I have found a new interest in life. How far will my scientific and
general knowledge take me? Can I learn to look at things with
clear, fresh eyes? How much can I take in at a single glance?
Can the grooves of old mental habits be effaced? This is what I
am trying to discover. The fact that I have to look after myself
keeps me mentally alert all the time and I find that I am develop-
ing a new elasticity of mind. I had become accustomed to only
having to think, will, give orders and dictate, but now I have to
occupy myself with the rate of exchange, changing money, paying
bills, taking notes and writing with my own hand.

From Bolzano to Trento one travels for nine miles through a
country which grows ever more fertile. Everything which, higher
up in the mountains, must struggle to grow, flourishes here in
vigour and health, the sun is bright and hot, and one can believe
again in a God.

A poor woman hailed me and asked me to let her child ride in
my coach because the hot ground was burning its feet. I performed
this deed of charity as an act of homage to the powerful Light of
Heaven. The child was dressed up in a peculiar and showy fashion,
but I could not get a word out of it in any language.

The Adige now flows more gently and in many places forms
broad islands of pebbles. Along the river banks and on the hills
everything is planted so thickly that you would imagine each
crop must choke the other – maize, mulberries, apples, pears,
quinces and nuts.

Walls are covered with a luxuriant growth of dwarf-elder, and
thick-stemmed ivy clambers and spreads itself over rocks; lizards
dart in and out of crevices, and everything that wanders about

reminds me of my favourite pictures. The women with their braided hair, the bare-chested men in light jackets, the magnificent oxen being driven home from the market, the little heavily laden donkeys – all this animated scene makes one think of some painting by Heinrich Roos.

As evening draws near, and in the still air a few clouds can be seen resting on the mountains, standing on the sky rather than drifting across it, or when, immediately after sunset, the loud shrill of crickets is heard, I feel at home in the world, neither a stranger nor an exile. I enjoy everything as if I had been born and bred here and had just returned from a whaling expedition to Greenland.

I even welcome the dust which now sometimes whirls about my coach, as it used to in my native land, and which I had not seen for so long. The bell-like tinkling noise the crickets make is delightful – penetrating but not harsh – and it sounds most amusing when some impish boys try to outwhistle a field of such singers: they seem to stimulate each other. Every evening is as perfectly calm as the day has been.

If someone who lives in the south or was born there were to overhear my enthusiasm at all this, he would think me very childish. But I already knew all about it when I was suffering, alas, under an unfriendly sky, and now I have the pleasure of feeling as an exception this happiness which by rights we ought to be able to enjoy as a rule of our nature.

Trento, 11 September. Evening

I wandered about the town, which is very old though there are a few well-built modern houses. In the church hangs a painting of the assembled Council listening to a sermon by the Vicar-General of the Jesuits. I should much like to know what he put over on them. The church of these Fathers is immediately recognizable by the pilasters of red marble on its façade. The door is covered by a heavy curtain to keep out the dust. I lifted it and stepped into a small antechapel. The church proper is closed off by a wrought-iron grille through which, however, one can view the whole without difficulty. It was quiet and empty, for it is no longer used for divine service. The door was open only because all churches must be open at the hour of vespers.

As I was standing there looking at the architecture, which seemed to me like that of all churches built by this order, an old man entered and immediately took off his black biretta.

His worn and dingy black habit showed that he was an impoverished priest. He knelt down before the grille, said a short prayer and got up. As he turned round he muttered to himself: 'Well, they have expelled the Jesuits but they ought at least to have paid them what the church cost them to build.* I know very well how many thousands they spent on it and on the Seminary.' With that he left and the curtain fell back behind him. I lifted it again and waited quietly. He was still standing at the top of the steps and talking to himself: 'The Emperor didn't do it. The Pope did it.' Unaware of my presence, he turned his face towards the street and continued: 'First the Spaniards, then we, then the French. The blood of Abel cries out against his brother Cain.' Then he descended the steps and walked down the street, still muttering continuously. Probably he was some poor old man who had been supported by the Jesuits, lost his wits after the tremendous fall of that order, and now comes every day to look in this empty shell for its former inhabitants, pray for them a little and then curse their enemies.

A young man from whom I had inquired about the points of interest in this town showed me a house which is called the Devil's House because the Devil, though usually bent on destruction, is said to have got the stones together and built it in a single night. The good fellow failed to notice what was really remarkable about it. It is the only house in good taste which I have seen in Trento and was probably built at an earlier period by some good Italian.

I left at five in the evening. Last night's performance was repeated, for immediately after sunset, the crickets began their shrill chorus. For nearly a mile the road ran between walls, over the tops of which I could see vineyards. Other walls which were not high enough had been built up with stones, brambles and so

---

* The Jesuit Order had been suppressed by Clement XIV in 1773.

forth to prevent passers-by from picking the grapes. Many vine-yard owners spray the vines nearest to the road with lime. This makes the grapes unpalatable but does not spoil the wine, since it is all eliminated during fermentation.

11 September. Evening

Here I am in Rovereto, where the language changes abruptly. North of this point it had wavered between German and Italian. Now, for the first time, I had a pure-bred Italian as a postilion. The innkeeper speaks no German and I must put my linguistic talents to the test. How happy I am that, from now on, a language I have always loved will be the living common speech.

Torbole, 12 September. Afternoon

How I wish my friends could be with me for a moment to enjoy the view which lies before me.

I could have been in Verona tonight, but I did not want to miss seeing Lake Garda and the magnificent natural scenery along its shores, and I have been amply rewarded for making this detour. After five, I started off from Rovereto up a side valley which discharges its waters into the Adige. At its head lies an enormous rocky ridge which one must cross before descending to the lake. I saw some limestone crags which would make fine subjects for pictorial studies. At the end of the descent one comes to a little village with a small harbour, or rather, landing place at the northern end of the lake. Its name is Torbole. On my way up the ridge I had frequently seen fig trees beside the road, and when I descended into the rocky amphitheatre I saw my first olive trees, which were laden with olives. I also saw, growing freely, the small white figs which Countess Lanthieri promised me.

From the room where I am sitting, a door opens on to the courtyard below. I placed my table in front of it and made a quick sketch of the view. Except for one corner to my left, I can see almost the entire length of the lake. Both shores, hemmed in by hills and mountains, glimmer with innumerable small villages.

After midnight the wind starts blowing from north to south. Anyone who wishes to travel down the lake must do so at this

hour, for some hours before sunrise the air current veers round
into the opposite direction. Now it is afternoon and the wind is
blowing strongly in my face, which is cooling and refreshing.
Volkmann* informs me that the lake was formerly called Benacus
and quotes a line from Virgil where it is mentioned:

Fluctibus et fremitu assurgens Benace marino.†

This is the first line of Latin verse the subject of which I have
seen with my own eyes. Today when the wind is increasing in
force and higher and higher waves are dashed against the landing
place, the verse is as true as it was many centuries ago. So much
has changed, but the wind still churns up the lake which a line of
Virgil's has ennobled to this day.

Written on a latitude of 45° 50'

In the cool of the evening I took a walk. Here I am really in a
new country, a totally unfamiliar environment. The people lead
the careless life of a fool's paradise. To begin with, the doors have
no locks, though the innkeeper assures me that I would not have
to worry if all my belongings were made of diamonds. Then the
windows are closed with oil paper instead of glass. Finally, a
highly necessary convenience is lacking, so that one is almost
reduced to a state of nature. When I asked the servant for a
certain place, he pointed down into the courtyard. '*Qui abasso può
servirsi!*' '*Dove?*' I asked. '*Da per tutto, dove vuol!*' was his friendly
answer. Everywhere one encounters the utmost unconcern, though
there is noise and lively bustle enough. The women of the neighbourhood chatter and shout all day long, but at the same time
they all have something to do or attend to. I have yet to see one
idle woman.

The innkeeper announced with a true Italian flourish that he
would have the happiness of serving me the most exquisite trout.
These are caught near Torbole where a brook comes down from
the mountains and the fish look for a way upstream. The

---

*J. J. Volkmann, author of *Historical and Critical News from Italy*,
Goethe's guidebook.

† *The Georgics* of Virgil, II, v, 159–60.

Emperor receives ten thousand gulden for the fishing rights. They are a large fish – some of them weigh over fifty pounds – speckled all over from head to tail. They are not the real trout, but their taste is delicate and excellent – something between that of trout and salmon.

What I enjoy most of all is the fruit. The figs and pears are delicious, and no wonder, since they ripen in a region where lemon trees are growing.

13 September. Evening

At three o'clock this morning I set off with two rowers. At first the wind was favourable and they could use the sails. At dawn the wind dropped and the morning, though cloudy, was glorious. We passed Limone, whose terraced hillside gardens were planted with lemon trees, which made them look at once neat and lush. Each garden consists of rows of square white pillars, set some distance apart and mounting the hill in steps. Stout poles are laid across these pillars to give protection during the winter to the trees which have been planted between them.

Our slow progress favoured contemplation and observation of such pleasing details. We had already passed Malcesine when the wind suddenly veered right round and blew northwards, as it usually does during the day. Against its superior force, rowing was of no avail and we were compelled to land at the harbour of Malcesine, the first Venetian town on the eastern shore of the lake. When one has water to deal with, it is no good saying: 'Today I shall be in this place or that.' I shall make as good use of this stop as possible, in particular, by drawing the castle, which is a beautiful building near the shore. I made a preliminary sketch of it while we were passing this morning.

14 September

The contrary wind which drove me yesterday into Malcesine harbour involved me in a dangerous adventure from which, thanks to keeping my temper, I emerged victorious and which highly amuses me in retrospect.

As I had planned, early in the morning I walked to the old castle, which, since it is without gates, locks or sentries, is accessible to anyone. I sat down in the courtyard facing the old tower, which is built upon and into the rock. I had found an ideal spot for drawing, at the top of three or four steps that led to a locked door. In the frame of this door stood a little carved stone seat of the kind one can still come across in old buildings in our country.

I had not been sitting there long before several persons entered the courtyard, looked me over and walked up and down. Quite a crowd gathered. Then they came to a stop and I found myself surrounded. I realized that my drawing had created a sensation, but I did not let this disturb me and went calmly on with my work. At last a somewhat unprepossessing-looking man pushed himself forward, came up close to me and asked what I was doing there. I replied that I was drawing the old tower so as to have a memento of Malcesine. This was not allowed, he said, and I must stop at once. Since he spoke in Venetian dialect which I hardly understand, I retorted that I didn't know what he was saying. At this, with typical Italian nonchalance he tore the page up, though he left it on the pad. When this happened I noticed that some of the bystanders showed signs of indignation, especially one old woman who said this wasn't right. They should call the *podestà*, who was the proper judge of such matters. I stood on the step with my back against the door and took in the faces of the crowd, which still kept growing. The eager stares, the good-natured expression on most of them and all the other characteristics of a crowd of strange people afforded me much amusement. I fancied I saw before me the chorus of 'Birds', whom, as the 'True Friend', I had so often made fun of on the stage of the Ettersburg theatre. By the time the *podestà* arrived on the scene with his actuary, I was in the highest spirits and greeted him without reserve. When he asked me why I had made a drawing of their fortress, I said modestly that I had not realized that these ruins were a fortress. I pointed to the ruinous state of the tower and the walls, the lack of gates, in short, to the general defenceless condition of the whole place, and assured him it had never crossed my mind that I was drawing anything but a ruin. He answered: If it were only a ruin, why was it worth noticing? Wishing to gain time and his good will, I went into a detailed exposition; they probably knew, I said, that a great many travellers came to Italy only to see ruins, that Rome, the capital of the world, had been devastated by the Barbarians and was now full of ruins which people had drawn hundreds of times, that not everything from antiquity had been as well preserved as the amphitheatre in Verona, which I hoped to see soon.

The *podestà* stood facing me, but on a lower step. He was a tall, though hardly a lanky, man of about thirty. The dull features of his stupid face were in perfect accord with the slow and obtuse way in which he put his questions. The actuary, though smaller and smarter, also did not seem to know how to handle such a novel and unusual case. I kept on talking about this and that. The people seemed to enjoy listening, and when I directed my words at some kindly-looking women, I thought I could read assent and approval in their faces.

But when I mentioned the amphitheatre in Verona, which is known here by the name 'arena', the actuary, who had been collecting his wits in the meantime, broke in: that might be all very well, he said, in the case of a world-famous Roman monument, but there was nothing noteworthy about these towers except that they marked the frontier between Venetia and the Austrian Empire, for which reason they were not to be spied upon. I parried this by explaining at some length that the buildings of the Middle Ages were just as worthy of attention as those of Greek and Roman times, though they could not be expected to recognize, as I did, the picturesque beauty of buildings which had been familiar to them since childhood. By good luck, the morning sun at this point flooded the tower, rocks and walls with a lovely light and I began describing the beauty of the scene with great enthusiasm. Since my audience was standing with their backs to it and did not want to withdraw their attention from me completely, they kept screwing their heads round, like wrynecks, in order to see with their eyes what I was praising to their ears. Even the *podestà* turned round, though with greater dignity; they looked so absurd that I became quite hilarious and spared them nothing, least of all the ivy which had luxuriantly covered the rocks and walls for so many centuries.

The actuary returned to his argument: this was all very well, but the Emperor Joseph was a troublesome *signore* who certainly had evil designs on the republic of Venice. I might well be a subject of his, sent to spy on the frontier.

'Far from being a subject of the Emperor,' I exclaimed, 'I can boast of being, like yourselves, the citizen of a republic which, though it cannot compare in power and greatness with the illustrious state of Venice, nevertheless also governs itself and, in its commercial activity, its wealth and the wisdom of its councillors, is inferior to no city in Germany. I am, that is to say, a native of Frankfurt-am-Main, a city of whose name and renown you must certainly have heard.'

'From Frankfurt-am-Main!' cried a pretty young woman. 'Now you will be able to find out at once, Signor Podestà, the kind of man this stranger is. I am certain he is honest. Send for Gregorio – he was in service there for a long time – he is the best person to clear up the whole matter.'

The number of kindly-disposed faces around me had increased, the original troublemaker had disappeared, and when Gregorio arrived, the tide turned definitely in my favour. Gregorio was a man in his fifties with one of those familiar olive-skinned Italian faces. He spoke and behaved like someone to whom anything strange is not strange at all. He at once told me that he had been in service with Bolongaro and would be happy to hear news from me about this family and about the city which he remembered with great pleasure. Fortunately, he had resided there when I was a young man, so that I had the double advantage of being able to tell him exactly what had happened in his day and what changes had taken place later. I had been acquainted with all the Italian families, so I gave him news of them all and he was delighted to hear many facts: that Signor Alessina, for instance, had celebrated his golden wedding in 1774, and that a medal, struck on that occasion, was in my possession. He remembered that the maiden name of this wealthy merchant's wife had been Brentano. I was also able to tell him many things about the children and grandchildren – how they had grown up, been provided for, married and had children in their turn.

While I gave him the most accurate information I could about everything, his features grew jovial and solemn by turns. He was moved and happy. The bystanders got more and more excited and hung on every word of our conversation, though he had to translate some of it into their dialect.

At the end he said: 'Signor Podestà, I am convinced that this man is an honest and educated gentleman who is travelling to enlarge his knowledge. We should treat him as a friend and set him at liberty, so that he may speak well of us to his countrymen and encourage them to visit Malcesine, the beautiful situation of which so well deserves the admiration of foreigners.'

I gave added force to these friendly words by praising the countryside, the town and its inhabitants, nor did I forget to mention the prudence and wisdom of its authorities.

All this was well received and I was given permission to look at anything in the neighbourhood I liked, in the company of Master Gregorio. The keeper of the inn where I had engaged a room now joined us and was delighted at the prospect of foreigners flocking to his inn, once the attractions of Malcesine were properly known. He examined my various articles of clothing with lively curiosity and was especially envious of my small pistols, which can be conveniently slipped into one's pockets. He thought people fortunate indeed who were allowed to carry such beautiful firearms, which were prohibited to them under the severest penalties. From time to time, I interrupted his friendly importunity to express my gratitude to my liberator.

'Do not thank me,' replied the honest fellow, 'you do not owe me anything. If the *podestà* knew his business and if the actuary thought about anything except his self-interest, you would not have been got off so easily. The one was more embarrassed than you were and the other had not a penny to gain by your arrest, the report he would have to make, or sending you to Verona. He realized this very soon and you were already at liberty before our conversation ended.'

Towards evening this good man came to take me to see his vineyard, which was pleasantly situated on the shore of the lake. His fifteen-year-old son accompanied us and was told to climb the trees and pick me the finest fruit, while his father selected the ripest grapes.

Alone with these two simple, kindhearted persons, in the immense solitude of this corner of the world, it struck me, as I meditated on my adventure of the morning, that man is indeed a strange creature, who, in order to enjoy something which he could perfectly well have enjoyed in peace and comfort and pleasant company, gets himself into trouble and danger because of an absurd desire to appropriate the world and everything it contains in a manner peculiar to himself.

Shortly before midnight the innkeeper accompanied me to the boat, carrying a little basket of fruit which Gregorio had given me as a present. And so, with a propitious wind, I left that shore which had threatened to become for me the coast of the Laestrygones.

Now about my trip down the lake. This ended happily, after the beauty of the mirror-like water and the adjacent shore of Brescia had refreshed my whole being. Along the western shore, where the mountains were no longer precipitous and the land sloped more gently down to the lake, Gargnano, Bogliaco, Cecina, Toscolano, Maderno, Gardone and Salò stretched in one long row for about an hour and a half. No words can describe the charm of this densely populated countryside. At ten in the morning I landed in Bardolino, loaded my baggage on to one mule and myself on to another. The road crossed a ridge which separates the lake basin from the Adige valley. The primeval waters from both sides probably met each other here, causing powerful currents which raised this gigantic dam of gravel. In quieter epochs fertile soil was then desposited on it, but the ploughmen are constantly bothered by the boulders which keep cropping up. They try to get rid of as many of them as possible by piling them on top of each other in rows, so that the road is lined by very thick and compact walls. Owing to the lack of moisture at this altitude, the mulberry trees are a sorry sight. There are no springs at all. Occasionally one comes across puddles of accumulated rain water, at which the mules and even the drivers quench their thirst. Below, along the river, waterwheels have been erected to irrigate the low-lying fields when necessary.

The magnificence of the new landscape which comes into view

as one descends is indescribable. For miles in every direction there stretches a level, well-ordered garden surrounded by high mountains and precipices. Shortly before one o'clock on 14 September I arrived in Verona, where I am writing this to complete the second instalment of my journal. Now I must sew the sheets together. I am greatly looking forward to seeing the amphitheatre tonight.

As to the weather during this period, I have the following to report. The night of the ninth and tenth was clear and cloudy by turns and there was a constant halo around the moon. At about 5 a.m. the whole sky became overcast with grey but not heavy clouds, which disappeared during the day. The lower I descended, the finer the weather became, and by the time we had reached Bolzano and left the great massif behind us, the whole character of the atmosphere had changed. Various shades of blue distinguished one part of the background landscape from another, and against this I could see that the atmosphere was charged with water vapour, evenly distributed, which it was able to hold in suspension, so that this moisture neither fell as dew or rain nor gathered into clouds. When I came down still further, I observed clearly how the water vapour rising from the Bolzano valley and the stratus clouds rising from the mountains to the south were moving towards the higher regions in the north, which they did not hide but veiled in a haze. Above the mountains in the far distance I could see a so-called water gall. South of Bolzano, the weather had been beautiful all summer with only occasionally a little 'water' (they say *acqua* when speaking of a light shower), followed immediately by sunshine. Yesterday a few drops fell now and then, but the sun shone all the time. They have not had such a good year for ages; all the crops have done well; the bad weather they have sent to us.

I shall only briefly mention the mountain rocks and minerals, since *Journey to Italy* by Ferber and Hacquet's *Across the Alps* have already dealt adequately with them.

At dawn, a quarter of an hour after crossing the Brenner Pass, I came, near Colma, to a marble quarry. Almost certainly this marble rests upon the same kind of schist as I saw on the other side of the pass. Further down, I saw indications of porphyry.

The cliffs were so splendid and the heaps of stones along the high
road of such a convenient size that, if I weren't so greedy and
were willing to limit myself to small specimens, I could easily
have made myself a little mineralogical museum like that of
Voigt's. Soon after leaving Colma, I found a kind of porphyry
which splits into regular horizontal plates, and between Bronzolo
and Egna another kind which splits vertically. Ferber took them
to be volcanic in origin, but that was fourteen years ago, when
eruptions were all the rage.* Even Hacquet ridiculed this hypothesis.

Of the inhabitants, I have little to say and that unfavourable.
After crossing the Brenner, I noticed as soon as it was daylight a
definite change in their physical appearance. I thought the sallow
complexion of the women particularly disagreeable. Their features
spoke of misery and their children looked just as pitiful. The men
looked little better. Their physical build, however, is well-propor-
tioned and sound. I believe that their unhealthy condition is due
to their constant diet of maize and buckwheat, or, as they call
them, yellow polenta and black polenta.

These are ground fine, the flour is boiled in water to a thick
mush and then eaten. In the German Tirol they separate the
dough into small pieces and fry them in butter, but in the Italian
Tirol the polenta is eaten just as it is or sometimes with a sprinkling of grated cheese. Meat they never see from one year's end to
the other. Such a diet makes the bowels costive, especially in
children and women, and their cachectic complexion is evidence
of the damage they do themselves. They also eat fruit, and green
beans which they boil in water and dress with garlic and olive oil.
I asked if there were no well-to-do peasants. 'Of course.' 'Don't
they ever treat themselves to something better?' 'No, that is all
they're used to.' 'But what do they do with their money? What
do they spend it on?' 'Oh, they have their masters all right, who
relieve them of it again.' This was the sum of a conversation I
had in Bolzano with the daughter of my innkeeper.

---

*An allusion to the controversy over the building of the earth's
crust between the Vulcanists who held volcanic action to be the
prime factor, and the Neptunists who held rock formations to be
oceanic deposits. Goethe was a Neptunist.

From her, too, I heard about the winegrowers. Though apparently the best off, their position is the worst of all. They are completely at the mercy of the merchants, who, in bad years, lend them money to keep them going and then, in good years, buy their wine for a mere song. But life is like that everywhere.

My theory about their diet is confirmed by the fact that the women in the towns all look healthier. I saw pretty plump faces with bodies that were a little too short for their weight and their big heads. Now and then I encountered some who looked really friendly and good-natured. The men we know from itinerant Tiroleans. In their own land they look less healthy than the women, probably because the women do more physical labour and take more exercise, while the men lead a sedentary life as shopkeepers or craftsmen. The people I met around Lake Garda were very dark-skinned without the least touch of red in their cheeks, but they looked cheerful and not at all unhealthy. Their complexion is probably due to their constant exposure to the rays of the sun, which beats so fiercely at the feet of their mountains.

FROM VERONA TO VENICE

Verona, 16 September

THE amphitheatre is the first great monument of the ancient world I have seen, and how well preserved it is! When I entered it, and even more when I wandered about on its highest rim, I had the peculiar feeling that, grand as it was, I was looking at nothing. It ought not to be seen empty but packed with human beings, as it was recently in honour of Joseph I and Pius VI. The Emperor, who was certainly accustomed to crowds, is said to have been amazed. But only in ancient times, when a people were more of a people than today, can it have made its full effect. Such an amphitheatre, in fact, is properly designed to impress the people with itself, to make them feel at their best.

When something worth seeing is taking place on level ground and everybody crowds forward to look, those in the rear find various ways of raising themselves to see over the heads of those in front: some stand on benches, some roll up barrels, some bring carts on which they lay planks crosswise, some occupy a neighbouring hill. In this way in no time they form a crater. Should the spectacle be often repeated on the same spot, makeshift stands are put up for those who can pay, and the rest manage as best they can. To satisfy this universal need is the architect's task. By his art he creates as plain a crater as possible and the public itself supplies its decoration. Crowded together, its members are astonished at themselves. They are accustomed at other times to seeing each other running hither and thither in confusion, bustling about without order or discipline. Now this many-headed, many-minded, fickle, blundering monster suddenly sees itself united as one noble assembly, welded into one mass, a single body animated by a single spirit. The simplicity of the oval is felt by everyone to be the most pleasing shape to the eye, and each head serves as a measure for the tremendous scale of the whole. But when the building is empty, there is no standard by which to judge if it is great or small.

The Veronese are to be commended for the way in which they preserved this monument. The reddish marble of which it is built is liable to weather, so they keep restoring the steps as they erode, and almost all of them look brand-new. An inscription commemorates a certain Hieronymus Maurigenus and the incredible industry he devoted to this monument. Only a fragment of the outer wall is left standing and I doubt if it was ever even completed. The lower vaults which adjoin a large square called *il Bra* are rented to some artisans, and it is a cheerful sight to see these caverns again full of life.

The most beautiful of the city gates is called *Porta stupa* or *del Palio*, but it has always been bricked up. From a distance it does not look well designed as a gate, and it is only when one gets close to it that one can recognize its beauty. All sorts of explanations are given for its being bricked up. Personally, I suspect that the artist intended it as a gateway to a new alignment of the Corso, for its relation to the present street is all wrong. To its left there are nothing but some barracks, and a line drawn at right angles to the gate through its centre leads to a nuns' convent, which it would certainly have been necessary to demolish. That was probably realized; also, the nobility and the men of wealth may have disliked the idea of building their houses in such a remote quarter of the town. Then, perhaps, the artist died, the gate was bricked up and the project abandoned for good.

16 September

The portico of the Teatro Filarmonico looks very impressive with its six tall Ionic columns. By comparison, the life-size bust of the Marchese Maffei in an enormous wig, situated in a painted niche over the door, supported by two Corinthian columns, looks all the more puny. The place is honourable enough, but to be worthy of the grandeur of the columns, the bust should have been colossal.

As it is, it stands ineffectually upon a little stone corbel and is out of harmony with the whole.

The gallery which runs around the vestibule is also too small, and the fluted Doric dwarfs look mean beside the smooth Ionic giants. But this must be forgiven for the sake of the fine museum which has been established under this colonnade. Here antique relics, most of them dug up in or around Verona, are arranged on exhibit. Some, even, are said to have been found in the amphitheatre. There are Etruscan, Greek and Roman works from the oldest times and some of more recent date. The bas-reliefs are set into the walls and bear the numbers Maffei gave them when he described them in his *Verona illustrata*. There are altars, fragments of columns and similar relics, also a beautiful tripod of white marble on which genii busy themselves with attributes of the gods. Raphael has copied and transfigured similar figures in the lunettes of the Farnesina.

The wind that blows from the tombs of the ancients is charged with fragrance as if it had passed over a hill of roses. The sepulchral monuments are intimate and moving and always represent scenes from everyday life. Here a husband and wife look out from a niche as from a window. Here a father and mother and son look at each other with an indescribable tenderness. Here a married couple join hands, here a father reclines on a couch and appears to be chatting with his family. To me, the immediacy of these sculptures was extremely moving. They date from a late period in art, but all are very simple, natural and expressive. There is no knight in armour kneeling in anticipation of a joyful resurrection. With varying degrees of skill, the artist has represented only the simple realities of human beings, perpetuating their existence and giving them everlasting life. No one folds his hands or looks up to heaven. Here they are still the people they were on earth, standing together, taking an interest in each other, loving each other. All this, despite a certain lack of craftsmanship, is charmingly expressed in these works. A richly ornamented marble pillar also gave me something to think about.

Admirable though this museum may be, it is clear that the noble desire to preserve which inspired its founders is no longer alive. The precious tripod will soon be ruined, for it stands in the open and is exposed on the western side to the inclemencies of the weather. This treasure could easily be preserved by providing it with a wooden cover.

Had the Palazzo del Provveditore ever been finished, it might have made a fine piece of architecture. The nobility still build a good deal, but, unfortunately, everyone builds on the site of his old residence – often, therefore, in small, narrow lanes. At the moment, for instance, they are putting a magnificent façade on a seminary which is situated on an alley in one of the remotest suburbs.

As I was passing the huge, sombre gateway of a strange-looking building in the company of a chance acquaintance, he good-naturedly asked me if I would like to enter the inner courtyard for a moment. The building was the Palazzo della Ragione, and on account of its height, the courtyard seemed nothing more than an enormous well. 'Here,' he told me, 'all criminals and suspects are held in custody.' Looking about me, I saw that on every floor there was an open corridor railed off by iron bars, which ran past numerous doors. Whenever a prisoner steps out of his cell to be brought for interrogation, he gets a breath of fresh air but he is also exposed to the eyes of the public; since, moreover, there must be a number of rooms for interrogation, chains kept rattling in the corridors, now on this floor, now on that. It was a horrid experience and I must confess that the good humour with which I shook off the 'Birds' would here have been put to a severer test.

At sunset I wandered along the rim of the crater-like amphitheatre, enjoying the view over the town and surrounding countryside. I was completely alone. Below me crowds of people were strolling about on the large flagstones of *il Bra* – men of all ranks and women of the middle class. From my bird's-eye view the women in their black outer garments looked like mummies.

The *zendale* and the *vesta* which constitute the whole *garderobe* of women of this class is a costume clearly suited to a people that does not care too much about cleanliness, but likes to move about in public all the time, now in church and now on the promenade. The *vesta* is a skirt of black taffeta worn over other skirts. If the woman has a clean white petticoat underneath, she knows how to lift the black one gracefully to one side. This is held in place by a belt which narrows the waistline and covers the lappets of the bodice, which may be of any colour. The *zendale* is a hooded shawl with long fringes; the hood is raised above the head on a wire frame and the fringes tied around the body like a scarf, so that their ends hang down at the back.

16 September

Today, about a thousand paces from the arena, I came upon a modern public spectacle. Four noblemen from Verona were playing a kind of ball game with four men from Vicenza. The Veronese play this game among themselves all year round for an hour or two before nightfall. On this occasion, because the match was with a foreign team, a vast crowd, at least four or five thousand, had gathered to watch. I could not see one woman of any rank in life.

When I spoke earlier of the needs of the crowd on such occasions, I described the kind of amphitheatre it makes accidentally, as those in the rear try to look over the heads of those in front. And this was what I now saw being created. Even at a distance I could hear the vigorous clapping which greeted every successful stroke. The game is played as follows: two slightly sloping planks are placed at an appropriate distance from each other. The striker stands at the top end of his plank, wielding in his right hand a large wooden ring set with spikes. When one of his own team throws the ball towards him, he runs down to meet it so as to increase the force of the stroke with which he hits it. The opposing team try to return the ball, and in this way it keeps flying back and forth until someone misses it and it falls to the ground. The postures the players assume during the game are often very beautiful and deserve to be imitated in marble, especially that assumed by the striker as he runs down the plank and raises his arm to hit the ball. I was reminded of the gladiator in the Villa Borghese. Almost all the players were well-developed muscular young men in short, tight-fitting white clothes. The teams were distinguished by badges of different colours. It seems odd that they should play this game near an old city wall where there is no proper provision for spectators. Why don't they play in the amphitheatre, where there is ample room?

17 September

I shall comment only briefly on all the pictures I have seen. My purpose in making this wonderful journey is not to delude myself but to discover myself in the objects I see. I must admit quite honestly that I understand very little about art or the craft of the artist, and must confine my observations to the subjects of the paintings and their general pictorial treatment.

The Church of San Giorgio is like an art gallery. All the pictures are altarpieces which vary in merit but all are well worth seeing. But what subjects these poor artists had to paint! And for what patrons! A rain of manna, thirty feet long and twenty feet high, and, as a companion picture, the miracle of the five loaves! What is there worth painting about that? Hungry persons pounce upon some small crumbs, bread is handed out to countless others. The painters have racked their brains to give these trivialities some significance. Still, genius, stimulated by these demands, has created many beautiful works. One painter, faced with the problem of representing St Ursula with her eleven thousand virgins, solved it very cleverly. The saint stands in the foreground, looking as though she has conquered the country. She has the noble, but quite unattractive, appearance of a virgin Amazon. In diminished perspective her little troop is seen stepping ashore from the ship and approaching in procession. Titian's *Assumption of the Virgin in the Cathedral* has become very black. One is grateful to this painter for letting the Goddess-to-be look down at her friends below, instead of gazing up to Heaven.

In the Gherardini Gallery I found some beautiful things by Orbetto. This was the first time I had heard of him. When one lives far away, one hears only of the major artists in the galaxy and is often satisfied with merely knowing their names; but when one draws closer, the twinkle of stars of the second and third magnitude becomes visible until, finally, one sees the whole constellation – the world is wider and art richer than one had hitherto supposed. One picture I must especially praise. It contains only two half-length human figures. Samson has just fallen asleep in the lap of Delilah, who is reaching furtively across his body for a pair of scissors which lies on a table by a lamp. The execution is very fine. I was also struck by a *Danaë* in the Palazzo Canossa.

The Palazzo Bevilacqua houses many treasures. A so-called *Paradise* by Tintoretto – actually it is the Coronation of Mary in the presence of all the patriarchs, prophets, apostles, saints, angels, etc. – gave that happy genius the opportunity to display all his riches. To appreciate his vision, the facility of his brush and the variety of his expressive means, one would have to own this composition and have it before one's eyes for a whole lifetime. The technique is flawless. Even the heads of the most distant angels, vanishing into the clouds of glory, have individual features. The tallest figures are about a foot high; Mary and Christ, who is placing the crown on her head, measure about four inches. The loveliest creature in the picture, without any doubt, is Eve – still, as of old, a bit voluptuous.

A few portraits by Paul Veronese have increased my respect for this artist. The collection of antiques is magnificent, especially a son of Niobe prostrate in death. Most of the portrait busts, which include an Augustus wearing the civic crown and a Caligula, are interesting in spite of their restored noses. My natural disposition is to reverence the good and the beautiful, so to be able to cultivate it day after day and hour after hour in the presence of such noble objects makes me feel very happy.

In a country where everyone enjoys the day but the evening even more, sunset is an important moment. All work stops; those who were strolling about return to their homes; the father wants to see the daughter back in the house – day has ended. We Cimmerians hardly know the real meaning of day. With our perpetual fogs and cloudy skies we do not care if it is day or night, since we are given so little time to take walks and enjoy ourselves out of doors. But here, when night falls, the day consisting of evening and morning is definitely over, twenty-four hours have been spent, and time begins afresh. The bells ring, the rosary is said, the maid enters the room with a lighted lamp and says: '*Felicissima notte!*' This period of time varies in length according to the season, and the people who live here are so full of vitality that this does not confuse them, because the pleasures of their existence are related, not to the precise hour, but to the time of day. If one were to force a German clock hand on them, they would be at a loss, for their own method of time measurement is closely bound up with their nature. An hour or an hour and a half before sunset, the nobility set out in their carriages; first they drive to the Bra, then down the long broad street to the Porta Nuova, through the gate and round the city walls. As soon as the hour of night rings, they all return; some drive to churches to recite the Ave Maria della Sera, others stop in the Bra, when the cavaliers approach the carriages and engage the ladies in conversation. This goes on for quite a while. I have never stayed to the end, but pedestrians remain in the streets until far into the night. Today it rained just enough to lay the dust. It was a gay and lively sight.

In order to adapt myself to one of the important customs of this country, I have invented a method which makes it easier for me to learn their system of counting the hours. The enclosed diagram will give you an idea of it. The inner circle shows our twenty-four hours from midnight to midnight, divided into two periods of twelve hours, as we count them and our clocks mark them. The middle circle shows how the bells are rung here at this time of year; they also ring up to twelve twice within twenty-four hours, but when our clocks would strike eight, they strike one, and so on till the twelve-hour cycle is completed. The outer circle shows how they reckon up to twenty-four. At night, for instance, if I hear seven strokes and I know that midnight is at five, I subtract five from seven and get the answer two in the morning. If, during the day, I hear seven rings and know that noon is at five, I do the same subtraction and the answer is two in the afternoon. But if I wish to refer to those hours according to local usage, I have to remember that noon is called seventeen hours; then I add this seventeen to the two and say nineteen hours. When you learn about this for the first time and start to figure it out, it seems extremely complicated and difficult to put into practice. But one soon gets used to it, and even finds the calculation as entertaining as the local inhabitants, who delight in this constant counting and recounting, like children who enjoy difficulties which are easy to master. They always have their fingers in the air, anyway, do all their counting in their heads and are fascinated by numbers.

Besides, the whole business is much easier for them because they do not pay the slightest attention to noon and midnight or compare, as we do, the two hands of a clock. They simply count the evening hours as they ring, and, during the day, add this number to the variable noon number with which they are familiar. The rest is explained by the table accompanying the diagram (see p. 61).

People here are always busily on the move, and certain streets where the shops and stalls of the artisans are crowded close together look especially merry. These shops have no front doors, but are open to the street, so that one can look straight into their interiors and watch everything that is going on – the tailors sewing, the cobblers stretching and hammering, all of them half out in the street. At night, when the lights are burning, it is a lively scene.

On market days the squares are piled high with garlic and onions and every sort of vegetable and fruit. The people shout, throw things, scuffle, laugh and sing all day long. The mild climate and cheap food make life easy for them. At night the singing and the music get even louder. The ballad of Marlborough* can be heard in every street, and here and there a dulcimer or a violin as well. They whistle and imitate all kinds of birdcalls; one hears the most peculiar sounds. In the exuberance of their life this shadow of a nation still seems worthy of respect.

The squalor and lack of comfort in their houses, which shock us so much, spring from the same source; they are always out of doors and too carefree to think about anything. The lower classes take everything as it comes, even the middle classes live in a happy-go-lucky fashion, and the rich and the nobility shut themselves up in their houses, which are by no means as comfortable

---

* Malbrouk [Marlborough] s'en va-t-en guerre. Popular satirical ballad on the English General dating from the Seven Years War (1707–13).

Comparative circle giving the Italian and German time measurements and the Italian hours for the latter half of September

Midday

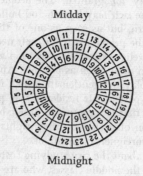

Midnight

From August to November the night increases in length by half an hour every half-month			From February to May the day increases in length by half an hour every half-month		
Month	Sunset by our clocks	Midnight by Italian time [hours]	Month	Sunset by our clocks	Midnight in Italy [hours]
Aug. 1	8.30 p.m.	3½	Feb. 1	5.30 p.m.	6½
Aug. 15	8.00 p.m.	4	Feb. 15	6.00 p.m.	6
Sept. 1	7.30 p.m.	4½	Mar. 1	6.30 p.m.	5½
Sept. 15	7.00 p.m.	5	Mar. 15	7.00 p.m.	5
Oct. 1	6.30 p.m.	5½	Apr. 1	7.30 p.m.	4½
Oct. 15	6.00 p.m.	6	Apr. 15	8.00 p.m.	4
Nov. 1	5.30 p.m.	6½	May 1	8.30 p.m.	3½
Nov. 15	5.00 p.m.	7	May 15	9.00 p.m.	3

In December and January the time does not change

In June and July the time does not change

Month	Sunset by our clocks	Midnight in Italy [hours]	Month	Sunset by our clocks	Midnight in Italy [hours]
Dec. Jan.	5.00 p.m.	7	July June	9.00 p.m.	3

as a house in the north. They entertain company in public buildings. The porticos and courtyards are filthy with ordure and this is taken completely for granted. The people always feel that they come first. The rich may be rich and build their palaces, the nobility may govern, but as soon as one of them builds a courtyard or a portico, the people use it for their needs, and their most urgent need is to relieve themselves as soon as possible of what they have partaken of as often as possible. Any man who objects to this must not play the gentleman, which means, he must not behave as though part of his residence was public property; he shuts his door and that is accepted. In public buildings the people would never dream of giving up their rights and that is what, throughout Italy, foreigners complain of.

Today I strolled about the city studying costumes and manners, especially those of the middle classes, who are the most numerous and the most active. They swing their arms as they walk. Persons of higher rank, who wear swords on occasion, only swing the right arm, since they are accustomed to keeping their left arm at their side.

Though the people go about their business with such unconcern, they have a sharp eye for anything unusual. When I first arrived, everybody looked at my high boots, which, even in winter, are not worn here because they are too expensive. Now that I am wearing shoes and stockings, nobody any longer pays me attention. But early this morning, when they were all running this way and that with flowers, vegetables, garlic and other market products, to my great surprise they could not take their eyes off some cypress branches I had in my hands. These branches had green cones hanging from them, and I was also carrying some sprigs of blossom from a caper bush. Everybody, young and old, kept staring at my fingers, and strange thoughts seemed to be passing through their heads.*

I had picked them in the Giardino Giusti, where huge cypresses soar into the air like awls. The yew trees, which, in our northern gardens, are clipped to a point, are probably imitations of this magnificent product of nature. A tree whose every branch, from

---

*Cypress branches were usually carried by mourners.

the lowest to the highest, aspires to heaven and which may live three hundred years deserves to be venerated. Judging from the date when the garden was planted, these cypresses must already have reached such a great age.

Vicenza, 19 September

The road from Verona to Vicenza runs in a north-westerly direction parallel to the mountains. To the left one sees a continuous range of foothills, composed of sandstone, limestone, clay and marl, dotted with villages, castles and isolated houses. A vast plain stretches to the right, across which we drove on a wide, straight and well-kept road through fertile fields. There trees are planted in long rows upon which the vines are trained to their tops. Their gently swaying tendrils hung down under the weight of the grapes, which ripen early here. This is what a festoon ought to look like.

The road is much used and by every sort of person. I was delighted to see carts with low wheels shaped like plates and drawn by four oxen carrying large tubs in which the grapes are brought from the vineyards to the wine presses. When the tubs are empty, the drivers stand in them. It reminded me very much of a triumphal Bacchanalian procession. The soil between the vine rows is used for the cultivation of all kinds of grain, especially maize and millet.

Near Vicenza a new range of hills rises, running north and south – they are said to be volcanic – which closes off the plain. At their feet, or rather in their semicircular recess, lies the city.

19 September

I arrived some hours ago and have already seen the Teatro Olimpico and other buildings by Palladio. An excellent little book with copperplates and a text has been published for the benefit of foreigners by someone with an expert knowledge of art. You have to see these buildings with your own eyes to realize how good they are. No reproductions of Palladio's designs give an adequate idea of the harmony of their dimensions; they must be seen in their actual perspective.

Palladio was a great man, both in his conceptions and in his power of execution. His major problem was that which confronts all modern architects, namely, how to make proper use of columns in domestic architecture, since a combination of columns and walls must always be a contradiction. How hard he worked at that, how the tangible presence of his creations makes us forget that we are being hypnotized! There is something divine about his talent, something comparable to the power of a great poet who, out of the worlds of truth and falsehood, creates a third whose borrowed existence enchants us.

The Teatro Olimpico is a re-creation of a Classical theatre on a smaller scale and indescribably beautiful. Yet, compared to our own modern theatres, it looks like an aristocratic, rich and well-educated child as against a clever man of the world who, though not as rich, distinguished or educated, knows better what it is within his means to do.

Looking at the noble buildings created by Palladio in this city, and noting how badly they have been defaced already by the filthy habits of men, how most of his projects were far beyond the means of his patrons, how little these precious monuments, designed by a superior mind, are in accord with the life of the average man, one realizes that it is just the same with everything else. One gets small thanks from people when one tries to improve their moral values, to give them a higher conception of themselves and a sense of the truly noble. But if one flatters the 'Birds' with lies, tells them fairy tales, caters daily to their weaknesses, then one is their man. That is why there is so much bad taste in our age. I do not say this to disparage my friends; I only say – that is what they are like, and one must not be surprised if things are as they are.

Beside the Basilica stands an old building resembling a citadel and studded with windows of unequal sizes. It is impossible to describe how wrong this looks. Undoubtedly the architect's original plan called for it to be demolished together with its tower. But I must control my feelings because here, as elsewhere, I so often come upon what I seek and what I shun side by side.

20 September

Yesterday I went to the opera, which lasted until long after midnight, and I was dying to get some sleep. Scraps of melodies from *The Three Sultanas* and *The Abduction from the Seraglio* had been not very skilfully pieced together. The music was easy to listen to, but probably the work of an amateur; there was not an idea in it which struck me as new. The two leading dancers performed an *allemande* with the utmost grace.

The theatre is new, of a modest elegance, and uniform in its decoration as befits a provincial town. From every box hangs a carpet of the same colour; only the box of the *Capitan grande* is distinguished by a slightly longer carpet.

The prima donna is very popular and received a tremendous ovation every time she came on stage, and the 'Birds' went wild with joy when she sang anything well, which she often did. She had a natural manner, a good figure, agreeable features, a beautiful voice, and behaved very modestly; only her arm gestures were a little lacking in grace. But I do not think I shall go again. As a 'Bird' I feel I am a failure.

21 September

Today I paid a visit to Dr Turra, who for five years devoted himself passionately to the study of botany, compiled a herbarium of Italian flora and laid out a botanical garden for the late Bishop. Now all this is over. His medical practice has crowded out the study of natural history, worms have eaten the herbarium, the Bishop is dead, and the botanical garden has been planted with useful cabbages and garlic.

Dr Turra is a civilized and learned man. He told me his history frankly and modestly and with unfailing courtesy, but he showed no inclination to show me his collections, which may not have been in a presentable state. So our conversation soon came to a standstill.

Evening

I called upon Scamozzi, an old architect who has brought out a
book on Palladio and is himself a competent and dedicated artist.
He showed great pleasure at my interest and gave me some
information. The building of Palladio's for which I have a special
predilection is said to be the house in which he himself lived.
Seen at close range, there is far more to it than one would imagine
from a picture. I should like to see a drawing of it in colour which
would reproduce the tints that the stone and the passage of time
gave it. But you must not think that the architect built himself a
palace. It is the most unpretentious house in the world and has
only two windows, separated by a wide expanse of wall which
would easily have admitted of a third. One might make an
amusing picture, showing how this house is wedged between
its neighbours. Canaletto would have been the man to do
this.

Today I went to see a magnificent house called the Rotonda.
It stands on a gentle elevation half an hour out of town. It is a
square block, enclosing a round hall lit from above. On each of
the four sides a broad flight of steps leads up to a portico of six
Corinthian columns. Architecture has never, perhaps, achieved
a greater degree of luxury. Far more space has been lavished on
the stairs and porticos than on the house itself, in order to give
each side the impressive appearance of a temple. The house itself
is a habitation rather than a home. The hall and the rooms are
beautifully proportioned, but, as a summer residence, they would
hardly satisfy the needs of a noble family. But from whatever
direction one approaches it, the Rotonda is a fine sight. If one
walks round it, the variety of visual effect created by the square
block and the projecting columns is quite extraordinary. The
owner's ambition, to leave his heirs an enormous *fideicommissum*
and a tangible memorial to his wealth, is perfectly realized. Just
as the house can be seen in all its splendour from every point
of the surrounding countryside, so the views of the countryside
from the house are equally delightful. You see the Bacchiglione
gliding along as they steer their barges downstream from Verona

to the Brenta, and you overlook the immense estates of the Marchese Capra, who desired that his family preserve them undivided. The inscriptions on the four gables, which together form a whole sentence, deserve to be recorded.

MARCUS CAPRA GABRIELIS FILIUS
QUI AEDES HAS
ARCTISSIMO PRIMOGENITURAE GRADUI SUBJECIT
UNA CUM OMNIBUS
CENSIBUS AGRIS VALLIBUS ET COLLIBUS
CITRA VIAM MAGNAM
MEMORIAE PERPETUAE MANDANS HAEC
DUM SUSTINET AC ABSTINET.

The last line is very odd; a man who had so much wealth at his disposal and could do what he liked with it still feels that he ought to sustain and abstain. That lesson, surely, could have been learned at less expense.

22 September

Tonight I attended a meeting at the Academy of the Olympians. It is hardly a serious affair but still a desirable one, for it adds some spice to the lives of these people. They had gathered in a large well-lit hall next door to the Teatro Olimpico. The Capitan and several representatives of the nobility were present. All told, there was an audience of about five hundred, all of them educated people.

The motion proposed by the President was: Which has been of greater benefit to the Arts – Invention or Imitation? Not a bad idea, for if one treats the alternatives as exclusive, one can go on debating it for centuries.

The Academicians took full advantage of the occasion and produced all sorts of arguments in prose and in verse, some of them very good ones. Moreover, they had an enthusiastic audience who shouted bravos, clapped and laughed. If only it were possible to stand up in front of one's own countrymen like this and entertain them in person, instead of having to confine one's best thoughts to the printed page of some book at which a solitary reader, hunched up in a corner, then nibbles as best he can.

Naturally, Palladio's name kept cropping up whenever the speakers were in favour of Imitation. At the end of the debate, when jokes are always expected, one of them wittily remarked that Palladio had already been taken care of by others, so he intended to praise Franceschini, the great silk manufacturer. Then he started to show how greatly his imitation of the fabrics of Lyon and Florence had profited this resourceful man and, through him, the town of Vicenza as well; therefore, Imitation was far superior to Invention. He said all this with such humour that the audience never stopped laughing. By and large, the advocates of Imitation received the greater applause because they voiced what the common herd thinks, so far as it is able to think.

At one point, for instance, the audience clapped enthusiastically at a very crude sophism because they had not felt the force of the many excellent arguments which had been offered in favour of Invention.

I am glad to have had this experience, and it was gratifying to see that, even after such a long time, Palladio is still revered by his fellow citizens as a lodestar and an example.

22 September

Early this morning I was in Thiene, which lies northward in the direction of the mountains. There they are putting up a new building on the ground-plan of the old, a laudable practice, showing a proper respect for the good heritage of the past. The castle is superbly situated on a wide plain against a background of limestone mountains without any intervening foothills. The traveller who comes by the road that runs in a dead-straight line towards the castle is greeted by lively streams on either hand, gushing down to water the vast rice fields he has just crossed.

So far I have seen only two Italian cities and only spoken to a few persons, but already I know my Italians well. They are like courtiers and consider themselves the finest people in the world, an opinion which, thanks to certain excellent qualities which they undeniably possess, they can hold with impunity. In my opinion, they are a very good people; to realize this, one has only to observe the children and the common folk as I do constantly, for I am in their company all the time and always enjoy it. And what beautiful faces and figures they have! I must particularly praise the people of Vicenza, for, in their town, one enjoys all the advantages of a great city. They do not stare at you, regardless of what you are doing; yet, when you speak to them, they are polite and ready to talk. I found the women especially agreeable. I do not wish to find fault with the women of Verona: they have well-developed figures and clear-cut features, but most of them are pale and the *zendale* is to their disadvantage, for, naturally, beneath such a charming costume one expects to see something especially fetching. Here, however, I have seen some very pretty creatures. Those with black curly hair were singularly attractive. There were blondes as well, but they are not really to my taste.

Padua, 26 September. Evening

I arrived here today, bag and baggage, after a three-and-a-half-hour drive from Vicenza in a single-seated little chaise called a *sediola*. The journey could have been made in half the time, but, as I wanted very much to enjoy a delightful day in the open air, I was not sorry that my *vetturino* failed to fulfil his obligation. We drove south-east across a fertile plain between hedges and trees without seeing anything special. At last, on the right, there rose a beautiful range of mountains stretching north and south. The profusion of flowers and fruits, hanging down from the trees and over the hedges and walls, was extraordinary. Roofs were laden with pumpkins, and the strangest-looking cucumbers hung from poles and trellises.

From the Observatory, I got a glorious view of the surrounding countryside. To the north lay the Tirolean Alps, snow-capped and almost hidden in clouds, and joined in the north-west by the hills of Vicenza. In the west and nearer, I could make out distinctly the folded shapes of the hills of Este. To the south-east an unbroken plain stretched away like a green sea, tree after tree, bush after bush, plantation after plantation, and, peeping out of this green, innumerable white houses, villas and churches. The

Campanile of San Marco and other lesser towers of Venice were
clearly visible on the horizon.

27 September

At last I have acquired the works of Palladio, not the original
edition with woodcuts, but a facsimile with copperplate engravings, published by Smith, an excellent man who was formerly
English consul in Venice. One must give the English credit for
having so long appreciated what is good and for their munificence
and remarkable skill in publicizing it.

On the occasion of this purchase, I had entered a bookshop,
which, in Italy, is a peculiar place. The books are all in stitched
covers and at any time of day you can find good company in the
shop. Everyone who is in any way connected with literature -
secular clergy, nobility, artists – drops in. You ask for a book,
browse in it or take part in a conversation as the occasion arises.
There were about half a dozen people there when I entered, and
when I asked for the works of Palladio, they all focused their
attention on me. While the proprietor was looking for the book,
they spoke highly of it and gave me all kinds of information about
the original edition and the reprint. They were well acquainted
both with the work and with the merits of the author. Taking
me for an architect, they complimented me on my desire to study
this master who had more useful and practical suggestions to
offer than even Vitruvius, since he had made a thorough study of
classical antiquity and tried to adapt his knowledge to the needs
of our times. I had a long conversation with these friendly men
and learned much about the sights of interest in the town.

Since so many churches have been built in honour of the saints,
it is good that a place should be found in them to erect memorials
to the intelligent. The portrait bust of Cardinal Bembo stands
between two Ionic columns. He has a beautiful face, withdrawn
upon itself by force of will, and an enormous beard. The inscription runs as follows :

Petri Bembi Card. imaginem Hier. Guerinus Ismeni f. in publico
ponendam curavit ut cujus ingenii monumenta aeterna sint ejus cor-
poris quoque memoria ne a posteritate desideretur.

As a building, in spite of all its fame, the university shocked me. I am glad I did not have to study there. Such a cramped school is unimaginable even to a German student, who often suffered agonies on the hard benches of the auditorium. The anatomical theatre, in particular, is an example of how to squeeze as many students together as possible. The listeners sit in tiers one above the other in a kind of high funnel. They look down from their precipice on to the narrow platform where the dissecting table stands. This gets no daylight, so that the professor has to demonstrate by the light of a lamp.

The Botanical Garden is much more cheerful. Many plants can stay in the ground all through the winter if they are planted near the walls. But towards the end of October the place is roofed over and kept heated during the short winter months. To wander about among a vegetation which is new to one is pleasant and instructive. It is the same with familiar plants as with other familiar objects : in the end we cease to think about them at all. But what is seeing without thinking? Here, where I am confronted with a great variety of plants, my hypothesis that it might be possible to derive all plant forms from one original plant becomes clearer to me and more exciting. Only when we have accepted this idea will it be possible to determine genera and species exactly. So far this has, I believe, been done in a very arbitrary way. At this stage in my botanical philosophy, I have reached an impasse, and I do not yet see how to get out of it. The whole subject seems to me to be profound and of far-reaching consequence.

The square called Prato della Valle, where the principal fair takes place in June, is of vast extent. The wooden stalls in the centre are not an attractive sight, but the Paduans assure me that they will soon have a *fiera* of stone like the one in Verona. Even now the surroundings of the square look impressive and promise well for this plan.

All around the edge of its enormous oval stand statues of famous men who either taught or studied here. Any native or foreigner is permitted to put up a statue of a certain size to any relative or fellow countryman, as soon as his merits and his connexion with the university have been proved.

The oval is surrounded by a canal. On the four bridges which

span it stand colossal statues of Popes and Doges, together with
smaller ones erected by guilds, private individuals and foreigners.
The King of Sweden has donated a statue of Gustavus Adolphus,
who, supposedly, once attended a lecture in Padua. The Arch-
duke Leopold has revived the memory of Petrarch and Galileo.
The statues are in a good modern style, very few over-mannered,
some quite lifelike, and all in the costume of their period and
their official rank. There is nothing undignified or in bad taste
about the inscriptions, either.

At any university this would have been a felicitous idea, but
nowhere so much as in Padua, for here one sees the evocation of
a past which is now closed.

In the place of assembly belonging to a religious brotherhood
dedicated to St Anthony, there are some ancient paintings, reminiscent of the old German school, among them some by Titian,
which show a progress in the art which no painter on the other
side of the Alps has so far made. I also saw some more modern
paintings. Though no longer able to reach the sublime dignity of
their predecessors, these artists have been extremely successful
in the lighter genre. The beheading of St John the Baptist by
Piazzetta is, after allowing for the mannerisms of this master, a
very good painting.

St John is kneeling, with his right knee against a rock and with
folding hands, looking up to heaven. Behind him, holding him
bound, a soldier bends forward to look into his face as if he
were surprised at the saint's composure. In the upper part of the
picture, another soldier is standing who is supposed to deal the
fatal blow; but he has no sword and is only making a gesture with
his hands as if he were practising the stroke beforehand. Below
him is a third soldier, drawing a sword out of a scabbard. The
idea, though not great, is felicitous, and the composition unusual
and effective.

In the Church of the Eremitani I saw some astonishing paintings
by Mantegna, one of the older masters. What a sharp, assured
actuality they have! It was from this actuality, which does not
merely appeal to the imagination, but is solid, lucid, scrupulously
exact and has something austere, even laborious about it, that
the later painters drew their strength, as I observed in Titian's

pictures. It was thanks to this that their genius and energy were able to rise above the earth and create heavenly forms which are still real. It was thus that art developed after the Dark Ages.

The audience chamber of the Palazzo Comunale, justly designated by the augumentative title *salone*, is such a vast closed-in shell that, even when one has just come from seeing it, one can hardly retain its image in one's mind. It is three hundred feet long, one hundred feet wide and, from floor to vaulted ceiling, one hundred feet high. People here are so used to living out of doors that the architects were faced with the problem of vaulting over a market square, so to speak. Such a huge vaulted space gives one a strange feeling. It is a closed-in infinity more analogous to human nature than the starry sky is. The sky draws us out of ourselves, but this gently draws us back into ourselves.

For the same reason, I like to rest for a while in the Church of St Giustina, which is four hundred and eighty-five feet long, and proportionately high and wide. Tonight I sat there meditating in a corner. I felt very alone, since no one in the world, even had he thought of me at that moment, would have looked for me in such a place.

I have now packed my bags once more. Tomorrow morning I am going to travel on the Brenta by boat. It rained today but it is now clear again, and I hope to see the lagoons in brilliant sunshine and send greetings to my friends from the embrace of the Queen Bride of the sea.

VENICE

It was written, then, on my page in the Book of Fate that at five in the afternoon of the twenty-eighth day of September in the year 1786, I should see Venice for the first time as I entered this beautiful island-city, this beaver-republic. So now, thank God, Venice is no longer a mere word to me, an empty name, a state of mind which has so often alarmed me who am the mortal enemy of mere words.

When the first gondola came alongside our boat – this they do to bring passengers who are in a hurry to Venice more quickly – I remembered from early childhood a toy to which I had not given a thought for perhaps twenty years. My father had brought back from his journey to Italy a beautiful model of a gondola; he was very fond of it and, as a special treat, he sometimes allowed me to play with it. When the gondolas appeared their shining steel-sheeted prows and black cages greeted me like old friends.

I have found comfortable lodgings in the Queen of England, not far from the Piazza San Marco. My windows look out on to a narrow canal between high houses; immediately below them is a single-span bridge, and opposite, a narrow, crowded passage. This is where I shall live until my parcel for Germany is ready and I have had my fill of sightseeing, which may be some time. At last I can really enjoy the solitude I have been longing for, because nowhere can one be more alone than in a large crowd through which one pushes one's way, a complete stranger. In all Venice there is probably only one person who knows me, and it is most unlikely that I shall meet him at once.

Venice, 28 September 1786

A few words about my adventures since leaving Padua. The passage down the Brenta in a public boat and in well-behaved company, since the Italians observe good manners among one another, was tolerably pleasant. The banks are studded with gardens and summer houses, small properties stretch down to the edge of the river and now and then the busy high road runs beside it. Since we descended the river by a chain of locks, there was a short delay every now and then when we could step ashore and enjoy the fruit which was offered us. Then we would board the boat again and continue gliding through a fresh and animated world.

To so many varied images was added a new apparition – two pilgrims who, though they came from Germany, seemed to have found their proper place here. They were the first I ever saw so close. They have right to free transportation on this public conveyance, but, since the other passengers avoided them, they did not sit in the covered space but astern with the steersman. Such pilgrims are rare in these days. They were stared at by everybody and treated with scant respect, for, in earlier times, many rascals roamed the countryside in this disguise. When I heard that they were Germans and could not speak any other language, I went aft to talk to them and learned that they came from the region of Paderborn. Both men were nearing fifty and had dark, good-natured faces. Their main goal had been the Shrine of the Three Magi in Cologne; then they had wandered across Germany and were now on their way to Rome. After that they planned to return to northern Italy; then one would wander back home to Westphalia, while the other made a further pilgrimage to S. Jago de Compostela.

Their habit was the conventional one but, with their tucked-up skirts, looked much better than the trailing taffeta habits we usually wear when we appear as pilgrims at our fancy-dress balls. The wide cape, the round hat, the scallop shell, that most primitive of drinking vessels, everything had its meaning and immediate use. Their passports were in a tin box. The most curious of their belongings were the small portfolios of red morocco in which they carried the small articles they needed for daily necessities. They had taken them out because they had found something in their clothes that needed mending.

Our steersman was happy to have found an interpreter and asked me to put various questions to them. In this way I learned

much about their opinions and their journey. They complained
bitterly of their fellow believers, even of secular priests and
monks. Piety, they said, seemed to be very rare, for no one was
inclined to believe in theirs, and in Catholic districts, almost
without exception, they were treated as vagabonds, even though
they immediately produced their itinerary, drawn up by their
superior, and their passports, issued by their bishop. On the other
hand, they told me with great feeling how well they had been
received by Protestants, particularly by a country pastor in Swabia
and even more so by his wife, who had persuaded her somewhat
reluctant husband to allow her to give them a much needed meal.
When they left, she even presented them with a *thaler*, which
had been a godsend to them as soon as they were back again in
a Catholic district. After telling me all this, one of them said with
the utmost seriousness: 'Of course, we remember this woman
every day in our prayers, praying that God may open her eyes
in the same way that He opened her heart to us, and that, even
this late, He may receive her into the bosom of the One True
Church. And so we hope and believe that we shall meet her
hereafter in Paradise.'

I sat on the small flight of stairs which led to the main deck
and interpreted what was relevant in this conversation to the
steersman and a few others who had left the cabin and crowded
into this narrow space. Meanwhile the pilgrims were given some
food, though not much, for Italians are not fond of giving. The
pilgrims then produced small consecrated slips of paper on which
were pictures of the Three Magi and appropriate devotional
prayers in Latin, and asked me to distribute them among the
small group of bystanders and explain their great value. I was
quite successful at this, too. When they seemed worried as to
how, in a great city like Venice, they would find the monastery
which puts up pilgrims, the sympathetic steersman promised that,
when they landed, he would give three *centavi* to a boy who
would guide them to that faraway place. He added, in an undertone, that they would find small comfort there. The institution
which had been founded on a grand scale to house God knows
how many pilgrims was now rather reduced and its revenues had
been turned over to other purposes. As we talked, we sailed down

the lovely Brenta, leaving behind us many wonderful gardens and magnificent palaces, and catching fleeting glimpses of prosperous coastal towns. At last we entered the lagoons and, immediately, gondolas swarmed around our boat. A passenger from Lombardy, a man well known in Venice, invited me to join him in one so that we might arrive in the city more quickly and avoid the ordeal of the Dogana. Some people wanted to detain us, but, with the help of a modest tip, we succeeded in shaking them off and, in the peaceful sunset, went gliding quickly towards our goal.

29 September. Michaelmas Eve

So much has been said and written about Venice already that I do not want to describe it too minutely. I shall only give my immediate impression. What strikes me most is again the people in their sheer mass and instinctive existence.

This race did not seek refuge in these islands for fun, nor were those who joined later moved by chance; necessity taught them to find safety in the most unfavourable location. Later, however, this turned out to their greatest advantage and made them wise at a time when the whole northern world still lay in darkness; their increasing population and wealth were a logical consequence. Houses were crowded closer and closer together, sand and swamp transformed into solid pavement. The houses grew upward like closely planted trees and were forced to make up in height for what they were denied in width. Avid for every inch of ground and cramped into a narrow space from the very beginning, they kept the alleys separating two rows of houses narrow, just wide enough to let people pass each other. The place of street and square and promenade was taken by water. In consequence, the Venetian was bound to develop into a new kind of creature, and that is why, too, Venice can only be compared to itself. The Canal Grande, winding snakelike through the town, is unlike any other street in the world, and no square can compete with the vast expanse of water in front of the Piazza San Marco, enclosed on one side by the semicircle of Venice itself. Across it to the left is the island of San Giorgio Maggiore, to the right the Giudecca with its canal, and still further to the right the Dogana with the entrance to the Canal Grande, where stand some great gleaming marble temples. These, in brief, are the chief objects which strike the eye when one leaves the Piazza San Marco between the two columns.

After dinner I hurried out without a guide and, after noting the four points of the compass, plunged into the labyrinth of this city, which is intersected everywhere by canals but joined together by bridges. The compactness of it all is unimaginable unless one has seen it. As a rule, one can measure the width of an alley with one's outstretched arms; in the narrowest, one even scrapes one's elbows if one holds them akimbo; occasionally there is a wider lane and even a little square every so often, but everything is relatively narrow.

I easily found the Canal Grande and its principal bridge, the Ponte Rialto, which is a single arch of white marble. Looking down, I saw the Canal teeming with gondolas and the barges which bring all necessities from the mainland and land at this point to unload. As today is the Feast of St Michael, the scene was especially full of life.

The Canal Grande, which separates the two main islands of Venice, is only spanned by a single bridge, the Rialto, but it can be crossed in open boats at various points. Today I watched with delight as many well-dressed women in black veils were ferried across on their way to the Church of the Solemnized Archangel. I left the bridge and walked to one of the landing points to get a closer look at them as they left the ferry. There were some beautiful faces and figures among them.

When I felt tired, I left the narrow alleys and took my seat in a gondola. Wishing to enjoy the view from the opposite side, I passed the northern end of the Canal Grande, round the island of Santa Chiara, into the lagoons, then into the Giudecca Canal and continued as far as the Piazza San Marco. Reclining in my gondola, I suddenly felt myself, as every Venetian does, a lord of the Adriatic. I thought with piety of my father, for nothing gave him greater pleasure than to talk of these things. It will be the same with me, I know. Everything around me is a worthy, stupendous monument, not to one ruler, but to a whole people. Their lagoons may be gradually silting up and unhealthy miasmas hovering over their marshes, their trade may be declining, their political power dwindling, but this republic will never become a whit less venerable in the eyes of one observer. Venice, like everything else which has a phenomenal existence, is subject to Time.

30 September

Towards evening I explored – again without a guide – the remoter quarters of the city. All the bridges are provided with stairs, so that gondolas and even larger boats can pass under their arches without difficulty. I tried to find my way in and out of the labyrinth by myself, asking nobody the way and taking my directions only from the points of the compass. It is possible to do this and I find my method of personal experience the best. I have been to the furthest edges of the inhabited area and studied the way of life, the morals and manners of the inhabitants. They are different in every district. Good heavens! what a poor good creature man is after all.

Many little houses rise directly from the canals, but here and there are well-paved footpaths on which one can stroll very pleasantly between water, churches and palaces. One agreeable walk is along the stone quay on the northern side. From it one can see the smaller islands, among them Murano, a Venice in miniature. The intervening lagoons are alive with innumerable gondolas.

Evening

Today I bought a map of the city. After studying it carefully, I climbed the Campanile of San Marco. It was nearly noon and the sun shone so brightly that I could recognize both close and distant places without a telescope. The lagoons are covered at high tide, and when I turned my eyes in the direction of the Lido, a narow strip of land which shuts in the lagoons, I saw the sea for the first time. Some sails were visible on it, and in the lagoons themselves galleys and frigates were lying at anchor. These were to have joined Admiral Emo, who is fighting the Algerians, but unfavourable winds have detained them here. North and west,

the hills of Padua and Vicenza and the Tirolean Alps made a
beautiful frame to the whole picture.

1 October

Today was Sunday, and as I walked about I was struck by the
uncleanliness of the streets. This set me thinking. There appears
to be some kind of police regulation on this matter, for people
sweep the rubbish into corners and I saw large barges stopping at
certain points and carrying the rubbish away. They came from
the surrounding islands where people are in need of manure. But
there is no logic or discipline in these arrangements. The dirt is
all the more inexcusable because the city is as designed for cleanliness as any Dutch town. All the street are paved with flagstones;
even in the remotest quarter, bricks are at least placed on the kerb
and, wherever it is necessary, the streets are raised in the middle
and have gutters at their sides to catch the water and carry it off
into covered drains. These and other technical devices are clearly
the work of efficient architects who planned to make Venice the
cleanest of cities as well as the most unusual. As I walked, I
found myself devising sanitary regulations and drawing up a
preliminary plan for an imaginary police inspector who was
seriously interested in the problem. It shows how eager man
always is to sweep his neighbour's doorstep.

2 October

I hurried off first thing to the Carità. I had discovered in the
writings of Palladio a reference to a monastery in which he had
intended to reproduce a typical private home of a rich and hos-
pitable man in classical times.

His plan, both in general design and in detail, had delighted
me and I expected to see a miracle of beauty. Alas, scarcely a tenth
of it has been built, but even this little is worthy of his divine
genius. I am convinced I am right when I say that I never saw
anything more sublime, more perfect, in my life. One ought to
spend years contemplating such a work.

The church is older. Leaving it, one enters an atrium of Corinthian columns which immediately makes one forget all ecclesiastical hocus-pocus. On one side is the sacristy, on the other the chapter house, and the most beautiful winding staircase in the world. This has a broad open newel and the stone steps are built into the wall and so tiered that each supports the one above it. How beautifully it is constructed can be gathered from the fact that Palladio himself was satisfied with it. From the atrium, one steps into a large inner courtyard. Unfortunately, of the building which was planned to surround it, only the left-hand side was finished – three superimposed orders of columns. The ground floor has porches, the first floor an arcade with cells opening into it; the top floor is a wall with windows.

Now a word about the construction. Only the capitals and bases of the columns and the keystones of the arches are carved in marble. All the rest is made, I cannot say of bricks, but of burnt clay. I never saw this kind of tile before. The friezes, the cornices and the sides of the arches are all made of it. The material was partly fired and the whole building held together with very little mortar. Even as it stands, it seems all of one piece, so what a wonderful sight it would have been if it had been finished and properly polished and coloured. But the scheme, as with so many buildings today, was on too large a scale. The artist had assumed, not only that the existing convent would be torn down, but also that some adjoining houses would be bought up. Probably the money ran out and he lost interest. O kindly Fates, who favour and perpetuate so many stupidities, why did You not allow this work to be completed !

3 October

The Church of Il Redentore, another noble work by Palladio, has an even more admirable façade than that of San Giorgio. Palladio was strongly imbued with the spirit of the Ancients, and felt acutely the petty narrow-mindedness of his times, like a great man who does not wish to conform to the world but to transform it in accordance with his own high ideals. From a casual remark in the book, I infer that he was dissatisfied with the custom of building Christian churches in the form of old basilicas, and tried

to make his sacred buildings approximate to the form of the
Classical temple. This attempt led to certain incongruities, which
seem to me to have been happily avoided in Il Redentore, but are
very conspicuous in San Giorgio. Volkmann says something
about this but he fails to hit the nail on the head.

The interior of Il Redentore is as admirable as the exterior.
Everything, including the altars, is by Palladio. Unfortunately,
the niches, which were meant to be filled with statues, are occupied by mediocre figures, carved in wood and painted all over.

3 October

The Capuchin friars had sumptuously decorated one of the side
altars in honour of St Francis. The only marble left visible was
the Corinthian capitals; all the rest was covered with what looked
like a magnificent arabesque embroidery. I was particularly impressed by the tendrils and leaves embroidered with gold thread,
and when I looked closer, I discovered an ingenious trick. Everything I had taken for gold was actually straw, pressed flat and
pasted on paper in beautiful designs. The ground was painted in
vivid colours and everything was executed in excellent taste.
If, instead of having been made in the convent for nothing, the
material of this piece of fun had been genuine gold, it would
probably have cost several thousand *thalers*. On occasions one
might very well follow their example.

On a quay overlooking the water I have several times noticed
a low fellow telling stories in Venetian dialect, of which, unfortunately, I cannot understand a word. His audience consisted for
the most part of people of the humblest class. No one laughed;
there was rarely even a smile. There was nothing obtrusive or
ridiculous about his manner, which was even rather sober; at the
same time the variety and precision of his gestures showed both
art and intelligence.

Map in hand, I tried to find my way through the labyrinth to
the Church of the Mendicants. Here is the Conservatorio, which
at the present time enjoys the highest reputation. The women
were singing an oratorio behind the choir screen; the church was

filled with listeners, the music beautiful and the voices superb. An alto sang the part of King Saul, the protagonist in the work. I have never heard such a voice. Some passages in the music were of infinite beauty and the text was perfectly singable – a kind of Italian Latin which made one smile at times but which gave the music wide scope.

The performance would have been even more enjoyable if the damned conductor had not beaten time against the screen with a rolled sheet of music as insolently as if he were teaching school-boys. The girls had so often rehearsed the piece that his vehement slapping was as unnecessary as if, in order to make us appreciate a beautiful statue, someone were to stick little patches of red cloth on the joints.

This man was a musician, yet he did not, apparently, hear the discordant sound he was making which ruined the harmony of the whole. Maybe he wanted to attract our attention to himself by this extraordinary behaviour; he would have convinced us better of his merits by giving a perfect performance. I know this thumping out the beat is customary with the French; but I had not expected it from the Italians. The public, though, seemed to be used to it. It was not the only occasion on which I have seen the public under the delusion that something which spoils the enjoyment is part of it.

Last night I went to the opera in San Mosè (here the theatres are named after the nearest church) and did not enjoy it much. The libretto, the music and the singers all lacked that essential energy which such performances need to reach perfection. One could not say that everything was bad, but only the two women took the trouble both to act well and to please. That, at least, was something to be thankful for. Both had beautiful figures and good voices and were lively, agreeable little creatures. The men, on the other hand, sang without any gusto and their voices lacked all brilliance.

The ballet was deficient in ideas and was booed most of the time. But one or two of the dancers, male and female, were wildly applauded. The girls considered it their duty to acquaint the audience with every beautiful part of their bodies.

Today I saw a very different kind of comedy which I enjoyed much more. In the Palazzo Ducale I witnessed an important trial, which, luckily for me, had come on during the vacation. One of the advocates was everything an exaggerated buffo should be: short and fat but agile, a very prominent profile, a booming voice and an impassioned eloquence, as though everything he said came from the bottom of his heart.

I call it a comedy because everything has probably already been settled before the public performance takes place; the judges know what they have to say, and the contending parties what they have to expect. Nevertheless, I much prefer this kind of proceeding to our fussy and complicated bureaucratic system. Let me try to give some idea of the amusing, informal and natural way in which such things are conducted here.

In a large hall of the palazzo, the judges sit on one side in a semicircle. Opposite them, on a platform large enough to seat several persons side by side, sit the advocates of both parties. On a bench facing them sit the plaintiff and the defendant. When I entered, the advocate for the plaintiff had left the platform, since today's session was not to be a legal duel. All the documents, pro and con, were to be read aloud, although they had already been printed. A scraggy clerk in a dingy black coat with a bulging file in his hands was preparing to perform his duties as a reader. The hall was packed and it was obvious that the legal issue was as important to the Venetian public as it was to the parties involved.

Fideicommissums enjoy a high legal status in the Republic. Once an estate is stamped with this character, it keeps it permanently, even though, for some special reason or other, it may have been sold several centuries ago and passed through many hands. If the question of ownership is ever raised, the descendants of the original family can claim their rights and the estate must be restored to them.

On this occasion the litigation was of particular importance because the complaint was against the Doge himself, or rather against his spouse, who was sitting there, on the little bench, wrapped in her *zendale*, with only a small space between her and the plaintiff. She was a lady of a certain age with a noble stature, regular features and a serious, even sour expression. The Venetians were very proud to see the princess appear before the court, in public and in her own palace.

The clerk started reading, and only then did I realize the significance of a little man sitting on a low stool behind a little table, not far from the advocates' platform, and of the hourglass he had in front of him. So long as the clerk is reading, the time is not counted, but if the advocate wishes to interrupt the reading, he is granted only a limited time. While the clerk reads, the hourglass lies on its side with the little man's hand touching it. As soon as the advocate opens his mouth, the hourglass is raised; as soon as he stops talking, it is laid down again.

Therefore, when the advocate wishes to attract the attention of the public or to challenge the evidence, it requires great skill on his part to do this effectively with brief comments. When he does, the little Saturn is completely nonplussed; he has to keep switching the hourglass from a horizontal to a vertical position and back every minute and finds himself in a similar situation to that of the evil spirits in the puppet play when the mischievous harlequin cries 'Berlicke! Berlocke!'* in such rapid succession that they never know whether they should come or go.

Only someone who has heard the collating of documents in a law court can have any idea of this method of reading – rapid monotonous, but quite articulate. A skilful advocate knows how to relieve the general boredom with facetious remarks, and the public responds to them with roars of laughter. I remember one joke, the most amusing of those I could understand.

The clerk was reciting a document in which the owner, whose right was in doubt, disposed of the property in question. The advocate asked him to read slower, and when the clerk came to the words 'I bestow, I bequeath' flew out at him, shouting: 'And what do *you* want to bestow? What do *you* want to bequeath? You poor starved devil, without a penny to your name! However,' he continued, apparently pulling himself together, 'the same could be said of our illustrious proprietor. He also wanted to bestow and to bequeath what belonged to him as little as it

---

* *Berlicke, Berlocke.* Magic spell from the old puppet play Dr *Faustus.*

belongs to you.' A burst of laughter ensued which went on for a long time, but the hourglass was immediately returned to its horizontal position, and the clerk went on droning and pulling faces at the advocate. All this clowning, however, is arranged in advance.

4 October

At the Teatro San Luca yesterday I saw an improvised comedy, played in masks with great bravura. The actors were, of course, unequal. Pantalone, very good; one woman, without being an outstanding actress, had an excellent delivery and stage presence. The subject was a fantastic one, similar to that which is played in our country under the title *Der Verschlag*.

We were entertained for more than three hours with one incredible situation after the other. But once again, the basis of everything is the common people; the spectators join in the play and the crowd becomes part of the theatre. During the daytime, squares, canals, gondolas and palazzi are full of life as the buyer and the seller, the beggar and the boatman, the housewife and the lawyer offer something for sale, sing and gamble, shout and swear. In the evening these same people go to the theatre to behold their actual life, presented with greater economy as make-believe interwoven with fairy stories and removed from reality by masks, yet, in its characters and manners, the life they know. They are delighted, like children, shouting, clapping and generally making a din. From sunset to sunset, from midnight to midnight, they are just the same. Indeed, I never saw more natural acting than that of these masked players, an art which can only be achieved by an extraordinarily happy nature and long practice.

As I write this, a regular bedlam has broken loose under my window, although it is past midnight. Whether for good or ill, they are always up to something together. Now I have heard three fellows telling stories on a square and a quay, also two lawyers, two preachers and a troupe of comic actors. All of them had something in common, not only because they are all natives of a country where people live in public all the time, and are all passionate talkers, but also because they imitate each other, and share a common language of gesture which accompanies what they say and feel.

Today is the feast of St Francis, and I went to the Church alle Vigne, which is dedicated to him. The loud voice of a Capuchin friar was accompanied like an antiphon by the shouts of the vendors in front of the church. I stood in the doorway between them and it sounded rather curious.

5 October

This morning I visited the Arsenal, which I found most interesting because I am ignorant of naval matters and managed to learn a few elementary facts there. It was like visiting some old family which, though past its prime, still shows signs of life. I always enjoy watching men at work and I saw many noteworthy things. I climbed up on to a ship of eighty-four cannon, the finished hull of which was standing there. Six months ago, in the Riva degli Schiavoni, a similar ship burned down to the waterline. The powder magazine was not very full, so not much harm was done when it exploded; all that happened was that the houses in the neighbourhood lost their windows.

Watching the men working with the finest Istrian oak provoked some mental reflections on the growth of this valuable tree. I cannot repeat often enough how much my hard-won knowledge of those natural things, which man takes as his raw material and transforms to suit his needs, helps me to get a clearer idea of the craftsman's technique. Just as my knowledge of mountains and the minerals extracted from them is of great advantage to me in my study of architecture.

To describe the *Bucentaur* in one word, I shall call it a show-galley. The old *Bucentaur*, of which pictures still exist, justifies the epithet still more than the present one which, by its splendour, makes one forget the original. I always return to my old contention that any artist can create something genuine if he is given a genuine task. In this case, he was commissioned to construct a galley worthy of carrying the heads of the Republic on their most solemn day to the sacrament of their traditional sea

power, and this task was admirably performed. One should not
say that it is overladen with ornaments, for the whole ship is one
single ornament. All the wood carving is gilded and serves no
purpose except to be a true monstrance showing the people their
masters in a splendid pageant. As we know, people who like to
decorate their own hats like to see their superiors elegantly
dressed as well. This state barge is a real family heirloom, which
reminds us of what the Venetians once believed themselves to be,
and were.

At night

I have just got back from the Tragedy and am still laughing, so
let me commit this farce to paper at once. The piece was not bad;
the author had jumbled together all the tragic matadors, and the
actors had good roles. Most of the situations were stale, but a few
were fresh and quite felicitous. Two fathers who hated each other,
the sons and daughters of these divided families passionately in
love crosswise, one couple even secretly married. Violent, cruel
things went on and in the end nothing remained to make the
young people happy but that their fathers should stab one
another, whereupon the curtain fell to thundering applause. The
audience did not stop shouting *'fuora'* until the two leading
couples condescended to creep round from behind one side of the
curtain, make their bows and go off on the other.

The audience was still not satisfied but continued clapping and
shouting *'I morti!'* until the two dead men also appeared and
bowed, whereupon a few voices cried: *'Bravi i morti'*; and it was
some time before they were allowed to make their exit. To get
the full flavour of this absurdity, one must see and hear it for
oneself. My ears are ringing with the *bravo! bravi!* which Italians
are for ever shouting, and now I have even heard the dead
acclaimed with this compliment. *Good night!* We northerners say
this at any time after sundown when we take leave of each other;
the Italian says *'Felicissima notte!'* only once, to wit, when the
lamp is brought into the room at the moment that separates day
from night, so that the phrase has quite a different meaning. The
idioms of every language are untranslatable, for any word, from

the noblest to the coarsest, is related to the unique character, beliefs and way of life of the people who speak it.

I learned many things from yesterday's tragedy. To begin with, I heard how the Italians declaim their iambic hendecasyllabics. Then I now see with what skill Gozzi combined the use of masks with tragic characters. This is the proper spectacle for a people who want to be moved in the crudest way. They take no sentimental interest in misfortune and enjoy themselves only if the hero declaims well. They set great store by rhetoric and, at the same time, they want to laugh at some nonsense.

Their interest in a play is limited to what they feel is real. When the tyrant handed his son a sword and ordered him to kill his own wife, who was standing before him, the public expressed its displeasure at such an unreasonable demand, and so noisily that they almost stopped the play. They yelled at the old man to take his sword back, an action which would, of course, have wrecked the subsequent situations in the play. In the end, the harassed son came down to the footlights and humbly implored the audience to be patient for a little because the business would certainly conclude exactly as they hoped. But, artistically speaking, the situation of which the public complained was absurd and unnatural, and I heartily approved of their feelings.

I now understood better the long speeches and the many passages of dialectic in Greek tragedy. The Athenians were even fonder of talking than the Italians, besides being better at it. Their dramatists must certainly have learned something at the tribunals, where they spent whole days.

Looking at the buildings which Palladio completed, in particular at his churches, I have found much to criticize side by side with great excellence. While I was asking myself how far I was right or wrong about this extraordinary man, he seemed to be standing beside me, saying: 'This or that I did against my will, nevertheless I did it because it was the closest approximation to my ideal possible under the circumstances.'

The more I think about him, the more strongly I feel that,

when he looked at the height and width of an old church or house for which he had to make a new façade, he must have said to himself: 'How can you give this building the noblest form possible? Because of contradictory demands, you are bound to bungle things here and there, and it may well happen that there will be some incongruities. But the building as a whole will be in a noble style, and you will enjoy doing the work.' It was in this way that he executed the great conception he had in mind, even when it was not quite suitable and he had to mangle it in the details.

The wing of the Carità, therefore, must be doubly precious to us because here the artist was given a free hand and could obey his genius unconditionally. Had the convent been finished, there would probably be no more perfect work of architecture in the whole world today.

The more I read his writings and note as I do his treatment of classical antiquity, the more clearly I understand how he thought and worked. He was a man of few words, but every one of them carries weight. As a study of Classical temples, his fourth volume is an excellent introduction for the intelligent reader.

7 October

Last night, at the Teatro San Crisostomo, I saw Crébillon's *Electra* – in translation, of course. I cannot express how tasteless I found it and how terribly bored I was.

As a matter of fact, the actors were quite good and knew how to put over certain passages on the public. In one scene alone Orestes has no less than three separate narrations, all poetically embroidered. Electra, a pretty, vivacious little woman, spoke the verse beautifully, but her acting was as extravagant as her role, alas, demanded. However, I again learned something. The Italian iambic hendecasyllabic is ill-suited to declamation because the last syllable is always short and this causes an involuntary raising of the voice at the end of every line.

This morning I attended High Mass at the Church of Santa Giustina, where, on this day of the year, the Doge has always to be present to commemorate an old victory over the Turks. The

gilded barges, carrying the Prince and some of the nobility, land
at the little square; oddly liveried boatmen ply their red-painted
oars; on shore the clergy and religious orders, holding lighted
candles on poles and silver candelabra, jostle each other and
stand around waiting; gangways covered with carpets are laid
across from the vessels to the shore : first come the *Savii* in their
long violet robes, then the Senators in their red ones, and, last,
the old Doge, in his long golden gown and ermine cape and
wearing his golden Phrygian cap, leaves the barge while three
servants bear the train of his robe.

To watch all this happening in a little square before the doors
of a church on which Turkish standards were displayed was like
seeing an old tapestry of beautiful colour and design, and to me,
as a fugitive from the north, it gave keen pleasure. At home,
where short coats are *de rigueur* for all festive occasions and the
finest ceremony we can imagine is a parade of shouldered muskets,
an affair like this might look out of place, but here these trailing
robes and unmilitary ceremonies are perfectly in keeping.

The Doge is a good-looking, imposing man. Although, apparently, in ill health, he holds himself, for the sake of dignity,
erect under his heavy gown. He looks like the grandpapa of the
whole race and his manner is gracious and courteous. His garments were very becoming and the little transparent bonnet he
wore under his cap did not offend the eye, for it rested upon the
most lovely snow-white hair.

He was accompanied by about fifty noblemen, most of them
very good-looking. I did not see a single ugly one. Some were tall
and had big heads, framed in blond curly wigs. As for their faces,
the features were prominent and the flesh, though soft and white,
had nothing repellently flabby about it. They looked rather
intelligent, self-assured, unaffected and cheerful.

When they had all taken their places in the church and High
Mass had begun, the religious orders entered in pairs by the
west door, were blessed with holy water, bowed to the high altar,
to the Doge and to the nobility, and then left by a side door to
the right.

For this evening I had made arrangements to hear the famous

singing of the boatmen, who chant verses by Tasso and Ariosto
to their own melodies. This performance has to be ordered in
advance, for it is now rarely done and belongs, rather, to the
half-forgotten legends of the past. The moon had risen when I
took my seat in a gondola and the two singers, one in the prow,
the other in the stern, began chanting verse after verse in turns.
The melody, which we know from Rousseau,* is something
between chorale and recitative. It always moves at the same
tempo without any definite beat. The modulation is of the same
character; the singers change pitch according to the content of
the verse in a kind of declamation.

I shall not go into the question of how the melody evolved. It
is enough to say that it is ideal for someone idly singing to himself
and adapting the tune to poems he knows by heart.

The singer sits on the shore of an island, on the bank of a canal
or in a gondola, and sings at the top of his voice – the people here
appreciate volume more than anything else. His aim is to make
his voice carry as far as possible over the still mirror of water.
Far away another singer hears it. He knows the melody and the
words and answers with the next verse. The first singer answers
again, and so on. Each is the echo of the other. They keep this up
night after night without ever getting tired. If the listener has
chosen the right spot, which is halfway between them, the further
apart they are, the more enchanting the singing will sound.

To demonstrate this, my boatmen tied up the gondola on the
shore of the Giudecca and walked along the canal in opposite
directions. I walked back and forth, leaving the one, who was
just about to sing, and walking towards the other, who had just
stopped.

For the first time I felt the full effect of this singing. The sound
of their voices far away was extraordinary, a lament without
sadness, and I was moved to tears. I put this down to my mood
at the moment, but my old manservant said: 'è singolare, come
quel canto intenerisce, e molto più, quando è più ben cantato.'
He wanted me to hear the women on the Lido, especially those
from Malamocco and Pellestrina. They too, he told me, sing

*J. J. Rousseau, Recueil d'Airs, Romances et Duos, Paris, 1750.

verses by Tasso to the same or a similar melody, and added : 'It is their custom to sit on the seashore while their husbands are out sea-fishing, and sing these songs in penetrating tones until, from far out over the sea, their men reply, and in this way they converse with each other.' Is this not a beautiful custom? I dare say that, to someone standing close by, the sound of such voices, competing with the thunder of the waves, might not be very agreeable. But the motive behind such singing is so human and genuine that it makes the mere notes of the melody, over which scholars have racked their brains in vain, come to life. It is the cry of some lonely human being sent out into the wide world till it reaches the ears of another lonely human being who is moved to answer it.

8 *October*

I visited the Palazzo Pisani Moretta to look at a painting by Paolo Veronese. The female members of the family of Darius are kneeling at the feet of Alexander and Hephaestus. The mother mistakes Hephaestus for the King, but he declines the honour and points to the right person. There is a legend connected with this picture according to which Veronese was for a long time an honoured guest in this palace and, to show his gratitude, painted it in secret, rolled it up and left it under his bed as a gift. It is certainly worthy of such an unusual history. His ability to create a harmony through a skilful distribution of light and shade and local colours without any single dominant tone is conspicuous in this painting, which is in a remarkable state of preservation and looks as fresh as if it had been painted yesterday. When a canvas of this kind has suffered any damage, our pleasure in it is spoiled without our knowing the reason.

Once it is understood that Veronese wanted to paint an episode of the sixteenth century, no one is going to criticize him for the costumes. The graded placing of the group, the mother in front, behind her the wife, and then the daughters in order, is natural and happy. The youngest princess, who kneels behind all the rest, is a pretty little mouse with a defiant expression. She looks as if she were not at all pleased at coming last.

My tendency to look at the world through the eyes of the painter whose pictures I have seen last has given me an odd idea. Since our eyes are educated from childhood on by the objects we see around us, a Venetian painter is bound to see the world as a brighter and gayer place than most people see it. We northerners who spend our lives in a drab and, because of the dirt and the dust, an uglier country where even reflected light is subdued, and who have, most of us, to live in cramped rooms – we cannot instinctively develop an eye which looks with such delight at the world.

As I glided over the lagoons in the brilliant sunshine and saw the gondoliers in their colourful costume, gracefully posed against the blue sky as they rowed with easy strokes across the light-green surface of the water, I felt I was looking at the latest and best painting of the Venetian school. The sunshine raised the local colours to a dazzling glare and even the parts in shadow were so light that they could have served pretty well as sources of light. The same could be said of the reflections in the water. Everything was painted clearly on a clear background. It only needed the sparkle of a white-crested wave to put the dot on the *i*.

Both Titian and Veronese possessed this clarity to the highest degree, and when we do not find it in their works, this means that the picture has suffered damage or been retouched.

The cupolas, vaults and lateral wall-faces of the Basilica of San Marco are completely covered with mosaics of various colours on a common gold ground. Some are good, some are poor, depending upon the master who made the original cartoon. Everything depends on that, for it is possible to imitate with square little pieces of glass, though not very exactly, either the Good or the Bad.

The art of mosaic, which gave the Ancients their paved floors and the Christians the vaulted Heaven of their churches, has now been degraded to snuff boxes and bracelets. Our times are worse than we think.

The Casa Farsetti houses a collection of casts taken from the finest pieces of antique sculpture, a few of which I had already seen in Mannheim and elsewhere. A colossal Cleopatra with the asp coiled around her arm, sleeping the sleep of death – a Niobe shielding her youngest daughter from the arrows of Apollo with her cloak – a few gladiators – a winged genius resting – sitting or standing philosophers.

Many striking portrait busts evoked the glorious days of antiquity. I feel myself, alas, far behind in my knowledge of this period, but at least I know the way. Palladio has opened it to me, and the way to all art and life as well. This may sound a little strange, but it is not quite so paradoxical as the case of Jacob Boehme, to whom Jove's thunderbolt revealed the secret of the universe while he was looking at a pewter bowl. The collection contains also a fragment of entablature from the temple of Antoninus and Faustina in Rome which, in its striking modernity, reminded me of the capital from the Parthenon which stands in Mannheim. How different all this is from our saints, squatting on their stone brackets and piled one above the other in the Gothic style of decoration, or our pillars which look like tobacco pipes, our spiky little towers and our cast-iron flowers. Thank God, I am done with all that junk for good and all.

Before the gate of the Arsenal, there are two enormous lions of white marble; one is sitting erect, planted firmly on his forepaws, the other is lying stretched out. They are so huge that they make everything around them look small, and one would feel crushed oneself if sublime works of art did not always elevate the spirit. They are said to belong to the best period of Greek art and to have been brought here from the Piraeus during the glorious days of the Republic.

Some bas-reliefs let into the wall of the Church of Santa Giustina, the vanquisher of the Turks, probably come from Athens as well, but they are difficult to see properly because of the high choir stalls. They show genii dragging about attributes of the gods. The sacristan drew my attention to them because, so the story goes, Titian took them as models for the angels in his painting: the *Murder of St Peter Martyr*. They certainly are indescribably beautiful.

In the courtyard of a palazzo, I saw a colossal nude statue of Marcus Agrippa; the wriggling dolphin at his side indicates that he was a naval hero. How true it is that a heroic representation of the human being simply as he is makes him godlike.

I took a close look at the horses on the Basilica of San Marco. From below one can see that in some places they have a beautiful yellow metallic sheen but in others show a copper-green tarnish. We are told that once they were gilded, and at close quarters one sees that they are scored all over, because the barbarians could not be bothered to file away the gold but hacked it off with chisels. Still, it might have been worse; at least their forms have been preserved.

Early this morning a gondola took me and my old factotum to the Lido. We went ashore and walked across the spit of land. I heard a loud noise: it was the sea, which presently came into view. The surf was breaking on the beach in high waves, although the water was receding, for it was noon, the hour of low tide. Now, at last, I have seen the sea with my own eyes and walked upon the beautiful threshing floor of the sand which it leaves behind when it ebbs. How I wished the children could have been with me! They would so have loved the shells. Like a child, I picked up a good many because I have a special use for them. There are plenty of cuttlefish about, and I need the shells to dry the inky fluid they eject.

Not far from the beach lies the Cemetery for the English and, a little further on, that for the Jews, neither of whom are allowed to rest in consecrated ground. I found the graves of the good consul Smith and his first wife. To him I owe my copy of Palladio, and I offered up a grateful prayer at his unconsecrated grave, which was half buried in the sand.

You must think of the Lido as a dune. The wind stirs up the sand, blows it in all directions and piles it up on all sides in drifts. Soon no one will be able to find this grave, though it is raised fairly high above the ground level.

What a magnificent sight the sea is! I shall try to go out in a boat with the fishermen; the gondolas dare not risk putting out to open sea.

Along the shore I found various plants whose common characteristics gave me a better understanding of their individual

natures. All are plump and firm, juicy and tough, and it is clear
that the salt content of the sand and, even more, the salt in the
air is responsible. They are bursting with sap like aquatic plants,
yet hardly like mountain flora. The tips of their leaves have a
tendency to become prickly like thistles, and when this happens,
the spikes grow very long and tough. I found a cluster of such
leaves which I took to be our harmless coltsfoot, but it was armed
with sharp weapons, and the leaves, the seed capsules and the
stalks were as tough as leather. Actually, it was sea holly (*Eryn-
gium maritimum*). I shall bring seeds and pressed leaves with me.

The fish market offers countless varieties of sea food. It is
delightful to wander through it inspecting the luckless denizens
of the sea which the nets have caught.

9 October

A precious day from beginning to end! I visited Pellestrina,
opposite Chioggia, where the Republic is constructing huge
defences against the sea called *i murazzi*. These are built of un-
cemented stone blocks and are intended to protect the Lido in
times of storm. The lagoons are a creation of nature. The interaction of tides and earth, followed by the gradual fall in level of
the primeval ocean, formed an extensive tract of swampland at
the extreme end of the Adriatic, which was covered at high tide
but partly exposed at low.

Human skill took over the highest portions of ground and thus
Venice came into being as a cluster of hundreds of islands surrounded by hundreds of other islands. At great cost and with
incredible energy, deep channels were dredged to enable warships
to reach the vital points even at low tide.

All that intelligence and hard work created in times past,
intelligence and hard work have now to preserve. There are only
two gaps in the Lido through which the sea can enter the lagoons
– one near the Castello and one near Chioggia. Normally the
tide flows in and out twice a day, and the current always follows
the same course. The high tide covers the marshy patches but
leaves the higher ground still visible, if not dry.

But it would be a very different matter if the sea should attack the spit of land and make new breaches so that it could flow in and out at will. Not only would the little towns on the Lido, Pellestrina, S. Pietro and others, be submerged, but also the system of communicating channels would be silted up. The Lido would be transformed into islands and the islands behind it into tongues of land. To prevent this, the Venetians must make every effort to protect the Lido, so that the angry element cannot destroy or alter that which man has already conquered and to which he has given shape and direction for his own purposes.

In times of abnormally high tides it is especially fortunate that the sea can only enter at two points and is shut out elsewhere. The fury of its entry is curbed and in a few hours it has to submit again to the law of reflux.

Actually, the Venetians have little to worry about: the slowness with which the sea is receding guarantees them security for millennia, and, by intelligently improving their system of dredged channels, they will do their best to keep their possessions intact.

If only they would keep their city cleaner! It may be forbidden, under severe penalties, to empty garbage into the canals, but that does not prevent a sudden downpour from sweeping into them all the rubbish that has accumulated at the street corners, or, what is worse, from washing it into the drains, which are only meant to carry off water, and choking them, so that the main squares are in constant danger of being flooded. I have even seen the drains in the little square of San Marco, which are as sensibly distributed as those on the big one, choked to overflowing.

On rainy days a disgusting sludge collects underfoot; the coats and *tabarros*, which are worn all year round, are bespattered whenever you cross a bridge, and, since everybody goes about in shoes and stockings – nobody wears boots – these get soiled, not with plain mud, but with a vile-smelling muck. Everybody curses and swears, but as soon as the weather clears up, nobody notices the dirt any more. It has been truly said that the public is for ever complaining that it is badly served but won't take the first step to see that it is served better. All this could be put right at once if the city authorities cared.

This evening I again climbed to the top of the Campanile. Last time I saw the lagoons in their glory at the hour of high tide;

this time I wanted to see them in their humiliation at low tide, so as to have a complete mental picture. It was very strange to see dry land all around where previously I had seen only a mirror of water. The islands were islands no longer but patches of higher ground rising from a large greenish-grey morass intersected by channels. The swampland is overgrown with aquatic plants and should, for that reason, be gradually rising, in spite of the pluck of the tides which never leave the vegetation alone.

To get back to the sea. Today I watched the amusing behaviour of the mussels, limpets and crabs. What an amazing thing a living organism is ! How adaptable ! How there, and how itself ! How useful my knowledge of natural history, scrappy though it is, has been to me, and how I look forward to increasing it ! But, when there is so much to share with them, I must not excite my friends with exclamations alone.

The sea walls of which I spoke are constructed as follows. First come some steep steps, then a gently inclined surface, then another step, then another incline and finally a vertical wall with a coping on top. The rising sea climbs the steps and slopes and only when exceptionally violent does it break against the wall and its coping.

In the wake of the tide come small mussels, univalved limpets and any other small creature that is capable of motion, crabs in particular. But they have hardly secured a hold on the sea wall before the tide begins to recede. At first the crawling swarm does not know what has happened to it, and expects the briny flood to return. But it does not return. The stone quickly dries in the blazing sun, and, at that, they begin to beat a hasty retreat. This gives the crabs their chance to go hunting. Nothing is more entertaining to watch than the movements of these creatures. All one can see is a round body and two long pincer claws; their spindly legs are invisible. They strut along as if on stilts, and as soon as a limpet starts moving, they rush forward and try to insert their claws into the narrow span between the limpet's shell and the ground so as to turn it upside down and devour the now defenceless molusc. But as soon as the limpet senses the presence of its enemy, it attaches itself to the stone by suction. Now the crab puts on a bizarre and graceful performance. It capers around the shell like a monkey, but lacks the strength to overpower the powerful muscle of the soft little creature. Presently it abandons its quarry and hurries off to stalk another wanderer, while the first limpet continues slowly on its way. I did not see a single crab succeed, although I watched for hours.

10 *October*

At last I have seen a real comedy! At the Teatro San Luca today they played *Le Baruffe Chiozzotte*, one of the few plays by Goldoni which is still performed. The title might be roughly translated as *The Scuffles and Brawls in Chioggia*. The characters are all natives of that town, fishermen and their wives, sisters and daughters. The habitual to-do made by these people, their quarrels, their outbursts of temper, their good nature, superficiality, wit, humour and natural behaviour – all these were excellently imitated. I was in Chioggia only yesterday, so their faces were still vivid in my mind's eye and their voices still ringing in my ears. I enjoyed the play immensely, and could follow it fairly well, even though I did not understand all the local allusions. The plot is as follows: The women of Chioggia are sitting as usual in front of their houses along the water front, spinning, knitting, sewing or making lace. A young man passes by and greets one of them with greater warmth than the others. This sets off a gibing match. Tongues grow sharper and more sarcastic, one insult outdoes another, accusations are hurled back and forth until one virago blurts out the truth. At this, all hell breaks loose and the authorities are forced to intervene.

The second act takes place in a courtroom. It is not allowed to represent the nobility on the stage, so the place of the *podestà* is taken by the actuary. He orders the women to appear before him one by one. This arouses suspicion because he is in love with the leading lady and is only too glad of an opportunity to speak with her in private. Instead of interrogating her, he declares his love.

Another woman, who is in love with him and madly jealous, bursts into the room, followed by the enraged lover of the first lady and then by all the others. Fresh accusations are hurled, and hell breaks loose again in the courtroom as it had previously on the quayside.

In the third act the fun reaches its climax and the play ends with a hasty forced solution.

One character is a very happy dramatic invention. Among all these scandal-loving, loquacious people, there is one old fisherman whose physical faculties are impeded as the result of a hard life since childhood. Speech, in particular, costs him immense effort. He has to move his lips and wave his hands violently in the air before he at last manages to stutter out what he is thinking. Since he can only express himself in short sentences, he has developed a laconic and solemn manner of speech, which gives all his remarks the character of a proverb or an aphorism. This provides a perfect counterbalance to the uninhibited passionate behaviour of the other characters.

I have never in my life witnessed such an ecstasy of joy as that shown by the audience when they saw themselves and their families so realistically portrayed on the stage. They shouted with laughter and approval from beginning to end. The actors did an excellent job. Between them they represented all the types of character one finds among the common people. The leading lady was particularly charming – much beter than she was the other day as a tragic heroine. By and large, all the actresses, but especially this one, imitated the voices, gestures and temperaments of the people with uncanny skill, but the highest praise is due to the playwright for creating such a delightful entertainment out of thin air. Only someone in intimate contact with this pleasure-loving people could have done it. It is written with an expert hand.

Of Sacchi's company, for which Gozzi wrote and which is now scattered, I have only seen Smeraldina, who is short and plump but full of vivacity, and Brighella, a lean, well-built man whose facial play and gestures are particularly expressive.

Masks, which in our country have as little life and meaning for us as mummies, here seem sympathetic and characteristic expressions of the country: every age, character type and profession is embodied in some extraordinary costume, and since people run around in fancy dress for the greater part of the year, nothing seems more natural than to see faces in dominoes on the stage as well.

11 *October*

Since solitude amid a large crowd does not, in the long run, seem possible, I have struck up an acquaintance with an old Frenchman. He does not know one word of Italian and, in spite of all his letters of introduction, feels completely at sea. He is a man of some standing and has perfect manners, but he cannot come out of his shell. He must be in his late fifties. He has left a seven-year-old son at home and is waiting anxiously for news of him. He is travelling through Italy in great comfort but at great speed. All he wants is to have at least seen the country and learned as much as possible in passing. I have managed to do him a few good turns and give him some useful information. As I was talking to him about Venice, he asked how long I had been there. When I told him: 'Two weeks and for the first time,' he remarked: '*Il paraît que vous n'avez pas perdu votre temps.*' This is the first testimonial to my good conduct that I can present. He had been here a week and is leaving tomorrow. To have met in a foreign country such an incarnation of Versailles is an experience I shall treasure. 'Now, here's another kind of traveller for you,' I said to myself. It was amazing to me that a man who, in this way, was well educated, brave and decent could travel without noticing anything in the world outside himself.

12 *October*

Yesterday, at San Luca, they played a new piece, *L'Inglicismo in Italia*. Since there are a great many Englishmen living in Italy, it is only natural that notice should be taken of their behaviour, and I hoped to hear what the Italians think about their wealthy and welcome guests. But the play amounted to nothing. There were a few of the usual farcical scenes, but the rest was heavy and pedantic. Moreover, there was not a trace of the English character; just the usual Italian moral platitudes about the most commonplace matters.

It was not a success and came near to being booed. The actors did not feel in their element as they had on the square of Chioggia. This was the last play I saw here, and it at least did one thing for me. By contrast, it heightened my enthusiasm for the representation of real Italian life as I saw it the other night.

Having gone over my journal for the last time and inserted a few observations from my notes, I shall now arrange everything in the proper order, roll it up and send it off, to be submitted to the judgement of my friends.

There is much in this record, I know, which I could have described more accurately, amplified and improved, but I shall leave everything as it stands because first impressions, even if they are not always correct, are valuable and precious to us. Oh, if only I could send my distant friends a breath of the more carefree existence here ! It is true that the Italian has only the shadowiest idea of the ultramontane countries, but Beyond the Alps now seems dim to me too, though friendly faces beckon to me all the time out of the mists. The climate alone would lead me to prefer these regions to all others, if birth and habit were not powerful bonds. I should not like to live here permanently or anywhere else where I had no occupation. For the present the novelty of everything keeps me constantly busy. Architecture rises out of its grave like a ghost from the past, and exhorts me to study its precepts, not in order to practise them or enjoy them as a living truth, but, like the rules of a dead language, in order to revere in silence the noble existence of past epochs which have perished for ever.

Since Palladio keeps referring to Vitruvius, I have bought Galliani's edition, but this tome weighs as heavy in my luggage as it weighs on my brain when I study it. I find Palladio, by his own way of thinking and creating, a much better interpreter of Vitruvius than his Italian translator. Vitruvius is not easy reading : the book is written in an obscure style and needs to be studied critically. I skim through the pages or, to be more exact, I read it like a breviary, more from devotion than for instruction. Already the sun sets earlier and I have more time for reading and writing.

Everything that was important to me in early childhood is

again, thank God, becoming dear to me, and, to my joy, I find
that I can once again dare to approach the classics. Now, at last,
I can confess a secret malady, or mania, of mine. For many years
I did not dare look into a Latin author or at anything which
evoked an image of Italy. If this happened by chance, I suffered
agonies. Herder often used to say mockingly that I had learned
all my Latin from Spinoza, for that was the only Latin book he
had ever seen me reading. He did not realize how carefully I
had to guard myself against the classics, and that it was sheer
anxiety which drove me to take refuge in the abstractions of
Spinoza. Even quite recently, Wieland's translation of Horace's
Satires made me very unhappy; after reading only a couple, I
felt beside myself.

My passionate desire to see these objects with my own eyes had
grown to such a point that, if I had not taken the decision I am
now acting upon, I should have gone completely to pieces. More
historical knowledge was no help. The things were in arm's
reach, yet I felt separated from them by an impenetrable barrier.
Now I feel, not that I am seeing them for the first time, but that
I am seeing them again.

14 October. Two hours after sunset

Written during my last moments here. The packet boat for
Ferrara is about to leave at any minute. I am not sorry to leave,
because if I were to stay longer with any pleasure and profit, I
should have to alter my original plan. Besides, everybody is
leaving Venice now for their gardens and estates on the mainland. I have only been here a short time, but I have absorbed the
atmosphere of this city sufficiently, and I know that I shall carry
a picture away with me which, though it may be incomplete, is
clear and accurate so far as it goes.

FROM FERRARA TO ROME

16 October. On the boat. Early morning

MY fellow travellers are still asleep in the cabin, but I have passed the last two nights on deck, wrapped in my cloak. It only cooled off in the early hours of the morning. I have now crossed the forty-fifth parallel and must return to my old song : I would gladly let the inhabitants of this country keep everything if only, like Dido, I could enclose in strips of bull's hide enough of their climate to surround our houses with it. Climate, truly, makes all the difference to one's life. The weather during the voyage was glorious, and the ever-shifting landscape idyllic. The Po runs gently between vast plains. One can see no distant views, only the bushy and wooded banks. I saw some of the same sort of childish levees I had seen on the Adige. They are just as inefficient as those along the Saale.

Ferrara, 16 October. Night

I arrived here at seven in the morning, German time, and expect to leave again tomorrow. For the first time on my trip, I am in low spirits and feel utterly indifferent to this beautiful, depopulated city in the middle of a flat plain. Once upon a time these same streets were animated by a brilliant court. Here Ariosto lived disappointed and Tasso unhappy, and we persuade ourselves that we are edified by visiting their shrines. The mausoleum of Ariosto contains a great deal of badly distributed marble. Instead of Tasso's prison we are shown a woodshed or coal cellar in which he was certainly not confined. At first nobody in the house knows what one wants to see. After a while they remember, but not before they have been tipped. I was reminded of Dr Luther's famous ink stain which is touched up from time to time by the custodian of the castle. There must be something of an itinerant journeyman about most travellers to make them want to look for such signs. I got more and more depressed and was only moderately attracted by a beautiful academic institute which a native-born cardinal had founded and endowed. But some monuments of antiquity restored me to life.

I was further cheered up by a painting of John the Baptist confronting Herod and Herodias. The prophet, in his conventional desert costume, is pointing at the lady with a vehement gesture. She looks impassively at the king sitting beside her, while he looks calmly but shrewdly at the enthusiast. At the feet of the king stands a white dog of medium size, while a small Bolognese dog peeps out from under Herodias' skirt. Both dogs are barking at the prophet. What a jolly idea!

Cento, 17 October. Evening

I am writing from Guercino's home town and in a better mood than I was in yesterday. Cento is a small, clean and friendly town of about five thousand inhabitants. As usual, the first thing I did was to climb the tower. I saw a sea of poplars among which were small farms, each surrounded by its own field. It was an autumn evening such as our summer rarely grants us. The sky, which had been overcast all day, was clearing as the cloud masses moved northward and southward in the direction of the mountains. I expect a fine day tomorrow.

I also got my first glimpse of the Apennines, which I am approaching. Here the winter is confined to December and January; April is the rainy month, and for the rest of the year they have fair, seasonable weather. It never rains for long. This year September was better and warmer than August. I welcomed the sight of the Apennines in the south, for I have had quite enough of flat country. Tomorrow I shall write from their feet.

Guercino loved his native town as most Italians do, for they make a cult of local patriotism. This admirable sentiment has been responsible for many excellent institutions and, incidentally, for the large number of local saints. Under the master's direction, an academy of painting was founded here, and he left the town several pictures which are appreciated by the citizens to this day, and rightly so.

I liked very much one painting of his which represents the risen Christ appearing to His mother. She is kneeling at His feet, looking up at Him with indescribable tenderness. Her left hand is touching His side just below the wound, which is horrible and spoils the whole picture. He has His arm around her neck and is bending backward slightly so as to see her better. The picture is, I will not say unnatural, but a little strange. In spite of it, the figure remains immensely sympathetic. He looks at her with a quiet, sad expression as if the memory of His suffering and hers had not yet been healed by His resurrection, but was still present in His noble soul. Strange has made an engraving of this picture and I should be happy if my friends could at least see that. I was also attracted by an exquisite picture of the Madonna. The Child is reaching for her breast, which she modestly hesitates to bare. In another, the Child is in the foreground facing us, while the Madonna behind Him is lifting His arm so that He may bless us with His raised fingers. A happy idea, and very much in the spirit of Catholic mythology.

As a painter, Guercino is healthy and masculine without being crude. His work has great moral beauty and charm, and a personal manner which makes it immediately recognizable, once one's eye has been trained to look for it. His brush work is amazing. For the garments of his figures he employs particularly beautiful shades of reddish-brown which harmonize very well with the blue he is so fond of using. The subjects of his other paintings are not so happy. This fine artist tortured himself to paint what was a waste of his imagination and his skill. I am very glad to have seen the work of this important school of painting, though such a hasty look is insufficient for proper enjoyment.

Bologna, 18 October. Night

I left Cento early this morning and arrived here soon after. As soon as he heard that I had no intention of staying long, an alert, well-informed guide raced me through the streets and so many churches and palaces that I scarcely had time to mark in my Volkmann the places I visited, and who knows, if I look at the marks in the future, how many of them I shall remember? But now for a few highlights.

First of all, the Cecilia by Raphael. My eyes confirmed what I have always known: this man accomplished what others could only dream of. What can one really say about this picture except that Raphael painted it! Five saints in a row – their names don't matter – so perfectly realized that one would be content to die so long as this picture could endure for ever. But, in order to understand and appreciate Raphael properly, one must not merely glorify him as a god who appeared suddenly on earth without a father or a mother, like Melchizedek; one must consider his ancestors, his masters. These were rooted in the firm ground of truth; it was their labour and scrupulous care which laid the broad foundation; it was they who vied with each other in raising, step by step, the pyramid, on the summit of which the divine genius of Raphael was to place the last stone and reach a height which no one else will surpass or equal.

My historical interest has been greatly stimulated by looking at paintings by some of the older masters, such as Francesco Francia, a very fine painter, or Pietro di Perugia, such a good man that one feels like calling him an honest German soul. If only Dürer had had the good fortune to go further south in Italy. Poor Dürer! To think how such a genius – I saw some incredibly great works by him in Munich — miscalculated in Venice and made a deal with a priestly gang which lost him months of his time, and how, when he was travelling in the Netherlands, he bartered the supreme works of art with which he had hoped to make his fortune for parrots, and made portraits of the servants, who had brought him a plate of fruit, to save himself tips! The thought of such a poor fool of an artist is especially moving to me because, at bottom, my fate is the same as his; the only difference is that I know better how to look after myself.

This is a venerable, learned city, thronged with people. They wander about under the arcades which line most of the streets and shelter them from sun and rain as they buy and sell, do business, or stand and gape. Towards evening I escaped from these crowds and climbed the tower to enjoy the fresh air and the view. To the north I could see the hills of Padua, and beyond them the

Swiss, Tirolean and Friulian Alps, the whole northern chain, in fact, which at the time was wrapped in mist; in the west, a limitless horizon, broken only by the towers of Modena; to the east, a dead level plain stretching to the Adriatic and, to the south, the foothills of the Apennines, cultivated right up to their summits and dotted with churches and country houses like the hills of Vicenza.

There was not a cloud in the sky, but on the horizon hung a haze which the watchman of the tower told me had not disappeared for the last six years. The hills of Vicenza with their houses and little churches used to be clearly visible through a telescope, but nowadays this is rare, even on the clearest days. This fog clings by preference to the northern mountain chain and it is this that makes our dear fatherland such a Cimmerian country. The watchman also pointed out that, thanks to the healthy air, all the roofs of the town looked brand-new; not a tile had been affected by damp or overgrown by moss. This was true, but probably the quality of the tiles has something to do with it. In former times, at least, the tiles baked in this region were of excellent quality.

The leaning tower is frightful to look at, but it was probably built that way on purpose. My theory is that, during the times of civic feuds, every great building became a fortress and every powerful family built its own tower. After a bit, this became both a hobby and a point of honour; everybody wished to boast of having a tower. In due time perpendicular towers became too commonplace, so someone built a leaning one. If so, one must admit that architect and owner achieved their aim, for people are no longer interested in all the straight towers but only in the crooked one. I went up it later. The layers of bricks run horizontally. Given a good mortar and iron bars, it is possible to build the craziest things.

19 October. Evening

I have spent the day well just looking and looking. It is the same in art as in life. The deeper one penetrates, the broader grows the view. In the sky of art countless new stars keep appearing, the Carracci, Guido, Domenichino, and they puzzle me. To enjoy these children of a later, happier period properly would require a knowledge and a competence of judgement which I lack and which can only be acquired gradually. The main obstacle to understanding these painters is their absurd subjects, which drive me mad, though I would like to admire and love them.

It is as if the sons of gods had married the daughters of men and begotten of them a variety of monsters. It is always the same, even with a genius like Guido. You find yourself in the dissecting room, at the foot of the gallows, on the edge of the corpse pit. His heroes always suffer and never act. Never an interest in everyday life, always the expectation of something fantastic about to appear from outside. The figures are either of criminals or lunatics except when, as a last resource, the painter introduces a nude boy or a pretty girl into the crowd of spectators or treats the saintly heroes as if they were mannequins, draping them in cloaks arranged in beautiful folds. That is no way to convey an idea of human beings. Out of ten subjects, only one should have been painted and even that one the artist was not allowed to paint from the proper angle.

The large picture by Guido in the Church of the Mendicanti is, technically, everything a painting should be, but the subject is the ultimate in absurdities which can be forced upon an artist. It is a votive picture. The Senate, I gather, unanimously praised it, and thought it up as well. Two angels, worthy of comforting a Psyche in distress, are obliged to mourn over a dead body.

St Proculo is a fine figure, but the others! – all these idiotic bishops and priests! Below them cherubs are playing with attributes; the painter, with the knife at his throat, did what he could for himself and tried his utmost to indicate that it was not he who was the barbarian.

Two nudes by Guido: a St John the Baptist in the desert and a Sebastian, exquisitely painted, but what do they *say*? One gapes, the other writhes.

When I look at history in this black mood, I feel inclined to say: First faith ennobled the arts, then superstition took over and ruined them.

After supper, feeling a little gentler and less arrogant than I did this morning, I jotted down the following notes:

In the Palazzo Tanari there hangs a famous picture by Guido of Mary suckling her child. She is larger than life and her head might have been painted by a god. Her expression, as she looks down on the child at her breast, is one of speechless and utter submission, as if it were not a child of love and joy to which she is giving her breast, but a heavenly changeling; she cannot do otherwise and, in her deep humility, cannot understand why this should have happened to her. The remaining space is filled by a voluminous garment which is highly admired by connoisseurs, but I did not know quite what to make of it. For one thing, the colours have darkened, the room is badly lit and it was a cloudy day.

In spite of my state of confusion, I already feel that using my eyes, experience and curiosity are beginning to help me through these mazes. I was, for instance, much impressed by a *Circumcision* of Guercino's, because, by now, I know his work fairly well and love it. I forgave him his indelicate subject and enjoyed his execution. He has left nothing to the imagination, but everything is painted in a decent manner and as perfectly as if it were done in enamel.

And so it is with me as it was with Balaam, the confused prophet who blessed when he had come to curse; and this would happen more often if I were to stay longer.

But as soon as I see a picture by Raphael again, or one which can probably be attributed to him, I am immediately and completely restored to health and happiness. I found a St Agatha, an exquisite picture, though not too well preserved. The painter has given her a healthy, self-confident virgin quality, yet devoid of either coldness or crudity. I have this figure firmly printed on my mind. To her, in the spirit, I shall read my *Iphigenie*, and I shall not allow my heroine to say anything this saint would not like to say.

Thinking again of this 'sweet burden', which I am carrying with me on my pilgrimage, compels me to confess that, along with all the great objects of art and nature I have to cope with, a train of new and rather disturbing poetic images keeps running through my mind. After I left Cento, I meant to start working again on *Iphigenie*, but what happened? My imagination conjured up a plot about Iphigenia in Delphi and I had to develop it. Here it is, in briefest outline.

Electra, confident that Orestes will bring the image of Diana from Tauris to Delphi, appears in the temple of Apollo carrying the cruel axe which had wrought such disaster in the House of Pelops and dedicates it to the god as a final expiatory offering. By ill luck, a Greek enters and tells her that he accompanied Orestes and Pylades to Tauris and saw the two friends being led to death, while he fortunately escaped. The passionate Electra is beside herself and does not know whether to vent her fury on the gods or on men.

In the meantime Iphigenia, Orestes and Pylades have also arrived in Delphi. When the two sisters meet without recognizing one another, Iphigenia's divine composure makes a strong contrast to the human passion of Electra. The Greek who had escaped sees Iphigenia and recognizes her as the priestess who, he believes, had sacrificed the friends, and discloses her identity to Electra. Electra snatches back the axe from the altar and is about to kill Iphigenia when a fortunate turn of events averts this horrible crime. If this scene were written properly, it could be as great as anything ever put on the stage, but, even if the spirit were willing, how should I find the time to write it?

Since this rush of so many good and desirable things rather alarms me, I must tell my friends of a dream I had about a year ago which I felt to be significant. I dreamed that I landed from a fairly large boat on the shore of a fertile island with a luxuriant vegetation, where I had been told one could get the most beautiful pheasants. I immediately started bargaining for these birds with the natives, who killed them and brought them to me in great numbers. I knew they were pheasants, although, since dreams usually transform things, they had long tails covered with iridescent eyelike spots similar to those of peacocks or rare birds of paradise. The natives brought them on board and neatly arranged them so that the heads were inside the boat and their long gaily-coloured feather tails hung outside. In the brilliant sunshine they made the most splendid pile imaginable, and there were so many of them that there was hardly room for the steersman and the rowers. Then we glided over calm waters and I was already making a mental list of the names of friends with whom I meant to share these treasures. At last we reached a great port. I lost my way among huge masted ships, and climbed from one deck to another, looking for some place where I could safely moor my little boat.

Such fantastic images give us great delight, and, since they are created by us, they undoubtedly have a symbolic relation to our lives and destinies.

I have visited the famous scientific academy called The Institute or The Studies. This large building, especially its inner courtyard, looks austere enough, although the architecture is not of the best. On the stairs and in the corridors, though there is no lack of stucco ornament and decorative frescoes, everything is correct and dignified and I was astounded, I must admit, by the wealth of beautiful and interesting things which have been collected here. But, as a German, accustomed to a more liberal system of education, I do not feel quite at ease.

An earlier observation came back to my mind : though Time changes everything, men cling to the form of a thing as they first knew it, even when its nature and function have changed. The Christian Churches still cling to the basilica form, though that of a temple would be better suited, perhaps, to their ritual. Scientific institutions still look like monasteries because it was in such pious precincts that study found its first quiet refuge. The law courts in Italy are as lofty and spacious as the wealth of the community permits – one might be in a market square out of doors, where in ancient times justice was administered. And do we not go on building our largest theatres with all their appurtenances under one roof, as though it were the first fair booth to be temporarily hammered together with a few boards and nails? At the time of the Reformation the great influx of people thirsty for knowledge compelled students to board in private houses, but how long it took us before we laicized our orphanages and gave poor children the secular education which is so necessary for them !

I spent the whole of this beautiful day in the open air. The moment I get near mountains, I become interested again in rocks and minerals. I seem to be an Antaeus who always feels new strength whenever he is brought into contact with his mother earth.

I rode on horseback to Paderno, where the so-called Bolognese heavy spar is found. This they make into little cakes which, after they have been calcined, glow in the dark if they have been previously exposed to the light. Here they simply call them *fosfori*.

On the way there, after leaving behind some sandstone hills, I came upon whole boulders of muscovite mica, sticking up out of the ground. The hill where the spar is found is not far from a brick kiln and a stream formed by the conjunction of a number of brooks. At first I thought it was alluvial clay which had probably been washed down from the mountains by rain, but, on closer inspection, I found that its solid rock was a finely laminated schist, alternating with bands of gypsum. The schist is so mixed with iron pyrites that, in contact with air and moisture, it undergoes a complete change. It swells, the lamina disappear and a kind of clayey slate is formed, conchoidal and crumbly, with surfaces that glitter like bituminous coal. Only after examining large specimens and breaking several in pieces so that I could clearly see both surfaces, could I convince myself of the transformation. The conchoidal surfaces are spotted with white particles and sometimes with yellow. Gradually the whole surface of the hill decomposes until it looks like a large mass of weathered iron pyrites. Among the solid layers, there are some green and red ones which are hardened. I also saw frequent traces of sulphur ore.

I then climbed up a boulder-strewn gulley washed out of the mountains by the rains, and was delighted to see many specimens of the spar I was looking for, sticking out of its weathered sides. Some were quite clean, others still encased in clay. One can see at once that they are not alluvial detritus, but to determine whether their formation was simultaneous with that of the schist, or a result of the tumefaction or decomposition of the latter, would require a more careful examination. The specimens I found, large and small, are roughly egg-shaped and the smallest look vaguely like crystals. The heaviest piece weighs eight ounces and a half. In the same clay I also found perfect loose crystals of gypsum. Experts will be able to draw more precise conclusions from the specimens I shall bring with me. So here I am again burdened with stones ! I have packed up more than twelve pounds of the heavy spar.

20 October. At night

How much I could write if I were to tell you of all the ideas which ran through my head today. But I feel irresistibly drawn onward and can only concentrate with an effort on the present moment. Heaven, it seems, has been listening to my prayers, for I have just heard that a *vetturino* is leaving for Rome, and I shall go with him the day after tomorrow. Tonight and tomorrow, therefore, I must make my preparations, settle many things and do some work.

Lojano, in the Apennines.
21 October. Evening

I don't know whether I drove out of Bologna today or was driven out. In other words, I was given an opportunity of leaving even earlier and I jumped at it. So now, here I am in a miserable inn, in the company of a papal officer who is going to his home town of Perugia. To start a conversation when I joined him in the two-wheeled carriage, I paid him a compliment. As a German, I said, accustomed to associating with soldiers, I was very happy to be travelling in the company of a papal officer. 'I can easily understand', he replied, 'that you have a sympathy for the military profession, since I have been told that, in Germany, everybody is a soldier, but please don't be offended if I say that, though our duties are light and I can live perfectly comfortably in my garrison at Bologna, I, personally, would rather be rid of this uniform and look after my father's small estate. But I am the younger son and must take things as they come.'

22 October. Evening

Giredo is a dismal little hole in the Apennines, but I am very happy, knowing that the road is leading me ever nearer to my heart's desire. Today we were joined by a couple, an Englishman and his so-called sister. They have beautiful horses and are travelling without servants, and the gentleman evidently acts as groom and valet combined. They grumble incessantly about everything and might come straight out of the pages of Archenholz.*

The Apennines are a curious part of the world. At the edge of the vast plain of the Po, a mountain range rises from the lowlands and extends to the southern tip of Italy with a sea on each side. If this range had not been so precipitous, lofty and intricate that tidal action in remote epochs could have little influence, it would be only slightly higher than the rest of the country, one of its most beautiful regions, and the climate would be superb. Instead, it is a strange network of criss-crossing mountain ridges; often one cannot even find out where the streams are running to. If the valleys were filled up and the level areas smoother and better watered, the country might be compared to Bohemia, except that the mountains look totally different. But you must not picture it as a desert. Though mountainous, it is well cultivated, the chestnuts thrive, the wheat is excellent and the crops are green already. The road is bordered with evergreen oaks, and around the churches and chapels stand slender cypresses.

Last night the sky was cloudy, but today it is again fair and clear.

Perugia, 25 October. Evening

For two evenings I have written nothing. The inns were so bad that I could not find room even to spread out a sheet of paper. Moreover, since leaving Venice, my travelling spool does not reel off as pleasantly and smoothly as it did before, and everything is beginning to get in a muddle.

At ten o'clock our time, on the twenty-third, we emerged from

----

*J. W. Archenholz (1743–1812), author of *England and Italy*.

the Apennines and saw Florence lying in a broad valley which was amazingly densely cultivated and scattered with villas and houses as far as the eye could see.

I took a quick walk through the city to see the Duomo and the Battistero. Once more, a completely new world opened up before me, but I did not wish to stay long. The location of the Boboli Gardens is marvellous. I hurried out of the city as quickly as I entered it.

One look is sufficient to show one that the people who built it were prosperous and enjoyed a lucky succession of good governments. The most striking thing about Tuscany is that all the public works, the roads and the bridges, look beautiful and imposing. They are at one and the same time efficient and neat, combining usefulness with grace, and everywhere one observes the care with which things are looked after, a refreshing contrast to the Papal States, which seem to keep alive only because the earth refuses to swallow them.

All that I recently said the Apennines might have been, Tuscany is, for it lies so much lower, the ancient sea has done its duty and piled up a deep loamy soil. This is light yellow in colour and easy to work. The peasants plough deep furrows but still in the old-fashioned manner. Their plough has no wheels and the share is not movable. Hunched behind his oxen, the peasant pushes his plough into the earth to break it up. They plough up to five times a year and use only a little light manure which they scatter with their hands. At sowing time they heap up small, narrow ridges with deep furrows between them in which the rain water can run off. The wheat grows on the top of the ridges, so that they can walk up and down the furrows when they weed. In a region where there is a danger of too much rain, this method would be very sensible, but why they do it in this wonderful climate, I cannot understand. I saw them doing this near Arezzo. It would be difficult to find cleaner fields anywhere; one cannot see the smallest clod of earth; the soil is as clean as if it had been sifted. Wheat seems to find here all the conditions most favourable to its growth, and does very well. Every second year, they grow beans for the horses, which are not fed on oats. The lupines are already green and will be ripe in March. The flax is coming up. It is left out all winter and the frost only makes it all the more hardy.

Olives are strange trees; they look almost like willows, for they lose their heartwood and their bark splits open, but they look sturdier. The wood grows slowly and is very fine-grained. The leaf is similar to a willow leaf, but there are fewer to a branch. Around Florence, all the hill slopes are planted with olives and vines, and the soil between them is used for grain. Near Arezzo and further on, the fields are less cluttered. In my opinion, they do not check the ivy enough; it does great damage to the olives and other trees, and it would be easy to destroy. There are no meadows anywhere. I was told that maize had exhausted the soil. Since it was introduced, agriculture has declined in other ways. I believe this comes from using so little manure.

Tonight I took leave of my papal captain after promising to visit him in Bologna on my way back. He is a perfect type of the average Italian. Here are a few anecdotes to illustrate his character.

Having often seen me lost in silent thought, he once said : 'Che pensa! Non deve mai pensar l'uomo, pensando s'invecchia,' or, in translation, 'Why do you think so much ! A man should never think. Thinking only makes him grow old.' Then, after we had talked a bit : 'Non deve fermarsi l'uomo in una sola cosa, perchè allora divien matto: bisogna aver mille cose, una confusione nella testa' – 'A man should never think about one thing only, because then he will go crazy : one should have a thousand things whirling about in one's head.' The mentality of such an Italian is even better revealed by the following conversation. He had obviously noticed that I was a Protestant, so, after some beating about the bush, he asked if I would mind answering a few questions, because he had heard so many odd things about Protestants and would like to obtain some first-hand information at last. 'Are you really allowed', he said, 'to have an affair with a pretty girl without being married to her? Do your priests permit you that?' I replied : 'Our priests are sensible men who do not bother themselves about such minor matters; of course, if we asked their permission, they would not give it.' 'And you really don't have to ask them?' he cried. 'Oh, you lucky people ! And, since you don't go to confession, they won't hear about it.' Whereupon he began abusing his priests and praising our blessed freedom. 'But confession,' he went on, 'what about that? We are told that all people, even those who are not Christians, must confess their sins. Since they are impenitent and cannot do it in the proper way, they make confession to an old tree, which is certainly silly and wicked, but still a proof that they recognize the necessity for confession.' I explained our views about confession and its practice. He thought it all very convenient but pretty much the same as confessing to a tree. He hesitated for a moment and then asked me in all earnestness to tell him the honest truth about another point. One of his priests, an absolutely truthful man, had told him personally that we were allowed to marry our sisters. This, after all, would be going rather far. When I denied this and tried to give him a few sane ideas about our beliefs, he seemed to think them too commonplace and paid no attention. Then he turned to another question. 'We have been told as a fact that Frederick the Great, who has won so many victories, even over true believers, and fills the world with his fame, is really a Catholic though everybody imagines he is a heretic. He has special dispensation from the Pope to keep his faith a secret. As you know, he never enters one of our churches, but worships in a subterranean chapel and is deeply contrite that he cannot publicly profess the sacred religion because, if he did, his Prussians, a brutish nation of fanatical heretics, would kill him immediately, and then he could be of no more help to the cause. That is why the Holy Father has given him this dispensation, and, in return, Frederick quietly favours and propagates the one true faith.' I let all this pass without argument and merely said that, as it was such a deep secret, no one could verify it. The rest of our conversation ran on the same lines. I was surprised at the shrewdness of the priests who deny or misrepresent anything which might infringe upon the mysterious circle of their traditional doctrine or cast doubts upon it.

Foligno, 26 October. Evening

I left Perugia on a glorious morning and felt the bliss of being once more alone. The situation of the town is beautiful and the

view of the lake charming. I shall remember them both. At first
the road went downhill, then it ran along a lovely valley, flanked
on either side by distant hills, until, finally, Assisi came into view.

From reading Palladio and Volkmann, I knew there was a
Temple of Minerva here, built during the reign of Augustus and
still perfectly preserved. When we got near Madonna degli Angeli,
I left my *vetturino* and let him go on to Foligno. I was longing
to take a walk by myself in this silent world, and climbed the
road to Assisi on foot with a high wind blowing against me. I
turned away in distaste from the enormous substructure of the
two churches on my left, which are built one on top of the other
like a Babylonian tower, and are the resting place of St Francis.
I was afraid that the people who gathered there would be of the
same stamp as my captain. I asked a handsome boy the way to
the Maria della Minerva, and he accompanied me up into the
town, which is built on the side of a hill. At last we arrived in
the Old Town and – lo and behold! – there it stood, the first
complete classical monument I have seen. A modest temple, just
right for such a small town, yet so perfect in design that it would
be an ornament anywhere.

Since I have read in Vitruvius and Palladio how cities should
be laid out and how temples and public buildings should be
situated, I have learned to treat these matters with great respect.
In this, as in so much else, the ancients were great by instinct.
The temple is situated halfway up the mountain at a point where
two hills meet and on a piece of level ground which today is
called the *piazza*. The square itself slopes slightly and four roads
meet there, two from above and two from below, forming an
irregular St Andrew's Cross. In ancient times the houses which
face the temple and obstruct the view probably did not exist. If
they were removed, one could look down on the fertile countryside to the south and the sanctuary of Minerva would be visible
from every side. The layout of the roads may be of early date,
since they follow the contours of the mountain. The temple does
not stand in the centre of the square but is so placed that it can
be seen in foreshortened perspective by anyone approaching it
from the direction of Rome. Besides drawing the building, one
ought to draw its well-chosen site.

One could never tire of looking at the façade and admiring the logical procedure of the architect. The order is Corinthian and the space between the columns about two modules. The bases of the columns and the plinths below them appear to be standing on pedestals, but this is only an illusion, for the stylobate has been cut through in five places, and through each gap five steps lead up between the columns. By these one reaches the platform on which the columns actually stand, and enters the temple. The bold idea of cutting through the stylobate was a very sensible one, given the site. Since the temple stands on a hill, the stairs up to it would otherwise have jutted out too far into the square and made it too cramped. How many steps there were originally is now impossible to determine, because, except for a few, they lie buried under the earth and paved over. I tore myself away reluctantly and firmly resolved to call the attention of all architects to this building so that an accurate plan may be made available to us. I realized once more how little accepted tradition is to be trusted. Palladio, on whom I had relied implicitly, made a sketch of this temple, but he cannot have seen it personally, for he puts real pedestals on the ground, which gives the columns a disproportionate height and makes the whole a Palmyra-like monstrosity instead of the great loveliness of the real thing. I cannot describe the sensations which this work aroused in me, but I know they are going to bear fruit for ever.

The evening was beautiful and I was walking down the Roman Road in a state of blissful content when suddenly behind me I heard loud, rough voices in lively argument. I thought they must be *sbirri*, for I had previously noticed some in the town. Without turning round, but straining my ears to catch what they were saying, I walked calmly on. Soon I realized that I was the subject of their quarrel. Four men, two of them armed with guns, passed me, muttering something. After a few steps they turned, surrounded me, and asked what I was doing here. I replied that I was a stranger and had walked to Assisi while my *vetturino* drove on to Foligno. This they found hard to believe – that someone should pay for a carriage and then walk. They asked if I had been to the Gran Convento. I said no, but assured them I had known the building for many years. This time, since I was an architect,

I had gone to look at the Maria della Minerva, which, as they knew, was an architectural masterpiece. This they did not deny, but they were offended because I had not paid my respects to the saint and did not conceal their suspicion that I might be a dealer in contraband goods. I pointed out how ridiculous it was to take someone for a smuggler who was walking by himself without a knapsack and with empty pockets. I offered to return to the town with them and go to the *podestà*. I would show him my documents and he would acknowledge me as a respectable foreigner. After muttering among themselves again, they said this would be unnecessary. I behaved all the time with dignity and, at last, they went away towards the town. I followed them with my eye. There, in the foreground, walked those rude fellows while, behind them, Minerva looked down on me kindly, as if she wanted to console me. I turned to look at the dreary Duomo of St Francis on my left and was just about to continue my way when one of the unarmed members of the band left it and approached me in a friendly manner. 'Dear Mr Foreigner,' he said, 'you ought, at least, to give me a tip, for, I assure you, I knew at once that you were an honest man and frankly told my companions so. But they are hot-headed, quick-tempered fellows who do not know the ways of the world. You must also have noticed that I was the first to applaud your words and back you up.' I complimented him on this and urged him to protect in future any distinguished foreigner who might come to Assisi for the sake of religion and art, especially any architect who might come to measure and sketch the Temple of Minerva, which had never yet been drawn or engraved. Such people would bring glory to the town, and if he gave them a helping hand, they would certainly show their gratitude – and with these words I pressed a few silver coins into his hand, which made him very happy, as they were more than he had expected. He begged me to come back to Assisi soon; I must on no account miss the feast of the saint, when I could certainly expect both edification and amusement. Indeed, if a good-looking man like me should wish to meet a handsome female, he could assure me that, on his recommendation, the most beautiful and respectable woman in Assisi would gladly receive me. He then took his leave, after solemnly promising that he would remember me that very evening in his devotions at the tomb of the saint and pray for the success of my journey. So we parted, and I felt much relieved at being alone again with Nature and myself. The road to Foligno along the side of the mountain overlooking the valley is beautiful, and my walk, which took fully four hours, was one of the most enchanting I have ever taken.

Travelling with *vetturini* is an exhausting affair; the only thing to be said for it is that one can always get out and walk. All the way from Ferrara I have submitted to being dragged along in this fashion. This Italy, so greatly favoured by Nature, has lagged far behind all other countries in mechanical and technical matters, which are, after all, the basis of a comfortable, agreeable life. The carriage of the *vetturino* is called *una sedia*, 'a seat', and is undoubtedly derived from the ancient litters in which women and elderly or prominent persons were carried by mules. The mule that was harnessed between the shafts of the rear has been replaced by two wheels, and that is all the improvement they have made. One is still joggled along as one was centuries ago. It is the same with their houses and everything else. The idyllic dream of the first men living out of doors and retiring to caves only in an emergency is a reality here, and to see it, one has only to enter their dwellings, especially in rural districts, which still preserve the character of caves.

They are utterly carefree because they are afraid that thinking might make them age quicker. With an unheard-of negligence they fail to make provision for the longer winter nights and, consequently, suffer like dogs for a considerable part of the year. The inn here in Foligno is exactly like a Homeric household. Everyone is gathered in a large vault around an open fireplace, shouting and talking. They all eat together at one long table, as in a painting of the Wedding Feast at Cana. To my great surprise, someone has brought me an inkwell, so I am taking the opportunity to write, though these pages will bear witness to the cold and the inconvenience of my writing table.

I have only just realized how bold I was to travel unprepared and alone through this country. The different currencies, the *vetturini*, the prices, the wretched inns are a daily nuisance, and anyone who travels along for the first time, hoping for

uninterrupted pleasures, is bound to be often disappointed and
have much to put up with. But, after all, my one wish has been to
see this country at any cost and, were I to be dragged to Rome on
Ixion's wheel, I should not utter a single word of complaint.

Terni, 27 October. Evening

Once again I am sitting in a cave which was damaged in an
earthquake last year. Terni lies between limestone hills on the
edge of a plain and, like Bologna on the other side, at the foot
of a mountain range.

Now that the papal officer has left me, I have a priest as a
travelling companion. He has of course recognized me as a
heretic, but is willing to answer all my questions about ritual
and similar matters. Through meeting new people all the time,
I am acquiring what I came for; it is only by listening to the
people talking among themselves that one can get a true picture
of the country. They are all bitter rivals; they indulge in the
oddest provincialism and local patriotism, and cannot stand each
other. There are eternal feuds between the different classes, conducted with such lively passion that one seems to be taking part
day and night in a comedy, in which everyone exposes himself.
Yet they can quickly control themselves too, and they immediately
notice when a foreigner disapproves of their behaviour.

I walked up to Spoleto and stood on the aqueduct, which also
serves as a bridge from one hill to the other. The ten brickwork
arches which span the valley have been quietly standing there
through all the centuries, and the water still gushes in all quarters
of Spoleto. This is the third work of antiquity which I have seen,
and it embodies the same noble spirit. A sense of the civic good,
which is the basis of their architecture, was second nature to the
ancients. Hence the amphitheatre, the temple, the aqueduct. For
the first time I understand why I always detested arbitrary
constructions, the Winterkasten* on the Weissenstein, for example, which is a pointless nothing, a monstrous piece of con-
fectionery – and I have felt the same about a thousand other

---

* Winterkasten. A huge octagonal castle on the Wilhelmshöhe near
Kassel.

buildings. Such things are still-born, for anything that does not have a true *raison d'être* is lifeless and cannot be great or ever become so. For how many pleasures and insights must I thank these last eight weeks! But they have also cost me a great deal of effort. I try to keep my eyes open all the time, remember as much as I can and not judge more than I can help.

The strange wayside chapel of San Crocefisso is not, in my opinion, the remnant of a temple which once stood there. Evidently, columns, pillars and entablatures have been found and patched together. The result, though not unskilful, is absurd. It is impossible to describe, but there certainly exists an engraving of it somewhere. The curious difficulty about trying to form an idea of antiquity is that we only have ruins to go by, so that our reconstructions must be inadequate.

The so-called classic soil is another matter. If we do not approach it fancifully but consider this soil in its reality as it presents itself to our senses, it still appears as the stage upon which the greatest events were enacted and decided. I have always looked at landscape with the eye of a geologist and a topographer, and suppressed my imagination and emotions in order to preserve my faculty for clear and unbiased observation. If one does this first, then history follows naturally and logically in all its astonishing wonder. One of the things I now most want to do is to read Tacitus in Rome.

I must not forget my observations of the weather. When I drove through the Apennines after leaving Bologna, the clouds were still drifting north, but later they changed their direction and moved towards Lake Trasimeno. There they were arrested and only a few moved on further south. This proves that, in summer, the great plain of the Po does not send all its clouds towards the Tirolean Alps, but sends some of them to the Apennines, which probably is the explanation of their rainy season. People are beginning to harvest the olives. Here they pick them by hand; in other places they knock them down with sticks. If winter comes early, the remaining fruit are left on the trees until the spring. I saw some very big and very old olive trees in a patch of very stony ground.

The Muses, like the daemons, do not always visit us at the right moment. Today they drove me to develop a most untimely idea. As I approached the centre of Catholicism, surrounded by Catholics, boxed up in a *sedia* with a priest and trying to feel and understand the truth of Nature and the nobility of Art, the thought rose unbidden in my mind that all traces of early Christianity have been obliterated. Indeed, when I visualized it in its purity, as recorded in the Acts of the Apostles, I shuddered at the thought of the distorted baroque paganism which has imposed itself upon those simple and innocent beginnings. Once again the legend of the Wandering Jew came to mind, who witnessed all these strange developments and lived to take part in that extraordinary scene when Christ returns to look for the fruits of His teaching and is in danger of being crucified a second time. The words *Venio iterum crucifigi* must serve me as an epigraph for this catastrophe.

Other dreams like it hover before me. In my impatience to get on, I sleep in my clothes and can think of nothing more agreeable than to be roused before dawn, quickly take my seat in the carriage and travel dayward half asleep, letting dream images do what they like with me.

Città Castellana, 28 October

My last day must not go unrecorded. It is not yet eight o'clock, but everybody is in bed and I am free to think of the past and look forward to the near future. The morning was very cold, the day clear and warm, the evening somewhat windy but beautiful. We left Terni very early and reached Narni before daybreak, so I could not see the bridge. All around were limestone hills without a trace of any other rock formation.

Otricoli lies on an alluvial mound, formed in an early epoch, and is built of lava taken from the other side of the river. As soon as one crosses the bridge, one is on volcanic terrain, either lava or an earlier metamorphic rock. We climbed a hill which I am inclined to define as grey lava. It contains many white crystals with the shape of garnets. The high road to Città Castellana is built of it and worn wonderfully smooth by the carriages. This town is built upon a volcanic tufa in which I thought I could recognize ashes, pumice stone and lava fragments. The view from the castle is magnificent. Soracte stands out by itself in picturesque solitude. Probably this mountain is made of limestone and belongs to the Apennines. The volcanic areas lie much lower, and it is only the water tearing across them which has carved them into extremely picturesque shapes, overhanging cliffs and other accidental features.

Well then, tomorrow evening Rome! Even now I can hardly believe it. When this wish has been fulfilled, what shall I wish for next? I can think of nothing better than safely landing at home in my pheasant-boat, to find my friends in good health, cheerful and happy to see me again.

ROME

At last I can break my silence and send my friends a joyful greeting. I hope they will forgive me for my secretiveness and my almost subterranean journey to this country. Even to myself, I hardly dared admit where I was going and all the way I was still afraid I might be dreaming; it was not till I had passed through the Porta del Popolo that I was certain it was true, that I really was in Rome.

Let me say this: here in Rome, in the presence of all those objects which I never expected to see by myself, you are constantly in my thoughts. It was only when I realized that everyone at home was chained, body and soul, to the north, and all desire to visit these parts had vanished, that, drawn by an irresistible need, I made up my mind to undertake this long, solitary journey to the hub of the world.

Now that this need has been satisfied, my friends and my native land have once again become very dear to my heart, and my desire to return very keen, all the keener because I am convinced that the many treasures I shall bring home with me will serve both myself and others as a guide and an education for a lifetime.

1 November

Now, at last, I have arrived in the First City of the world! Had I seen it fifteen years ago with an intelligent man to guide me, I should have called myself lucky, but, since I was destined to visit it alone and trust to my own eyes, I am happy, at least, to have been granted this joy so late in life.

Across the mountains of the Tirol I fled rather than travelled. Vicenza, Padua and Venice I saw thoroughly, Ferrara, Cento, Bologna casually, and Florence hardly at all. My desire to reach Rome quickly was growing stronger every minute until nothing could have induced me to make more stops, so that I spent only three hours there. Now I have arrived, I have calmed down and feel as if I had found a peace that will last for my whole life. Because, if I may say so, as soon as one sees with one's own eyes the whole which one had hitherto only known in fragments and chaotically, a new life begins.

All the dreams of my youth have come to life; the first engravings I remember – my father hung views of Rome in the hall – I now see in reality, and everything I have known for so long through paintings, drawings, etchings, woodcuts, plaster casts and cork models is now assembled before me. Wherever I walk, I come upon familiar objects in an unfamiliar world; everything is just as I imagined it, yet everything is new. It is the same with my observations and ideas. I have not had a single idea which was entirely new or surprising, but my old ideas have become so much more firm, vital and coherent that they could be called new.

When Pygmalion's Galatea, whom he had fashioned exactly after his dreams, endowing her with as much reality and existence as an artist can, finally came up to him and said: 'Here I am,' how different was the living woman from the sculptured stone.

Besides, for me it is morally salutary to be living in the midst of a sensual people about whom so much has been said and written, and whom every foreigner judges by the standard he brings with him. I can excuse those who criticize and disapprove of them because their life is so far removed from ours that it is difficult and expensive for a foreigner to have dealings with them.

3 *November*

One of the main reasons I had given myself as an excuse for hurrying to Rome, namely, that All Saints' Day was on 1 November, turned out to be a delusion. If, I had said to myself, they pay such high honours to a single saint, what a spectacle it must be when they honour them all at once. How utterly mistaken I was. A conspicuous general feast has never become popular in the Church; originally, perhaps, each religious order celebrated the memory of its patron saint privately, for now the feast on his name day, the day appointed for his veneration, is the one on which each appears in all his glory.

Yesterday, however, which was the Feast of All Souls, I had better luck. The Pope* celebrated their memory in his private chapel on the Quirinal. Admission was free to all. I hurried with Tischbein to the Monte Cavallo. The square in front of the palazzo, though irregular in shape, is both grand and graceful. There I set eyes on the two Colossi. To grasp them is beyond the power of the eye or the mind. We hurried with the crowd across the spacious courtyard and up an enormous flight of stairs, and into the vestibules opposite the chapel. To think that I was under the same roof as the Vicar of Christ gave me a strange feeling. The office had begun and the Pope and cardinals were already in the church – the Holy Father, a beautiful and venerable figure of a man, the cardinals of various ages and statures.

I was suddenly seized by the curious wish that the Head of the Church would open his golden mouth and, in speaking of the transports of joy felt by the souls of the blessed, transport us with joy as well. When I saw him merely moving from one side of the altar to the other and muttering just like any ordinary priest, the original sin of the Protestant stirred in me and I felt no pleasure whatsoever in the sacrifice of the Mass as it is traditionally offered here. Did not Christ, even as a child, interpret the Scriptures in a loud voice? As a young man, He certainly did not teach or work miracles in silence, for, as we know from the Gospels, He liked to speak and He spoke well. What would He say, I thought, if He were to see His representative on earth droning and tottering about? The words *Venio iterum crucifigi* came to mind and I nudged my companion to come out with me into the free atmosphere of the vaulted and frescoed rooms. There we found a lot of people who were looking at the paintings, for the Feast of All Souls is also the feast of all artists in Rome. On this day not only the chapel but also all the rooms in the palazzo are open to the public for many hours. Entrance is free and one is not molested by the custodian.

I looked at the frescoes and found some excellent ones by

---

* Pius VI (1775–99).

artists whose names I hardly knew – Carlo Maratti, for example, whom I soon came to love and admire. But it was the master-pieces of the artists whose style I had already studied which gave me the keenest pleasure. I saw a St Petronilla by Guercino. This canvas was formerly in St Peter's, where it has now been replaced by a copy in mosaic. The body of the dead saint is lifted out of the tomb, restored to life and received into Heaven by a divine youth. Whatever objections there may be to this twofold action, the painting is beyond price.

I was even more surprised by a Titian which outshines all of his pictures which I have seen so far. Whether it is only that my visual sense is now more trained, or whether it really is his most stupendous picture, I cannot judge. It shows the imposing figure of a bishop, enveloped in a gorgeous chasuble stiff with gold embroideries and figures. Holding a massive crozier in his left hand, he gazes up to Heaven, rapt in ecstasy. In his right hand he holds an open book, from which he seems to have just received divine inspiration. Behind him, a beautiful virgin, carrying a palm, looks with tender interest into the book. On his right, a grave old man is standing quite close to the book but does not seem to be paying it any attention. Perhaps the keys in his hand assure him that he can elucidate its secrets by himself. Facing this group, a nude, well-shaped young man, bound and pierced with arrows, looks out with humble resignation. In the space between them two monks, bearing a cross and a lily, turn their devout gazes heavenward, where, above the semicircular ruin which encloses all the human figures, a mother in her highest glory looks down in compassion while the radiant child on her lap holds out a wreath with a gay gesture as if eager to throw it down. Above them and the triple aureole, like a keystone, hovers the Holy Dove.

Behind this composition there must lie some ancient tradition which made it possible to combine all these various and seemingly incongruous figures into a significant whole. We do not ask how or why; we take it as it is and marvel at its inestimable art.

Less enigmatic but still mysterious is a fresco by Guido. A childlike Virgin sits quietly sewing, flanked by two angels who are ready at the slightest gesture to minister to her wishes. What this charming picture says is that youthful innocence and diligence are protected and honoured by the Heavenly Powers. No legend or interpretation is necessary.

But now for an amusing anecdote to lighten these somewhat ponderous reflections on art. For some time I had been aware that some German artists, evidently acquaintances of Tischbein's, would give me a stare, go out and come back for another look. Presently Tischbein, who had left me alone for a few minutes, returned and said: 'This is going to be great fun. The rumour that you are in Rome has already spread and aroused the curiosity of the artists about the only foreigner whom nobody knows. One of our circle has always boasted of having met you and even lived with you on terms of intimacy, a story we found hard to believe. So we asked him to take a look at you and resolve our doubts. He promptly declared that it was not you but a stranger without the slightest resemblance to you. So your incognito is safe, at least for the moment, and later we shall have something to laugh about.'

Since then, I have moved more freely among these artists and asked them to tell me the authors of various paintings, the style of which is still unfamiliar to me. I was especially attracted by a painting of St George, the slayer of the dragon and the liberator of virgins. Nobody could tell me the name of the master until a short, modest man, who had not opened his mouth before, stepped forward and said it was by the Venetian painter Pordenone, and one of his finest paintings. I realized then why I had been drawn to it; being already familiar with the Venetian school, I could better appreciate the virtues of its members. The artist who gave me this information is Heinrich Meyer, a Swiss, who has been studying here for several years in the company of a friend named Cölla. He makes remarkable drawings in sepia of antique busts and is well versed in the history of art.

5 November

I have been here now for seven days and am gradually beginning to get a general idea of the city. We walk about a good deal, I study the layout of Ancient Rome and Modern Rome, look at ruins and buildings and visit this villa or that. The most important monuments I take very slowly; I do nothing except look, go away, and come back and look again. Only in Rome can one educate oneself for Rome.

I find it a difficult and melancholy business, I must confess, separating the old Rome from the new, but it has to be done and I can only hope that, in the end, my efforts will prove worthwhile. One comes upon traces both of magnificence and of devastation, which stagger the imagination. What the barbarians left, the builders of Modern Rome have destroyed.

Here is an entity which has suffered so many drastic changes in the course of two thousand years, yet is still the same soil, the same hill, often even the same column or the same wall, and in its people one still finds traces of their ancient character. Contemplating this, the observer becomes, as it were, a contemporary of the great decrees of destiny, and this makes it difficult for him to follow the evolution of the city, to grasp not only how Modern Rome follows on Ancient, but also how, within both, one epoch follows upon another. I shall first of all try to grope my way along this half-hidden track by myself, for only after I have done that shall I be able to benefit from the excellent preliminary studies to which, from the fifteenth century till today, eminent scholars and artists have devoted their lives.

As I rush about Rome looking at the major monuments, the immensity of the place has a quietening effect. In other places one has to search for the important points of interest; here they crowd in on one in profusion. Wherever you turn your eyes, every kind of vista, near and distant, confronts you – palaces, ruins, gardens, wildernesses, small houses, stables, triumphal arches, columns – all of them often so close together that they could be sketched on a single sheet of paper. One would need a thousand styluses to write with. What can one do here with a single pen? And then, in the evening, one feels exhausted after so much looking and admiring.

7 November

My friends must excuse me if, in future, I become rather laconic. When one is travelling, one grabs what one can, every day brings something new, and one hastens to think about it and make a judgement. But this city is such a great school and each day here has so much to say that one does not dare say anything about it oneself. Even if one could stay here for years, it would still be better to observe a Pythagorean silence.

7 November

I am feeling in fine shape. The wind is *brutto*, as the Romans say. There is a wind at noon, the sirocco, which brings some rain daily, but I do not find this sort of weather disagreeable because it is warm all the time, which it never is on rainy days in our country.

I am coming to appreciate Tischbein more and more, his talents, his ideas on art and his aims as a painter. He showed me his drawings and sketches. Many are very promising. His stay with Bodmer has turned his thoughts towards the earliest ages of man when he found himself on earth and was expected to solve the problem of becoming the lord of creation.

As an introduction to a series of pictures, he has tried to represent this great age symbolically – mountains covered with majestic forests, ravines carved out by torrents, moribund volcanoes emitting only a thin column of smoke, and, in the foreground, the massive stump of an ancient oak with its roots uncovered on which a stag is testing the strength of its antlers – all well conceived and charmingly executed.

He has made one very curious drawing showing man as the tamer of horses, superior not in strength but in cunning to all the beasts of the field, the air and the waters. This composition is of extraordinary beauty and should look most effective when done in oils. We must certainly acquire a drawing of it for Weimar. He also plans to paint an assembly of wise old men, which will give him an opportunity of doing some real figures. At the moment he is enthusiastically making sketches for a battle scene in which two bands of horsemen are attacking each other with equal fury. They are separated by a tremendous ravine over which a horse can vault only by a tremendous effort. Defence is out of the question. Bold attack, reckless decision, victory or a plunge into the abyss. This picture will give him a chance to reveal his knowledge of the anatomy and movements of the horse.

He would like to see this planned series of scenes linked together by a poem which would explain their meaning and itself gain in substance from the figures in them. The idea is an excellent one, but, to bring it to fruition, we should have to spend years together.

The loggias of Raphael, the huge paintings of the School of Athens, etc., I have seen only once. This was much like studying Homer from a faded and damaged manuscript. A first impression is inadequate; to enjoy them fully, one would have to look at them again and again. The best preserved are those on the ceiling with Biblical stories for their subjects; these look as fresh as if they had been painted yesterday. Even though only a few of them are by Raphael himself, they were all done from his designs and under his personal supervision.

When I was a young man, I sometimes indulged in a daydream of being accompanied to Italy by an educated Englishman, well versed in general history and the history of art. This has now come to pass in a still happier way than I dreamed of. Tischbein has long been devoted to me, and has always wanted to show me Rome, where he has lived for so long. We were old friends by correspondence and now we are new friends in the flesh. Where could I have found a better guide? Thanks to him, I shall be able to learn and enjoy as much as possible in the limited time I have. As I see things at present, when I leave here, I shall wish I was arriving instead.

8 November

My peculiar and perhaps capricious semi-incognito has some
unforeseen advantages. Since everyone feels it his duty to ignore
my identity, no one can talk to me about me; so all they can do
is talk about themselves and the topics which interest them. In
consequence I get to know all about what everyone is doing and
about everything worthwhile that is going on. Even Hofrat
Reiffenstein* respects my whim, but since for some reason of his
own he dislikes the name I adopted, he soon made me a Baron
and now I am known as The-Baron-who-lives-opposite-the-
Rondanini. This title is sufficient because Italians always call
people by their first names or their nicknames. This is the way I
wanted it, and I escape the endless annoyance of having to give
an account of myself and my writings.

9 November

Sometimes I stand still for a moment and survey, as it were, the
high peaks of my experiences so far. I look back with special joy
to Venice, that great being who sprang from the sea like Pallas
from the head of Jupiter. In Rome the Pantheon, so great within
and without, has overwhelmed me with admiration. St Peter's
has made me realize that Art, like Nature, can abolish all standards of measurement. The Apollo Belvedere has also swept me
off my feet. Just as the most accurate drawings fail to give an
adequate idea of these buildings, so plaster casts, good as some
I have seen are, can be no substitute for their marble originals.

10 November

I am now in a state of clarity and calm such as I had not known
for a long time. My habit of looking at and accepting things as
they are without pretension is standing me in good stead and

---

* Hofrat Reiffenstein (1719–93). Diplomat, formerly in the service of
Gotha and Russia, archaeologist and art connoisseur.

makes me secretly very happy. Each day brings me some new remarkable object, some new great picture, and a whole city which the imagination will never encompass, however long one thinks and dreams.

Today I went to the pyramid of Cestius and in the evening climbed to the top of the Palatine, where the ruins of the imperial palaces stand like rocks. It is impossible to convey a proper idea of such things. Nothing here is mediocre, and if, here and there, something is in poor taste, it, too, shares in the general grandeur.

When I indulge in self-reflection, as I like to do occasionally, I discover in myself a feeling which gives me great joy. Let me put it like this. In this place, whoever looks seriously about him and has eyes to see is bound to become a stronger character: he acquires a sense of strength hitherto unknown to him.

His soul receives the seal of a soundness, a seriousness without pedantry, and a joyous composure. At least, I can say that I have never been so sensitive to the things of this world as I am here. The blessed consequences will, I believe, affect my whole future life.

So let me seize things one by one as they come; they will sort themselves out later. I am not here simply to have a good time, but to devote myself to the noble objects about me, to educate myself before I reach forty.

11 November

Today I visited the Nymph Egeria, the Circus of Caracalla, the ruined tombs along the Via Appia and the tomb of Metella, which made me realize for the first time what solid masonry means. These people built for eternity; they omitted nothing from their calculations except the insane fury of the destroyers to whom nothing was sacred.

I also saw the ruins of the great aqueduct. What a noble ambition it showed, to raise such a tremendous construction for the sake of supplying water to a people. We came to the Colosseum at twilight. Once one has seen it, everything else seems small. It is so huge that the mind cannot retain its image; one remembers

it as smaller than it is, so that every time one returns to it, one
is astounded by its size.

Frascati, 15 November

The rest of our company are already in bed, and I am writing
in the sepia I use for drawing. We have had a few rainless days
of genial sunshine, so that we don't long for the summer.
This town lies on the slope of a mountain, and at every turn the
artist comes upon the most lovely things. The view is unlimited;
you can see Rome in the distance and the sea beyond it, the hills
of Tivoli to the right, and so on. In this pleasant region the villas
have certainly been built for pleasure. About a century ago,
wealthy and high-spirited Romans began building villas on the
same beautiful spots where the ancient Romans built theirs.
For two days we have roamed the countryside, always finding
some new attraction.

Yet I find it hard to decide which are the more entertaining,
our days or our evenings. As soon as our imposing landlady has
placed the three-branched brass lamp on the table with the
words 'Felicissima notte!' we sit down in a circle and each brings
out the drawings and sketches he has made during the day. A
discussion follows : shouldn't the subject have been approached
from a better angle? Has the character of the scene been hit off?
We discuss, in fact, all those elements in art which can be judged
from a first draft.

Thanks to his competence and authority, Hofrat Reiffenstein
is the natural person to organize and preside at these sessions,
but it was Philipp Hackert who originated this laudable custom.
An admirable landscape painter, he always insisted on everyone,
artists and dilettantes, men and women, young and old, whatever
their talents, trying their hand at drawing, and he himself set
them a good example. Since his departure this custom of gathering together an interested circle has been faithfully kept up by
Hofrat Reiffenstein; and one can see how worthwhile it is to
stimulate in everyone an active interest.

The individual characters of the members of our circle are
charmingly revealed. Tischbein, for example, being a painter of

historical scenes, looks at landscape in a completely different way from a landscape painter. He sees important groupings and significant objects where another would see nothing and then manages to catch many traits of simple humanity, in children, country folk, beggars and other similar unsophisticated people, even in animals, which he can render most successfully with a few characteristic strokes, providing us with new topics for discussion.

When we run out of conversation, some pages are read aloud from Sulzer's *Theory*, another custom introduced by Hackert. Though, judged by the strictest standards, this work is not altogether satisfactory, I have observed with pleasure its good influence on people of a middling level of culture.

Rome, 17 November

Here we are back again! Tonight there was a tremendous downpour with thunder and lightning. It still goes on raining, but remains warm. Today I saw the frescoes by Domenichino in Sant' Andrea della Valle and the Carracci in the Farnese Gallery. Too much for months, let alone for a single day.

18 November

The weather has been fine and clear. In the Farnesina I saw the story of Psyche, colour reproductions of which have for so long brightened my rooms. Later I saw Raphael's *Transfiguration* in San Pietro in Montorio. These paintings are like friends with whom one has long been acquainted through correspondence and now sees face to face for the first time. The difference when one lives with them is that one's sympathies and antipathies are soon revealed.

In every corner there are magnificent things which are almost never mentioned and have not been disseminated over the world in etchings and reproductions. I shall bring some with me, done by excellent young artists.

Tischbein is well versed in the various types of stone used both
by the ancient and the modern builders. He has studied them
thoroughly and his artist's eye and his pleasure in the physical
texture of things have greatly helped him. Some time ago he sent
off to Weimar a choice collection of specimens which will welcome me on my return. Meanwhile, an important addition to
them has turned up. A priest who is now living in France
planned to write a book on Stones in Antiquity and, by special
favour of the Propaganda, received some sizeable pieces of marble
from the island of Paros. They range in grain from the finest to
the coarsest and are of perfect purity except for a few which
contain some mica. These were used for building, whereas the
pure marble was used for sculpture. In judging the works of
artists, an exact knowledge of the material they used is obviously
a great help.

There are plenty of opportunities here for assembling such a
collection. Today we walked in the ruins of Nero's palace over
fields of banked-up artichokes and could not resist the temptation
to fill our pockets with tablets of granite, porphyry and marble
which lay around in thousands, still bearing witness to the splendour of the walls which they once covered.

I must now speak of a curious, problematic painting which is
one of the most extraordinary things I have ever seen.

There was a Frenchman living here some years ago who was
well known as a collector and lover of the arts. He came into
possession, nobody knows how, of an antique chalk drawing, had
it restored by Mengs and added it to his collection as an item of
great value. Winckelmann mentions it somewhere with enthusiasm. It shows Ganymede offering Jupiter a cup of wine and
receiving a kiss in return. The Frenchman died and, in his will,
left the picture to his landlady, stating it to be an antique. Then
Mengs died and on his deathbed declared that it was not an
antique but had been done by him. This started an endless feud
between all parties. One person swore that Mengs had dashed it
off as a joke, another that Mengs could never have done anything

like it, that it was almost too beautiful for a Raphael. Yesterday I saw it for myself and I must confess that I do not know of anything more beautiful than the figure of Ganymede, especially the head and the back – all the rest has been much touched up. However, the picture is discredited and no one wants to relieve the poor woman of her treasure.

20 November

Experience has taught us often enough that there is a demand for drawings and etchings to go with every kind of poem, and that even a painter himself will dedicate his most descriptive pictures to some passage of poetry, so Tischbein's idea, that in order to achieve a proper unity poets and painters should collaborate from the start, is a very praiseworthy one. The difficulty would obviously be greatly lessened if the poems were short enough to be composed at a sitting and read at a glance. Tischbein, it so happens, has pleasing idyllic subjects in mind and, to my surprise, they are of a character which neither poetry nor painting by itself could treat adequately. On our walks he has told me all about them and urged me to fall in with his plan. He has already designed a frontispiece for our joint effort. If I were not afraid to embark on something new, I might perhaps be tempted.

22 November
On the Feast of St Cecilia

I must write a few lines to keep alive the memory of this happy day or, at least, make a historical report of what I have been enjoying. The day was cloudless and warm. I went with Tischbein to the square in front of St Peter's. We walked up and down until we felt too hot, when we sat in the shadow of the great obelisk – it was just wide enough for two – and ate some grapes we had bought nearby. Then we went into the Sistine Chapel, where the light on the frescoes was at its best. Looking at these marvellous works of Michelangelo's, our admiration was divided between the Last Judgement and the various paintings on the

ceiling. The self-assurance, the virility, the grandeur of conception of this master defy expression. After we had looked at everything over and over again, we left the chapel and entered St
Peter's. Thanks to the brilliant sunshine outside, every part of the
church was visible. Since we were determined to enjoy its magnitude and splendour, we did not, this time, allow our overfasti-
dious taste to put us off and abstained from carping criticism. We
enjoyed everything that was enjoyable.

Then we climbed up on to the roof, where one finds a miniature copy of a well-built town with houses, shops, fountains,
churches (at least they looked like churches from the outside) and
a large temple – everything in the open air with beautiful walks
between. We went into the Cupola and looked out at the Apennines, Mount Soracte, the volcanic hills behind Tivoli, Frascati,
Castel Gandolfo, the plain and the sea beyond it. Below us
lay the city of Rome in all its length and breadth with its hill-
perched palaces, domes, etc. Not a breath of air was stirring, and
it was as hot as a greenhouse inside the copper ball. After taking
in everything, we descended again and asked to have the doors
opened which lead to the cornices of the dome, the tambour
and the nave. One can walk all the way round and look down
from the height on the whole church. As we were standing on
the cornice of the tambour, far below us we could see the Pope
walking to make his afternoon devotions. St Peter's had not
failed us. Then we climbed all the way down, went out into the
square and had a frugal but cheerful meal at an inn nearby, after
which we went on to the church of St Cecilia.

It would take pages to describe the decorations of this church,
which was packed with people. One could not see a stone of the
structure. The columns were covered with red velvet wound
around with ribbons of gold lace, the capitals with embroidered
velvet conforming more or less to their shape – so, too, with the
cornices and pillars. All the intervening wall space was clothed in
brightly coloured hangings, so that the whole church seemed to
be one enormous mosaic. More than two hundred candles were
burning behind and at the sides of the high altar, so that one
whole wall was lined with candles, and the nave was fully illuminated. Facing the high altar, two stands, also covered with

velvet, had been erected under the organ loft. The singers stood
on one; the orchestra, which never stopped playing, on the other.

Just as there are concertos for violins or other instruments,
here they perform concertos for voices: one voice – the so-
prano, for instance – predominates and sings a solo while, from
time to time, the choir joins in and accompanies it, always supported, of course, by the full orchestra. The effect is wonderful.

All good days must come to an end and so must these notes.
In the evening we got to the opera house, where *I litiganti**
was being given, but we were so sated with good things that we
passed it by.

23 November

Useful as I find my incognito, I must not forget the fate of the
ostrich who believed that he could not be seen when he buried
his head in the sand. While sticking to it on principle, there are
occasions when I must relax my role. I was not unwilling to
meet Prince Liechtenstein, the brother of Countess Harrach, since
I have the greatest regard for her, and I have dined several times
at his house. I soon realized, however, that my surrender to his
invitations would have further consequences, and so it did. I
had heard in advance about the Abbate Monti and his tragedy
Aristodemo, which was soon to be performed, and I had been
told that the author had expressed a wish to read it to me and get
my opinion. Without actually refusing, I did nothing about it,
but at last I met the poet and one of his friends at the Prince's
house, where the play was read aloud.

The hero, as you know, is a king of Sparta who, to satisfy
various conscientious scruples, commits suicide. It was tactfully
insinuated that the author of *Werther* would certainly not resent
finding that some passages from his admirable book had been
used in the play. So, even within the walls of Sparta, I was not to
be allowed to escape the angry manes of that unfortunate young
man.

The work reveals a remarkable talent. It moves simply and
quietly, and both the sentiments and the language, strong but

---

* *Tra i due litiganti il terzo gode.* Operetta by Giambattista Lorenzi.

delicate, are in accord with the theme. In my own fashion, if not in the Italian one, I pointed out the virtues of the play, and everybody was fairly satisfied, though, with southern impatience, they had expected something more. In particular, they wanted to hear from my lips some prophetic words about the impression it would make on the public.

I evaded this by saying that I was unfamiliar with this country, its preconceptions and its taste. But I was sincere enough to add that Roman audiences were spoiled, being accustomed to a three-act comedy with a complete two-act opera as an interlude or to a grand opera with utterly irrelevant ballets as intermezzi, so that I could not see them enjoying the noble calm progression of a tragedy without interruptions. Moreover, I said, it seemed to me that, to Italians, suicide was something utterly outside the range of their comprehension. One killed other people. Yes. That one heard of almost every day. But to take one's own precious life, or even contemplate doing so, that I had never heard of in Rome. I would be glad, however, to hear any evidence and arguments which would prove that my doubts were mistaken, for nothing would please me better than to see the play performed and to applaud it sincerely and loudly with a chorus of friends.

This statement was very warmly received and I had every reason this time to be glad I had unbent. Prince Liechtenstein is kindness itself, and, more than once, he has given me the opportunity to see in his company treasures of art which can only be seen by special permission of the owners, and to get that, one must be influential in high circles.

But it was asking too much of my good humour when the daughter of the Young Pretender also expressed her wish to see the 'rare marmoset'. I refused and have very firmly gone underground again.

Yet there is something unsatisfactory about this. I am more convinced than ever of a conclusion I came to earlier in my life: a man of good will should be just as active and energetic in social life as the egotistic, the narrow-minded and the evil. It is easy to see the truth of this, but difficult to put it into practice.

All I can say about the Italians is this: they are children of
Nature, who, for all the pomp and circumstance of their religion and art, are not a whit different from what they would be
if they were still living in forests and caves. What strikes any
foreigner are the murders which happen almost every day. In
our quarter alone there have been four in the last three weeks.
Today again the whole city is talking of one, but it only *talks*. An
honest artist called Schwendimann, a Swiss medallist and the
last pupil of Hedlinger, was assaulted exactly like Winckelmann.
His assailant, with whom he had got into a scuffle, stabbed him
twenty times, and when the guards arrived, the villain stabbed
himself. This is not the fashion here. Usually, the murderer
takes sanctuary in a church, and that is the end of that.

   Truth demands that I put some shadows into my rosy picture
by reporting crimes, disasters, earthquakes and floods. Most of
the foreigners are wildly excited over the present eruption of
Vesuvius, and it takes a strong character not to be swept away
oneself.

   This natural phenomenon has something of the irresistible
fascination of a rattlesnake. At the moment it seems as if all the
art treasures of Rome were of no account; all the foreigners have
interrupted their sightseeing tour and are hurrying off to Naples.
But I shall resist the temptation and stay here, trusting that the
mountain will keep something in reserve for me.

Moritz is here, who first attracted my attention by his biography,
Anton Reiser, and his travel book, *Wanderings in England*. He
is a really first-rate man and we greatly enjoy his company.

   In Rome, where there are so many foreigners who have not
come to study its art but for quite other kinds of amusement,
one must be prepared for anything.

   There are certain half-arts, calling for manual dexterity and a
taste for handicrafts, which have been highly developed here and

attract the interest of many foreigners. One of these is encaustic painting. From the first preliminaries to the final firing, it is a mechanical process which anyone who has worked a little with water colours can learn, and the novelty of the undertaking makes up for the often small artistic value of the result. There are clever artists who teach this process. Under the pretext of giving instruction, they often do the best part of the work themselves, so that the fair pupil, when she finally sees the picture raised in wax relief and brilliant in its gold frame, is amazed at her unrecognized talent.

Another pretty occupation is to take coins or incised stones and impress them in a sheet of fine clay so that both sides are reproduced at the same time.

The preparation of the glass pastes themselves requires more skill and concentration. For all these crafts, Hofrat Reiffenstein keeps the necessary tools and equipment in his house or at least in his neighbourhood.

2 December

By chance, I came across Archenholz's book on Italy. When one reads it here, it is incredible how such a scribble shrinks to nothing. It's as if one had thrown it in the fire, and watched it slowly turn brown and black, till the pages curled and went up in smoke. The author has seen everything, of course; but he knows far too little to excuse his overbearing, contemptuous tone, and, whether he is praising or blaming, he makes blunders all the time.

To have beautiful warm weather, with only an occasional rainy day, at the end of November is a new experience for me. We spend the fine days out of doors, the wet ones in our room, and always find something to enjoy, to study or to do.

On 28 November we visited the Sistine Chapel again and got them to open the gallery for us, because from there the ceiling can be seen at closer range. The gallery is rather narrow and we squeezed into it along the iron railing with some difficulty and some feeling of danger – people who suffer from vertigo would be advised to stay below – but this was more than made up for by the masterpiece which met our eyes. At present I am so enthusiastic about Michelangelo that I have lost all my taste for Nature, since I cannot see her with the eye of genius as he did. If only there were some means of fixing such images firmly in one's memory! At any rate, I shall bring home as many engravings and drawings made after his work as I can get hold of. From the chapel we went to the loggias of Raphael, and, though I hardly dare admit it, I could not look at them any longer. After being dilated and spoiled by Michelangelo's great forms, my eye took no pleasure in the ingenious frivolities of Raphael's arabesques, and his Biblical stories, beautiful as they are, do not stand up against Michelangelo's. What a joy it would give me if I could see the works of both more frequently and compare them at leisure without prejudice, for one's initial reactions are bound to be one-sided.

The sun was almost too warm as we dragged ourselves to the Villa Pamfili and stayed in its lovely gardens until evening. A large meadow, bordered with evergreen oaks and tall stone-pines, was dotted with daisies which all had their little heads turned to the sun. This set me off again on botanical speculations, which I resumed the next day during a walk to Monte Mario, Villa Mellini and Villa Madama. It is fascinating to observe how a vegetation behaves when its lively growth is never interrupted by severe cold. One sees no buds here and realizes for the first time what a bud is. The arbutus is again in bloom while its last fruits are still ripening. The orange trees also show blossoms, as well as half- and fully-ripe fruits, but these, unless they stand between buildings, are covered at this time of year. There is room for speculation about the cypress, which, when it is very old and full-grown, is the most dignified of all trees. Soon I shall pay a visit to the Botanical Garden, where I hope to learn a good deal. Nothing, above all, is comparable to the new life that a reflective person experiences when he observes a new country. Though I am still always myself, I believe I have been changed to the very marrow of my bones.

3 December

Till now the weather has followed a six-day cycle – two cloudless days, one overcast day, two or three wet days and then again fine weather. I try to make the best use I can of each one of them.

The noble objects with which I am surrounded never lose their freshness for me. I did not grow up with them. I have not wrung from each its peculiar secret. Some attract me so powerfully that, for a while, I become indifferent, even unjust, to others. For example, the Pantheon, the Apollo Belvedere, one or two colossal heads and, recently, the Sistine Chapel have so obsessed me that I see almost nothing else. But how can we, petty as we are and accustomed to pettiness, ever become equal to such noble perfection? Even when one has adjusted oneself to some degree, a tremendous mass of new things crowd in on one, facing one at every step, each demanding the tribute of one's attention. How is one to find one's way through? Only by patiently allowing it all to grow slowly inside one, and by industriously studying what others have written for one's benefit.

I immediately bought the new edition of Winckelmann's *History of the Art of Antiquity*, translated by Fea. Read on the spot where it was written and with an able and learned company to consult, I find it a great help.

Roman antiquity is beginning to give me about as much pleasure as Greek. History, inscriptions, coins, in which hitherto I took no interest, are forcing themselves on my attention. My experience with natural history is repeating itself here, for the entire history of the world is linked up with this city, and I reckon my second life, a very rebirth, from the day when I entered Rome.

5 December

In the few weeks I have been here, I have already seen a number of foreigners come and go, and have been amazed at the lack of respect so many of them show for all these objects which are so worth seeing. In the future, thank God, none of these birds

of passage will ever be able to impress me again. If, when I get
back to the north again, one of them should start telling me about
Rome, he will never again make me sick with envy. I have seen
her for myself and I already know more or less where I stand.

8 December

Now and again we get a really beautiful day. The rain that falls
from time to time is making the grass grow and the gardens
green. The presence of evergreens here and there prevents one
from noticing the fallen leaves of the others. The orange trees in
the gardens, growing uncovered straight out of the ground, are
heavy with fruit.

I meant to give a full account of a carriage drive we took to
the sea and of the fishing catch we saw there, but our good friend
Moritz returned in the evening on horseback and broke his arm
when his horse took a fall on the slippery Roman pavement.
This has put a stop to our merrymaking and brought domestic
calamity into our little circle.

13 December

I am so happy that you have taken my disappearance as well as
I hoped you would. Please make my peace with any heart that
may be offended at it. I did not mean to upset anyone
and I cannot yet say anything to justify myself. God forbid that
the motives which led to my decision should ever hurt the feelings of a friend.

I am slowly recovering from my *'salto mortale'*, and I study
more than I amuse myself. Rome is a world, and it would take
years to become a true citizen of it. How lucky those travellers
are who take one look and leave.

This morning I came by chance on the letters which Winckelmann wrote from Italy, and you can imagine with what emotion
I have started to read them. Thirty-one years ago, at the same
time of year, he arrived here, an even greater fool than I was.
But, with true German seriousness, he set himself to make a
thorough and accurate study of antiquity and its arts. How

bravely he worked his way through! And, in this city, what it means to me to remember him!

Aside from the objects of Nature, who in all her realms is true and consistent, nothing speaks so loudly as the impression left by a good and intelligent man, or by authentic works of art which are just as unerring as Nature. One feels this particularly strongly in Rome, where so many caprices have been given free rein and so many absurdities perpetuated by wealth and power.

I was especially delighted by one passage in a letter of Winckelmann's to Francke. 'In Rome you must seek out everything with a certain phlegm, otherwise you are taken for a Frenchman. I believe that Rome is the school for the whole world and I, too, have been purged and tested here.'

What he says exactly describes my methods of investigation. No one who has not been here can have any conception of what an education Rome is. One is, so to speak, reborn and one's former ideas seem like a child's swaddling clothes. Here the most ordinary person becomes somebody, for his mind is enormously enlarged even if his character remains unchanged.

This letter will reach you in time for the New Year. May its beginning bring you much happiness and may we all meet again before its end! What a joy that will be! The past year has been the most important in my life; whether I die tomorrow or live yet awhile, it has been good to me. Now a few words for the children, which you may read to them or tell them in your own words.

Here you do not notice the winter. The only snow you can see is on the mountains far away to the north. The lemon trees are planted along the garden walls. By and by they will be covered with rush mats, but the orange trees are left in the open. Hundreds and hundreds of the loveliest fruits hang on these trees. They are never trimmed or planted in a bucket as in our country, but stand free and easy in the earth, in a row with their brothers. You can imagine nothing jollier than the sight of such a tree. For a few pennies you can eat as many oranges as you like. They taste very good now, but in March they will taste even better.

The other day we went to the seashore and saw fishermen hauling in their nets. The oddest creatures came up – fish, crabs and weird freaks of nature. Among them was the fish which gives anyone who touches it an electric shock.

20 December

But all this is more effort and trouble than it is pleasure. The rebirth which is transforming me from within continues.

Though I expected really to learn something here, I never thought I should have to start at the bottom of the school and have to unlearn or completely relearn so much. But now I have realized this and accepted it, I find that the more I give up my old habits of thought, the happier I am. I am like an architect who wanted to erect a tower and began by laying a bad foundation. Before it is too late, he realizes this and deliberately tears down all that he has built so far above ground. He tries to enlarge and improve his design, to make his foundations more secure, and looks forward happily to building something that will last. May Heaven grant that, on my return, the moral effect of having lived in a larger world will be noticeable, for I am convinced that my moral sense is undergoing as great a transformation as my aesthetic.

Dr Münter is here, having returned from Sicily. He is an energetic, impetuous man. I don't know his plans, but he is going to visit you in May and will have much to tell you. He has been travelling in Italy for two years, but is very disappointed with the Italians because they have paid too little respect to the important letters of recommendation he carried, which were supposed to give him access to certain archives and private libraries. As a result, he has failed to do as much as he hoped. He has collected some beautiful coins and is, so he tells me, in possession of a manuscript which classifies coins historically by certain specific characteristics, on similar lines to Linnaeus's classification of plants. Herder will probably be able to get more information about this. Perhaps permission will be given to have a copy made. Something of this kind can and must be done, and, sooner or later, we too will have to concern ourselves more seriously with this field.

I am now starting to look at the best things for the second time.
As my initial amazement changes to a feeling of familiarity, I
acquire a clearer sense of their value. For a profound understanding of what man has created, the soul must first have won
its complete freedom.

Marble is an extraordinary material. Because of it, the Apollo
Belvedere gives such unbounded pleasure. The bloom of eternal
youth which the original statue possesses is lost in even the best
plaster cast.

In the Palazzo Rondanini opposite, there is an over-lifesize
mask of a Medusa in which the fearful rigidity of death is admirably portrayed. I own a good cast of it, but nothing is left of the
magic of the original. The yellowish stone, which is almost the
colour of flesh, has a noble, translucent quality. By comparison,
plaster always looks chalky and dead. And yet, what a joy it is to
enter a caster's workshop and watch the exquisite limbs of the
statues coming out of the moulds one after the other. It gives one
a completely fresh view of the figures. All the statues which are
scattered over Rome can here by seen set side by side. This is
invaluable for purposes of comparison. I could not resist buying
the cast of a colossal head of Jupiter. It now stands in a good
light facing my bed, so that I can say prayers to him the first
thing in the morning. However, for all his majesty and dignity,
he has been the cause of a comic incident.

When our old landlady comes in to make our beds, she is
usually accompanied by her favourite cat. I was sitting outside
in the hall and heard her busying herself in my room. Suddenly
she flung the door open – to hurry is not like her – and called
to me to come quickly and witness a miracle. When I asked her
what had happened, she replied that her cat was worshipping
God the Father.

She had noticed for some time that the creature had the
intelligence of a Christian, but, even so, this was a miracle. I ran
into the room to see for myself, and it really was miraculous.
The bust stands on a high pedestal, and the body is cut off far

below the chest, so that the head is near the ceiling. The cat had jumped up on to the pedestal, placed its paws on the chest of the God and stretched itself up until its muzzle could just reach the sacred beard, which it was now gracefully licking, oblivious of the exclamations of the landlady or my entrance.

I did not spoil the enthusiasm of the good woman by telling her my own explanation for this strange feline devotion. Cats have a keen sense of smell and probably it had scented the grease from the mould, some of which still remained sunk in the grooves of the beard.

29 December

I must tell you more about Tischbein and his admirable qualities: how, for instance, true German that he is, he has educated himself. I must also say with gratitude what a true friend he has been to me during his second stay in Rome. He has looked after me constantly and had a whole series of copies from the best masters made for me, some in black crayon, others in sepia and water colour. These will be invaluable to me in Germany when I am far away from the originals.

Tischbein at first set out to become a portrait painter, and in the course of his career has come into contact with eminent men, especially in Zurich, who improved his taste and enlarged his vision.

I brought along with me *Scattered Leaves*, which are doubly welcome here. As a reward, Herder ought to be told in full detail what a good impression this little book makes at repeated readings. Tischbein could hardly believe that its author could have written it without ever having been in Italy.

In this artistic colony one lives, as it were, in a room full of mirrors where, whether you like it or not, you keep seeing yourself and others over and over again.

I had often noticed Tischbein giving me a close scrutiny and now the reason has come out; he is thinking of painting my portrait. The sketch is finished, and he has already stretched the canvas. The portrait is to be life-size. He wants to paint me as a traveller, wrapped in a white cloak, sitting on a fallen obelisk and looking towards the ruins of the Campagna di Roma in the background. It is going to be a fine painting, but it will be too large for our northern houses. I shall, I hope, again find some corner for myself, but there will be no room for my portrait.

In spite of all the attempts that are made to draw me out of my obscurity, in spite of all the poets who read me their productions in person or get others to do so, and though I would only have to say the word to cut quite a figure here, I stick to my resolution. I am only amused at discovering what they are after. Each little circle, though they all sit at the feet of the Queen of the world, now and then displays the spirit of a small provincial town. In fact, they are no different here than they are anywhere else. I am already bored at the thought of what they would like to do with me and through me. It would mean joining a clique, championing its passions and intrigues, praising its artists and dilettantes, belittling their rivals, and putting up with everything that pleases the Great and the Rich. Why should I add my prayer to this collective litany which makes me wish I were on another planet, and what good would it do?

No, I refuse to become any more deeply involved, and for my part, I mean to keep away, and when I get home, to discourage in myself and others the desire to gad about the wide, wide world.

What I want to see is the Everlasting Rome, not the Rome which is replaced by another every decade. If I had more time, I would use it better. It is history, above all, that one reads quite differently here from anywhere else in the world. Everywhere else one starts from the outside and works inward; here it seems to be the other way around. All history is encamped about us and all history sets forth again from us. This does not apply only to Roman history, but to the history of the whole world. From here I can accompany the conquerors to the Weser and the Euphrates, or, if I prefer to stand and gape, I can wait in the Via Sacra for their triumphant return. In the meantime I have lived on doles of grain and money, and have my comfortable share in all this splendour.

2 *January* 1787

One may say what one likes in praise of the written or the
spoken word, but there are very few occasions when it suffices.
It certainly cannot communicate the unique character of any
experience, not even in matters of the mind. But when one
has first taken a good look for oneself at an object, then it is a
pleasure to read or hear about it, for now the word is related
to the living image, and thought and judgement become
possible.

You often used to make fun of my passion for observing
stones, plants and animals from certain definite points of view,
and tried to make me give it up. Now my attention is fixed on
the architect, the sculptor and the painter and in them, too, I
shall learn to find myself.

6 *January*

I have just come back from seeing Moritz, whose arm is now
out of a cast. Things are going well. What I learned during
these two weeks I spent with my suffering friend as nurse, confessor, confidant, finance minister and private secretary may
bear good fruit in the future. During all this time the acutest
suffering and the rarest pleasure went hand in hand.

Yesterday, for my eye's delight, I set up in the hall outside
my room a new cast, a colossal head of Juno, the original of
which is in the Villa Ludovisi. She was my first Roman love
and now I own her. No words can give any idea of this work. It
is like a canto by Homer. But I really deserve such good company
because I can now announce that *Iphigenie* is finished at last, that
is to say, it lies on the table before me in two almost identical
copies, one of which will soon be on its way to you. Please
receive it kindly. Though you will not, of course, find in its
pages what I should have written, you will at least be able to
guess what I would like to have written.

You have complained several times about obscure passages in
my letters which hinted at some conflict under which I was

suffering, even in the midst of the noblest sights. My Greek travelling companion was in no small part responsible by urging me to work when I ought to have been looking about me.

It reminds me of an excellent friend who had made all the preparations for a journey which might well have been called a journey of exploration. For years he studied and saved up his money and then, thinking to kill two birds with one stone, he suddenly eloped with the daughter of a distinguished family.

In a similar reckless mood I decided to take *Iphigenie* with me to Carlsbad. Let me now tell you briefly of the places where I was most occupied with my heroine.

After leaving the Brenner behind me, I took her out of the largest parcel and took her to my heart. On the shores of Lake Garda, where the strong noonday wind was dashing the waves against the shore and I felt at least as lonely as my heroine on the shores of Tauris, I drafted the first lines of a new version. I continued this in Verona, Vicenza, Padua, and with especial ardour in Venice. After that I came to an impasse and even felt tempted to write a new play, *Iphigenie in Delphi*. This I would have done at once if distractions and my sense of obligation towards the older play had not deterred me.

But once in Rome I began working again steadily. In the evening, before going to bed, I prepared myself for the next morning's allotted stint, which I attacked the moment I woke. My method was very simple. I wrote a rough draft straight off, then I read this aloud to myself, line by line, period by period, until it sounded right. The result is for you to judge. In writing it, I have learned more than I have achieved. I shall enclose some comments with the play itself.

6 January

Again I have some more ecclesiastical matters to tell you about. We spent a roaming Christmas Eve visiting the churches where services were being held. One of the most popular is equipped with a special organ and other musical devices, so that not a pastoral sound is lacking, from the shepherd's pipes to the chirping of birds and the bleating of sheep.

On Christmas Day I saw the Pope with the assembled clergy in St Peter's, where he celebrated High Mass. At times he sat on his throne, at others he stood in front of it. It is a spectacle unique in its kind, magnificent and dignified. But I am so old a protestant Diogenes that the effect on me of this splendour was more negative than positive. Like my pious predecessor, I should like to say to these spiritual conquerors of the world: Do not come between me and the sun of sublime art and simple humanity.

Today is the Feast of the Epiphany, and I have heard Mass said according to the Greek rite. These ceremonies seemed to me more impressive, austere and thoughtful than the Latin ones.

As I watched, I again felt that I am too old for anything but truth. Rites, operas, processions, ballets, they all run off me like water off a duck's back. But an operation of Nature, like the sunset seem from the Villa Madama, or a work of art, like my revered Juno, leaves a deep and lasting impression.

I am already beginning to shudder at the thought of the forth-coming theatre season. Next week seven theatres will open. Anfossi himself is here and will perform *Alexander in India*. *Cyrus* will also be given and a ballet, *The Conquest of Troy*. This would be something for the children.

10 January

Here, then, is my 'child of sorrows'. *Iphigenie* deserves the epithet in more senses than one. When I read it to our circle I marked several lines. Some of them I think I have improved; others I have left as they stood, hoping Herder will put them right with a stroke or two with his pen. I have worked myself into a stupor over it.

The main reason why, for several years, I have preferred to write prose is that our prosody is in a state of great uncertainty. My intelligent and scholarly colleagues left the decision on such matters to instinct and taste. What has been lacking is any prosodic principle. I would never have dared rewrite *Iphigenie* in iambics if I had not found my guiding star in Moritz's *Prosody*. My association with the author, especially while he was laid up, has enlightened me still further on the subject, and I ask my friends to give his theory sympathetic consideration.

It is a striking fact about our language that we have very few syllables which are definitely long or short; with most of them, it is a matter of taste and option. Moritz has now worked out that there exists a certain syllabic hierarchy. The syllable which is more important to the meaning of a word is long and makes the less important syllable next to it short. On the other hand, the same syllable is short if it comes before or after a syllable which carries a greater weight of meaning. Here is certainly something to hold on to, and, even if not everything has been solved, we have at least a thread by which we can grope our way along. I have often obeyed the advice of this maxim and found it conform to my own feelings about language.

I mentioned earlier my reading of the play. Let me now tell you briefly how it turned out. Accustomed to my earlier impassioned and explosive work, these young men were expecting something in the manner of *Berlichingen* * and at first could not reconcile themselves to the calm flow of the lines, though some elevated and simple passages did not fail to make their effect. Tischbein, who also has little taste for such emotional restraint, expressed this in a charming allegory or symbol. He compared my work to a burnt offering, the smoke from which is prevented from rising by a gentle air current and creeps along the ground, while its flame struggles to rise upward. His drawing, which I enclose, has both charm and point, I think.

And so this work which I had expected to finish much sooner has entertained, detained, occupied and tortured me for three whole months. It is not the first time I have treated what was most important as if it were a side issue; but we won't wrangle or philosophize any more over this.

I enclose a pretty carved stone – a little lion with a gadfly buzzing in front of its nose. This was a favourite subject of the Ancients, who treated it time and time again. I should like you to seal your letters with it in future so that the little thing may serve as a kind of artistic echo travelling back and forth between you and me.

* *Götz von Berlichingen*, early drama by Goethe, 1773.

Every day I have so much to tell and every day activities and distractions prevent me from putting one sensible word down on paper. Furthermore, the days are getting chilly and one is better off anywhere than indoors when the rooms have neither stoves nor fireplaces and are only good for sleeping or feeling uncomfortable in. Still, there are some incidents of the past week which must not go unrecorded.

In the Palazzo Giustiniani there stands a statue of Minerva which I admire very highly. Winckelmann scarcely mentions it, and when he does, in the wrong context. And I do not feel myself competent to say anything about it. We had been standing for a long time looking at the statue when the wife of the custodian told us that it had once been a sacred image. The *inglesi*, she said, who belong to the same religious cult, still come to worship it and kiss one of its hands. (One hand, indeed, is white, while all the rest of the statue is a brownish colour.) She went on to say that a lady of this religious persuasion had been here recently, thrown herself on her knees and worshipped it. She herself, being a Christian, had found this behaviour so funny that she had run out lest she should burst out laughing. Seeing that I could not tear myself away from the statue either, she asked me if I had a sweetheart whom it resembled. Worship and love were the only things the good woman understood; disinterested admiration for a noble work of art, brotherly reverence for another human spirit were utterly beyond her ken. We were delighted with the story of the English lady and left with the desire to return soon. If my friends want to hear more about the High Style of the Greeks, they should read what Winckelmann has to say about it. He does not mention this Minerva in his discussion, but, if I am not mistaken, the work is a late example of the high, austere style at the point of its transition to the style of beauty : the bud is about to open. A transitional style is appropriate to her character as Minerva.

Now for a spectacle of another sort ! On the Feast of Epiphany, which celebrates the bringing of the Glad Tidings to the Heathen, we went to the Propaganda. There, in the presence of three cardinals and a numerous auditory, we first heard an address on the theme: In what place did Mary receive the three Magi? In a stable? If not, where else? Then some Latin poems on similar themes were read, and after that about thirty seminarists appeared and read, one after another, little poems, each in his native tongue: Malabarian, Epirotian, Turkish, Moldavian, Hellenic, Persian, Colchic, Hebrew, Arabic, Syrian, Coptic, Saracenic, Armenian, Iberian, Madagassic, Icelandic, Egyptian, Greek, Isaurian, Ethiopian, etc., and several others which I could not understand. Most of the poems seemed to be written in their national metres and were recited in their national styles of declamation, for some barbaric rhythms and sounds came out. The Greek sounded as if a star had risen in the night. The audience roared with laughter at all the foreign voices, and so this performance, too, ended in farce.

Here is another little story to show how lightly the sacred is taken in holy Rome. The late Cardinal Albani was once present at just such a festive gathering as I have described. One of the seminarists turned towards the Cardinal and began in his foreign tongue with the words 'gnaja! gnaja!' which sounded more or less like the Italian 'canaglia! canaglia!' The Cardinal turned to his colleagues and said: 'This fellow certainly knows us!'

13 January

In spite of all he did, Winckelmann left much undone and his work leaves much to be desired. With the materials he had assembled, he built quickly so as to get a roof on his house. If he were still alive and in good health, he would be the first to revise what he wrote. How much more he would have added to his observations, what good use he would have made of all that others, following in his footsteps, have done and of all the results of recent excavations. And then Cardinal Albani, for whom he wrote so much and for whose sake, perhaps, he left many things unsaid, would be dead.

Well, *Aristodemo* has been performed at last and with great success. Since Abbate Monti is related to the Pope's nephew and is very popular in high society, one could take it for granted that nothing but good would be heard from that quarter, and, sure enough, the boxes were generous with their applause. From the start the parterre was captivated by the poet's beautiful diction and the excellent delivery of the actors, and let no occasion pass to voice its satisfaction. The German artists in the back rows were no less vociferous, appropriately for once, since they are apt to be noisy on all occasions.

The author was so nervous about the reception of his play that he stayed at home, but after each act he received favourable reports, which by degrees transformed his anxiety into joy. There will be no lack of repeated performances and everything looks fine. The success of the play proves that a strong dramatic contrast, provided each element has any obvious real merit on its own, can win the approval of both the connoisseur and the general public.

It was a praiseworthy performance, and the acting and delivery of the chief actor, who is on stage nearly all the time, were excellent; it was like seeing one of the kings of antiquity in person. The costumes which impress us so much when we see them on statues had been most successfully imitated in the actor's costume and it was obvious that he had studied the antique period well.

16 *January*

Rome is threatened with a great loss. The King* of Naples is going to transport the Farnese Hercules to his palace. All the artists are in mourning. However, as a result, we are going to see something our predecessors never saw. The upper part of the statue, from the head to the knees, and the feet with the pedestal on which they stand were discovered on the estates of

---

* Ferdinand IV (1751–1825).

the Farnese. The legs from the knees to the ankles were missing, and Guglielmo della Porta had made substitutes for them, upon which Hercules had been standing up till now. But recently the original legs were discovered on the Borghese estates and have been on exhibit in the Villa Borghese.

Prince Borghese has now decided to present these precious fragments to the King of Naples. The legs which Porta made have been removed and replaced by the authentic ones. Though everyone up till now has been perfectly satisfied with the statue as it was, there is a hope that we may be going to have the pleasure of seeing something quite new and more harmonious.

18 January

Yesterday, the Feast of St Anthony, we had a wonderful time. Though there had been frost in the night, the day turned out beautifully warm and clear.

It is a matter of historical observation that all religions, as their ritual or their theological speculation expands, must sooner or later reach the point of allowing the animals to share to some extent in their spiritual patronage. St Anthony, abbot or bishop, is the patron saint of all four-footed creatures and his feast is a saturnalia for these otherwise oppressed animals and for their keepers and drivers as well. The gentry must either walk or stay at home, and the people love to tell fearful stories of unbelieving masters who forced their coachmen to drive on this day and were punished by serious accidents.

The church stands on a square which is so large that, normally, it looks empty, but today it is full of life. Horses and mules, their manes and tails gorgeously braided with ribbons, are led up to a small chapel, detached from the church proper, and a priest, armed with an enormous brush, sprinkles them with holy water from tubs and buckets in front of him. He does this generously, vigorously and even facetiously so as to excite them. Devout coachmen offer candles of various sizes, their masters send alms and gifts, so that their valuable, useful beasts may be protected against every kind of accident during the coming year. Donkeys and horned cattle also get their modest share of blessing.

Later we took a long diverting walk under the blesssed Italian sky. We were surrounded by objects of interest, but this time we ignored them and abandoned ourselves to fun and frolics.

19 January

We took another holiday today and looked at a part of the Capitol which I had hitherto neglected. Then we crossed the Tiber and drank Spanish wine aboard a ship which had just landed. Romulus and Remus are said to have been found in this neighbourhood. For us it was a triple Pentecost as we got drunk on the holy spirit of art, the memories of the ancient past and the sweet wine simultaneously.

20 January

The enjoyment which a beginner derives from his first superficial look depresses him later when he realizes that, without solid knowledge, such pleasure is an illusion.

I am fairly well up in anatomy and have acquired some knowledge of the human body, though not without much effort. Now, thanks to my constant observation of statues, I find myself becoming more and more interested in the subject and at a more serious level. In surgical anatomy, knowledge of the part is the only thing which matters, and for that, one wretched little muscle is quite sufficient. But in Rome the parts are of no account except in so far as they contribute to a shape which is noble and beautiful.

In the large military hospital of Santo Spirito they have made a model of the muscular system for artists to study, which is universally admired. It looks just like a Marsyas or a saint who has been flayed alive.

I am also educating myself by following the customs of the Ancients and studying the skeleton, not as an artificially assembled mass of bones, but with the natural ligaments to which it owes life and motion.

If I now tell you that I am also studying perspective in the evenings, it will show, I hope, that I have not been idle. For all

that, I am always hoping to do more than I actually manage to
do.

As for the artistic tastes of the German colony here, I can only
say : the bells ring loudly enough, but not in unison.

When I think what wonderful things there are all around us
and how little advantage I have taken of them, I could despair.
But now I look forward eagerly to returning and hope that, next
time, I shall see clearly these masterpieces, after which I was,
until now, groping like a blind man.

Even in Rome, too little provision is made for the person who
seriously wants to study the city as a whole. He is compelled
endlessly to piece it together from fragments, though these are
certainly superabundant. The truth is, few visitors are really
serious about seeing and learning anything that matters. They
are governed by their caprices and their vanity, as all who have
dealings with them are well aware. Every guide has his designs
on one, everybody wants to recommend some tradesman or
other, or promote the career of his favourite artist. And why
shouldn't he? Don't these ignoramuses reject the best when it is
offered them?

It would be of the greatest advantage to the serious student
if the government, which must give its permission before an
antique work of art is exported, would insist in such cases
that a cast be made first. These casts might be collected in a
special museum. But even if a Pope were to have such an idea, he
would have all the traders against him because, in a few years,
there would be an outcry at the loss of so many valuable and
important works, for which, in some cases, the permission to
export has been obtained by secret and devious ways.

For some time, but particularly since the performances of
Aristodemo, the patriotic feelings of the German colony have
been aroused. They never stopped singing the praises of my
Iphigenie. Again and again I was asked to read excerpts and in
the end I was forced to repeat my reading of the whole work.
When I did this, I found several more lines which sounded

better when read than they looked on paper, which proves that poetry is not written for the eye.

Rumours of this reading at last reached the ears of Reiffenstein and Angelica,* and I was urged to give another at their house. I asked for some days' grace, but gave them a lengthy outline of the story and the plot development. This presentation was more favourably received by the aforesaid than I had dared hope; even Signor Zucchi, from whom I expected it least, showed a sincere and sympathetic interest. This, however, is easy to explain, for in its formal structure my play conforms more or less to the traditional form of Greek, Italian and French drama. And this still has the greatest appeal for those who have not yet grown accustomed to the English audacities.

25 January

I find it becoming more and more difficult to give a proper account of my stay in Rome. The more I see of this city, the more I feel myself getting into deep waters.

It is impossible to understand the present without knowing the past, and, to compare them with each other, I should need more time and fewer distractions. The very site of the city takes one back to the time of its foundation. We soon see that it was no great, wisely led people who settled here and prudently established it as the centre of an empire. No powerful ruler chose it as a suitable spot for the seat of a colony. No, it began as a refuge for shepherds and riffraff. A couple of vigorous young men laid the foundations for the palaces of the masters of the world on the very same hill at the foot of which a despotic usurper had once had them exposed among reeds and swamps. In relation to the land behind them, the seven hills are not hills at all; it is only in relation to the ancient river bed of the Tiber, which later became the Campus Martius, that they appear to be heights. If the spring allows me to make further excursions possible, I shall be able to describe the disadvantages of the site more fully. Even now, with pity in my heart, I can hear the

---

*Angelica Kauffmann, Swiss painter, married to the Italian painter Antonio Zucchi.

anguished lamentations of the women of Alba as they see their
city destroyed and are driven from that beautiful location which
some intelligent leader had chosen. I can picture them, huddled
on the miserable Coelian hill and exposed to the mists of the
Tiber, looking back at their lost paradise. I still know little of the
surrounding country, but I am convinced that no inhabited site
among the peoples of old was as badly placed as Rome. In the
end, when they had swallowed up everything, in order to live
and enjoy life, the Romans had to move out again and build
their country villas on the sites of the cities they had destroyed.

25 January

It is comforting to observe how many people here live quietly,
each pursuing his own interests. In the house of a priest who,
though without original talent, has devoted his life to art, we
saw some interesting copies of great paintings which he had reproduced in miniature. The best of all was of the Last Supper by
Leonardo da Vinci. Christ is sitting at the table with His intimate
disciples, and the painter has chosen the moment when He
prophesies and says: 'Verily, one of you shall betray me.'

I am trying to make arrangements to have an etching made,
either after this copy or another. It would be the greatest
blessing if a faithful reproduction could become available to a
wide public.

Some days ago I visited a Franciscan called Father Jacquier
who lives on the Trinità dei Monti. He is a Frenchman by birth
and well known for his books on mathematics. He is very old, but
very nice and sympathetic. He has known many eminent men
in his time and even spent some months with Voltaire, who
grew very fond of him.

I have made the acquaintance of many other good and sound
people among the clergy. There are plenty of them about but,
because of some priestly mistrust, they avoid each other.

The bookshops here are not centres for the exchange of ideas
and the literary novelties seldom have much in them. The proper
thing, therefore, for a solitary man to do is to seek out the her-
mits.

After the success of *Aristodemo* which I really did a good deal to promote, I was again led into temptation. But it soon became only too obvious that they were not interested in me personally. They wanted to use me as a tool to strengthen their party and, if I had been prepared to come out and take sides, I too could have played a brief shadowy role. But now that they have seen I am not to be made use of, they leave me alone, and I go my own way in peace.

Yes, my life has acquired a ballast which gives it the proper balance; I am no longer afraid of the ghosts who so often used to make me their sport. Be of good cheer yourselves; that will give me added strength to stand on my own feet and will draw me back to you.

28 January

Everything I see around me suggests two lines of inquiry which I shall not fail to pursue when I see my way more clearly. The first is this:

At the sight of the immense wealth of this city, even though it consists of scattered fragments, one is inevitably led to ask about the age when it came into being. It was Winckelmann who first urged on us the need of distinguishing between various epochs and tracing the history of styles in their gradual growth and decadence. Any true art lover will recognize the justice and importance of this demand.

But how are we to obtain this insight? Little spade-work has been done; the general principle has been clearly laid down, but the details remain uncertain and obscure. A special training of the eye over many years would be required, and we must first learn what questions to ask. But hesitating and temporizing are no help. Once his attention has been drawn to the question and its importance realized, any serious student will understand that, in this field as in others, judgement is impossible without a knowledge of historical development.

The second line of inquiry is concerned exclusively with the art of the Greeks: What was the process by which these incomparable artists evolved from the human body the circle of their god-like shapes, a perfect circle from which not one essential, incidental or transitional feature was lacking? My instinct tells me that they followed the same laws as Nature, and I believe I am on the track of these. But there is something else involved as well which I would not know how to express.

2 February

Nobody who has not taken one can imagine the beauty of a walk through Rome by full moon. All details are swallowed up by the huge masses of light and shadow, and only the biggest and most general outlines are visible. We have just enjoyed three clear and glorious nights. The Colosseum looked especially beautiful. It is closed at night. A hermit lives in a small chapel and some beggars have made themselves at home in the crumbling vaults. These had built a fire on the level ground and a gentle breeze had driven the smoke into the arena, so that the lower parts of the ruins were veiled and only the huge masses above loomed out of the darkness. We stood at the railing and watched, while over our heads the moon stood high and serene. By degrees the smoke escaped through holes and crannies and in the moonlight it looked like fog. It was a marvellous sight. This is the kind of illumination by which to see the Pantheon, the Capitol, the square in front of St Peter's, and many other large squares and streets.

Like the human spirit, the sun and the moon have a quite different task to perform here than they have in other places, for here their glance is returned by gigantic, solid masses.

13 February

I must mention a stroke of luck. It was a small one, but, great or small, luck is luck and always welcome. On the Trinità dei Monti they are digging the foundation for a new obelisk. The top of the hill is covered with mounds of earth taken from the ruins of the Gardens of Lucullus, which were later inherited by the Caesars. My wig-maker was passing by one morning and found in the rubble a flat piece of terra-cotta with some figures on it. He washed it and showed it to us, and I promptly bought it. It is almost as big as my hand and seems to be part of a large bowl. The figures on it are two griffins flanking a sacrificial altar; they are beautifully done and give me extraordinary pleasure. If they had been carved in stone, they would have made a lovely seal.

15 February

Before leaving for Naples, I could not escape giving another reading of *Iphigenie*. The audience consisted of Signora Angelica, Hofrat Reiffenstein and even Signor Zucchi, who insisted on coming because his wife wished him to. At the time he was working on a large architectural drawing done in decorative style, at which he is a master. He used to be closely associated with Clerisseau and they were in Dalmatia together. He drew the figures for the buildings and ruins which Clerisseau later published. In doing so, he learned so much about perspective and effects that now, in his old age, he can amuse himself with a sheet of paper in a worthwhile way.

Angelica, tender soul that she is, responded to my play with a sympathetic understanding that astounded me. She has promised to make a drawing based on one passage and give it to me as a souvenir. And so, just as I am on the point of leaving Rome, I have become tenderly attached to these kindhearted people. It is both a pleasure and a pain for me to know that someone will be sorry to see me go.

16 February

The safe arrival of *Iphigenie* was announced to me in a surprising and pleasant way. Just as I was leaving for the opera, a letter in a familiar hand was brought to me – doubly welcome because it had been sealed with the little lion, so that I knew that my package must have arrived safely. I pushed my way into the opera house and looked for a seat under the large chandelier. There, in the middle of a crowd of strangers, I suddenly felt so close to my distant friends that I wished I could jump up and embrace them. I thank you heartily for the bare notice of its arrival. I hope your next letter will be accompanied by some kind word of approval.

Here follows a list, telling you how the copies which are due to me from Göschen are to be distributed among my friends. I don't care in the least how the general public responds to my piece, but I do wish to give my friends some pleasure with it.

I am always inclined to undertake too much. If I think of my next four volumes as a whole, my head swims; when I think of them separately, I feel a little better. Perhaps it would have been wiser to have done as I originally intended, and sent these things out into the world in fragments. Then I could have embarked with fresh courage and strength on new subjects in which I felt a fresher interest.

Would I not have done better to write *Iphigenie in Delphi* instead of grappling with the moods of Tasso? But I have already put much too much of myself into the play, fruitlessly to abandon it now.

I am sitting in the hall by the fireplace, and the heat of a fire that is, for once, well fed gives me the courage to start a new page. How wonderful it is that one can reach out so far into the distance with one's latest thoughts and transport thither one's immediate surroundings.

The weather is beautiful, the days are becoming visibly longer, the laurel and boxwood are in flower and so are the almond trees. This morning I came upon an unusual sight. In the distance I saw what looked like some tall poles which were the most beautiful purple all over. On closer inspection, they turned out to be what in our hothouses is called the Judas tree and, by botanists, *Cercis siliquastrum*. Its violet, butterfly-shaped flowers blossom directly out of the trunk. They had been lopped during the winter, which accounted for the poles I had seen, and flowers had burst forth from the bark by the thousands. Daisies are pushing up out of the ground in swarms like ants. The crocus and the adonis appear less often but look all the more decorative and graceful when they do.

What new joys and profitable experiences the southern regions

of this country must have in store for me! It is the same with
the works of Nature as with works of art: so much has been
written about them and yet anyone who sees them can arrange
them in fresh patterns.

When I think of Naples or, even more, of Sicily as I know
them from stories and pictures, it strikes me that these earthly
paradises are precisely the places where volcanoes burst forth in
hellish fury and have for centuries terrified and driven to despair
the people who live there and enjoy these regions.

But, important though I hope they will be to me, I must banish
these things from my thoughts so that I may make the most of
my last few days in the ancient capital of the world.

For two weeks now I have been on the go from morning to
night, seeing the things I had not seen before and giving the best
a second or third look. Everything is beginning to make a
pattern; the major works fall into their proper places and there is
room between them for many minor ones. My preferences are
becoming clearer and my emotional response to what is greatest
and most authentic is now freer and more relaxed.

At this stage one naturally envies the artist, who, through
reproducing and imitating these great visions, comes closer to
them in every way than the person who merely looks and
thinks. Still, after all, each can do only what lies in his power, and
so I spread all the sails of my spirit that I may circumnavigate
these coasts.

Today the grate has been stacked up with the finest coal,
something which rarely happens, since it is hard to find someone
with the time or the inclination to devote an hour or two to
looking after the fire. I shall take advantage of the agreeable
temperature to rescue some of my notes before they become
completely illegible.

On February the second we went to the Sistine Chapel for the
ceremony of the blessing of the candles. This upset me very much
and I soon left with my friends. I thought to myself: These are
the very candles which for three centuries have blackened the
frescoes, and this is the very incense which, with sacred insolence,
not only wraps the sun of art in clouds, but also makes it grow
dimmer every year and in the end will totally eclipse it.

We went outside and, after a long walk, came to Sant'Onofrio, where Tasso lies buried in a corner. His bust stands in the convent library. The face is of wax, and I can well believe that it is a death mask. It is a little blurred and damaged in places, but it still reveals better than any of his other portraits a gifted, delicate, noble and withdrawn personality.

So much for today. Now I must tackle the honest Volkmann's second volume on Rome and copy out excerpts concerning the things I have not yet seen. Before I go to Naples, the harvest should at least be reaped. The good day will certainly come when I can gather it into sheaves.

17 *February*

Except for four rainy days, all through February the sky has been cloudless, and in the middle of the day it is almost too warm. Everyone prefers to be out of doors. Hitherto we gave ourselves up to gods and heroes, but now the landscape comes into its rights, and the beauty of these days draws us into the countryside. I sometimes remember how in the north artists tried to make something of thatched roofs and ruined castles, to capture a picturesque effect from brooks, bushes and dilapidated rocks, and then I wonder at the change in myself, all the more so because these things still cling to me from habit. In the last two weeks, however, I have plucked up courage and have been going out, equipped with small pieces of drawing paper, to the hills and valleys where the villas are. Without too much deliberation I make sketches of typical southern or Roman subjects, chosen at random, and, trusting to luck, try to give them some light and shade. I can see clearly what is good and what is even better, but as soon as I try to get it down, it somehow slips through my fingers and I capture, not the truth, but what I am in the habit of capturing. Progress would require the discipline of steady practice, but where shall I find the time for such concentration? Still, I feel I have improved in many ways during these two weeks of passionate endeavour.

The artists like giving me lessons because I am quick to understand. But understanding is not the same as doing. Quickness of understanding is a mental faculty, but right doing requires the practice of a lifetime. However, feeble as his efforts may be, the amateur should not despair. The few lines I draw on the paper, often too hasty and seldom exact, help me to a better comprehension of physical objects. The more closely and precisely one observes particulars, the sooner one arrives at a perception of the whole.

One must not, however, compare oneself with the artist, but proceed in one's own manner. Nature has provided for all her children: even the least of them is not hindered in his existence by the existence of the greatest. 'A little man is still a man.' * Let us leave it at that.

I have seen the sea twice, first the Adriatic, then the Mediterranean, but both, as it were, only in passing. In Naples we shall get better acquainted. Everything in me is suddenly beginning to merge clearly. Why not earlier? Why at such a cost? I have so many thousands of things, some new, some from an earlier time, which I would like to tell you.

> In the evening, when the Carnival madness
> has abated

I am not happy about leaving Moritz alone when I go away. He has made good progress, but the moment he is left to look after himself, he immediately withdraws into his favourite hiding holes. With my encouragement he has written a letter to Herder, which I enclose, and I hope that the answer will contain some useful advice. Moritz is an unusually good person; he would have made better progress if, now and then, he had met sympathetic people capable of explaining his condition to him. At the moment, if Herder would allow him to write a letter once in a while, it would do him more good than anything. He is engaged on an archaeological work which really deserves to be encouraged. Our friend Herder could not easily have lent his kind offices to a better cause, nor sown his teachings in a more fertile field.

---

* A little man. A quotation from Goethe's satirical puppet play *Das Jahrmarktsfest zu Plundersweilern*, 1773.

The large portrait of me, which Tischbein has started on, is already beginning to grow out of the canvas. He has ordered a small clay model from a skilful sculptor and draped it elegantly in a cloak. From this model he is now hard at work painting, for the picture ought, of course, to be brought to a certain stage before we leave for Naples, and merely to cover such a large canvas with paint takes plenty of time.

19 February

To my annoyance, I wasted the whole day among the fools. When night fell, I went for a walk in the Villa Medici to recover. The new moon is just past. Next to its tenuous sickle, I could almost make out the dark portion of the disc with the naked eye, and through a telescope it was clearly visible. During the day a haze hovers over the earth like that I know from the drawings and paintings of Claude Lorrain, but this phenomenon cannot easily be seen in Nature more beautifully than here. The almond trees, blossoming among the dark-green oaks, are a new vision of grace. The sky is like a light-blue piece of taffeta, lit up by the sun. But how much more beautiful it will be in Naples! All this confirms my botanical fancies, and I am on the way to establishing important new relations and discovering the manner in which Nature, with incomparable power, develops the greatest complexity from the simple.

Vesuvius is throwing up stones and ashes, and at night people can see the summit glowing. I hope that ever-active Nature will make me the present of a flow of lava. I can hardly wait to make these mighty objects my own.

21 February. Ash Wednesday

At last the folly is over. Yesterday evening the innumerable little candles created another scene of Bedlam. One has to see the Roman Carnival to lose all wish ever to see it again!

It is not worth writing about, though it might make an amusing topic of conversation. What I find unpleasant about it is the lack of genuine gaiety in the people, who have not enough money to gratify the few desires which they may still have. The great are stingy about spending, the middle class is impecunious and the populace without a penny. On the last day the noise was incredible, but there was no genuine merriment. The pure and lovely sky looked down in innocence on all these buffooneries.

Since, however, one cannot entirely refrain from describing such scenes and to amuse the children, I am sending you some coloured drawings of carnival masks and characteristic Roman costumes. The dear little ones may use them to replace some missing chapter in their Orbus Pictus.

I am using the moments between packing to write down a few things I forgot to mention. Tomorrow we leave for Naples. I am looking forward to finding a new freedom in that paradise of Nature, and a fresh impulse to resume my study of art when I return to the solemnities of Rome.

Packing is no trouble. I do it with a lighter heart than I did six months ago when I severed my ties with all that was dear to me. Yes, that was six months ago already, and of the four I have spent in Rome, not a moment has been wasted. That is saying a good deal, but it is no exaggeration.

I know that *Iphigenie* arrived; by the time I reach the foot of Vesuvius, I hope I shall hear that she has been kindly received.

To be travelling in Tischbein's company, who has such a remarkable eye for nature and art, is a great privilege for me. Like true Germans, we cannot refrain from making plans to work. We have bought the finest drawing paper, though the number and splendour of the objects we shall encounter will probably set limits to our good intentions.

I have made up my mind about one thing: the only one of my poetic works which I shall take with me is *Tasso*. I set great hopes on him. If I only knew your opinion of *Iphigenie*, this might serve me as a guide, for *Tasso* is a similar work. The subject, which is even more strictly circumscribed than the former play, needs still further elaboration in detail. All I have written so far must be thrown away; it has been lying around too long and neither the characters, the plot nor the tone have the slightest affinity with my present views.

As I was putting my things in order I came across your reproach that I contradict myself in my letters. I was not aware of this, but, since I always send them off the moment I have written them, it is highly probable. I feel myself being tossed about by tremendous powers, and it is only to be expected that I do not always know where I stand.

There is a tale about a fisherman who was caught at night by a storm and was trying to steer his boat homeward. His little son clung to him and asked: 'Father, what is that funny little light I see, now above us, now below?' His father promised to give him the answer the next day. It turned out to have been the beacon of the lighthouse, which to the child's eyes, as the boat rocked up and down on the wild waves, had appeared now below him, now above.

I too am steering my boat towards port over a wild sea and am keeping a steady eye on the lighthouse beam, even though to me too it seems to be constantly shifting its position, so that at last I may come safe and sound to shore.

At any departure, one inevitably thinks of earlier journeys and of that final future one. The thought is borne in on me, more forcibly than ever, that we make far too many provisions for life. Tischbein and I, for example, are about to turn our backs on so many wonderful things, including our well-stocked private museum. We now have three Junos standing side by side for comparison, but we are leaving them behind as though we had none.

PART TWO

NAPLES

WE made good time getting here. Two days ago the sky grew overcast, but there were some signs in the atmosphere which promised the return of good weather, and so it was. The clouds gradually dispersed, patches of blue sky appeared from time to time and, finally, the sun shone upon our course. We passed through Albano, and, before reaching Genzano, made a stop at the gates of a park which the owner, Prince Chigi, might be said to retain but not to maintain. Perhaps that is why he does not want anyone to look at it. It has turned into a complete wilderness – trees, shrubs, weeds, creepers grow as they like, wither, tumble down and rot. The valley of the park is enclosed by a high wall, but there is a little lattice gate through which one can peer into it, and see the hill slope beyond and the castle on its crown. It would make a fine subject for a good painter.

Enough of description. Let me merely add that, from this high ground, we could see the mountains of Sezze, the Pontine Marshes, the sea and the islands. A heavy shower was moving seaward over the marshes, and ever-changing patterns of light and shade played over the level waste. Some columns of smoke rising from scattered and barely visible huts gave an added beautiful effect as the sunlight struck them.

Velletri stands on a volcanic hill which is joined to other hills only on its northern side and commands a wide view in the other three directions.

We paid a visit to the museum of the Cavaliere Borgia, who, thanks to his connexions with the Cardinal and the Propaganda, has been able to collect some remarkable antiques – Egyptian idols, carved in the hardest kind of stone, metal figurines from earlier and later periods, and terracotta bas-reliefs which were dug up in this region. These last lead one to conclude that the ancient Volsci had a style of their own.

Among the many other rare objects in this museum, I particularly noticed two small paint-boxes of Chinese origin. On one the whole process of raising silkworms was portrayed, on the other the cultivation of rice, both very naïvely imagined and elaborately executed.

It is disgraceful, I know, that one does not come more often to look at these treasures, seeing how near to Rome they are. One's only excuse is the discomfort of any excursion into these parts and the binding spell of the Roman magic circle. As we were walking towards our inn, we passed some women sitting in front of their houses who called out to us and asked if we would like to buy some antiques. When we showed an eager interest, they brought out old kettles, fire-tongs and other worthless household utensils, and split their sides with laughter at having made fools of us. At first we were furious, but our guide set matters right when he assured us that this trick was an old custom here and every foreign visitor must submit to it with good grace.

I am writing this in a miserable inn and am too tired and uncomfortable to write any more. So – a very, very good night !

Fondi, 23 February

As early as three in the morning we were again on our way. Daybreak found us in the Pontine Marshes, which do not actually look as dreary as people in Rome usually describe them.

From one cross-journey, one cannot, of course, really judge such a vast and ambitious project as the drainage operations which have been undertaken at the Pope's orders, but it looks to me as though they are going to be largely successful.

Imagine a wide valley running from north to south with hardly any fall, but dipping towards the mountains in the east and rising towards the sea in the west. Down its whole length runs the straight line of the restored Via Appia, flanked on its right by the main canal which drains all the land on the seaward side, so that this has now been reclaimed for agriculture. Except for a few patches which lie too low, it is in cultivation as far as the eye can see, or would be if the farmers could be found to lease it.

The land on the mountain side of the road presents a more difficult problem. Cross-channels emptying into the main canal have been dug through the embankment of the road, but these cannot drain off the water. I am told there is a plan for digging a second drainage canal along the base of the mountains. Over large areas, especially around Terracina, willows and poplars have been accidentally sown by the wind.

Each posting station is merely a long shed with a thatched roof. Tischbein drew one and was rewarded by a sight such as only he can fully enjoy. A white horse had broken loose on the drained land and was rejoicing in its freedom, galloping over the brown earth like a flash of light. It looked superb, and Tischbein's rapture gave it added significance.

On the site of the former village of Mesa, at the very centre of the area, the Pope has erected a beautiful great building to inspire hope and confidence in the whole undertaking. So on we rolled in animated conversation but remembering the warning not to fall asleep on this road. If we had forgotten, the blue exhalation which, even at this time of year, hangs above the ground at a certain height would have reminded us of the dangerous miasma. It made the rocky perch of Terracina all the more desirable, and presently we saw the sea before us. The other side of that rock city offered us a view of a vegetation which was entirely unfamiliar. Indian figs forced their large, fleshy leaves between humble grey-green myrtles, yellow-green pomegranates and pale-green olive branches. Beside the road grew flowers we had never seen before. The meadows were full of narcissus and adonis. We had the sea on our right for a time, but the limestone hills close on our left remained unbroken. They are a continuation of the Apennines and run down from Tivoli till they reach the sea from which they have been separated, first by the Campagna di Roma, then by the extinct volcanoes of Frascati, Albano and Velletri, and finally by the Pontine Marshes. Monte Circello, the promontory which faces Terracina and marks the end of the Pontine Marshes, is probably limestone as well.

We now turned away from the sea and soon reached the plain of Fondi. This small area of fertile soil enclosed by not too rugged mountains welcomes every traveller with a smile. Most of

the oranges are still hanging on the trees, the young crops –
chiefly wheat – are showing green in the fields and there, below
us, lay the little town. A solitary palm tree stood out, and we
gave it a greeting. So much for tonight. Forgive my hasty pen.
The objects of interest are too many and our quarters too
miserable. But I could not resist my desire to get something
down on paper. We arrived here at sunset and now it is time for
bed.

Sant'Agata, 24 February

The room is cold, but I must give you some account of a perfect
day. Dawn had just broken when we drove out of Fondi, and we
were immediately greeted by oranges hanging over the walls on
either side of the road. The trees are so loaded with fruit, I could
hardly believe my eyes. On top, the young foliage is yellowish,
but below, a very lush green. Mignon * was quite right to yearn
for this country.

Then we came to well-tilled wheat fields planted with properly
spaced olive trees. When the wind stirred, they turned the
silvery undersides of their leaves to the light while the branches
swayed gracefully. It was a grey morning, but a strong north
wind promised to disperse the clouds.

Presently the road ran along a valley between fields which
were full of stones but well cultivated, their young crops of the
freshest green. In several places we saw large, circular, paved
threshing floors enclosed in low walls. They do not bring the
corn home in sheaves, but thresh it on the spot. The valley narrowed, the road climbed steadily, sheer limestone crags rose on
either side, the storm blew violently at our backs, and sleet fell
which melted very slowly.

Our curiosity was aroused by the walls of some old buildings
which were laid out in a network pattern. The high ground was
rocky but planted with olive trees wherever there was the
smallest patch of soil for them to grow in. Next we crossed a
plain covered with olive groves and came to a small town. There

---

* The poem *Mignon* (*Nur wer die Sehnsucht kennt . . .*) was written
in 1785.

we noticed, built into garden walls, ancient tombstones and all sorts of fragments, and the well-constructed floors of ancient villas, now filled up with earth and overgrown with thickets of olives. And then ... then, there was Vesuvius, capped with a cloud of smoke.

When we reached Mola di Gaeta, we were again greeted by orange trees in profusion. We stayed there a few hours. The bay in front of the little town commands a beautiful vista of sea and shore. The coast is the shape of a crescent moon. The tip of the right horn, the rock on which stands the fortress of Gaeta, is not far away, but its left horn extends much further. Following it with the eye, one sees first a chain of mountains and then Vesuvius and the islands beyond. Facing the crescent and almost at its centre lies the island of Ischia.

On the beach I found my first starfish and sea urchins, which had been washed ashore. I also picked up a lovely green leaf, as thin as the finest vellum, and some curious pebbles. Limestone pebbles were the most common, but serpentine, jasper, quartz, granite, porphyry, various kinds of marble and green-blue glass were also to be seen. These last can hardly come from this region and are most probably fragments from ancient buildings. Thus one can watch the waves playing before one's eyes with the splendour of an earlier world. We tarried with pleasure and were much amused by the nature of the people, whose behaviour was rather like that of some primitive tribe. After leaving Mola behind us, we had beautiful views all the way, even after the sea left us. The last we saw of it was a lovely cove, which we sketched. A good fruit country followed, fenced in by hedges of aloes. We also saw an aqueduct which ran from the mountains towards some unrecognizable jumble of ruins.

After crossing the river Garigliano, the road ran in the direction of a mountain range through a fairly fertile but uninteresting region. At last, the first hill of volcanic ash. From then on we entered a vast system of hills and valleys with snow-capped mountains rising in the background. A straggling town on a nearby hill caught my eye. In the valley lay Sant'Agata, where a respectable inn welcomed us with a cheerful fire burning in a fireplace built like a cabinet. Our room, however, is icy

cold and has no windows, only shutters – so I must hurry to
finish this.

Naples, 25 February

We have arrived safely at last and the omens are favourable. I
haven't much to report about the last day of our journey. We
left Sant'Agata at sunrise. All day a north-east wind blew fiercely
at our backs without slackening, but it was afternoon before it
succeeded in dispersing the clouds, and we suffered acutely
from the cold.

Our road led us again between and over volcanic hills, among
which, so far as I could tell, limestone formations occurred much
less frequently. At last we came to the plain of Capua and soon
afterwards to the town itself, where we made our midday halt.
In the afternoon a beautiful, flat expanse lay before us. The broad
high road ran between fields of green wheat; this is already a
span high and spread out before our eyes like a carpet. Rows of
poplars are planted in the fields and vines trained between their
widespreading branches. It was like this all the way to Naples.
The soil is loose, free from stones and well cultivated. The
stems of the vines are unusually strong and tall and the tendrils
sway like nets from one poplar to another.

Vesuvius was on our left all the time, emitting copious clouds
of smoke, and my heart rejoiced at seeing this remarkable
phenomenon with my own eyes at last. The sky grew steadily
clearer and, finally, the sun beat down on our cramped and
jogging quarters. By the time we reached the outskirts of Naples
the sky was completely cloudless, and now we are really in
another country. The houses with their flat roofs indicate another climate, though I dare say they are not so comfortable
inside. Everybody is out in the streets and sitting in the sun as
long as it is willing to shine. The Neapolitan firmly believes that
he lives in Paradise and takes a very dismal view of northern
countries. *Sempre neve, case di legno, gran ignoranza, ma denari
assai* – that is how he pictures our lives. For the edification of all
northerners, this means: 'Snow all the year round, wooden
houses, great ignorance, but lots of money.'

Naples proclaims herself from the first as gay, free and alive. A numberless host is running hither and thither in all directions, the King is away hunting, the Queen is pregnant and all is right with the world.

26 February

Alla Locanda de Sgr Moriconi al Largo del Castello – at this jolly, high-sounding address, letters from all four quarters of the globe can reach us from now on.

In the vicinity of the great citadel by the sea there is a vast space which, though it is surrounded on all sides by houses, is not called *piazza* but *largo* – the Broad Place, a name which probably dates from a time long ago when it was still open country. At one corner stands a large house in which we have taken a spacious corner room so that we can enjoy an uninterrupted view of the ever-lively square. An iron balcony runs along the outside past many windows and even round the corner. One would never leave it if the nipping wind did not chill one to the bones. Our room is gaily decorated, especially the elaborately coffered ceiling, where hundreds of arabesques announce that we are not far from Pompeii and Herculaneum. All this would be very fine, but there is neither fireplace nor stove, and, since February exercises its rights even here, I was longing for some means of keeping warm.

They brought me a tripod, high enough to hold one's hands over without stooping. To this is fastened a shallow pan filled with very fine live charcoal which is covered by an even layer of ashes. As we learned in Rome, it has to be used very economically. From time to time the overlying ashes must be carefully pushed aside with the head of a key, in order to let a little air reach the coals. If one gets impatient and stirs up the glowing embers, one may feel warmer for the moment, but very soon they burn themselves out, and then one must pay something to get the brazier refilled.

I was not feeling very well, so, naturally, I wanted more comfort. A rush mat protected me against the worst consequences of the cold stone floor. Since furs are unknown here, I decided to put on a pea-jacket which we had brought with us as a joke. This served me in good stead, especially after I fastened it round my waist with a cord from my valise. I must have looked a comic sight, something between a sailor and a Capuchin friar. When Tischbein returned from visiting some friends, he could not stop laughing.

27 February

Yesterday I spent indoors reading, waiting for my slight indisposition to pass. We spent today in ecstasies over the most astonishing sights. One may write or paint as much as one likes, but this place, the shore, the gulf, Vesuvius, the citadels, the villas, everything, defies description. In the evening we went to the Grotta di Posillipo and reached it just at the moment when the rays of the setting sun were shining directly into the entrance. Now I can forgive anyone for going off his head about Naples, and think with great affection of my father, who received such lasting impressions from the very same objects as I saw today. They say that someone who has once seen a ghost will never be happy again; vice versa, one might say of my father that he could never be really unhappy because his thoughts could always return to Naples. In my own way, I can now keep perfectly calm and it is only occasionally, when everything becomes too overwhelming, that my eyes pop out of my head.

28 February

Today we paid a visit to Philipp Hackert, the famous landscape painter, who enjoys the special confidence and favour of the King and Queen. One wing of the Palazzo Francavilla has been reserved for his use He has furnished this with the taste of an artist and lives very contentedly. He is a man of great determination and intelligence who, though an inveterate hard worker, knows how to enjoy life.

Afterwards we went to the seashore and saw all kinds of fish and the weirdest-shaped creatures being hauled in out of the waves. The day was lovely, the tramontana bearable.

1 *March*

In Rome I had already been obliged, more often than I liked, to abandon my obstinate hermit existence and take some part in social life. It does seem rather odd, I must admit, to go into the world with the intention of remaining alone. I was unable, for instance, to resist Prince Waldeck's kind invitations, and, thanks to his rank and influence, I was able to see many good things in his company.

For some time now, he has been staying in Naples, and we had hardly arrived before he sent us an invitation to take a drive with him out to Pozzuoli and the neighbouring countryside. I had been thinking of a trip to Vesuvius today, but Tischbein persuaded me to accept, saying that, in this perfect weather and the company of such a cultured prince, the other excursion promised to be as profitable as it certainly would be pleasant. While in Rome we made the acquaintance of a beautiful lady and her husband who are both inseparable friends of the Prince's. She is to be one of the party, so we are counting on having a delightful time.

I was already well known in this high circle from an earlier occasion. At our first meeting, the Prince had asked me what I was working on, and I was so preoccupied with my *Iphigenie* that one evening I told them the whole story in considerable detail. There was some discussion afterwards, but I got the impression they had been expecting something livelier and more violent.

1 *March. Evening*

Who has not had the experience of being swept off his feet and perhaps decisively influenced for life by a cursory reading of a book which, when he read it again and thought about it, had hardly anything more to say to him? (This happened once to me with *Sakuntala*.*) And does not much the same thing happen to us in our encounters with eminent persons?

---

* *Sakuntala*, dramatic poem by the sixth-century Indian poet Kalidasa. Since it was not translated into German until 1791, the view of most commentators is that Goethe only wrote S— and probably meant Spinoza.

How shall I describe a day like today? – a boat trip; some short drives in a carriage; walks on foot through the most astonishing landscape in the world; treacherous ground under a pure sky; ruins of unimaginable luxury, abominable and sad; seething waters; caves exhaling sulphur fumes; slag hills forbidding all living growth; barren and repulsive areas; but then, luxuriant vegetation, taking root wherever it can, soars up out of all the dead matter, encircles lakes and brooks, and extends its conquest even to the walls of an old crater by establishing there a forest of noble oaks.

Thus one is tossed about between the acts of nature and the acts of men. One would like to think, but feels too incompetent. Meanwhile the living merrily go on living. We, of course, did not fail to do the same, but people of culture, who belong to the world and know its ways, and are also warned by grave events, are inclined to reflections. As I was lost in contemplation of an unlimited view over earth, sea and sky, I was called back to myself by the presence of an amiable young lady who is accustomed to receive attentions and is not indifferent to them.

But even in my transports, I did not forget to take some notes. For a future redaction, the map I made on the spot for our use and a quick sketch of Tischbein's will be of great help. Today I am incapable of adding another word.

2 *March*

Today I climbed Vesuvius, although the sky was overcast and the summit hidden in clouds. I took a carriage to Resina, where I mounted a mule and rode up the mountain through vineyards. Then I walked across the lava flow of 1771 which was already covered with a fine but tenacious moss, and then upward along its edge. High up on my left I could see the hermit's hut. Climbing the ash cone, which was two-thirds hidden in clouds, was not easy. At last I reached the old crater, now blocked, and came to the fresh lava flows, one two months, one two weeks, and one only five days old. This last had been feeble and had already cooled. I crossed it and climbed a hill of ashes which had been recently thrown up and was emitting fumes everywhere. As the smoke was drifting away from me, I decided to try and reach the crater. I had only taken fifty steps when the smoke became so dense that I could hardly see my shoes. The handkerchief I pressed over my mouth was no help. In addition, my guide had disappeared and my steps on the little lava chunks which the eruption had discharged became more and more unsteady. I thought it better, therefore, to turn back and wait for a day with less cloud and less smoke. At least I now know how difficult it is to breathe in such an atmosphere.

Otherwise the mountain was perfectly calm, with none of the flames, rumbling or showers of stone there had been during the weeks before we arrived. Well, I have now made a reconnoitre, so that I can make my regular attack as soon as the weather clears.

Most of the types of lava I found were already known to me, but I discovered one phenomenon which struck me as unusual and which I intend to investigate more closely after I have consulted experts and collectors. This was the lining of a volcanic chimney which had once been plugged up, but then burst open and now juts out from the old filled-up crater. This hard, greyish, stalactitic mass seems to me to have been produced simply by the condensation of the finest volcanic vapours, unassisted by moisture or chemical action. This gives matter for further thought.

3 March

Today the sky is overcast and a sirocco is blowing – just the weather for writing letters.

Besides, I have seen quite enough people (and a mixed bag they are), beautiful horses and extraordinary fish.

I won't say another word about the beauties of the city and its situation, which have been described and praised so often. As they say here, 'Vedi Napoli e poi muori! – See Naples and die!' One can't blame the Neapolitan for never wanting to leave his city, nor its poets for singing the praises of its situation in lofty hyperboles: it would still be wonderful even if a few more Vesuviuses were to rise in the neighbourhood.

I don't want even to think about Rome. By comparison with

Naples's free and open situation, the capital of the world on the Tiber flats is like an old wretchedly placed monastery.

The sea and shipping make one aware of new possibilities. Yesterday the frigate for Palermo sailed before a strong tramontana, and her passage cannot have taken more than thirty-six hours.

With longing, I watched her spread sails as she passed between Capri and Cape Minerva and finally disappeared. If I were to watch a person I loved sail away in this fashion, I should pine away and die. Today a sirocco is blowing; if the wind increases, the waves near the harbour wall should be a merry sight. It being a Friday, the great coach drive of the nobility took place, when they show off their carriages and even more their horses. Nothing could be more graceful than these creatures. For the first time in my life, my heart went out to them.

3 March

I am sending you some pages, summarizing my first days in this new world, and enclose with them the envelope of your last letter, scorched in one corner, as evidence that it has been with me on Vesuvius.

You mustn't, either in your dreams or your waking hours, think of me as surrounded by dangers; where I go, I can assure you, I am in no greater peril than I would be on the high road to Belvedere.* I can aptly quote the Psalmist: 'The earth is the Lord's and all that is in it.' I don't seek adventure out of idle curiosity or eccentricity, but, since I have a clear mind which quickly grasps the essential nature of an object, I can do more and risk more than others. The voyage to Sicily is perfectly safe, and Sicily itself is by no means as dangerous as people who have never come within miles of it like to make out.

No earthquakes have been felt in southern Italy recently; only Rimini and neighbouring places in the north have suffered any damage. Earthquakes have moods of their own; here people talk of them as they talk of the weather or as, in Thuringia, they talk of forest fires.

---

*The summer residence of the Dukes of Weimar.

I am glad you have now taken kindly to the new version of *Iphigenie*; I should be still happier if you were more aware of how much it differs from the first. I know what I have done to it and am entitled, therefore, to talk about it. I could have gone much further. If what is good gives one joy, what is better gives one even more, and, in art, only the best is good enough.

5 March

We have spent the second Sunday in Lent wandering from one church to another. What is treated in Rome with the utmost solemnity is treated here with a lighthearted gaiety. The Neapolitan school of painting, too, can only be properly understood in Naples.

We were amazed to see the whole west front of a church painted from top to bottom. Over the portal, Christ was driving the money-changers out of the temple; on both sides, the latter were falling gracefully down a flight of stairs with a startled look on their faces.

In the interior of another church the span above the entrance is copiously decorated with a fresco depicting the expulsion of Heliodorus. No wonder Luca Giordano had to be quick, having such vast spans to fill. Even the pulpit is not always, as it is else-where, a cathedra, a chair for a single preacher. One I saw was a gallery up and down which walked a Capuchin, scolding the congregation for their sins, now from one end, now from the other.

I can't begin to tell you of the glory of a night by full moon when we strolled through the streets and squares to the endless promenade of the Chiaia, and then walked up and down the seashore. I was quite overwhelmed by a feeling of infinite space. To be able to dream like this is certainly worth the trouble it took to get here.

During the last few days I have made the acquaintance of a remarkable man, the Cavaliere Filangieri, who is well known for his work *Science of Legislation*. He is one of those noble-hearted young men to whom the happiness and freedom of mankind is a goal they never lose sight of. His manners are those of a gentleman and a man of the world, but they are tempered by a delicate moral sense which pervades his whole personality and radiates charmingly from his speech and behaviour. He is devoted to his King and the present monarchy, even though he does not approve of everything that is going on. He is also oppressed by his fears of Joseph II. The thought of a despot, even as a phantom possibility, is horrible to noble minds. He told me quite frankly what Naples might expect from this man. He likes to talk about Montesquieu, Beccaria and his own writings – all in the same spirit of good will and of a sincere youthful desire to do good. He must still be in his thirties.

Soon after we met, he introduced me to the work of an older writer, whose profound wisdom is so refreshing and edifying to all Italians of this generation who are friends of justice. His name is Giambattista Vico, and they rank him above Montesquieu. From a cursory reading of the book, which was presented to me as if it were sacred writ, it seems to me to contain sibylline visions of the Good and the Just which will or should come true in the future, prophecies based on a profound study of life and tradition. It is wonderful for a people to have such a spiritual patriarch: one day *Hamann* will be a similar bible for the Germans.

6 March

Reluctantly, but out of loyal comradeship, Tischbein accompanied me today on my ascent of Vesuvius. To a cultured artist like him, who occupies himself only with the most beautiful human and animal forms and even humanizes the formless – rocks and landscapes – with feeling and taste, such a formidable, shapeless heap as Vesuvius, which again and again destroys itself and declares war on any sense of beauty, must appear loathsome.

We took two cabriolets, since we didn't trust ourselves to find our own way through the turmoil of the city. The driver shouted incessantly, 'Make way! Make way!' as a warning to donkeys, burdened with wood or refuse, carriages going in the opposite direction, people walking bent down under their loads or just strolling, children and aged persons, to move aside so that he could keep up a sharp trot.

The outer suburbs and gardens already gave sign that we had entered the realm of Pluto. Since it had not rained for a long time, the leaves of the evergreens were coated with a thick layer of ash-grey dust; roofs, fascias and every flat surface were equally grey; only the beautiful blue sky and the powerful sun overhead gave witness that we were still among the living.

At the foot of the steep slope we were met by two guides, one elderly, one youngish, but both competent men. The first took me in charge, the second Tischbein, and they hauled us up the mountain. I say 'hauled', because each guide wears a stout leather thong around his waist; the traveller grabs on to this and is hauled up, at the same time guiding his own feet with the help of a stick.

In this manner we reached the flat base from which the cone rises. Facing us in the north was the debris of the Somma. One glance westward over the landscape was like a refreshing bath, and the physical pains and fatigue of our climb were forgotten. We then walked round the cone, which was still smoking and ejecting stones and ashes. So long as there was space enough to remain at a safe distance, it was a grand, uplifting spectacle. After a tremendous, thundering roar which came out of the depth of the cauldron, thousands of stones, large and small, and enveloped in clouds of dust, were hurled into the air. Most of them fell back into the abyss, but the others made an extraordinary noise as they hit the outer wall of the cone. First came the heavier ones, struck with a dull thud and hopped down the slope, then the lighter rattled down after them and, last, a rain of ash descended. This all took place at regular intervals, which we could calculate exactly by counting slowly.

However, the space between the cone and the Somma gradually narrowed till we were surrounded by fallen stones which made walking uncomfortable. Tischbein grew more depressed than ever when he saw that the monster, not content with being ugly, was now threatening to become dangerous as well.

But there is something about an imminent danger which challenges Man's spirit of contradiction to defy it, so I thought to myself that it might be possible to climb the cone, reach the mouth of the crater and return, all in the interval between two eruptions. While we rested safely under the shelter of a projecting rock and refreshed ourselves with the provisions we had brought with us, I consulted our guides. The younger one felt confident that we could risk it; we lined our hats with linen and silk handkerchiefs, I grabbed his belt, and, sticks in hand, we set off.

The smaller stones were still clattering, the ashes still falling about us as the vigorous youth hauled me up the glowing screes. There we stood on the lip of the enormous mouth; a light breeze blew the smoke away from us but also veiled the interior of the crater; steam rose all around us from thousands of fissures; now and then we could glimpse the cracked rock walls. The sight was neither instructive nor pleasing, but this was only because we could not see anything, so we delayed in the hope of seeing more. We had forgotten to keep our slow count and were standing on a sharp edge of the monstrous abyss when, all of a sudden, thunder shook the mountain and a terrific charge flew past us. We ducked instinctively, as if that would save us when the shower of stones began. The smaller stones had already finished clattering down when, having forgotten that another interval had begun and happy to have survived, we reached the foot of the cone under a rain of ashes which thickly coated our hats and shoulders.

After an affectionate scolding from Tischbein and some refreshment, I was able to make a careful examination of both the older and the fresher lavas. The older guide could pick them out and give the exact year of each. The more ancient were already covered with ash and quite smooth; the more recent, especially those which had flowed more sluggishly, looked very peculiar.

When lava flows sluggishly, the surface cools into solid masses. From time to time some obstruction brings these to a standstill. The masses behind are borne forward on the molten stream beneath and forced over the stationary ones. This process is repeated again and again until finally the whole flow petrifies in jagged shapes. Something similar happens with ice floes on a river, but it looks odder in lava. Among the formless melted products there were some large chunks which, on fracture, showed a resemblance to a type of more primitive rock. The guides maintained that they were old lavas from the lowest depths of the volcano which it expels from time to time.

On our way back to Naples I noticed some one-storey little houses constructed in a curious way without windows; the only light the rooms receive comes through the door opening on to the street. From early morning until late into the night, the occupants sit outside until it is time to retire into their caves.

This city, which, even in the evening, is in an uproar too, though one of a somewhat different kind, makes me wish I could stay here longer to make such sketches as I can of its animated scenes. But nothing so nice, I fear, is likely to happen.

7 March

This week Tischbein has conscientiously taken me to see most of the art treasures in Naples and explained them to me. As a connoisseur and excellent painter of animals, he had already aroused my interest in the bronze head of a horse in the Palazzo Colubrano, and today we went to see it. This amazing fragment stands in a niche above the courtyard fountain, directly facing the front gates. What an effect it must have produced when it was seen in relation to the limbs and body as a whole.

The horse, as it was originally, must have been much larger than the horses on the Basilica of San Marco, and, even from the head alone, when examined closely and in detail, one gets an overwhelming impression of character and power. The magnificent frontal bone, the snorting nostrils, the pricked ears, the bristling mane! What a passionate, powerful creture!

When we turned round, we noticed a female statue standing in a niche over the gates. Winckelmann held that it represents a dancer, for he believed that it was the lively and ever-changing motions of such performers which the sculptors immortalized for us in the frozen marble forms of nymphs and goddesses. This one is very graceful and lovely; at some time or other her head must have come off, but it has been skilfully replaced; the rest is perfectly intact, and she really deserves a better place.

Today I received your dear letters of 16 February. Please go on writing. I have given precise orders about my mail while I am away and shall go on doing so if I should travel further. At such a distance, it seems strange to me to read that my friends do not come together more often, but of course, when people live so near each other, it is quite natural if they seldom meet.

The weather has become gloomier – a sign of change. Spring is near and we are going to have rain. The summit of Vesuvius has not been visible since I was up there. During the last few nights we sometimes saw flames, but now everything is quiet again. A more violent eruption is expected.

The storms of the last days have presented us with the picture of a magnificent sea and allowed me to study the motions and the forms of the waves. Nature is, indeed, the only book whose every page is filled with important content.

The theatre, on the other hand, no longer gives me any pleasure. Here, during Lent, they perform sacred operas. The only difference between them and profane operas is that they have no ballets between the acts; otherwise, they are as gay as possible. At the Teatro San Carlo they are giving *The Destruction of Jerusalem by Nebuchadnezzar*. To me the theatre is merely a peepshow on a larger scale. I seem to have lost my taste for such things.

Today we paid a visit to the Prince of Waldeck in the Palazzo Capodimonte, which houses a large collection of paintings, coins, etc., not too well displayed, but including some precious things. What I saw clarified and confirmed many traditional concepts for me.

In our northern countries we know such things, coins, carved gems, vases, even lemon treees, only from single specimens; seen here, where they belong, and in profusion, they look quite different. For where works of art are rare, rarity itself is a value; it is only where they are common, as they are here, that one can learn their intrinsic worth.

Large sums are currently being paid for Etruscan vases and,

to be sure, you can find some beautiful and exceptional pieces among them. Every foreigner wants to possess one. You grow less cautious with your money here than you would be at home. I am afraid that I myself will be tempted.

One agreeable aspect of travel is that even ordinary incidents, because they are novel and unexpected, have a touch of adventure about them. After returning from Capodimonte, I made still another visit in the evening to the Filangieri's. There, on the sofa with the lady of the house, sat a young person whose outward appearance did not seem to me to be quite in keeping with her free-and-easy behaviour. Dressed in a light little frock of striped silk, with her hair arranged in a capricious fashion, the pretty little creature looked like one of those modistes who spend so much time dressing other women that they can't be bothered to pay attention to their own appearance. Since they are accustomed to getting paid for their work, they cannot see why they should look after themselves for nothing. My entrance did not disturb her in the least, and on she chattered, telling a number of droll little stories about things which had happened to her during the last few days, or rather, things which her harum-scarum behaviour had caused to happen.

The lady of the house tried to help me to get a word in edge-wise by talking about Capodimonte and its magnificent situation and art treasures, but all in vain. The lively little lady jumped up – when standing, she looked even prettier – took her leave, ran to the door and, as she passed me, said : 'The Filangieri are coming to dine with me one of these days. I hope to see you too.' And off she went before I could open my mouth to accept. I was then told that she was the Princess –,* and closely related to the family. The Filangieri are not rich and live in modest but decent style. I fancied that the little Princess must be in the same position, especially since I know that such high-sounding titles are not rare in Naples. I wrote down her name, the day and the hour, to be certain of turning up at the right place and the right time.

* Filangieri's sister, Teresa, Princess Ravaschieri di Satriano.

Since my stay in Naples is not going to be a long one, I visit the
more distant points of interest first; those nearby offer themselves of their own accord. As Tischbein and I drove to Pompeii,
we saw on every hand many views which we knew well from
drawings, but now they were all fitted together into one splendid
landscape.

Pompeii surprises everyone by its compactness and its small-
ness of scale. The streets are narrow, though straight and provided with pavements, the houses small and windowless – their
only light comes from their entrances and open arcades – and
even the public buildings, the bench tomb at the town gate, the
temple and a villa nearby look more like architectural models
or dolls' houses than real buildings. But their rooms, passages
and arcades are gaily painted. The walls have plain surfaces with
richly detailed frescoes painted on them, most of which have now
deteriorated. These frescoes are surrounded by amusing arabesques in admirable taste :   from one, enchanting figures of children and nymphs evolve, in another, wild and tame animals
emerge out of luxuriant floral wreaths. Though the city, first
buried under a rain of ashes and stones and then looted by the
excavators, is now completely destroyed, it still bears witness to
an artistic instinct and a love of art shared by a whole people,
which even the most ardent art lover today can neither feel nor
understand and desire.

Considering the distance between Pompeii and Vesuvius, the
volcanic debris which buried the city cannot have been driven
here, either by the explosive force of the eruption or by a strong
wind : my own conjecture is that the stones and ashes must have
remained suspended in the air for some time, like clouds, before
they descended upon the unfortunate city.

To picture more clearly what must have happened historically
one should think of a mountain village buried in snow. The
spaces between the buildings, and even the buildings themselves,
crushed under the weight of the fallen material, were buried and
invisible, with perhaps a wall sticking up here and there; sooner

or later, people took this mound over and planted vineyards and gardens on it. It was probably peasants digging on their allotments who made the first important treasure hauls.

The mummified city left us with a curious, rather disagreeable impression, but our spirits began to recover as we sat in the pergola of a modest inn looking out over the sea, and ate a frugal meal. The blue sky and the glittering sea enchanted us, and we left hoping that, on some future day, when this little arbour was covered with vine leaves, we would meet there again and enjoy ourselves.

As we approached Naples, the little houses struck me as being perfect copies of the houses in Pompeii. We asked permission to enter one and found it very clean and neatly furnished – nicely woven cane chairs and a chest which had been gilded all over and painted with brightly coloured flowers and then varnished. Despite the lapse of so many centuries and such countless changes, this region still imposes on its inhabitants the same habits, tastes, amusements and style of living.

12 *March*

Today I rambled through the city in my usual fashion, noting many points which I hope to describe more fully later, for now, unfortunately, I have not the time.

Everything one sees and hears gives evidence that this is a happy country which amply satisfies all the basic needs and breeds a people who are happy by nature, people who can wait without concern for tomorrow to bring them what they had today and for that reason lead a happy-go-lucky existence, content with momentary satisfaction and moderate pleasures, and taking pain and sorrow as they come with cheerful resignation. Here is an amazing illustration of this.

The morning was cold and damp, for it had been raining a little. I came to a square where the large paving stones seemed to me to have been swept unusually clean, and was surprised to see a number of ragamuffins squatting in a circle with their hands pressed to the flat stones as if they were warming them. At first I thought they were playing a game, but the serious

expression on their faces suggested some more practical purpose
for their behaviour. I racked my brains trying to guess what
they were up to, but found no satisfactory explanation, so I had
to ask someone why these little monkeys formed this circle and
took up such a peculiar posture.

I was told that a blacksmith in the neighbourhood had been
putting a tyre on a cartwheel. This is done as follows: the iron
band is laid on the ground, shavings are piled on it in a circle
and set alight to make the iron sufficiently malleable. When the
shavings have burnt themselves out, the tyre is fitted on to the
wheel, and the ashes are carefully swept up. The little street arabs
take advantage of the fact that the paving stones are still hot
and stay there till they have absorbed the last bit of warmth
from them.

I could give you countless other examples of this capacity to
get the most out of the least and make careful use of what would
otherwise be wasted. This people displays the most ingenious
resource, not in getting rich, but in living free from care.

Evening

In order to get to the whimsical little Princess on time, and not
to miss the right house, I hired a servant, who conducted me to
the gates of a large palazzo. Since I did not credit her with living
in such a magnificent residence, I spelled out her name once
more, letter by letter, but he assured me that this was the right
place. I entered a spacious empty courtyard, enclosed by the
main building and several annexes – all in the gay Neapolitan
style of architecture – and faced an enormous portal and a wide
though not very long staircase, on either side of which servants
in splendid livery were lined up, who bowed deeply as I passed.
I felt like the sultan in Wieland's Fairy Tale and, following his
example, took my courage in both hands. At the head of the
staircase, I was received by the upper servants, and, in due course,
the grandest of them opened a door and I was confronted by a
magnificent but perfectly empty salon. As I paced up and down
I caught a glimpse of a side gallery where a table was laid for
about forty persons on the same scale of splendour as everything

else. A secular priest entered : without asking who I was or where I came from, he took my presence for granted and made polite conversation.

Double doors were thrown open to admit an elderly man, and immediately closed behind him. The priest advanced to meet him, so I did the same. We greeted him with a few polite words to which he replied with some barking and stammering noises. For all that I could make of them, he might have been speaking Hottentot. When he had taken up a position by the fireplace, the priest stepped back and I followed his example. Now an impos-ing Benedictine entered, accompanied by a younger brother. He, too, greeted our host and, after being barked at, withdrew and joined us by the window. The members of religious orders, especi-ally the more elegantly dressed ones, are at great advantage in society; their habit, though it indicates humility and renunci-ation, at the same time lends them a decided dignity. They can appear submissive without abasing themselves, and when they draw themselves up to their full height, they are invested with a certain self-complacency which would be intolerable in any other profession but becomes them rather well. The Benedictine was this kind of man. I asked him about Monte Cassino; he invited me to come there and promised me the warmest reception. In the meantime, officers, courtiers, secular priests, even some Capuchins had arrived, and the salon was full of people.

I looked in vain for a lady. At last, the double doors opened and closed again and a lady entered who looked even older than the master of the house. The presence of the lady of the house – for that is what I took her to be – convinced me that I was in the wrong palazzo and a total stranger to its owners.

Dinner was now announced and I stuck close to the ecclesi-astics, hoping to sneak in with them into the paradise of the dining room. At this moment Filangieri and his wife entered hurriedly, apologizing for being late; and a moment later the little Princess came running into the salon, curtsying, bowing, and nodding to all the guests as she passed, and made straight for me. 'How nice of you to keep your promise !' she cried. 'Sit next to me at table, and you shall have all the titbits. But wait a moment ! First I have to find my place. Then you must immediately take the chair next to me.' Thus bidden, I followed her various gyrations and at last we reached our places. The Benedictines were seated opposite me and Filangieri on my right. 'The food is excellent,' said the Princess, 'everything Lenten fare but choice. I will tell you which dishes are the best. But first I must take our precious clerical friends down a peg. I can't abide them. They're all knaves. Every time they come to the house they make off with some food. What we have, we should eat with our friends.'

The soup had been served, and the Benedictine was eating it with decorum. 'Don't be shy, your Reverence!' she cried gaily. 'Is your spoon too small? Let me send for a bigger one! You gentlemen must be used to large mouthfuls.' The Father replied that, in this princely home, everything was so well ordered that even guests who were accustomed to far greater comforts than he would be perfectly satisfied.

When little tarts were offered, he took only one. Why, she cried, didn't he take half a dozen? Surely he must know that puff-paste is easy on the bowels. The sensible man took another one and thanked her for her kind attentions, as if he hadn't heard her indelicate joke.

A more substantial piece of pastry gave her a further opportunity for venting her malice. 'Take a third one, Father! You seem determined to lay a good foundation.' 'When such excellent materials are provided,' replied the priest, 'the builder has an easy time.' And so she went on and on, only pausing now and then to help me select the most delicious morsels. Meanwhile I talked with my neighbour on serious topics. As a matter of fact, I have never heard Filangieri say anything commonplace. In this respect, as in so many others, he resembles my friend Georg Schlosser,* except that, being a Neapolitan and a man of the world, he has a softer nature and is more approachable.

Throughout the meal, the mischievous lady on my left did not leave the clergy in peace for a moment. During Lent the fish is served in forms which make it look like meat, and this gave her inexhaustible opportunities for making irreverent and un-

---

* J. G. Schlosser, advocate and Goethe's brother-in-law.

seemly comments. She made great play with the expressions 'a liking for flesh' and 'a fleshly liking', saying that one ought at least to enjoy the form, even though the substance was forbidden. I heard her make more jokes of the same kind, but have not the courage to repeat them. Certain things may sound tolerable when spoken, especially on beautiful lips, but set down in black and white, they lose all charm for me. An impudent remark is peculiar in that it amuses at the moment because one is taken aback, but if repeated later, it sounds merely offensive.

Dessert was served, and I was afraid she would continue her banter, but, unexpectedly, she turned to me and said with good humour : 'The dear clergy shall swallow their Syracusan wine in peace. I have never yet succeeded in teasing one of them to death or even in spoiling his appetite. But now, let's talk sense. What were you and Filangieri talking about so seriously? That good man worries too much. As I keep telling him : if you make new laws, we shall have all the bother of devising ways and means to break them; we already know what to do about the old ones. Just think what a nice city Naples is, and how long people have lived here carefree and contented. From time to time, of course, someone gets hanged, but life goes on swimmingly for the rest.'

She then suggested that I go and stay on her large estate in Sorrento; her agent would serve me the finest fish and delicious *mungana*, the meat of suckling calves. The mountain air and heavenly view would soon cure me of all philosophy; later, she would come herself and then all my wrinkles – at my age I had no business to have any – would vanish without trace, and we would lead a very jolly life together.

13 March

Today I shall write a few more words and let one letter chase after another. I am well, but I see less than I should. This place encourages languor and an easygoing life. In spite of this, I am rounding out my picture of the city bit by bit.

On Sunday we went to Pompeii again. There have been many disasters in this world, but few which have given so much delight to posterity, and I have seldom seen anything so interesting. The

city gate and the avenue of tombs are unusual. There is one
tomb of a priestess, shaped like a semicircular bench and with an
inscription carved in large letters on its stone back. As I looked
over it, I saw the sun setting into the sea.

We met a company of lively Neapolitans, who were as natural
and lighthearted as could be, and we all ate at the Torre dell'An-
nunziata. Our table was set close to the shore with a delightful
view of Castellammare and Sorrento, which seemed very near.
One of the Neapolitans declared that, without a view of the sea,
life would not be worth living. Personally, it is enough for me
that I now carry this picture in my memory and I shall quite
happily return to the mountains, when the time comes.

We are lucky to have a very accurate landscape painter here,
who captures the atmosphere of these rich and open surroundings in his drawings. He has already done some work for me.

I have now carefully studied my Vesuvian specimens; things
look quite different when seen in relation to each other. If, as
perhaps I should, I were to devote the rest of my life to observation, I might discover some things which would enlarge human
knowledge.

Please tell Herder that my botanical insights are taking me
further and further. My basic hypothesis remains the same, but
to work everything out would take a lifetime. One day, perhaps,
I shall be capable of giving a general outline.

I am now looking forward to seeing the Portici museum. For
most people it is the place they visit first; for us it will be the
last. I still don't know where I am going next; they all want me
to be back in Rome for Easter. I shall wait and see.

Angelica is engaged in painting a scene from my *Iphigenie*.
Her idea is a very happy one and she will carry it out admirably.
She has chosen the turning point in the play, the moment
when Orestes comes out of his swoon and finds himself in the
presence of his sister and his friend. She has transformed the lines
which the three characters speak one after another into simultaneous gestures. This shows both her delicate sensibility and
her capacity to translate life into terms of her own medium.

Farewell and keep on loving me! Everyone here treats me
kindly, even though they do not know what to make of me. They

find Tischbein more congenial. This evening, immediately after supper, he painted some life-size heads, and they reacted like Maoris at the sight of their first man-of-war. Tischbein has a great gift for sketching in pen and ink the figures of gods and heroes, large as life or larger. He dashes them off with a few strokes and then puts in the shadows with a broad brush, so that the head stands out in relief. The company were amazed at the ease with which he did this and expressed their enthusiastic delight. Then their fingers began itching to try it themselves. They picked up the brushes and started daubing beards on each other's faces.

This happened in a cultured circle and in the house of a man who is himself a sound painter and draughtsman. Is not such behaviour an expression of some primitive trait in the human race?

Caserta, 14 March

Saw Hackert at his apartment in the old castle where he lives very comfortably and has room enough to entertain his guests. The new castle is a palace worthy of a king, a huge quadrilateral building like the Escorial with a number of inner courtyards. Its location is extraordinarily beautiful – upon one of the most fertile plains in the world with a park extending to the feet of the mountains. From the latter an aqueduct carries a whole river to supply the castle and surrounding countryside with water. This can be released to hurl itself over some artificially arranged rocks in a stupendous cascade. The gardens are beautifully laid out and in perfect harmony with a region that is itself a garden.

The castle, though truly regal, seemed to lack life, and people like myself cannot feel at ease in its immense empty rooms. The King probably feels the same, for he has been provided with a lodge in the mountains, the scale of which is less out of proportion to a human being and better suited to hunting and other pleasures of this life.

Though Hackert is always busy drawing and painting, he remains sociable and has a gift for attracting people and making them become his pupils. He has completely won me over as well, since he is patient with my weaknesses and stresses to me the supreme importance of accuracy in drawing and of a confident and clearheaded approach. When he paints, he always has three shades of colour ready. Using them one after the other, he starts with the background and paints the foreground last, so that a picture appears, one doesn't know from where. If only it were as easy to do as it looks! With his usual frankness he said to me: 'You have talent but you don't know how to use it. Stay with me for eighteen months and then you will produce something which will give pleasure to yourself and others.' Is this not a text on which one should never stop preaching to all dilettantes? What fruit it is going to bear in me remains to be seen.

The fact that he is not only giving drawing lessons to the Princesses but is also called upon in the evening to give lectures on art and other related subjects is evidence of the special trust with which the Queen honours him. For his talks he uses Sulzer's dictionary as a textbook, selecting some passage or other which he likes or believes in.

I could not but approve, but, at the same time, I could not help smiling at myself. What a difference there is between a person who wishes to build his life from within and one who wishes to influence the world and instruct others for domestic uses. I have always hated Sulzer's theory because its basic principles are false, but I realize now that his book contains much which people need to know. The many pieces of information which it offers and the way of thinking which satisfied the worthy Sulzer make it good enough, surely, for society people.

We spent many interesting hours with Andres, the restorer of old paintings, who has been summoned from Rome and is also living in the old castle. The King takes a great interest in his work. I shall not try to describe his unique craftsmanship because I would have to begin by enlarging upon the difficulty of the task and the immense labour required to arrive at a successful solution.

16 March

Your welcome letter of 19 February reached me today and shall be answered at once. I am always happy to be brought to my senses again by thinking of my friends.

Naples is a paradise; everyone lives in a state of intoxicated self-forgetfulness, myself included. I seem to be a completely different person whom I hardly recognize. Yesterday I thought to myself: Either you were mad before, or you are mad now.

From here I went to see the remains of the ancient town of Capua and its environs. Only in these regions can one understand what vegetation really is and what led man to invent the art of cultivation. The flax is already in bloom and the wheat a span and a half high. The country round Caserta is completely flat and the fields are worked on till they are as smooth and tidy as garden beds. All of them are planted with poplars on which vines are trained, yet in spite of the shadow they cast, the soil beneath them produces the most perfect crops. How will they look later, when spring is come in all its power? Till now, though we have had lovely sunshine, the wind has been cold and there is snow on the mountains.

During the next two weeks I must make up my mind whether to go to Sicily or not. I have never before been so torn by conflicting feelings as I am now when I contemplate this decision. One day something happens which makes me in favour of the trip, the next some circumstance turns me against it. Two spirits are fighting over me.

And now, for my friends of the gentler sex, in strict confidence – don't breathe a word to the men! I am quite aware that my *Iphigenie* has met with a strange reception. Everyone was used to the original version and, through hearing and reading it so often, knew some passages almost by heart. Now it all seems different, and I realize well enough that, at bottom, nobody appreciates

the endless pains I have taken over the play. A work of this kind
is never really finished; one only calls it finished because one has
done all that is possible in the time and the circumstances.

But this is not going to discourage me from trying to perform
a similar operation on *Tasso*. Sometimes I feel like throwing it
into the fire, but I shall stick to my resolution, and I intend, if
things go as they should, to make it an unusual work. So I am
rather glad that the printing of my writings is proceeding so
slowly. On the other hand, it is always good for me to feel the
distant threat of the compositor. Strangely enough, even the
things I undertake purely for love benefit from some kind of
external pressure.

In Rome I was glad to study: here I want only to live, forgetting myself and the world, and it is a strange experience for me to
be in a society where everyone does nothing but enjoy himself.
Sir William Hamilton, who is still living here as English ambassador, has now, after many years of devotion to the arts and the
study of nature, found the acme of these delights in the person
of an English girl of twenty with a beautiful face and a perfect
figure. He has had a Greek costume made for her which becomes
her extremely. Dressed in this, she lets down her hair and, with a
few shawls, gives so much variety to her poses, gestures, expressions, etc., that the spectator can hardly believe his eyes. He sees
what thousands of artists would have liked to express realized
before him in movements and surprising transformations –
standing, kneeling, sitting, reclining, serious, sad, playful,
ecstatic, contrite, alluring, threatening, anxious, one pose follows another without a break. She knows how to arrange the
folds of her veil to match each mood, and has a hundred ways of
turning it into a head-dress. The old knight idolizes her and is
enthusiastic about everything she does. In her, he has found
all the antiquities, all the profiles of Sicilian coins, even the
Apollo Belvedere. This much is certain: as a performance it's
like nothing you ever saw before in your life. We have already
enjoyed it on two evenings. This morning Tischbein is painting
her portrait.

Everything I have been told (or learned for myself by putting
two and two together) about the personages and conditions at

the Court must now be sorted out and checked. Today the King has gone wolf-hunting; they expect to kill at least five.

Every time I wish to write words, visual images come up, images of the fruitful countryside, the open sea, the islands veiled in a haze, the smoking mountain, etc., and I lack the mental organ which could describe them.

Here the soil produces everything, and one can expect from three to five harvests a year. In a really good year, I am told, they can grow maize three times in the same fields.

I have seen much and thought even more. The world is opening itself to me more and more, and all that I have long known intellectually is now becoming part of me. What an early-to-know, late-to-practise creature man is !

It is only a pity that, at the moment, I have nobody with whom I can share my thoughts. Tischbein is with me, to be sure, but, both as a man and an artist, his mind is the shuttlecock of a thousand ideas, and hundreds of people have a claim on his time. His is a curious case : a man who cannot take an unforced interest in the existence of anyone else because he feels so frustrated in his own efforts.

Certainly the world is only a simple wheel and every point on its circumference is equidistant from its centre. It only looks so strange to us because we ourselves are revolving with it.

What I have always said has been confirmed : there are certain natural phenomena and certain confused ideas which can be understood and straightened out only in this country.

As for my voyage to Sicily – the gods still hold the scales in their hands. The little needle still oscillates back and forth.

Who can the friend be whose coming has been so mysteriously announced to me? I hope I shan't miss him because of my erratic excursions and my proposed trip to the island.

The frigate has returned from Palermo. In a week from today she will sail back. I still don't know whether I shall sail with her or return to Rome in time for Holy Week. Never in my life have I felt so undecided. A single moment, a trifle, may turn the scales.

I am beginning to get along better with other people. The important thing to remember is always to weigh them by the shop-keeper's scales and never by the goldsmith's, as friends, in hypochondriac or exacting moods, are only too apt to do with each other, alas.

Here people know nothing whatever about each other. Each runs hither and thither and hardly notices his neighbours. All day long they race back and forth in their paradise, without looking about them much, and when the mouth of hell nearby begins to roar, they have recourse to the blood of St Januarius. Well, in the rest of the world, too, in their fight with death and devil, people resort to blood, or would if they could.

To thread one's way through an immense and ever-moving crowd is a peculiar and salutary experience. All merge into one great stream, yet each manages to find his way to his own goal. In the midst of so many people and all their commotion, I feel peaceful and alone for the first time. The louder the uproar of the streets, the quieter I become.

I sometimes think of Rousseau and his hypochondriac outpourings of misery. I can quite understand how a mind as delicately organized as his could become deranged. If I didn't take such an interest in the things of nature, or see that there are ways of sorting out and comparing hundreds of observations despite their apparent confusion – as a surveyor checks many separate measurements with a single straight line – I should often think I was mad myself.

We could not put off any longer going to see Herculaneum and the Portici museum of objects excavated there. Herculaneum lay at the foot of Vesuvius and was completely buried under lava, to which subsequent eruptions added fresh layers, so that the ancient city is now sixty feet below ground level. It was discovered when, in the course of digging a well, some workmen came upon floors of paved marble. It is a thousand pities that the site was not excavated methodically by German miners, instead of being casually ransacked as if by brigands, for many noble works of antiquity must have been thereby lost or ruined.

We descended a flight of sixty steps to a vault, where we admired by torchlight the former open-air theatre, while the guard told us about the things which were found there and brought to the light of day.

We had good letters of recommendation to the museum and were well received, but we were not allowed to make any drawings. Perhaps this made us pay attention all the more closely to what we saw, so that we were all the more vividly transported into the past, when all these objects were part and parcel of their owners' daily life. They quite changed my picture of Pompeii. In my mind's eye its homes now looked both more cramped and more spacious – more cramped because I now saw them crowded with objects, and more spacious because these objects were not made merely for use but were decorated with such art and grace that they enlarged and refreshed the mind in a way that the physical space of even the largest room cannot do.

There was one beautiful jar, for example, with an exquisitely wrought rim which, on closer inspection, turned out to be two hinged semicircular handles, by which the vessel could be lifted and carried with ease. The lamps are decorated with as many masks and scrolls of foliage as they have wicks, so that each flame illuminates a different work of art. There were high, slender bronze pedestals, evidently intended as lamp stands. The lamps which were suspended from the ceiling were hung with all sorts of cunningly wrought figures which surprise and delight the eye as they swing and dangle.

We followed the custodians from room to room, trying to enjoy and learn as much as possible in the little time we had. We hope to come back.

19 *March*

In the last few days I have entered into a new and intimate relationship. For four weeks Tischbein has been a loyal and useful partner in all my excursions into the realm of nature and art. When we were at Portici yesterday we had a talk and both of us came to the conclusion that his artistic career, his duties at court and in the city, which may lead to a permanent post in Naples, were incompatible with my plans and particular interests. Helpful as ever, he suggested as a possible companion a young man whom I have seen a lot of ever since we arrived, and not without interest and sympathy.

His name is Kniep. He lived for some time in Rome, then came to Naples, the ideal place for a landscape painter. In Rome I had already often heard that his draughtsmanship was admirable, though the same could not be said for his willingness to work. Now that I have got to know him pretty well, I think that this fault for which he is blamed is really a lack of self-confidence which can certainly be overcome if we spend some time together. In confirmation of this, he has made a good start already, and, if things go as I wish, we are going to be good travelling companions for quite some time.

19 *March*

One has only to walk the streets and keep one's eyes open to see the most inimitable pictures.

Yesterday, at the Molo, which is the noisiest corner of the city, I came across a wooden stage on which a Pulcinella was having a quarrel with a monkey. On a balcony overhead a pretty girl exposed her charms to all. Beside the stage with the monkey stood a quack offering his nostrums against all ailments to a credulous crowd. Painted by Gerard Dow, such a scene would delight our contemporaries and posterity.

Today is the Feast of St Joseph, the patron saint of all *frittaruoli*, or pastry cooks, using the word 'pastry' in its crudest sense. Since, under the black, boiling oil they use for frying, there is a constant flare of flame, all fiery torments are assigned to their mystery. Last night they decorated their house fronts with appropriate paintings: Souls in Purgatory and Last Judgements were blazing on all sides. In front of their doors large frying pans stood on hastily erected stoves. One apprentice kneaded the dough, while a second shaped it into crullers and threw them into the boiling oil. A third stood beside the pan with a small skewer, picked out the crullers when they were cooked and put them on another skewer, held by a fourth apprentice, who then offered them to the bystanders. The third and fourth apprentices were young boys wearing blond, elaborately curled wigs, which are regarded as the attribute of angels. To complete the group, there were some persons who handed wine to the cooks, drank themselves and cried their wares. Angels, cooks, everybody shouted at the top of their voices. They drew a great crowd because, on this night, all pastry goods are sold at greatly reduced prices and even a portion of the profits is given to the poor.

One could go on for ever describing similar scenes, each crazier than the last, not to mention the infinite variety of costumes or the hordes of people you can see on the Toledo alone.

You can find many other original entertainments if you live among these people, who are so natural that one might even become natural oneself. As an example, take Pulcinella, the mask native to this country, as Harlequin is to Bergamo or Hanswurst to the Tirol. Pulcinella is the imperturbable servant, somewhat careless, almost lazy, but humorous. You can find waiters or house servants of this type everywhere. I got enormous fun today out of ours, though it was over nothing more than sending him to buy me paper and pens. Partial misunderstanding, procrastination, good will and a touch of roguery combined created a charming scene which would be successful on any stage.

The news that another emission of lava had just occurred, invisible to Naples since it was flowing towards Ottaiano, tempted me to make a third visit to Vesuvius. On reaching the foot of the mountain, I had hardly jumped down from my two-wheeled, one-horse vehicle before the two guides who had accompanied us the last time appeared on the scene and I hired them both.

When we reached the cone, the elder one stayed with our coats and provisions while the younger followed me. We bravely made our way towards the enormous cloud of steam which was issuing from a point halfway below the mouth of the cone. Having reached it, we descended carefully along its edge. The sky was clear and at last, through the turbulent clouds of steam, we saw the lava stream.

It was only about ten feet wide, but the manner in which it flowed down the very gentle slope was most surprising. The lava on both sides of the stream cools as it moves, forming a channel. The lava on its bottom also cools, so that this channel is constantly being raised. The stream keeps steadily throwing off to right and left the scoria floating on its surface. Gradually, two levels of considerable height are formed, between which the fiery stream continues to flow quietly like a mill brook. We walked along the foot of this embankment while the scoria kept steadily rolling down its sides. Occasionally there were gaps through which we could see the glowing mass from below. Further down, we were also able to observe it from above.

Because of the bright sunshine, the glow of the lava was dulled. Only a little smoke rose into the pure air. I felt a great desire to get near the place where the lava was issuing from the mountain. My guide assured me that this was safe, because the moment it comes forth, a flow forms a vaulted roof of cooled lava over itself, which he had often stood on. To have this experience, we again climbed up the mountain in order to approach the spot from the rear. Luckily, a gust of wind had cleared the air, though not entirely, for all around us puffs of hot vapour were emerging from thousands of fissures. By now we were actually standing on the lava crust, which lay twisted in coils like a soft mush, but it projected so far out that we could not see the lava gushing forth.

We tried to go half a dozen steps further, but the ground under our feet became hotter and hotter and a whirl of dense fumes darkened the sun and almost suffocated us. The guide who was walking in front turned back, grabbed me, and we stole away from the hellish cauldron.

After refreshing our eyes with the view and our throats with wine, we wandered about observing other features of this peak of hell which towers up in the middle of paradise. I inspected some more volcanic flues and saw that they were lined up to the rim with pendent, tapering formations of some stalactitic matter. Thanks to the irregular shape of the flues, some of these deposits were in easy reach, and with the help of our sticks and some hooked appliances we managed to break off some pieces. At the lava dealer's I had already seen similar ones, listed as true lavas, so I felt happy at having made a discovery. They were a volcanic soot, precipitated from the hot vapours; the condensed minerals they contained were clearly visible.

A magnificent sunset and evening lent their delight to the return journey. However, I could feel how confusing such a tremendous contrast must be. The Terrible beside the Beautiful, the Beautiful beside the Terrible, cancel one another out and produce a feeling of indifference. The Neapolitan would certainly be a different creature if he did not feel himself wedged between God and the Devil.

22 March

If my German temperament and my determination to study and practise rather than amuse myself did not drive me on, perhaps I might tarry a little longer in this school for easy, happy living and try to profit more from it. It is possible to live very comfortably in this city on only a small income. The situation and the climate are beyond praise; but they are all the resources the foreigner has. Of course, someone with leisure, money and talent could settle down here and live most handsomely. This is what Sir William Hamilton has done in the evening of his days. The rooms in his villa, which he has furnished in the English taste, are charming and the view from the corner room may well be unique. The sea below, Capri opposite, Mount Posillipo to the right, near by the promenade of the Villa Reale, to the left an old building of the Jesuits, in the distance the coast line from Sorrento to Cape Minerva – probably nothing comparable could be found in the whole of Europe and certainly not in the middle of a great city.

But now the Sirens from beyond the sea are luring me away from this delight and a hundred others, and, if the wind is favourable, I shall be leaving at the same time as this letter – it will go north as I go south.

Man is headstrong in spirit, and at this moment I am in particular need of unconfined spaces. It is not perseverance I have to learn so much as quickness of perception. Once I can get hold of a matter by its fingertip, listening and thinking will enable me to grasp the whole hand.

Strangely enough, a friend recently spoke of *Wilhelm Meister* and begged me to go on with it. Under these skies, I doubt if it would be possible, but perhaps in the last books I shall manage to capture something of this heavenly air. I pray that my existence may develop further, the stem grow taller, the flowers blossom forth in greater abundance and beauty. If I cannot come back reborn, it would be much better not to come back at all.

Today I saw a painting by Correggio which is up for sale. Though not in perfect condition, it still retains an indelible charm. It depicts a Madonna and Child at the moment when the latter is hesitating between her breast and some pears offered Him by a cherub – in other words, The Weaning of Christ. It immediately reminded me of the Betrothal of St Catherine, and is also, I am convinced, from the hand of Correggio.

23 *March*

My relationship with Kniep has been put to a practical test and
promises to give great satisfaction to us both. We made an
excursion to Paestum together, and he proved himself a most
hard-working draughtsman. The fruits of our journey are some
superb sketches, and he is very happy because he finds that this
exacting busy life stimulates his talent, which he had come to
doubt. Drawing calls for resolution and it is just in this that his
precise and tidy proficiency becomes evident. He never forgets
to draw a square round the paper on which he is going
to make a drawing, and sharpening and resharpening his excellent English pencils gives him almost as much pleasure as
drawing. In consequence, his outlines leave nothing to be
desired.

We have made the following bargain: from now on we shall
live and travel together and all he will be expected to do is draw.
All his drawings will become my property, but, in order that they
may serve as a basis for further activity on our return, he is
going to execute a number of subjects, selected by me, which I
shall buy till I have spent a certain sum, after which, thanks to
his skill and the importance of the views he has drawn, he will be
able to sell the rest. I am very happy about this arrangement.

Now let me give a brief account of our excursion. Our carriage
was a light two-wheeled affair, and our groom a rustic but good-
natured boy. He stood behind us as, taking the reins in turn, we
rolled through an enchanting countryside which Kniep greeted
with a painter's eye. Soon we came to a mountain defile through
which we sped on the smoothest of roads past picturesque
groups of trees and rocks. Near La Cava we halted because Kniep
could not resist making a drawing of a splendid mountain which
stood out sharply against the sky. His neat and characteristic
sketch took in the whole mountain from its summit to its base.
The pleasure it gave us both seemed a good beginning to our
friendship.

That same evening he made another drawing from the window
of our inn in Salerno, which will make any description of this

lovely region superfluous. Who would not have felt inclined to study in this place when the university was in its heyday?

Very early next morning, we drove by rough and often muddy roads towards some beautifully shaped mountains. We crossed brooks and flooded places where we looked into the blood-red savage eyes of buffaloes. They looked like hippopotamuses.

The country grew more and more flat and desolate, the houses rarer, the cultivation sparser. In the distance appeared some huge quadrilateral masses, and when we finally reached them, we were at first uncertain whether we were driving through rocks or ruins. Then we recognized what they were, the remains of temples, monuments to a once glorious city. Kniep quickly chose a favourable spot from which to draw this very unpicturesque landscape, while I found a countryman to conduct me round the temples. At first sight they excited nothing but stupefaction. I found myself in a world which was completely strange to me. In their evolution from austerity to charm, the centuries have simultaneously shaped and even created a different man. Our eyes and, through them, our whole sensibility have become so conditioned to a more slender style of architecture that these crowded masses of stumpy conical columns appear offensive and even terrifying. But I pulled myself together, remembered the history of art, thought of the age with which this architecture was in harmony, called up images in my mind of the austere style of sculpture – and in less than an hour I found myself reconciled to them and even thanking my guardian angel for having allowed me to see these well-preserved remains with my own eyes. Reproductions give a false impression; architectural designs make them look more elegant and drawings in perspective more ponderous than they really are. It is only by walking through them and round them that one can attune one's life to theirs and experience the emotional effect which the architect intended. I spent the whole day doing this, while Kniep was busy making sketches. I felt happy to know that I had nothing to worry about on that score, but could be certain of obtaining faithful records to assist my memory. Unfortunately, there was no place nearby where we could stay the night, so we returned to Salerno and drove back to Naples early the next morning. This time we saw Vesuvius from its other side. The country was fertile and the main road was lined with poplars, as colossal as pyramids. We made a brief halt to make this pleasing picture our own. Then we came to the top of a ridge and a grand panorama unfolded before us: Naples in all its glory, rows of houses for miles along the flat coast line of the Gulf, promontories, head-lands, cliffs, then the islands and, beyond them, the sea. A breath-taking sight!

A horrible noise, more a screaming and howling for joy than a song, startled me out of my wits. It came from the boy who was standing behind me. I turned on him furiously. He was a good-natured lad, and this was the first time he had heard a harsh word from either of us.

For a while he neither moved nor spoke; then he tapped me on the shoulder, thrust his right arm between Kniep and myself, pointed with his forefinger and said: *'Signor, perdonate! Questa è la mia patria!'* which means: 'Sir, forgive me. This is my native land!' And so I was startled for the second time. Poor northerner that I am – something like tears came into my eyes.

25 March. Lady Day

Although I felt Kniep was very glad to be accompanying me to Sicily, I could not help noticing that there was something he hated to leave. Thanks to his sincerity, it did not take me long to discover that this something was a sweetheart to whom he is deeply attached. His story of how they became acquainted was touching. The girl's conduct so far spoke highly in her favour: now he wanted me to see how pretty she was. A meeting place was arranged where I could, incidentally, enjoy one of the most beautiful views over Naples. He led me on to the flat roof of a house, directly overlooking the lower part of the city and facing towards the harbour mole, the Gulf and the coast of Sorrento. Everything that lies to the right takes on a peculiar perspective which cannot easily be seen from any other point.

While we were admiring this view, all of a sudden the pretty little head we had been expecting popped up out of the floor, for the only access to this kind of terrace is through a square opening which can be closed by a trap door. When the little angel had emerged completely, it suddenly occurred to me that some old masters depict the Angel of the Annunciation as coming up a staircase. Our angel had a lovely figure, a charming little face and natural good manners. I was glad to see my new friend so happy under this wonderful sky and in view of the loveliest landscape in the world.

After the girl left us, he confessed to me that the reason why he had so far endured voluntary poverty was because it had enabled him to enjoy her love and learn to prize her simple and modest way of life. Now, however, he welcomed the prospect of improving his circumstances, mainly because this would enable him to make her life more comfortable as well as his own.

After this agreeable encounter, I took a walk along the seashore. I was feeling calm and happy. Suddenly I had a flash of insight concerning my botanical ideas. Please tell Herder I am very near discovering the secret of the Primal Plant. I am only afraid that no one will recognize in it the rest of the plant world. My famous theory about the cotyledons has now been so elaborated that it would be difficult to take it any further.

26 March

I shall send this letter off tomorrow. On Thursday the twenty-ninth I am due to sail for Palermo at last on the corvette which, in my ignorance of things nautical, I promoted in an earlier letter to the rank of a frigate.

During my stay here, my state of indecision – should I go or not? – made me restless and irritable at times; now I have made up my mind, I feel much better. Given my temperament, this trip is salutary and even necessary. To me Sicily implies Asia and Africa, and it will mean more than a little to me to stand at that miraculous centre upon which so many radii of world history converge.

In Naples I have lived like a Neapolitan. I have been anything but studious, and when I get back I must make up for a few of my omissions – but only a few, I'm afraid, since I have to be in Rome by 29 June. Having missed Holy Week, I want at least to celebrate the Feast of St Peter. I must not let my Sicilian trip make me deviate too far from my original plan.

The day before yesterday there was a violent thunderstorm and torrents of rain; now it is clear again and a tramontana is blowing from the north. If it keeps up, we shall have a very swift passage.

Yesterday Kniep and I visited the corvette to take a look at our cabin. A sea voyage is something I still have to experience. This short crossing and perhaps a cruise along the coast will stimulate my imagination and enlarge my vision of the world. The captain is a likeable young man; the ship, built in America, is neat, elegant and sails well.

Here everything is beginning to turn green; in Sicily it will be even greener. By the time you get this letter, I shall already have left Trinacria* behind me and be on my return voyage. There's man for you! For ever jumping backwards and forwards in his thoughts. I have not yet been there but already I am with you again. It is not my fault if this letter is confused. I am interrupted all the time, but I should at least like to finish this page.

I have just had a visit from the Marchese Berio, a young man who appears well informed. He wished to make the acquaintance of the author of *Werther*. By and large, the Neapolitans have a great desire for culture and a thirst for knowledge, but they are too happy-go-lucky to set about it in the right way. If I had more time, I would gladly give them more. Four weeks – what are they to set against the immensity of life?

And now, farewell! On this journey I shall certainly learn how to travel; whether I shall learn how to live, I don't know. The people I meet who possess this art are so different from me in their nature and habits that I doubt whether I have the talent.

Farewell, and think of me with the same love that I cherish for you in my heart.

28 *March*

What with packing, saying goodbye, shopping, paying bills,

---

*Trinacria, the Three-Pointed, i.e., Sicily.

catching up with this and preparing that, these last days have been completely wasted.

My peace of mind has been disturbed at the last minute by the Prince of Waldeck. When I went to say good-bye to him, he would talk of nothing else but the arrangements I was to make after my return to accompany him to Greece and Dalmatia. Once one has stepped into the great world and accepted its ways, one has to be careful not to get trapped or even spirited away. I am too exhausted to write another word.

                                                  29 March

For some days the weather has been uncertain, but on this day of our departure, it is as beautiful as could be. A favourable tramontana, a sunny sky, just the day for wishing to go round the world. Once more, I sincerely bid farewell to all my friends in Weimar and Gotha. May your love accompany me; I shall certainly always need it. Last night I dreamed I was at home and again at my usual occupations. I know this much: I could never unload my boat of pheasants anywhere but on your shores. Let us hope that by then it will be laden with precious cargo.

SICILY

ON her last voyage the packet set sail with a favourable north-east wind behind her. Not so this time. The wind had veered to the south-west and we were forced to learn how dependent the navigator is upon the moods of the weather. We spent an impatient morning between the shore and the café. At noon we went on board at last. The corvette was anchored not far from the Molo. Bright sunshine and a slight haze made the shadows of the cliffs of Sorrento look intensely blue; Naples was full of life and a blaze of colour. It was sundown before the boat began to move and very slowly at that. The head wind drove us towards Posillipo and its promontory. Throughout the night the ship made its quiet progress. The cabins below deck are pleasant and furnished with single berths. Our fellow passengers, opera singers and dancers with engagements in Palermo, are gay and well behaved.

Daybreak found us between Ischia and Capri and about a mile from the latter, as the sun rose magnificently behind the crags of Capri and Cape Minerva. Kniep kept himself busy drawing the shifting outlines of the coast and islands as we sailed along, and the slowness of our progress was to his advantage. The wind remained slack. By about four in the afternoon we lost sight of Vesuvius, but Cape Minerva and Ischia were still visible. As evening drew near, they too disappeared. The sun sank into the sea accompanied by clouds and a streak of purple light a mile long. Kniep made a drawing of this phenomenon as well. Now there was no more land to be seen, the horizon was a circle of water and the night sky was lit up by the moon.

But I was not to enjoy this gorgeous sight for long before I was overcome by seasickness. I retired to my cabin, assumed a horizontal position, took nothing but some bread and red wine, and soon felt very snug. Isolated from the outside world, I let my thoughts run freely on the inner one, and, since I anticipated a slow passage, I set myself forthwith a serious task which would keep me fully occupied. The only manuscripts I had taken with me on this voyage were the first two acts of *Tasso*. These, though roughly similar in plot and action to the ones I have now done, were written ten years ago in a poetic prose. I found them too weak and nebulous, but these defects vanished when, in accordance with my present ideas, I introduced a metre and let the form dominate.

31 March

The sun rose out of the sea into a clear sky. At seven we caught up with a French boat which sailed two days before we did. Although we had sailed much faster, the end of our voyage was still not in sight. The appearance of the island of Ustica gave us some encouragement, but, alas, it lay on our left when we should have left it, like Capri, on our right. By now the wind was completely adverse and we could not move an inch. The waves were running high and almost everybody on board was sick.

I remained in my horizontal position, revolving and reviving my play in my mind. The hours passed by and I would not have known what time of day it was if Kniep had not periodically brought me bread and wine. The rough sea had not affected his appetite in the least, and he took a malicious glee in telling me what an excellent dinner they had had, and how sorry our nice young captain was that I couldn't be with them to eat my share. The various ways in which the passengers behaved, as good cheer and pleasure gave way to discomfort and sickness, also provided him with rich material for mischievous description.

At four in the afternoon the captain changed course. The mainsails were hoisted again and we steered in a straight line towards Ustica, beyond which, to our great delight, we could see the mountains of Sicily. We now had the wind with us and the speed of the ship increased as we headed for Sicily. We passed several other islands. The setting sun was veiled in an evening haze. The wind remained fairly propitious. About midnight the sea began to get very rough.

1 April

By three in the morning, it was blowing a gale. Half awake, half asleep, I kept thinking about my drama. On deck there was a great commotion as the sails were taken in. The sea was high and the boat tossed and rolled. Towards dawn the sky cleared and the storm subsided. Ustica was now definitely on our left. The sailors pointed out a large turtle swimming in the distance, and through our telescopes we could follow its living dot quite clearly. By noon we could make out the promontories and bays of the Sicilian coast, but the ship had fallen considerably to leeward. Now and then we tacked. In the afternoon we came closer to the shore, where the west coast, from Cape Lilibeo to Cape Gallo, lay in bright sunshine. A school of dolphins accompanied our ship on both sides of the prow, always darting ahead. It was delightful to watch them swimming through the transparent waves and often leaping clean out of the water, so that their fins and the spines along their backs made an iridescent play of green and gold.

Since we were still too far to leeward, the captain set a straight course for a bay beyond Cape Gallo. Kniep did not lose this good opportunity to make detailed sketches of the various vistas. At sunset the captain again turned out to sea and headed north-eastward in order to reach the latitude of Palermo. Once in a while I ventured on deck but kept my poetic project always in mind – by now I had almost mastered the whole play.

The sky was slightly overcast, but the moon was bright and its reflection in the sea incredibly beautiful. For the sake of the effect, many painters would have us believe that the reflection of the celestial lights in the water is at its widest where it is strongest, that is to say, at the point nearest the observer. But now I saw for myself that the reflection was widest on the horizon and tapered, as it approached the ship, till it ended, like a glittering pyramid, in a point. During the night the captain repeated his manoeuvre several times.

2 April

By eight in the morning we stood directly opposite Palermo. I was in high spirits. During these last days in the belly of the whale, I have made considerable progress in planning my play. I felt so well that I was able to stand on the foredeck and devote my attention to the coast of Sicily. Kniep kept sketching all the time. Thanks to his skill and accuracy, several sheets of paper have become valuable records of our belated arrival.

Palermo, 2 April

After a great deal of trouble and effort, we finally reached port at three in the afternoon. I had completely recovered and was able to enjoy everything thoroughly. The city faces north with high mountains rising behind it. The rays of the afternoon sun were shining across it, so that all the buildings facing us were in shadow but lit by reflected light. The delicate contours of Monte Pellegrino to the right were in full sunshine, and a shore with bays, headlands and promontories stretched far away to the left.

In front of the dark buildings, graceful trees of a tender green, their tops illuminated from behind, swayed like vegetal glow-worms. A faint haze tinted all the shadows blue.

Instead of hurrying impatiently ashore, we remained on deck until we were driven off. It might be long before we could again enjoy such a treat for the eyes from such a vantage point.

We entered the city through a wonderful gate, consisting of two huge pillars but no crosspiece, so that the towering chariot of Santa Rosalia can pass through on her famous feast day, and were taken to a large inn. The landlord was a jovial old man who had long been accustomed to receiving strangers of all national-ities. He led us to a spacious room with a balcony overlooking the harbour and the mountain of Santa Rosalia. We were so delighted with the location of our room that at first we didn't notice a raised alcove, whose curtains concealed an enormous sprawling bed surmounted by a silk canopy. This was quite in keeping with the rest of the old-fashioned, stately furniture. A little embarrassed by such pomp and splendour, we were prepared, as is customary, to haggle about terms, but the old man said he would leave it to us to name them; he only hoped we would like it here. We might also, he added, use the *sala* adjoining our room, which, thanks to its wide balcony, was light, airy and cheerful

For an artist, there was an inexhaustible wealth of vistas to be seen, and we studied them one by one with an eye to painting them all.

The same evening the bright moonlight tempted us to take a walk down to the harbour and back. Before going to bed, we stood for a long time on our balcony. The light was unusual and all was stillness and charm.

3 April

We went out first thing to take a closer look at the city, which is easy to grasp in its overall plan, but difficult to get to know in detail. A street a mile long runs from the lower to the upper gate; this is bisected by another street, so that everything which lies along these axes is easy to find. But the inner part of the city is a confusing labyrinth, where a stranger can find his way about only with the help of a guide.

Towards evening we watched with great interest the famous carriage parade of the nobility, who at that hour drive out of the town towards the harbour in order to take the air, chat with each other and, above all, flirt with the ladies. Two hours before sunset, a full moon rose, bathing the evening in an inexpressible glory. Owing to the mountains behind Palermo to the south, sunlight and moonlight are never seen reflected in the water at these hours. Even on this brightest of days, the sea was dark blue, sombre and, so to speak, intrusive, whereas in Naples, from noon on, it always becomes increasingly serene, brilliant and, so to speak, extensive.

Kniep went off to make a drawing of Monte Pellegrino and left me to take walks and make observations by myself.

Here are a few more notes, hastily thrown together :

We left Naples at sundown on Thursday, 29 March, and did
not reach Palermo till three in the afternoon four days later. I
have never set out on a journey as calmly as I did on this one
and have never had a quieter time, though our voyage was much
prolonged by continuously adverse wind, and for the first days I
was violently seasick and confined to my cabin. If anything was
ever a decisive event for me, it is this trip.

No one who has never seen himself surrounded on all sides by
nothing but the sea can have a true conception of the world and
of his own relation to it. The simple, noble line of the marine
horizon has given me, as a landscape painter, quite new ideas.

My artist-companion is a merry, loyal and warmhearted young
man who makes very accurate drawings, which you will enjoy
when I bring them back with me. To shorten the long hours of
the voyage, he had written down a description of the technique
of water-colour painting, showing me how to use certain colours
to produce certain tones. If one were not told, one could mix
away for ever trying to discover the secret. I had already
heard something about it in Rome, but only scrappily. In no
country has this art been brought to such perfection as in Italy.

I cannot begin to describe the way in which this Queen of the
Islands has received us – with mulberry trees in their freshest
green, evergreen oleanders, hedges of lemon trees, etc. In a public garden I saw great beds of ranunculi and anemones. The air is
mild, warm and fragrant. Furthermore, the full moon rose over
a promontory and was reflected in the sea, and all this after being
tossed by the waves for four days and nights ! Forgive my scrib-
bling with a blunt pen dipped in the sepia which my friend uses
when he retraces his drawings. It will come to you like a whisper
while I am preparing another memorial to these happy hours.
I shan't tell you what it is, and I can't tell you when you will
receive it.

3 April

The enclosed sheet, dear friends, is meant to let you share a
little in our joys and give you some idea of the vast expanse of

water which this incomparable bay encloses. Starting in the east, where a low promontory extends far out into the sea, and moving west, the eye passes from wooded crags to the suburbs where the fishermen live, then to the city itself, where all the houses, which like ours line the waterfront, face the sea, then to the gate through which we entered, then to the landing-place for smaller boats, then to the port proper, the Molo and the anchorage for large ships. Beyond that rises graceful Monte Pellegrino, which shelters all vessels from the winds, and finally, stretching down to the sea on the other side of the mountain, a lovely, fertile valley. Kniep made a drawing and I made a rough sketch. We both had great fun doing this and came home in high spirits. We have not yet felt strong and brave enough to work over it and finish it properly, so our sketches must stay as they are for the time being. This sheet is merely a proof of our incapacity to cope with such subjects, or rather of our presumption in trying to master them in such a short time.

4 April

This afternoon we visited the pleasant valley in the mountains to the south of Palermo, along which meanders the river Oreto. To make a good picture of this valley calls for a skilful hand and an unerring eye for colour. Kniep succeeded in finding an excellent viewpoint for one. In the foreground water cascades over a dilapidated weir, which lies in the shadow of a cheerful-looking clump of trees; in the background an unobstructed vista of the valley with a few farm buildings.

The fair spring weather and the luxuriant vegetation lent an air of grace and peace to the whole valley, which our stupid guide proceeded to ruin with his erudition, for he started telling us in great detail how, long ago, Hannibal* had given battle here and what stupendous feats of valour had taken place on this very spot. I angrily rebuked him for such an odious evocation of defunct ghosts. It was bad enough, I said, that from time to time crops have to be trampled down, if not always by elephants, still

---

*It was not Hannibal but Hasdrubal who was defeated near Panormus by Caecilius Metellus in 251 B.C.

by horses and men, but at least one need not shock the imagination out of its peaceful dreams by recalling scenes of savage
violence from the past.

He was very astonished that I, on such a spot, should not want
to hear anything about classical times, and, of course, I could not
make him understand my objections to this mixing-up of the
past and the present.

He must have thought me still more of an eccentric when he
saw me searching for pebbles in the shoals which the river had
left high and dry, especially when I pocketed several specimens.
Again, I could not explain to him that the quickest way to get an
idea of any mountainous region is to examine the types of rock
fragments washed down by its streams, or that there was any
point in studying rubble to get the idea of these eternal classical
heights of the prehistoric earth.

My haul from the river turned out to be a rich one. I collected
nearly forty specimens, though I must admit they could possibly
all be classified under a few rubrics. The majority are probably
some kind of jasper or chert or schist. Some were round and
smooth, some shapeless rubble, some rhomboid in form and of
many colours. There was no lack, either, of pebbles of shell-
limestone.

Shell-limestone underlies the plain on which Palermo stands,
the region outside the city, called Ai Colli, and part of the Baghe-
ria. The city has been built of it, hence the large quarries in the
neighbourhood. Near Monte Pellegrino there is one quarry more
than fifty feet deep. The lower strata are whiter than the upper
and contain many fossil corals and shellfish, scallop shells in
particular. The uppermost stratum is mixed with red clay and
contains few fossils, if any. Above this there is only a very thin
layer of red clay.

The limestone of Monte Pellegrino itself is an older formation
and full of holes and fissures; these are irregularly distributed,
but, when examined carefully, they seem to follow the lines of
demarcation between the strata. The rock is compact and
resonant when struck with a hammer.

There are no meadows, so there is no hay. In spring the horses
are fed on barley fresh from the ear, '*per rinfrescar* – to refresh

them' as they say; at other seasons on chaff and bran. There is some pasture in the mountains and some in the fields, for a third of them lie fallow. There are some sheep of a breed introduced from Barbary, but very few, and more mules than horses, because the dry food agrees better with the former.

5 April

We explored the city thoroughly. The architecture is similar to that of Naples, but the public monuments – the fountains, for instance – are even further removed from the canons of good taste. There is no instinctive feeling for art here, as there is in Rome, to set a standard. The monuments owe their existence and their form to accidental circumstances. One fountain, much admired by all the islanders, would not exist had Sicily not happened to have deposits of beautiful marble of every colour at a time when a sculptor who was an expert in making animal figures happened to be in high favour. This fountain is hard to describe.

In a square of moderate size stands a circular stone construction a little less than one storey high, the socle, wall and cornice of which are coloured marble. Let into it all the way round are niches from which all sorts of animal heads, carved in white marble, look out, craning their necks – horses, lions, camels, elephants in succession. Within this circular menagerie, one is rather surprised to see a fountain. Four flights of marble steps lead up it from openings cut in the enclosing wall, allowing people to draw the copiously flowing water.

It is the same with the churches, which surpass even those of the Jesuits in splendour, but accidentally, not deliberately. It's as if an artisan, a carver of figures or foliage, a gilder, a varnisher or a worker in marble, without taste and without guidance, had wished to show what he could do in a given spot.

On the other hand, one finds plenty of talent for the realistic imitation of Nature; for example, the animal heads I mentioned are very well done. This, of course, is just what the masses admire, for the only artistic pleasure they know lies in finding that the copy is like the original.

Towards evening I made an amusing acquaintance when I entered a modest shop on the main street to buy various odds and ends. While I was standing outside looking at the goods, a gust of wind whirled down the street, stirring up a cloud of dust which blew into the shops and covered the windows. 'By all the saints,' I cried when I went in, 'why is your city so filthy? Can nothing be done about it? In its length and beauty this street would stand comparison with the Corso in Rome; it has pavements which every shopkeeper and owner of a workshop keeps clean by continually sweeping everything into the middle of the street. At the slightest breeze all the rubbish which has accumulated there is blown back again and everything is dirtier than it was before. In Naples the refuse is carried away daily to the gardens and fields on the backs of donkeys. Couldn't some similar measure be devised for your city?' 'That is the way things have always been,' he replied. 'What we throw out of our homes immediately starts to rot on our doorsteps. As you can see, there are piles of straw, weeds, kitchen garbage, and rubbish of every kind. It all dries and is blown back with the dust. We fight it all day and what happens? Our busy pretty little brooms wear out and go to increase the rubbish.'

The joke was that this was quite true. They have pretty little brooms, made from dwarf palms, which with hardly any alteration would make fine fans, but these are soon worn out, and when this happens, they are left lying in the streets in thousands. When I asked him once again if they could not adopt some other method, he answered: 'People say that the very persons who are responsible for keeping the city clean have too great political influence to be forced to spend the public funds as they are in duty bound; they are further afraid that, if all the muck were removed, the disgraceful condition of the paving would clearly reveal the embezzlement of the public money. But all this', he added with a waggish look, 'is what malicious people say. Personally, I share the view of those who maintain that the nobility keep the streets this way because they like a soft, elastic surface for their carriages over which they can take their usual evening drive in comfort.' Having got into his stride, he went on to poke fun at various examples of police corruption, giving me a reassur-

ing proof that man still retains enough sense of humour to mock
at what he cannot mend.

Santa Rosalia, the patron saint of Palermo, has become so universally famous through Brydone's description of her feast day
that my friends will certainly be pleased to read something about
the spot where she is especially venerated.

Monte Pellegrino is a huge mass of rock, broader than it is
high, which stands at the north-west end of the Gulf of Palermo.
There is an inaccurate picture of it in *Voyage pittoresque de la
Sicile*. It is composed of a grey limestone from an early epoch.
Its cliffs are completely barren without so much as a tree or a
shrub, and even its level patches are only scantily covered with
a little turf and moss.

At the beginning of the last century, the bones of the saint
were discovered in one of its caves and brought down to Palermo.
Her presence delivered the city from the plague and, from that
moment on, Rosalia became its patron saint, chapels were built
in her honour and magnificent ceremonies observed. Her devotees
made frequent pilgrimages up the mountain, and, at great cost,
a road was constructed, supported on piers and arches like an
aqueduct, which zigzags upward between two crags.

The shrine itself is more appropriate to the humility of the
saint who took refuge there than the pomp of the festival which
is celebrated in honour of her renunciation of the world. In all
Christendom, which for eighteen hundred years has founded its
wealth, its splendours, its solemn festivities upon the poverty
of its first founders and most fervent confessors, there may well
be no other sacred spot as naïvely decorated and touchingly
venerated as this.

On reaching the top of the mountain, one turns a corner and
faces a steep cliff to which the church and convent appear to be
joined. There is nothing particularly attractive or interesting
about the façade of the church, and one opens the door expecting
little, but, once inside, one gets an extraordinary surprise. One
finds oneself in a great hall which runs the whole breadth of the

church and opens into the nave. There are the usual holy-water
stoups and a few confession boxes. The nave is an open courtyard
bounded on its right by rugged rocks and on the left by a continuation of the hall. It is paved with stone slabs set at a slight
angle to drain off the rain water, and at its centre stands a small
fountain. The cave itself has been transformed into a chancel
without robbing it of its natural, rugged character.

After climbing a few steps which lead up to it, one is confronted by a high lectern with choir stalls on either side. The
only daylight comes from the courtyard and from the nave. In
the centre, right at the back of the dark cave, stands the high
altar.

As I said, the cavern has not been altered, but since there is a
constant trickle of water from the rocks, some means had to be
devised to keep the place dry. Leaden pipes, interconnected in
various ways, have been attached to the face of the rock. These
are wide at the top and narrow at the bottom and painted a drab
green, so that the interior of the cave seems to be overgrown with
some large species of cactus. The pipes catch the water as it drips
from the sides and back of the cave and conduct it into a clear
cistern from which the faithful scoop it to use it as a protection
against every kind of ill.

As I was looking at all this, a priest approached and asked me
if I were a Genoese and would like to have some masses said. I
told him that I was visiting Palermo with a Genoese who would
come up for the feast day tomorrow. Since one of us always has
to stay at home, I had come up today to look around. He said I
was quite free to look at everything I liked and make my devotions. He drew my attention to a side altar on the left which was
especially sacred and went away.

Through a large trellis of wrought brass I could see lamps
gleaming under the altar. I knelt down and peered through.
Inside there was another screen of very fine brass wire, so that the
object behind it appeared as if through gauze.

By the quiet light of the lamps I saw a beautiful woman who
seemed to be reclining in a kind of ecstacy; her eyes were half
closed and her head rested on her right hand, which was heavily
adorned with rings. Her garment of gilded tinfoil was a perfect

imitation of a cloth richly woven with gold thread. Her head and hands, made of white marble, were perhaps not in the best style, but had been carved so naturally that one expected her to start breathing and moving at any moment. At her side a cherub seemed to be fanning her with a lily. I could not take my eyes off this picture, which seemed to me to possess a quite extraordinary charm.

In the meantime, the priests had entered the cave, taken their seats in the stalls and were saying vespers. I sat down on a bench facing the altar and listened for a while, then I returned to the altar, knelt down and gazed once more at the beautiful image of the saint, surrendering myself completely to the magic of the figure and the place.

The chanting died away; the water trickled down into the cistern. The church had again become an empty desert, as it were, a savage cave, where a great silence, a great purity now reigned. The tinsel trappings of Catholic worship, especially in Sicily, were displayed here in all their artlessness. The illusion created by the figure of the fair sleeper appealed even to a discriminating eye. It was only with difficulty that I tore myself away, and I got back to Palermo very late at night.

7 April

I spent some happy, peaceful hours alone in the Public Gardens close to the harbour. It is the most wonderful spot on earth. Though laid out formally and not very old, it seems enchanted and transports one back into the antique world. Green borders surround exotic plants, espaliers of lemon trees form gracefully arched walks, high hedges of oleander, covered with thousands of red blossoms which resemble carnations, fascinate the eye. Strange trees, probably from warmer climes, for they are still without leaves, spread out their peculiar ramifications. At one end there is a bank with a bench on it from which one can overlook the garden and intricate vegetation; at the other are some large ponds in which goldfish swim about gracefully, now hiding under moss-grown pipes, now swarming together in great numbers, attracted by a piece of bread.

The green of the plants is of a different shade, either more yellow or more blue, than the green we are used to. What gives this scenery its greatest charm, however, is the haze uniformly diffused over everything, which has a peculiar effect. Even when one object is only a few steps further away than another, the difference in depth is clearly distinguished by a different tint of light blue. If one looks at them for long, their own colour is lost and they appear, at least to the eyes, to be blue all over.

The enchanting look which distant objects like ships and promontories take on in this haze is most instructive for a painter who has to learn to distinguish distances and even measure them exactly, as I discovered when I walked to the top of a hill. I no longer saw Nature, but pictures; it was as if some very skilful painter had applied glaze to secure a proper gradation of tone.

The enchanted garden, the inky waves on the nothern horizon, breaking on the curved beaches of the bays, and the peculiar tang of the sea air, all conjured up images of the island of the blessed Phaeacians.

I hurried off to buy myself a Homer so that I could read the canto in which he speaks of them. When I got back, I found Kniep enjoying a well-earned rest after a hard day's work, and I recited to him a hastily improvised translation as we sat over our glasses of good red wine.

8 April. Easter Sunday

The noisy rejoicing in the Resurrection of the Lord began at dawn : rockets, firecrackers, squibs and the like exploded in great numbers in front of the churches, while crowds of the faithful fought their way in through the open doors. Bells rang, organs pealed, processions sang in unison, priestly choirs chanted antiphonally – to ears unaccustomed to such a rowdy worship of God, the noise was quite deafening.

The first Mass had hardly ended before two runners, in the elegant livery of the Viceroy, arrived at our inn on a double errand : first, to bring greetings to all foreigners on this feast day and receive tips in return; second, to invite me to dinner, a message which obliged me to increase my donation.

After spending the morning visiting churches and studying the faces and behaviour of the people, I drove to the Viceroy's palace, which is situated at the upper end of the city. I arrived a little early, and the reception rooms were empty except for one cheerful little man whom I recognized at once as a Knight of Malta.

When he heard that I was a German, he asked if I could give him any news of Erfurt, where he had once spent a pleasant time. He mentioned the Dacheröden family and the Coadjutor von Dalberg, and I was able to give him news which pleased him very much. Then he inquired about the rest of Thuringia and, with special interest, about Weimar. 'Whatever happened to the man – in my day he was young and high-spirited – who at that time set the tone in Weimar? What *was* his name? You know – the author of *Werther*.' I paused for a moment, as if I was trying to remember, and then said: 'As a matter of fact, the person you ask about so kindly is myself.' He was visibly taken aback and exclaimed: 'Then how things must have changed!' 'Yes, indeed,' I replied, 'between Weimar and Palermo I have changed in many ways.'

At this moment the Viceroy entered with his suite. He behaved with the dignified ease which befits a gentleman of his rank, but he could not help smiling when the Knight of Malta went on and on expressing his amazement at seeing me here. At dinner I was seated next to the Viceroy, who discussed my journey with me and promised that he would send out orders that I be allowed to see everything in Palermo and given every assistance on my way across Sicily.

9 April

Our entire day has been taken up with the madness of the Prince of Pallagonia. His follies turned out to be quite different from anything I had imagined after hearing and reading about them.

When a person is expected to describe some absurdity, he is always at a loss, because however great his love for the truth, merely by describing it, he makes it something, whereas, in fact, it is nothing that wants to be taken for something. So let me preface my remarks with another general reflection : neither tasteless vulgarity nor assured excellence is the creation of one single man or one single epoch; on the contrary, with a little thought, one can trace the genealogy of both.

The fountain I mentioned earlier can be counted as one of the ancestors of the Pallagonian mania, the only difference being that the latter has its own territory where it has complete liberty to display itself on a grand scale. I shall now try to trace its history.

In these regions country houses are built in the middle of the estate, so that, to reach the house itself, one has to drive through cultivated fields, vegetable gardens and other agriculturally useful premises. But people are more economical here than they are in northern countries, where a large acreage of valuable soil is often sacrificed to the layout of a park so that the eye may be flattered by unprofitable shrubs. These southerners, on the contrary, erect two walls between which one reaches the big house without being aware of what is happening on either side. The drive usually begins with a huge gateway – sometimes there is a vaulted hall as well – and ends in the courtyard of the house.

To give the eye something to look at, a moulding runs along the top of the walls, decorated with scrolls and brackets on which vases are sometimes placed. The wall surfaces are divided into whitewashed panels. The circular courtyard of the big house is surrounded by one-storey dwellings where the servants and farm labourers live, and high above all this rises the rectangular block of the house itself.

This is the traditional layout, and probably existed long before the Prince's father built the house. His taste, if not the best, was still tolerable, but his son, the present owner, without departing from the general design, has given free rein to his passion for deformed and revolting shapes, and it would be paying him too great a compliment to credit him with the faintest spark of imagination.

On entering the great hall on the boundary of the estate, we found ourselves in an octagon, very high in proportion to its width. Four colossal giants in modern gaiters support the cornice over which, facing the gate, hovers the Holy Trinity. The drive to the house is unusually broad, and each wall has been transformed into an uninterrupted socle on which excellent pedestals sustain strange groups interspersed with vases. The repulsive appearance of these deformities, botched by inferior stonecutters, is reinforced by the crumbly shell-tufa of which they are made, but a better material would, no doubt, have made the worthlessness of the form still more conspicuous. I called them groups, but the word is inappropriate, for they are not the products of calculation or even of caprice; they are merely accidental jumbles.

Each square pedestal carries three groups, the bases of which are so arranged that, together, their various postures fill the whole space. The predominant group usually consists of two figures and its base takes up a great part of the front of the pedestal. These figures are mostly animal and human monsters. Two more pieces are needed to fill up the space at the rear. There is one of medium size which usually represents a shepherd or a shepherdess, a cavalier or a lady, a dancing monkey or a dog. The last gap is most often filled by a dwarf, since this unfortunate race is a great subject for boorish jokes.

The following list may give you a better idea of what Prince Pallagonia has perpetrated in his madness.

Human beings. Beggars of both sexes, men and women of Spain, Moors, Turks, hunchbacks, deformed persons of every kind, dwarfs, musicians, Pulcinellas, soldiers in antique uniforms, gods and goddesses, persons dressed in French fashions of long ago, soldiers with ammunition pouches and leggings, mythological figures with grotesque accessories; for instance: Achilles and Chiron with Pulcinella.

Animals. Only parts of them; a horse with human hands, the head of a horse on a human body, deformed monkeys, many dragons and snakes, every kind of paw attached to every kind of body, double heads and exchanged heads.

Vases. Every kind of monster and scroll, emerging from their bellies or their bases.

Now imagine similar figures multiplied *ad infinitum*, designed without rhyme or reason, combined without discrimination or point, pedestals and monstrosities in one unending row, and the painful feelings they must inspire, and you will sympathize with anyone who has to run the gauntlet of this lunacy.

When we reached the big house, we were received into the arms of a semicircular courtyard and faced a gateway and a wall constructed like a fortress. Here we found an Egyptian figure built into the wall, a fountain without water, a monument and, scattered about everywhere, overturned vases and statues deliberately laid on their noses.

The inner courtyard is the traditional circular shape, but, just so that there should be no lack of variety, the low buildings which surround it have been built in small semicircles. The paving was overgrown with grass, and the courtyard looked like a dilapidated graveyard. Oddly scrolled marble urns, inherited from the owner's father, and dwarfs and freaks of a later date, lay higgledy-piggledy, waiting to be found their right place. In addition there was an arbour, crammed with antique vases and stone scrolls of various shapes.

But the bad taste and folly of an eccentric mind reaches its climax in the cornices of the low buildings which slant this way and that, so that our sense of hydrostatic balance and the perpendicular, which is what primarily makes us human beings and is the fundamental principle of all eurhythmics, is upset and tortured. Even these roofs are also decorated with hydras and small busts, an orchestra of monkeys and similar absurdities; dragons alternate with gods, and an Atlas carries a wine cask instead of the celestial globe.

If one hopes to escape all this by entering the house, which, since his father built it, looks relatively sane from the outside, just inside the door one is confronted by the laurel-wreathed head of a Roman emperor on the body of a dwarf who sits on a dolphin.

In the house the fever of the Prince rises to a delirium. The legs of the chairs have been unequally sawn off, so that no one can sit on them, and we were warned by the castellan himself not to use the normal chairs, for they have spikes hidden under their velvet-cushioned seats. In corners stood candelabra of Chinese porcelain, which turned out, on closer inspection, to be made up of single bowls, cups and saucers, all glued together. Some whimsical object stares out at you from every corner.

Even the unrivalled view of the sea beyond the foothills is spoiled because the panes of coloured glass in the windows either make warm tones look cold or cold tones blazing. I must not forget a cabinet. Its panels are made from antique gilt frames which have been sawn in pieces and then put together again. The hundred different styles of carving, ancient and modern, crammed into these panels, from which the gilt was peeling when it wasn't smothered in dust, made it look like a mangled piece of junk.

A description of the chapel alone would fill a book. Here lies the clue to the whole madness. Only in the brain of a religious fanatic could it have grown to such rampant proportions. I must leave you to imagine how many caricatures of a perverted piety have been assembled here, and only mention the most conspicuous one.

A carved crucifix of considerable size, painted in realistic colours and varnished and gilded in places, is fixed flat to the ceiling. Into the navel of the Crucified a hook has been screwed from which hangs a chain. The end of this chain is made fast to the head of a man, kneeling in prayer and painted and varnished like everything else. He hangs suspended in the air as a symbol of the ceaseless devotions of the present owner.

The house is only partly built; a large hall, designed and elaborately decorated, though not at all in atrocious taste, remains unfinished. There are some limits, it seems, to what even the Prince can do to indulge his mania.

It was the first time I had seen Kniep lose patience. His feelings as an artist were outraged by this madhouse, and when I tried to study the details of these misbegotten horrors, he hustled me away. But, good-natured fellow that he is, he finally drew one of the groups, the only one that at least made some sort of picture. A woman with a horse's head is seated in a chair playing cards with her vis-à-vis, a cavalier in old-fashioned clothes. He has a griffin's head, dressed in a full-bottomed wig with a crown perched on top of it. Which reminds me: the coat-of-arms of the House of Pallagonia is a satyr holding up a mirror to a woman with a horse's head. Even after having seen the other absurdities, this seems to me the most peculiar of all.

10 April

Today we drove up the hill to Monreale on an excellent road built by an abbot of the monastery at the time of its enormous wealth. The road was broad, its gradient easy, with trees here and there and, more conspicuously, both high-spouting and running fountains, decorated with scroll ornaments of an almost Pallagonian eccentricity, but refreshing, nevertheless, to beasts and men.

The monastery of San Martino is a venerable institution. One confirmed old bachelor by himself has rarely produced anything sensible – witness the case of Prince Pallagonia – but a celibate group can create the greatest of works, as many churches and cloisters testify. But the real reason why religious communities have achieved so much is probably that, unlike the other kind of family father, they can count upon an unlimited number of descendants.

The monks showed us their museum. They own many beautiful things, both objects of antiquity and products of Nature. We were especially taken by a coin bearing the figure of a young goddess. The good fathers would have gladly given us a replica but they hadn't anything handy which might have served as a mould.

After showing us everything, not without some melancholy comparisons between the past and the present day, they took us to a pleasant little room with a lovely view from its balcony. Here a table had been laid for the two of us, and nothing was lacking to make an excellent meal. After the dessert had been served, the abbot came in, accompanied by his oldest monks, sat down with us and stayed for almost half an hour, during which time we had to answer many questions. They bade us a very cordial farewell; the younger monks took us back to the museum and then walked us to our carriage.

We returned home in a very different frame of mind from that of yesterday. It seemed deplorable that such a great institution should be in decline at the very time when an enterprise as vulgar as the one we had seen the day before should be vigorously flourishing.

The road to San Martino climbs limestone hills of an early formation. The stone is quarried, crushed and burned to a very white lime. For fuel they use a long, strong kind of grass which is dried in bundles. In this way they obtain what they call *calcara*. The topsoil right up the the steepest heights is a red alluvial clay. The greater the height, the redder it becomes, as it is less darkened by vegetation. In the distance I saw a quarry with walls almost the colour of cinnabar.

The hills among which the monastery stands are well cultivated and rich in springs.

11 April

Having seen the two principal places of interest outside the city, we now visited the Palazzo Reale, where the Viceroy's obliging runner showed us around. To our dismay, the hall where the antiques usually stand was in a state of the greatest disorder, because the walls were being redecorated.

The statues had been moved, covered with sheets, and hidden from view by scaffolding, so that, despite the good will of our guide and occasional help from the workmen, we couldn't see them properly. I was mainly interested in two bronze rams, which, even in these unpropitious circumstances, delighted me. They are represented in a reclining position with one hoof stretched out and their two heads turned in opposite directions, so that they complement each other. Their fleeces are not short and curly but flow in long waves. Two powerful figures from the mythological family, worthy of carrying Phrixus and Helle; a

work of great veracity from the best Greek period. They are said
to have stood in the port of Syracuse.

The runner then took us to see the catacombs outside the city.
These must have been designed by someone with a feeling for
architecture; they do not look in the least like quarries which
happen to have been used as a burial place. The sides are perpendicular and made of a compact tufa. Vaulted openings were
dug into them, and in these the stone coffins were placed, one
on top of the other. Those above are smaller than those below,
and in the space over the pilasters there are niches for the coffins
of children. Everything is of tufa without any masonry to support it.

12 *April*

Today we were shown Prince Torremuzza's collection of coins.
I went there almost reluctantly. I understand too little about
this field, and a merely inquisitive tourist is the bane of the true
connoisseur. But after all, one has to begin somewhere, so I
relented and derived great pleasure and some profit from our
visit.

The ancient world was dotted with cities and even the smallest
of them has left us, in its precious coins, a record, if not of the
whole course of art history, at least of some epochs of it. An
eternal spring of art's immortal fruits and flowers smiled up at
us out of these drawers, telling of a craftsmanship perfected and
practised over a lifetime, and of much else besides.

Alas, we others possessed in our youth nothing but family
medals which say nothing and coins bearing the portraits of
emperors in which the same profile is repeated *ad nauseam*, of
overlords who cannot be regarded as paragons of humanity. It
makes me sad to think that in my youth my historical knowledge was limited to Palestine, which had no images at all, and
Rome, which had far too many. Sicily and Magna Graecia have
given me hope of a new life.

The fact that I indulge in general reflections on these objects
is proof that I still know precious little about them; but I hope
I shall gradually improve in this, as in everything else.

This evening another of my wishes was fulfilled and in a surprising fashion. I was standing in the main street, joking with my old shopkeeper friend, when I was suddenly accosted by a tall, well-dressed runner who thrust a silver salver at me, on which lay several copper coins and a few pieces of silver. Since I had no idea what he wanted, I shrugged my shoulders and ducked my head, the usual gesture for showing that one has not understood or does not wish to. He left as quickly as he had come, and then I saw another runner on the opposite side of the street, occupied in the same fashion.

I asked the shopkeeper what all this was about, and he pointed with a meaningful, almost furtive glance to a tall, thin gentlemen, dressed in the height of fashion, who was walking down the middle of the street through all the dung and dirt with an air of imperturbable dignity. In a freshly curled and powdered wig, carrying his hat under his arm and wearing a silk coat, a sword and neat shoes with jewelled buckles, the elderly gentleman walked solemnly on, ignoring all the eyes that were turned in his direction.

'That is Prince Pallagonia,' said the shopkeeper. 'From time to time he walks through the city collecting ransom money for the slaves who have been captured by Barbary pirates. The collection never amounts to much, but people are reminded of their plight, and those who never contribute during their lifetime often leave a considerable legacy to this cause. The Prince has been president of this charity for many years now, and has done a great deal of good.'

'If,' I said, 'instead of spending vast sums on follies for his villa, he had used them for this cause, no prince in the world would have accomplished more.' My shopkeeper disagreed: 'Aren't we all like that? We pay gladly for our follies but we expect others to pay for our virtues.'

13 April

Anyone with an interest in mineralogy who goes to Sicily must feel highly indebted to Count Borch, who was the first to make a thorough study of its minerals. To honour the memory of a predecessor is at once a pleasure and a duty. After all, what am I, both in my life and my travels, but a precursor of those who shall come after me?

The Count's industry seems to me to have been superior to his learning; his approach is somewhat self-complacent, lacking in the modesty and seriousness with which important issues should be treated. On the other hand, his quarto volume devoted to the minerals of Sicily is extremely useful, and with its help I prepared myself for a visit to the stone polishers. Though they are not as busy as they used to be, when churches and altars had to be faced with marble and agate, they still carry on their craft. I ordered specimens of soft stones and hard stones – these are their terms for marble and agate, the only difference in their eyes being a difference in price. They are also showing great skill in handling another material which is a by-product from their lime kilns. Among the calcined lime they find lumps of a sort of glass paste, varying in colour from a very light to a very dark or almost black blue. These, like other minerals, are cut into thin sheets and priced according to their purity and brilliance of colour. They can be used as successful substitutes for lapis lazuli in the veneering of altars, tombs and other church ornaments.

I have ordered a complete collection, but it is not yet ready and will have to be sent to Naples. The agates are of a rare beauty, especially those in which irregular specks of yellow or red jasper alternated with a white and, as it were, frozen quartz. An exact imitation of these, produced by coating the back side of thin glass panes with lacquer dyes, was the only sensible thing I saw in the Pallagonian madhouse. They have a more decorative effect than windows made with true agate, because, instead of having to piece together many small stones, the architect can make the panes any size he likes. This artistic trick deserves to be more widely used.

13 *April*

To have seen Italy without having seen Sicily is not to have seen Italy at all, for Sicily is the clue to everything.

We are now in the rainy season – today we had a thunderstorm – but this is continually interrupted by fine days, and how powerfully everything waxes green ! Some of the flax has already formed nodules, some is still in flower, and the blue-green fields of flax at the bottom of the valleys look like little ponds. My companion is a true 'Hopewell' * to whom I shall continue to play the 'True Friend'. He has already made many sketches and will continue to do so. The thought of one day coming home with all my treasures fills me with joy.

So far I have said nothing about the food – an important subject, after all. The vegetables are delicious, especially the lettuce, which is very tender and tastes like milk; one can understand why the Ancients called it *lactuca*. The oil and the wine are also good, but would be even better if prepared with greater care. The fish – excellent and of a most delicate flavour. We have always had good beef, too, though most people here do not recommend it.

But let's leave the table now and go to the window to look down into the street. As always happens at this season, a criminal has been reprieved in honour of Holy Week, and is being accompanied by a religious brotherhood to a mock gallows. There he says his prayers, kisses the ladder and is led away again. He is a good-looking, well-kempt man of the middle class, dressed completely in white, white tail coat, white hat. He carries his hat in his hand. Pin some coloured ribbons on him here and there, and he could attend any fancy-dress ball as a shepherd.

13 and 14 April

I must now set down the details of a singular adventure which befell me just before I left Palermo.

During my stay I have often heard people at our public eating place discussing Cagliostro, where he came from and what has happened to him. The people of Palermo are all agreed on one point : that a certain Giuseppe Balsamo was born in their city, became notorious for his many hoaxes and was exiled. But opinions are divided as to whether this man and Count Cagliostro are one and the same person. Some who once knew Balsamo

---

* *Hopewell (Hoffegut)*. Like *Truefriend*, a character in *The Birds*.

insist that they can recognize his features in the well-known engraving which has also reached Palermo. During these discussions one guest mentioned the efforts which a Palermo lawyer has made to clear up the whole question. He has been commissioned by the French authorities to investigate the early history of the man who, in the course of an important and dangerous trial,* had the insolence to insult the intelligence of France and, indeed, the whole world with the most ridiculous cock-and-bull stories.

This lawyer, someone told me, has drawn up Giuseppe Balsamo's family tree, and sent it, along with an explanatory memoir and certified appendices, to France, where it will probably be published.

Everybody spoke highly of this lawyer, and when I expressed a wish to make his acquaintance, my informant offered to take me to his house and introduce me.

A few days later we went there together and found him in consultation with some clients. When he had finished with them, he produced a manuscript containing Cagliostro's family tree, the necessary confirmatory documents and the draft of his memoir.

He gave me this family tree to look at while he explained it. I shall quote enough of what he said to make it intelligible.

Giuseppe Balsamo's great-grandfather on his mother's side was Matteo Martello. The maiden name of his great-grandmother is unknown. There were two daughters of this marriage: Maria, who married Giuseppe Bracconeri and became the grandmother of Giuseppe Balsamo; and Vincenza, who married Giuseppe Cagliostro, a native of La Noara, a village eight miles from Messina. (Incidentally, two bell-founders named Cagliostro are still living in Messina.) This Vincenza Cagliostro subsequently stood godmother to her grand-nephew, who received at baptism the Christian name of her husband, Giuseppe. When, later, this Giuseppe Balsamo went to live abroad, he also adopted his great-uncle's surname, Cagliostro. Giuseppe and Maria Bracconeri had three children: Felicitas, Matteo and Antonino.

Felicitas married Pietro, the son of Antonino Balsamo, a Pal-

---

* The famous 'Diamond Necklace Affair', 1783–4.

ermo haberdasher who seems to have been of Jewish extraction. Pietro Balsamo, the father of the notorious Giuseppe, went bankrupt and died at the age of forty-five. His widow, who is still alive, bore him one other child, a daughter, Giovanna Giuseppe-Maria. This daughter married Giovanni Batista Capitummino, who died, leaving her with three children.

The memoir which the author obligingly read to me and, at my request, lent me for a few days is based on baptism certificates, marriage contracts and other legal instruments which he has collected with great care.* It describes the good use Giuseppe made of his gift for imitating any hand. He forged, or rather manufactured, an old document, on the strength of which the ownership of certain estates was contested in court. He fell under suspicion, was examined and imprisoned, but succeeded in escaping and was cited edictally. He travelled through Calabria to Rome, where he married Lorenza, the daughter of a brassworker. From Rome he went to Naples under the name of Marchese Pellegrini. He took the risk of returning to Palermo, was recognized and imprisoned, but managed to get himself set free. The story of how this happened deserves telling.

A prominent Sicilian prince, a great landowner who held several high offices at the court of Naples, had a son who combined a violent temper and powerful physique with all the arrogance to which, when they lack culture, the rich and the great imagine themselves to be entitled.

Donna Lorenza Cagliostro, alias Pellegrini, succeeded in ingratiating herself with the son, and the bogus Marchese pinned his hopes on this. The young Prince made no secret of being the protector of the newly arrived couple. But the party who had

---

*Added by Goethe some years later. It contained, as I see from an extract I made at the time, more or less the same particulars as those given in the minutes of the Roman trial, namely, that Giuseppe Balsamo was born in Palermo at the beginning of June 1743, that, in his youth, he took the habit of the Brothers of Mercy, an order dedicated to the care of the sick, that he showed early promise of an unusual intelligence and talent for medicine but was expelled from the order for bad conduct, and that afterwards he posed in Palermo as a magician and treasure seeker.

been injured by the fraud lodged an appeal, and Giuseppe Balsamo was again thrown into prison. The Prince, naturally, was furious. He tried by various means to have him set free and, when these failed, he made a scene in the very antechamber of the President, when he threatened to give the plaintiff's attorney a thrashing if he did not immediately revoke Balsamo's arrest. The attorney refused, whereupon the Prince grabbed him, threw him on the floor, trampled on him and would have assaulted him still further had not the President, hearing the fracas, hurried out in person and put a stop to it. But, being a weak and servile man, he did not dare punish the offender; the plaintiff and his attorney lost heart and Balsamo was released. There is no record in the official files of who ordered this or of the circumstances in which it came about.

Balsamo left Palermo soon afterwards, and the author of the memoir has only incomplete reports to give of his subsequent travels. It ended with a closely reasoned proof that Cagliostro and Balsamo are one and the same person.*

---

* Added by Goethe some years later. At that time this thesis was more difficult to sustain than it is today when all the facts are known and we can see how the story hangs together. If I had not had reason to suppose that this document was to be made public in France, so that, on my return, I should probably find it in print, I would have made a copy and my friends and the public would have learned many interesting facts much earlier. Since then we have learned most of its contents from a source which has usually been a source of errors only. Who would have thought that Rome, of all places, would contribute so much to the enlightenment of the world and the unmasking of an impostor by publishing a précis of the court minutes! Though this précis could be and should have been more interesting than it is, every sensible reader will be grateful for it. For years we had to look on in dismay while the deceived, the half-deceived and the deceivers worshipped this man and his conjuring tricks, prided themselves upon their association with him, and from the height of their credulous conceit pitied those who had common sense enough not to be impressed.

Who did not prefer to keep silent during those times? Only now, when the whole affair is closed and beyond discussion, can I bring myself to complement the official document by telling what I know.

When I saw from the genealogical tree that several members of the family, Cagliostro's mother and sister in particular, were still living, I told the author of the memoir that I would like to see them and make the acquaintance of the relatives of such an extraordinary personality. He replied that this would be difficult, since they were poor but respectable people who lived a very retired life and were not used to meeting strangers. Furthermore, Sicilians are very suspicious by nature, and my visit might be misinterpreted in various ways. He promised, however, to send me his clerk, who had access to the family and had procured all the information and documents for him.

Next day the clerk appeared but expressed some scruples about the business. 'So far', he told me, 'I have always avoided letting these people see my face again because, in order to get my hands on their marriage contracts, baptismal certificates, etc., and make legal copies of them, I had to resort to a deception. I mentioned casually one day that there was a family stipendium vacant somewhere for which the young Capitummino was probably qualified, but to see if this were so, the first thing which would have to be done would be to draw up a family tree. After that, of course, everything would depend upon negotiations. I would take care of these, if they would promise me a compensation.

'The good people agreed with alacrity. I received the necessary document, the copies were made and the family tree drawn up, but since then I have been careful to keep out of their way. Only a few weeks ago I ran into Mother Capitummino, and the only excuse I could make was the slowness with which all such negotiations are transacted here.'

That is what the clerk said, but when he saw that I did not want to give up my idea, we agreed after some deliberations that I should introduce myself as an Englishman, delegated to bring his family news of Cagliostro, who had been released from the Bastille and had just arrived in London.

At the appointed hour – it must have been about three in the afternoon – we set off together. The house stood at the end of an alley not far from Il Cassaro, the main street. We climbed some dilapidated stairs which led directly into the kitchen. A woman of medium height, broad and sturdy without being stout,

was busy washing dishes. Her dress was clean, and when we
entered, she turned up one corner of her apron to hide the part
which was dirty. She seemed glad to see the clerk and said:
'Signor Giovanni, have you good news for us? Have you
straightened things out?' He replied: 'I still haven't settled our
business yet, but here is a foreigner who brings you greetings
from your brother and can tell you how he is.'

The greetings I was supposed to bring were something I hadn't
bargained for, but at least I had been introduced. 'You know my
brother?' she asked. 'The whole of Europe knows him,' I replied,
'and I think you will be happy to hear that he is well and safe, for
you have probably been worried about his fate.' 'Go in,' she said,
'I won't be long.' So the clerk and I entered the next room.

It was what we would call a parlour, spacious and lofty, but it
also seemed to be almost the entire living space for the family.
There was only one window. The walls, which had once been
painted, were covered with the blackened pictures of saints in gold
frames. Two large beds without curtains stood against one wall,
a small cupboard, shaped like a secretaire, against another. Old
chairs, with rush bottoms and backs which had once been gilt,
stood around, and the tiles of the floor were worn out in places,
but everything was very clean. We now approached the family,
who were assembled at the other end of the room near the
window. While the clerk was explaining the reason for my visit
to old Mother Balsamo – the old woman was very deaf – I had
time to take a good look at the others. By the window stood a
girl of about sixteen, with a good figure but a face scarred from
smallpox, and beside her a young man whose face was also pock-
marked and who looked disagreeable. In an armchair facing the
window sat, or rather slumped, a very ugly person who seemed to
be afflicted with some kind of lethargy.

When the clerk had finished, they invited us to sit down. The
old woman asked me several questions in Sicilian dialect, which
had to be translated for me, since I could not understand every
word. She was pleasant to look at; the regular lines of her face
expressed a serenity which one often notices on the faces of
deaf people, and her voice sounded gentle and agreeable.

I answered her questions, and my answers had to be translated as well. The slowness of our conversation gave me the chance to weigh my words carefully. I told her that her son had been acquitted in France and was now in England, where he had been well received. The happiness she voiced on hearing this news was accompanied by expressions of deep piety. Now that she spoke louder and slower, I could understand her better.

Meanwhile her daughter had come in and sat down next to the clerk, who repeated to her all I had said. She had put on a fresh apron and arranged her hair neatly under a net. She must have been a woman of about forty. The more I looked at her and compared her with the mother, the more I was struck by the difference between them. The daughter's whole bearing expressed determination and a lively, healthy sensuality. She looked about her with intelligent gay blue eyes in which I could not detect the slightest shade of suspicion. She sat leaning forward on her chair with her hands resting on her knees, and looked better in this position than she had standing up. Her unpronounced features reminded me of her brother's as we know him from an engraving of his portrait. She asked me several questions about my journey and my reasons for visiting Sicily, and was convinced that I would return to celebrate with them the feast of Santa Rosalia.

The grandmother again had some questions to ask me, and while I was answering them, her daughter spoke with the clerk in an undertone. When I got the chance, I asked what they were talking about. The clerk said that Signora Capitummino had told him her brother still owed her fourteen ounces. When he had to leave Palermo in a hurry, she had redeemed some of his belongings from the pawnshop. She had never heard from him since, and although she had heard that now he was very rich and lived like a lord, he had never repaid her or given her any financial help. Would I, she asked, when I returned to England, please take it upon me to remind him in a friendly way of this debt and obtain some support for her? Would I also take a letter with me and, if possible, deliver it personally? I said I would, where-upon she asked where I was staying so that she could send me this letter. As I did not want her to know my address, I offered to come the next evening to fetch it. She then began to tell me about her precarious situation. She was a widow with three children. One of them, a girl, was being educated in a convent; the other two, a girl and a boy, were living at home – the latter had just left for school. Besides them, she had her mother to support and, out of Christian charity, she had taken in the poor sick person I had seen, which made her burden still heavier. All her industry was hardly sufficient to procure the bare necessities for herself and her family. She knew, of course, that God would not let her good works go unrewarded, but nevertheless, she groaned under the burden which she had borne for such a long time.

The young people now joined in the conversation, which became more lively. While I was talking with them, I heard the old woman ask her daughter if she thought I was a devotee of her sacred religion. The daughter cleverly evaded the question by telling her mother, so far as I could understand, that the foreigner seemed to have their welfare at heart and it would not be proper to question anyone about this matter on the first meeting.

When they heard that I intended to leave Palermo soon, they again urged me to be sure to return and praised the paradisiacal days of the Feast of Santa Rosalia. Nothing like it, they said, was to be seen and enjoyed in the whole world. My companion, who had wanted to leave long before and had repeatedly made signs to me that we should go, at last brought the conversation to an end, and I repeated my promise to come next day in the late afternoon to fetch the letter. The clerk was glad that our visit had gone off so well, and we parted from each other with expressions of mutual satisfaction.

You can imagine the impression this poor, pious, friendly family made on me. My curiosity had been satisfied, but their unaffected good manners had aroused an interest which increased the more I thought about them. At the same time I was worried about the next day. It would be only natural if, after I left, my surprise visit had set them thinking. From their family trees I knew that several other members of the family were still living, and they would, of course, call them and their friends together to discuss the amazing news they had heard from me. I had achieved my purpose and the only thing left for me to do was to bring this adventure to an end as tactfully as possible. Accordingly, the next day, soon after my midday meal, I went to the house by myself. They were astonished to see me so early. The letter, they said, was not ready yet. Furthermore, several relatives were coming in that evening who also wished to make my acquaintance. I told them I had to leave early the next morning and still had to pay some other visits and do my packing, so I had decided to come early rather than not come at all.

Meanwhile the grandson, who had not been there the day before, came in carrying the letter I was to take. This had been written, as is customary here, by one of the public scribes who sit in the squares. In height and build, the young man resembled the sister I had already seen, and his manner was quiet, melancholy and modest.

He asked me about his uncle's wealth and expensive style of living, remarking sadly: 'Why has he so completely forgotten about his family? How fortunate it would be for us if he would only return to Palermo. But how,' he continued, 'did he come to tell you that he still has relatives in Palermo? They say he passes himself off as a man of noble birth and denies any connexion with us.' I answered this question, for which the clerk's imprudence had been inadvertently responsible, as plausibly as I could by saying that his uncle might have reasons for concealing his humble birth from the general public, but that he made no secret of it to his friends.

His sister, encouraged by the presence of her brother and also, perhaps, by the absence of her friend of yesterday, now joined in our conversation and began to talk in a very well-mannered and lively way. Both of them implored me to remember them to their uncle, if I should write to him. They also insisted that, after travelling across the kingdom, I was to come back and celebrate the Feast of Santa Rosalia with them. Their mother supported them in this. 'Signor,' she said, 'although it is not proper for me, really, with a grown-up daughter in the house, to invite foreigners to call, since one has to be wary not only of danger but also of gossip, you will always be welcome here whenever you come back to this city!'

'Yes, yes,' said her children. 'We shall show him round and

sit with him on the stands from which you get the best view of the festivities. How he will admire the great car of the Saint and the magnificent illuminations!'

Meanwhile their grandmother had read through the letter several times. When she heard I was about to leave, she rose from her chair and handed me the folded sheet of paper. 'Tell my son how happy the news you have brought has made me! Tell him also that I take him to my heart – like this.' With these words she opened her arms wide and pressed them again to her breast. 'Tell him that I recommend him every day in my prayers to God and the Blessed Virgin, that I send him and his wife my blessing, and that my only wish is to see him again before I die, with these eyes which have shed so many tears for him.'

The graceful music which only the Italian language possesses enhanced the choice and noble arrangement of her words, which were further accompanied by those lively gestures with which the southern peoples give such extraordinary fascination to their speech. Deeply moved, I bade them farewell. All shook hands with me. The young people saw me to the door, and when I descended the stairs, they ran to the kitchen balcony overlooking the street and, as they waved goodbye, called out repeatedly that I was on no account to forget to come back. They were still standing on the balcony when I turned the corner.

I need hardly say that the interest I took in this family made me keenly anxious to do something practical to relieve their need. They had been twice deceived: first by the lawyer's clerk, now by an inquisitive North European, and it looked as if their hopes of help out of the blue were going to be dashed for the second time.

My first idea was to send them, before I left, the fourteen ounces which the fugitive owed them, under the pretext that I could count on Cagliostro reimbursing me. But when I had paid my bill at the inn and made a rough estimate of what I had left in cash and letters of credit, I realized that, in a country where lack of communications makes all distances infinite, so to speak, I would find myself in difficulties if I presumed, out of kindness of heart, to remedy the injustice of a scoundrel.

That same evening I went to see my friend, the shopkeeper,

and asked him how the feast tomorrow would pass off. A great procession, headed by the Viceroy, was to move through the city, accompanying the Host on foot, and it was inevitable that the slightest wind would wrap God and man in a dense cloud of dust. The cheerful little fellow said that the people of Palermo are content to rely on a miracle. On several similar occasions a heavy downpour had washed down the sloping street and made a fairly clean road for the procession. The same thing was expected this time, and not without reason, for clouds were beginning to gather in the sky, promising rain during the night.

15 April

And so it happened! Last night a torrent of rain came down from heaven. First thing next morning, I hurried down into the street to witness the miracle. It was indeed extraordinary. The flood, channelled between the pavements, had dragged the lighter rubbish down the street, pushing some of it into the sea and some into the drains, at least into those which were not choked. It had shifted the coarser litter from one place to another, so that curious meanders had been formed on the paving stones. Hundreds and hundreds of people with shovels, brooms and pitchforks were now busy enlarging these clean patches and joining them together by piling the remaining refuse on one side or the other. In consequence, when the procession started, it could proceed down a clean road, serpentining between the mud, and the clergy in their long skirts and the Viceroy and nobility in their elegant footwear could pass without being incommoded and bespattered. In my imagination I saw the Children of Israel, for whom the angel prepared a dry path through the midst of swamp and slough, and tried to ennoble with this simile the shocking spectacle of so many devout and proper people praying and parading their way down an avenue of wet piles of muck.

Where the streets have pavements, it is always possible to walk without getting dirty, but today, when we visited the inner city in order to see various things we had neglected so far, despite all the sweeping and heaping that had gone on, we found it almost impossible to get through.

Today's ceremonies gave us occasion to visit the cathedral and see its remarkable monuments. As we were stretching our legs in any case, we thought we would visit some more buildings. Among them a well-preserved Moorish house delighted us. It was not a big house, but its rooms were spacious and well proportioned; in a northern country it would not really be habitable, but in a southern it would make a most desirable residence. Expert architects should make a ground plan and a perspective view of it.

In a dismal quarter we saw several fragments of antique marble statues, but we hadn't the patience to try and identify them.

16 April

Since we have now to reckon with our imminent departure from this paradise, I hoped today to find a few more hours of perfect peace in the Public Gardens, and then to take a walk in the valley at the foot of the mountain of Santa Rosalia, so that I could do my daily stint of the Odyssey and consider the dramatic possibilities of Nausicaa. All this came to pass, and if I did not have perfect luck, I had much to be satisfied with. I made a draft of the whole, and could not resist roughing out and even composing several passages which particularly tempted me.

17 April

It is really and truly a misfortune to be haunted and tempted by so many spirits. Early this morning I went alone to the Public Gardens with the firm intention of meditating further upon my poetic dreams, but, before I knew it, another spirit seized me, one that had already been haunting me during the last few days.

Here where, instead of being grown in pots or under glass as they are with us, plants are allowed to grow freely in the open fresh air and fulfil their natural destiny, they become more intelligible. Seeing such a variety of new and renewed forms, my old fancy suddenly came back to mind: Among this multitude might I not discover the Primal Plant? There certainly must be one. Otherwise, how could I recognize that this or that form *was* a plant if all were not built upon the same basic model?

I tried to discover how all these divergent forms differed from one another, and I always found that they were more alike than unlike. But when I applied my botanical nomenclature, I got along all right to begin with, but then I stuck, which annoyed me without stimulating me. Gone were my fine poetic resolutions – the garden of Alcinous had vanished and a garden of the natural world had appeared in its stead. Why are we moderns so distracted, why do we let ourselves be challenged by problems which we can neither face nor solve !

Alcamo, 18 April

Very early in the morning we left Palermo on horseback. Kniep and the *vetturino* had proved themselves most efficient at packing and loading. We rode slowly up the excellent road we had travelled on before when we visited San Martino, and once more admired the magnificent fountains along it. Then an incident occurred which taught us something about the temperate habits of this country. Our groom was carrying a small barrel of wine slung over his shoulder like one of our *vivandières*. This looked big enough to hold sufficient wine to last us a few days. So we were surprised when he rode up to one of the water spouts, took out the spigot of the barrel and let water run in. Being Germans, we were flabbergasted and asked what he was doing. Wasn't the barrel full of wine? He replied, with the utmost nonchalance, that he had left a third of it empty because nobody ever drank unmixed wine. It was better to add the water while the wine was still in the barrel because then they would mix better. Besides, one couldn't always be certain of finding water. By this time, the barrel was full and there was nothing to be done but accept what used to be the custom at Oriental wedding feasts in days of old.

After passing Monreale and reaching the top of the ridge, we saw a beautiful landscape which spoke more of history than of agriculture. On our right stretched the level horizon of the sea, interrupted by picturesque foothills and wooded or treeless shores, its absolute calm in perfect contrast to the rugged limestone cliffs. Kniep quickly made some thumbnail sketches.

We are now in Alcamo, a quiet, clean little town with a well-appointed inn and within convenient distance of the Temple of Segesta, which we can see standing in solitary grandeur not so far off.

19 April

Our lodgings are so attractive that we have decided to spend the whole day here.

First, let me say something about our experiences yesterday.

After Monreale, we left the good road and entered a region of rocky mountains. High up on the ridge, I came across stones which, judging by their weight and sparkle, I took to be iron pyrites. All the flat land is cultivated and fairly fertile. The outcrops of limestone are red in colour like the weathered soil. This red, calcareous clay covers a wide area and makes a heavy soil with no sand in it, but nevertheless yields excellent wheat. We saw some lopped olive trees, old and very sturdy.

Under the shelter of an airy pergola attached to a miserable inn, we took a light midday meal. Dogs greedily gobbled up the discarded skins of our sausages; a beggar boy chased them away and hungrily consumed our apple parings until he, in his turn, was chased away by an old beggar. Professional jealousy is to be found everywhere. The old beggar ran up and down in his tattered toga, acting as both boots and waiter. I had observed on earlier occasions that if you order anything from an innkeeper which he hasn't got in the house at the moment, he calls a beggar to fetch it from the grocer's.

As a rule we are spared such slovenly service, thanks to our excellent *vetturino*, who is groom, guide, watch, buyer and cook in one.

On the higher slopes of the mountains we still found olive, carob and mountain ash. Here cultivation follows a three-year cycle – beans, corn and rest. Manure, the peasants say, works greater miracles than the saints. The vines are trained very low.

Alcamo stands on a hill at some distance from the Gulf. The landscape is impressive in its majesty – high crags, deep valleys, vastness and variety. Beyond Monreale one enters a beautiful double valley, divided down the middle by a mountain ridge. The cultivated fields lie green and still, the broad road is lined with wild bushes and tangled shrubs lavishly decked with brilliant blossoms: the lentisk, so covered with yellow, papilionaceous flowers that not a green leaf is visible, bush after bush of hawthorn, aloes, already tall and showing signs of bloom, rich carpets of amaranthine clover, insect-orchids, small alpine roses, hyacinths with closed bells, borage, alliums, asphodels.

The stream which comes down from Segesta carries with it not only calcareous debris but also many particles of hornstone which are very compact and in every shade of dark blue, yellow and brown. Before one reaches Alcamo, one finds complete hills of such deposits. In the limestone cliffs I also saw veins of hornstone and silica with a *salband* of lime.

Segesta, 20 April

The Temple of Segesta was never completed. They never levelled the area around it, only the periphery on which the columns were to be set up. One can tell this from the fact that in some places the steps are sunk nine or ten feet into the ground, though there is no hill nearby from which the stones and earth could have been washed down. Moreover, the stones are still lying in their natural places and there are no broken fragments among them.

All the columns are standing, the two which had fallen having recently been raised again. It is difficult to decide whether or not they were meant to have socles, and it is difficult for me to explain why this is so, without a drawing. In some places it looks as though the columns must have stood on the fourth step, in which case one would have had to descend a further step to enter the temple. In other places the top step has been cut through and it looks as though the columns had bases. But then one comes to places where there is no cut and one is back at the first hypothesis. Some architect ought to settle this point definitely.

The two long sides have twelve columns each, not counting the
corner columns; the façade and the rear side have six each, including the corner ones. One sign that the temple was never
completed is the condition of the temple steps. The peglike projections to which ropes were attached when the blocks were
transported from the quarry to the site have not been hewn off.
But the strongest evidence is the floor. Here and there slabs indicate where its edges must have been, but the centre is natural
rock which rises higher than the sides, so that the floor can never
have been paved. In addition, there is no trace of an inner hall,
and the temple was never coated with stucco, though one can
presume that this was intended, because, on the abaci of the
capitals, there are projections where stucco could possibly be
applied. The whole temple is built of a travertine type of limestone, which is now very badly weathered. The restoration of
1781 has done a lot of good. The new stonework is simple but
beautiful. I could not find the particular great blocks Riedesel
speaks of: perhaps they were used up when the columns were
restored.

The site of the temple is remarkable. Standing on an isolated
hill at the head of a long, wide valley and surrounded by cliffs,
it towers over a vast landscape, but, extensive as the view is,
only a small corner of the sea is visible. The countryside broods
in a melancholy fertility; it is cultivated but with scarcely a
sign of human habitation. The tops of the flowering thistles were
alive with butterflies; wild fennel, its last year's growth now
withered, stood eight or nine feet high and in such profusion and
apparent order that one might have taken it for a nursery garden.
The wind howled around the columns as though they were a
forest, and birds of prey wheeled, screaming, above the empty
shell.

The fatigue of clambering about among the unimpressive ruins
of a theatre discouraged us from visiting the ruins of the city.
At the foot of the temple, I found large pieces of hornstone, and
on our way back to Alcamo, I saw that the road bed was largely
composed of this rock, to which the soil owes the silica content
that makes it friable. Examining a young fennel, I noticed a
difference between the upper and the lower leaves; the organism

is always one and the same, but it evolves from simplicity to multiplicity. The peasants are now busy weeding, walking up and down their fields like men on a *battue*. There are some insects about. (In Palermo I saw only glow-worms.) The leeches, lizards and snails here are no more beautiful in colour than ours; indeed, all those I saw were grey.

Castelvetrano, 21 April

From Alcamo up to Castelvetrano one approaches the limestone mountains over gravel hills. Between the steep barren mountains lie broad upland valleys – the ground is all cultivated, but there are scarcely any trees. The extensive alluvial deposits which form the gravel hills indicate by their alignment the course of the currents in the primeval ocean. The soil is well mixed and, owing to its sand content, more friable. Salemi lay to our right, an hour's ride away. We crossed hills where the limestone was overlaid with beds of gypsum, and the composition of the soil improved still further. The foreground was all hills; far away to the west we could see the sea. We came upon fig trees in bud and, to our delight, great masses of flowers, which had formed colonies on the broad road and kept repeating themselves, one large multicoloured patch following closely on the last. Beautiful bindweeds, hibisci, rose-mallows and a great variety of clovers predominated by turns, interspersed with allium and bushes of goat's rue. We wound our way on horseback, crossing and recrossing narrow paths. Russet-coated cattle grazed here and there, small but well built and with small, graceful horns.

In the north-east the mountains stood in row after row with the peak of Il Cuniglione soaring up in their midst. Among the gravel hills there were no signs of a spring or a stream, and evidently there is little rainfall here, since we saw neither ravines nor debris from flash floods.

During the night I had a strange experience. We were dead tired and had thrown ourselves on our beds in an inn which was anything but elegant. At midnight I woke up and saw over my head a star so beautiful that I thought I had never seen one like it. Its enchanting light seemed a prophecy of good things to come and my spirit felt utterly refreshed, but soon it disappeared, leaving me alone in the dark. It was not till daybreak that I discovered what had caused this miracle. There was a crack in the roof and I had woken up just at the very moment when one of the most beautiful stars in the firmament was crossing my private meridian. The travellers, of course, unhesitatingly interpreted this natural phenomenon as an omen in their favour.

Sciacca, 22 April

The road from Castelvetrano ran all the time over gravel hills and was devoid of mineralogical interest. When it reached the seashore, we could see a few limestone cliffs. The whole plain is immensely fertile; the oats and barley were in excellent condition, *salsola kali* had been planted, the fruit stalks of the aloes were higher than those we saw during the past two days, and the various clovers never left us. We came to a copse – mostly bushes, but with a tree rising here and there. And then, at last, corktrees.

Girgenti, 23 April. Evening

From Sciacca to this place is a good day's ride. Shortly after Sciacca we halted to look at the thermal baths. A hot spring, with a pungent odour of sulphur, gushes out of a rock. The water tastes salty but not foul. Can it be that the sulphur fumes are not produced till it issues into the open air? A little higher up, there is a spring of cool, odourless water, and on top of the hill stands the cloister where the steam baths are: a dense cloud of vapour was rising from them into the pure air.

The beach here is made up of limestone fragments only; quartz and hornstone have abruptly disappeared. I inspected the small rivers: Caltabellotta, Macaluba and Platani. The first two carried limestone debris only, but in the bed of the Platani I found yellow marble and iron pyrites, the eternal companions of that more noble rock. Some small pieces of lava caught my eye, for I did not expect to find any volcanic material in these parts. I even believe they must have been transported here from far away to serve human purpose; probably they were fragments of old millstones. In the neighbourhood of Monteallegro thick beds of solid gypsum overlie and interlie the beds of limestone. The little town of Caltabellotta looks so odd, perched up on its crag.

24 April

I swear that I have never in my whole life enjoyed such a vision of spring as I did at sunrise this morning. The new Girgenti stands on the site of the ancient citadel, which covers an area large enough to house a city. From our windows we look down over a wide, gentle slope, now entirely covered with gardens and vineyards, so that one would never guess this was once a densely populated urban quarter. All one can see rising out of this green and flowering area is the Temple of Concord near its southern edge and the scanty ruins of the Temple of Juno to the east. All the other sacred ruins, which lie along a straight line between these two points, are invisible from this height. At the foot of the slope, looking south, lies the shore plain, which extends for about two miles till it reaches the sea. We had to forgo an immediate descent through branches and creepers into that marvellous zone of green foliage with its flowers and promise of fruit, because our guide, a good-natured little secular priest, begged us to devote our first day to seeing the city.

First he showed us its well-built streets, then he led us to some higher ground to enjoy an even more extensive view and finally, to satisfy our artistic appetite, brought us to the cathedral. This contains an ancient sarcophagus which, since it was converted into an altar, has been well preserved. It depicts Hippolytus with his hunting companions and horses. Phaedra's nurse has bidden them halt and is about to hand Hippolytus a small tablet. The artist's main concern was to portray beautiful young men. In order that the eye should concentrate its attention on them, he has made the old nurse very small, almost a dwarf. I have never seen a bas-relief as wonderful or as well preserved. If I am not mistaken, it is an example of Greek art from its most graceful period.

A priceless vase of considerable size carried me back to some still more remote epoch, and, in the structure of the church itself, there were places where the pieces of antique buildings seemed to have been incorporated.

Since there are no inns in Girgenti, a family kindly made room for us in their own house and gave us a raised alcove in a large chamber. A green curtain separated us and our baggage from the members of the household, who were manufacturing macaroni of the finest, whitest and smallest kind, which fetches the highest price. The dough is first moulded into the shape of a pencil as long as a finger; the girls then twist this once with their finger tips into a spiral shape like a snail's. We sat down beside the pretty children and got them to explain the whole process to us. The flour is made from the best and hardest wheat, known as *grano forte*. The work calls for much greater manual dexterity than macaroni made by machinery or in forms. The macaroni they served us was excellent, but they apologized for it, saying that there was a much superior kind, but they hadn't enough in the house for even a single dish. This kind, they told us, was only made in Girgenti and, what is more, only by their family. No other macaroni, in their opinion, can compare with it in whiteness and softness.

In the evening our guide again managed to appease our impatient longing to walk down the hill by leading us to other points along the heights from which, as we gazed at the noble view, he gave us a general survey of the position of all the remarkable things we were to see on the morrow.

25 April

At sunrise we were at last permitted to walk down the hill, and at every step the scenery became more picturesque. Convinced that he was only serving our best interests, the little man led us through the lush vegetation without stopping once, though we passed thousands of singular views, any one of which would have made a subject for an idyllic picture. The ground beneath our feet was undulated like waves over the hidden ruins. The shell-tufa of which these were built ensures the fertility of the soil which now covers them. In due course we came to the eastern limit of the city where, year after year, the ruins of the Temple of Juno fall into ever greater decay because their porous stone is eroded by wind and weather. We only meant to make a cursory examination today, but Kniep has already chosen the points from which he will sketch tomorrow.

This temple stands on a foundation of weathered rock. From this point the city wall ran due east along the edge of a limestone hill which falls in precipices to the shore plain. The sea which once washed the base of these cliffs must have receded to its present shoreline in a fairly remote age. The city walls were partly built of quarried stone and partly hewn out of the solid rock. Behind the walls rose the temple. It is easy to imagine what a stupendous sight the rising tiers of Girgenti must have looked from the sea.

The slender architecture of the Temple of Concord, which has withstood so many centuries, already conforms more nearly to our standard of beauty and harmony than the style which preceded it – compared to Paestum, it is like the image of a god as opposed to the image of a giant.

Since the intention was so laudable, one ought not to complain, I suppose, but what has recently been done to preserve these monuments is in very poor taste. The cracks have been repaired with a dazzling white gesso which quite spoils the look of the whole temple. It would have been so easy to give the gesso the colour of the weathered stone. On the other hand, when one sees of what friable shell-limestone the walls and columns are built, one must admit that it is surprising the temple has survived at all. It is clear, though, that the builders themselves, in the hope of a grateful posterity, took steps for its preservation; on the columns one can still see traces of a thin coat of plaster which they applied both to flatter the eye and to ensure durability.

Next we stopped before the ruins of the Temple of Jupiter, which lie scattered far and wide like the disjointed bones of a gigantic skeleton, amid and beneath several smallholdings, which are divided by fences and overgrown with plants of every size. The only recognizable shapes in all this heap of rubble are a triglyph and half of a column, both of gigantic proportions. I

tried to measure the triglyph with my outstretched arms and
found I could not span it. As for the column, this will give you
some idea of its size. When I stood in one of the flutings as in a
niche, my shoulders barely touched both edges. It would take
twenty-two men, placed shoulder to shoulder, to form a circle
approximating in size to the circumference of such a column.
We left with a feeling of disappointment because there seemed
nothing here for a draughtsman to do.

The Temple of Hercules, on the other hand, still reveals traces
of the classic symmetry. The two rows of columns on its front
and rear side all lie pointing north and south, one row uphill, the
other down, as if they had all fallen together at the same moment. The hill itself may have been formed from the ruins of its
cella. The columns which were probably held together by the
entablature may have been blown down in a raging storm. The
separate blocks of which they were composed are still lying in
their proper order. Kniep has already mentally sharpened his
pencils in anticipation of depicting this unusal occurrence.

The Temple of Aesculapius, standing in the shade of a lovely
carob tree and almost walled in by some kind of small farm buildings, makes a pleasant picture.

Last we climbed down to the Tomb of Theron and felt happy
to be standing in the presence of a monument we had seen in so
many reproductions. It provides the foreground to an extraordinary vista. The eye travels faster from west to east along the
rocky cliff with its crumbling walls, through which and above
which it sees the remains of the temples. This view has been
painted by Hackert with a skilful hand, and Kniep will certainly
sketch it too.

26 April

By the time I woke up, Kniep was all ready to set off on his artistic excursion with a boy he had hired to carry his cardboard
sheets. I stood by the window and shared the glory of the morning with my secret, quiet, but by no means speechless friend. A
certain shy reverence has hitherto kept me from pronouncing the
name of this mentor to whom I turn and listen from time to

time. It is von Riedesel,* that excellent man whose little book I carry near my heart like a breviary or a talisman.

I have always enjoyed seeing myself in the mirror of natures who possess what I lack, and he is one of them. Calm resolution, sureness of aim, apt and precise method, good grounding and scholarship, intimate association with a masterly teacher, in his case, Winckelmann – I lack them all, and everything which comes from having them. So I cannot blame myself for trying to gain, by stealth, storm and cunning, what my life has so far not permitted me to acquire in the ordinary way. Would that this good man, amid the tumult of this world, could be aware that, at this very moment, a grateful disciple is doing homage to his merits, lonely in a lonely place which had so much attraction for him that he wished to spend his lifetime here, far from family and friends, forgetting and forgotten.

So, consulting my assiduous friend from time to time, I walked the roads of yesterday with my clerical guide, looking at the same objects from many different angles.

He drew my attention to a beautiful custom of this powerful, ancient city. Set in the rocks and masses of masonry which once served Girgenti as ramparts are tombs which were probably reserved for the Brave and the Good. What fairer resting-place could they have found as a memorial to their glory and an immortal example to the living?

In this wide plain between the cliffs and the sea are the remains of a small temple which has been converted into a Christian chapel. The harmonious combination of the half-columns and the square blocks of the walls was a joy to the eye. I felt I was witnessing the exact moment when the Doric order reached its highest measure of perfection. We took a brief look at some insignificant monuments of antiquity and a longer one at the large subterranean vaults in which wheat is stored at the present day. My good old guide gave me much information about the conditions here, both civil and ecclesiastical, Nothing he told me sounded very encouraging, and our conversation seemed in keep-

---

*J. H. von Riedesel (1740–85), Prussian ambassador to the Court of Vienna, author of *Journey across Sicily and Magna Graecia.*

ing with our surroundings, where everything is steadily crumbling away. I learned from him, incidentally, that there is still
much hatred of the French for having made peace with the
Barbaresques. They are accused of betraying Christendom to the
infidels.

Looking at the cliffs, one observes that all the strata dip
towards the sea. The lower layers have eroded, so that the upper
overhang like suspended fringes.

Halfway up the road from the shore plain there is an ancient
gate hewn out of the rock. The walls which still stand are built
on rock foundations in tiers.

Our *cicerone* is called Don Michele Vella, the-antiquary-who-
lives-near-Santa-Maria-in-the-house-of-Mastro-Gerio.

The broad beans are planted thus: they dig holes in the soil
at suitable intervals, put in a handful of manure, wait for rain
and then sow the beans. The bean-straw is burned and the ashes
used for washing their linen. They never use soap. Instead
of soda, they use the burned outer shells of almonds. They
wash their laundry first with water and then with this kind
of lye.

The rotation of crops is as follows: broad beans, wheat, tumenia; during the fourth year, the field lies fallow and serves as
pasture. Tumenia – the name is said to be derived from either
bimenia or *trimenia* – is a precious gift from Ceres. It is a kind of
summer corn and takes three months to ripen. They keep sowing
it from January till June, so that, at any given moment, some of
it is ripe. It needs little rain but much heat. At first it has a very
tender leaf, but it grows as fast as wheat and when ripe is very
strong. Wheat is sown in October and November and is ripe in
June, barley in November. Here the latter is ripe by the first of
June, but earlier along the coast and later in the mountains.

The flax is ripe already. The acanthus has unfolded its magnificent leaves. *Salsola fruiticosa* grows luxuriantly, and sainfoin is
abundant on the uncultivated slopes. Some of these crops are
leased to people who carry them to the city in sheaves. The oats
which they weed out of the wheat are also sold in sheaves.

When they plant cabbages, they dig neat trenches with little borders of soil to catch the rain. The fig trees are showing all their leaves; the figs have begun to form and will be ripe by St John's Day. Later in the year, however, the trees will bear a second crop. The almond trees are laden with fruit. I saw a lopped carob tree bearing innumerable pods. The vines which yield eating grapes are trained over pergolas, supported on high poles. Melons are planted in March and ripe in June. I saw them cheerfully growing among the ruins of the Temple of Jupiter, though there was no moisture for them at all.

Our *vetturino* eats raw artichokes and kohlrabi with the greatest gusto; it must be said, though, that these are much tenderer and more succulent here than they are in our climate. The same is true of other vegetables. When one passes through the fields, the peasants let one eat, for example, as many young broad beans as one likes, pods and all.

When I showed interest in some black stones that resembled lava, the antiquary told me that they came from Mount Etna, and that more specimens could be found near the harbour, or rather, the anchorage.

Except for quails, there are few birds in this region. The other migrants are swallows, *rinnine* and *ridene*. *Rinnine* are small black birds which come from the Levant, breed and nest in Sicily and then either fly back or further on. *Ridene*, or wild duck, arrive from Africa in December and January, descend on Acragas in great numbers and then move off into the mountains.

A word about the vase in the cathedral. It shows a hero in full armour, a stranger apparently, who has just arrived and is standing in the presence of a seated old man whose wreath and sceptre show him to be a king. Behind the King stands a woman with lowered head, supporting her chin with her left hand in a watchful and pensive pose. Behind the hero facing them, another old man, also wearing a wreath, is talking to a man who carries a spear and is possibly a member of the King's bodyguard. He appears to have introduced the hero and to be saying to the guard: 'Just let him speak to the King, he is a good man.' The

ground colour of this vase seems to have been red and the figures
to have been painted over it in black; the woman's garment is
the only place where red seems to have been laid on black.

                                                            27 April

If Kniep really means to carry out all his plans, he will have to
draw without stopping, while I roam about with my little old
guide. Today we walked as far as the seashore, from which, the
ancients assure us, Girgenti was a wonderful sight.

As we gazed out at the vast watery expanse, my guide pointed
to a long bank of cloud like a mountain ridge on the southern
horizon; this, he said, indicated the coast of Africa. I was struck
by another strange phenomenon: a slender arc of light clouds,
with one foot resting on Sicily and the other on the sea somewhere
in the south, vaulted into the blue sky, which was otherwise
cloudless. Almost motionless and richly dyed by the rays of the
setting sun, it was a strange and a beautiful spectacle. My guide
told me that its other foot probably rested on Malta, which lay
exactly in the direction to which the arc pointed, and that this
phenomenon was not rare. It would really be very odd if the
mutual attraction between the two islands should manifest itself
atmospherically in this way.

Our conversation revived an idea I had once had and dismissed
as being too difficult and dangerous: Why not take a trip to
Malta? But the same objections remained and I decided to keep
our *vetturino* till we reached Messina.

In taking this decision, I was influenced by another of my
stubborn fancies. So far, on my excursions through Sicily I had
only seen a few regions which were rich in wheat; the horizon
had always been limited by mountains, so that my impression
was of an island entirely lacking in plains, and I could not understand why Ceres was said to have shown it such especial favour.
When I asked about this, I was told that, instead of going along
the coast by way of Syracuse, I should cut straight across the
interior; then I would see wheat fields in plenty. Though it
meant leaving out Syracuse, Kniep and I readily yielded to this
tempting suggestion because we had heard that little now re-

mained of that once glorious city but its name. Besides, it would
be easy to visit it from Catania.

Caltanissetta, 28 April

At last we can say we have seen with our own eyes the reason
why Sicily earned the title of 'The Granary of Italy'. Soon after
Girgenti, the fertility began. There are no great level areas, but
the gently rolling uplands were completely covered with wheat
and barley in one great unbroken mass. Wherever the soil is
suitable to their growth, it is so well tended and exploited that
not a tree is to be seen. Even the small hamlets and other
dwellings are confined to the ridges, where the limestone rocks
make the ground untillable. The women live in these hamlets
all the year round, spinning and weaving, but during the season
of field labour, the men spend only Saturdays and Sundays with
them; the rest of the week they spend in the valleys and sleep
at night in reed huts. Our desire had certainly been granted;
indeed, we soon came to long for the winged chariot of Trip-
tolemus to bear us away out of this monotony.

After riding through this deserted fertility for hours under a
scorching sun, we were glad to arrive in the well-situated and
well-built town of Caltanissetta. However, we looked in vain for
a tolerable inn. The mules are housed in superbly vaulted stables,
the farm hands sleep on the heaps of clover which is used for
fodder, but the foreigner has to start his housekeeping from nothing. Even when he has found a room which might possibly do,
this has first to be cleaned. Chairs, benches, even tables do not
exist; one sits on low blocks of solid wood.

If one wants to convert these blocks into the legs of a bed, one
goes to the carpenter and rents as many boards as are needed.
The large leather bag which Hackert lent us was temporarily
filled with chaff and proved a godsend. But first we had to do
something about our meals. On our way we had bought a chicken,
and our *vetturino* went off at once to buy rice, salt and spices.
But since he had never been near this place before, it was some
time before we could solve the question of where we could do our
cooking, as there were no facilities for this at the inn. At last

an elderly citizen offered, in return for a small sum, to provide firewood, to lend us a stove, kitchen utensils and table requisites, and, while the meal was being prepared, to conduct us round the town.

This he did and brought us finally to the market square, where, in accordance with immemorial custom, the town notables were sitting around, talking among themselves and expecting us to entertain them as well.

We had to tell them stories about Frederick the Second, and the interest they showed in that great king was so lively that we kept his death a secret for fear we might become objects of hatred to our hosts as bearers of ill tidings.

A few more geological observations. As one descends from Girgenti, the soil turns whitish: the older type of limestone appears to be followed immediately by gypsum. Then comes a new type of limestone, more friable, slightly decomposed and, as one can see from the tilled fields, varying in colour from a light yellow to a darker, almost violet tint. Halfway between Girgenti and Caltanissetta, gypsum reappears. This favours the growth of a beautiful purple, almost rose-red sedum, while the limestone harbours a bright yellow moss.

Near Caltanissetta the decomposed limestone frequently outcrops again. Its strata contain few fossilized shells, and the outcrops have a reddish, slightly violet colour, almost like red lead. I had observed similar ones on the hills near San Martino.

Quartz I only saw once, halfway down a little valley, enclosed on three sides and opening in the east towards the sea. In the distance on our left the high mountain which rises above Camerata came into view and another shaped like a truncated cone. The immense wheatfields looked incredibly clean – no weeds at all. At first we saw nothing but green fields, then ploughed ones, and here and there, where the ground was moister, a patch of pasture. Trees are very rare; we came upon a few apple and pear trees soon after leaving Girgenti, and fig trees on the summits of ridges and in the neighbourhood of the occasional villages.

The valleys are beautiful in shape. Even though their bottoms are not completely level, there is no sign of heavy rain, for it immediately runs off into the sea; only a few little brooks, which one hardly notices, trickle along.

The dwarf palms and all the flowers and shrubs of the south-western zone had disappeared and I did not see much red clover. Thistles are allowed to take possession only of the roads, but all the rest is Ceres' domain. As a matter of fact, the whole region looks very like certain hilly, fertile regions in Germany, that between Erfurt and Gotha, for example, especially when one looks in the direction of the Gleichen.* It took a combination of many factors to make Sicily one of the most fertile countries in the world. They plough with oxen and it is forbidden to slaughter cows or calves. We have met many goats, donkeys and mules on our trip, but few horses. Most of these were dapple greys with black feet and black manes. They have magnificent stables with built-in stone mangers.

Manure is used only in growing beans and lentils; the other crops are grown after they have been harvested. Red clover and sheaves of barley, in the ear but still green, are offered for sale to passing riders.

On the mountain above Caltanissetta we saw a hard fossiliferous limestone : the large shells lay below, the small on top. In the paving stones of the little town we found pectinites.

After Caltanissetta the hills descend steeply into a number of valleys which discharge their waters into the river Salso. The soil is reddish and very clayey. Much of the land lies fallow, and, where it is cultivated, the crops, though tolerably good, are far behind those of the regions we had traversed earlier.

Castrogiovanni, 29 April

Today we saw an even more fertile and even more uninhabited region. It rained steadily, which made travelling very unpleasant, since we had to cross several rivers which were in flood. When we came to the bank of the Salso and looked in vain for a bridge, a surprising adventure awaited us. Some sturdy men grabbed the mules by the girth in pairs and led them, with their riders and

---

*Gleichen. Three mountains near Gotha.

baggage, across a deep arm of the stream to a gravel bank, alternately checking and pushing the beasts to keep them on the right course and prevent them from being swept off their feet by the current. After the whole cavalcade had assembled on the bank, they transported us across the second arm of the river in the same fashion.

Brushwood grew along the banks but soon disappeared after we reached dry land. The Salso carries down particles of granite, a metamorphosed gneiss, and marble, both speckled and plain.

Presently we saw ahead of us the isolated crest on which Castrogiovanni is perched. It gives the whole landscape a curiously sombre character.

As we ascended the flank of this hill by a long, winding road, we saw that it was made of shell-limestone. We picked up some specimens containing large calcified shells. Castrogiovanni itself is not visible until one reaches the summit, since it is built on the northern slope. The little town, the tower and the village of Calascibetta a little way off to the left confront each other very solemnly. The beans were blossoming in the plains below, but who could enjoy the view! The roads were horrible, the more so because they had once been paved, and the rain beat down without stopping. The ancient Enna gave us a most unfriendly welcome – a room with a plastered stone floor and shutters but no windows, so that either we had to sit in the dark or put up with the drizzling rain, from which we had just escaped. We consumed some of our remaining provisions, spent the night in misery and took a solemn vow never to let ourselves be tempted again on our travels by a mythological name.

30 April

We left Castrogiovanni by a path so steep and rugged that we had to lead the mules. For most of the descent, everything at eye level was wrapped in clouds, but at a great height we were astonished to see a grey-and-white-striped something which seemed to be a solid body. How could there be a solid body in the sky? Our guide explained that it was one flank of Etna, seen through rents in the clouds; the stripes were snow and the bare rock of the ridge; even so, the ridge we could see was not the summit.

Leaving the steep rock of the ancient Enna behind us, we rode through long, long, lonely valleys, uncultivated, uninhabited, abandoned to pasturing cattle which were as graceful and lively as deer. These good creatures had pasture acreage enough, but they were hemmed in by enormous masses of encroaching thistles which were steadily reducing their grazing ground. Here these plants find the ideal conditions for increasing and multiplying their kind. The area they have usurped would provide sufficient pasture for several large estates. Since they are not perennials, they could easily be exterminated at this season by mowing them down before they have flowered.

As we were solemnly making strategic plans for our war on the thistles, we were put to shame by the discovery that they were not quite as useless as we thought. At a lonely inn where we had halted to fodder our mules, two Sicilian noblemen had just arrived. They were on their way across country to Palermo to settle a lawsuit. To our amazement, we saw these two dignified gentlemen standing in front of a clump of thistles and cutting off the tops with their sharp pocket knives. Carefully holding their prickly acquisitions by the finger tips, they pared the stalk and consumed the inner portion with great gusto, an operation which took them some time. Meanwhile we refreshed ourselves with some wine, undiluted for once, and some good bread. Our *vetturino* prepared some of this thistle pith for us, insisting that it was both healthy and refreshing, but to us it seemed as tasteless as the raw kohlrabi of Segesta.

On the way, 30 April

In the pleasant valley down which the S. Paolo river zigzags its course, the soil, a dark-red decomposed limestone, is twenty feet deep in places. The aloes had grown tall, the harvest looked good, though here and there spoiled by weeds and far behind the crops in the south of the island. Much fallow land, wide fields, an occasional small house and, except just below Castrogiovanni, no trees. Along the river banks, extensive pasture land crowded with enormous clumps of thistles. In the detritus of the river, more quartz, some plain, some like breccia.

Molimenti is a modern hamlet, with a good location on the bank of the S. Paolo and beautiful fields all round it. In this neighbourhood the wheat is ready for harvesting by the twentieth of May. The district shows as yet no trace of a volcanic character; even the river carries no volcanic detritus. The soil is a good mixture, rather heavy, and usually of a coffee-brown purplish colour. The mountains along the left bank of the river are limestone and sandstone. I was unable to examine the order of the strata, but undoubtedly the decomposition of these two rocks has contributed to the great and constant fertility of the valley. Shortly after leaving Molimenti, we saw peasants harvesting the flax.

1 *May*

Down this so diversely cultivated valley, destined by Nature to universal fertility, we rode in rather a gloomy mood because, in spite of all our hardships, we had not seen anything which was paintable. Kniep made one sketch of an interesting distant view, but the middle and foreground were so awful that he introduced into the latter an elegant group in the style of Poussin which cost him little trouble and transformed the drawing into a delightful little picture. I wonder how many 'Travels of a Painter' contain such half-truths.

In an effort to put us in a better temper, our muleteer had promised us good lodgings for this evening and actually brought us to a real inn which was built only a few years ago. As it is situated at just a day's journey from Catania, it must be welcome to any traveller. The accommodation was tolerable, and, after our twelve days' journey, we were able to make ourselves fairly comfortable at last. But, to our surprise, we found an inscription pencilled on the wall in a beautiful English script, which read:

Traveller, bound for Catania, whoever you may be, beware of staying at the Golden Lion; it is worse than falling into the clutches of the Cyclops, the Sirens and Scylla.

Though we fancied that the benevolent warning was probably a mythological exaggeration, we nevertheless made up our minds to give a wide berth to this fierce beast of a Golden Lion, so, when our muleteer asked us where we wanted to put up in Catania, we said: 'Anywhere, except at the Lion.' At this, he suggested that we might be satisfied with the place where he stabled his mules, though we would have to provide our own food, as we have done hitherto. So great was our wish to escape the jaws of the lion, that we readily agreed.

Near Hybla Maior, pieces of lava begin to appear which the stream has brought down from the north, and, on the far side of the ferry, limestone, mixed with particles of hornstone and lava, and hardened volcanic ash coated with a tufa of lime. The alluvial hills continue all the way to Catania; beside them and over them lie lava flows from Mount Etna. On our left we passed what was probably a crater. Here Nature shows her predilection for high colours and amuses herself by arraying the black-blue-grey lava in vivid yellow moss, red sedum, and a variety of purple flowers. Cacti and vines give evidence of meticulous cultivation. Lava everywhere, one enormous flow after another. Motta is a beautiful and imposing crag. The beans grow in tall bushes. The fields vary in quality; in some the soil is of good composition, in others very flinty.

Our *vetturino*, who had probably not seen this spring vegetation of the south-east coast for a long time, broke out into loud exclamations of joy at the beauty of the crops and asked us with complacent patriotism if we knew anything like it in our country. A girl with a pretty face and lovely figure – an old acquaintance of his – ran along beside his mule, chattering and spinning her thread at the same time. Now yellow flowers began to predominate. As we neared Misterbianco, cacti reappeared in the hedges, but entire hedges of these bizarre-shaped plants, each more beautiful than the last, appeared more frequently as we reached the outskirts of Catania.

It is no good denying that, as regards lodging, we found ourselves very badly off. Such fare as our muleteer could manage
was not of the best. A chicken boiled with rice is certainly not
to be despised, but an immoderate use of saffron made it as
yellow as it was inedible. Our sleeping-quarters were so uncomfortable that we seriously thought of having recourse again
to Hackert's leather bag. Early next morning, therefore, we had a
talk with our friendly host, who expressed his regrets at being
unable to provide us with better accommodation. 'But over there,'
he said, pointing to a large corner house across the street, 'you will
be well looked after and have every reason to be satisfied.' From
the look of the place, it promised well and we hurried over immediately. The proprietor was not at home, but an alert-looking
man, who introduced himself as a waiter, assigned us a pleasant
room next to a large sitting room and assured us that the
terms would be reasonable. We asked him, as we always do, for
precise details about the price of lodging, meals, wine, breakfast,
etc. Everything did sound very cheap, so we moved our few
belongings across the street and stowed them in the drawers of
the spacious gilded commodes. For the first time Kniep had a
chance to sort out his cardboard sheets and put his drawings in
order, while I did the same with my notes.

Feeling very happy about the rooms, we stepped out on to the
balcony to enjoy the view. When we had admired it long enough,
we were just turning to go back to our work when – lo and
behold ! – there above our heads, like a threat, was a big golden
lion. Our eyes met, and our smiles turned to laughter. From now
on we would be on constant watch lest one of the Homeric bogies
should suddenly appear out of some corner. But nothing of the
sort happened; all we found in the sitting room was a pretty
young woman playing with a two-year-old child. Our semi-
landlord told her in harsh tones to clear out at once. She had no
business there. 'Don't be so cruel,' she said, 'don't drive me away.
I cannot manage the child at home when you are not there.
Surely these gentlemen won't mind my soothing it in your

presence.' The husband would not leave it at that, but tried to
drive her away. The child stood in the doorway howling, so
that, in the end, we were obliged to beg that she be allowed to
stay where she was.

After the Englishman's warning, it didn't take a genius to see
through the comedy : we played the innocent greenhorns and he
played the loving father to perfection. Strangely enough, the
child seemed to like him better than the pretended mother;
probably, she had given it a pinch on the sly. When the man left
to take a letter of recommendation for us to the house chaplain
of Prince Biscari, she remained and, with the most innocent air
in the world, went on playing with the child till he returned to
report that the Abbé would come in person to show us round.

3 May

Early this morning, the Abbé, who had already come yesterday to pay his respects, arrived and took us to the palace, a
one-storey building on a high foundation. We first visited the
museum with its collection of marble and bronze statues, vases
and many other such-like antiquities.

We were fascinated by a torso of Jupiter, which I knew already
from a cast in Tischbein's studio, but which has greater merits
than one would guess from the cast. A member of the household
gave us the most essential historical information, and then we
moved on into a large, high-ceilinged room. The many chairs
along the walls indicated that it was sometimes used for large
social gatherings. We sat down, expecting a gracious reception.
Two ladies entered the salon and walked up and down its
whole length, engaged in lively conversation. When they noticed
us, the Abbé rose, we did the same, and we all bowed. I asked
who they were and was told that the younger one was the Princess, the older a noblewoman from Catania. We sat down again,
and the ladies continued to walk up and down like people in
a public square.

Next we were taken to the Prince, who showed us his collection of coins. This was a special mark of confidence, since, both in
his father's day and in his own, several objects were missing after

they had been shown to visitors, and he was now chary of showing them. I had learned a good deal from looking at Prince Torremuzza's collection, and added to my knowledge by reading
Winckelmann, whose book provides a reliable thread to guide us
through the various epochs of art, so this time I was able to do
much better. When he saw that, though amateurs not connoisseurs, we were observant, the Prince, who is an expert in these
matters, willingly explained to us everything we wanted to know.
After spending quite some time, though not enough, over these
objects, we were about to take our leave when he took us to his
mother's suite to see the rest of his smaller works of art.

There we were introduced to a distinguished-looking lady,
with an air of instinctive breeding, who received us with the
words: 'Look around, gentlemen; you will find everything just
as my dear husband arranged it. This I owe to the filial devotion
of my son, who not only allows me to live in his best rooms, but
also will not allow a single object in his father's collection to be
removed or displaced. In consequence I enjoy the double advantage of living in the fashion I have been accustomed to for so
long, and of making the acquaintance of eminent foreigners who,
as in former times, come here from far-off countries to look at
our treasures.'

With that she opened the glass cabinet in which the amber
collection was kept. What distinguishes Sicilian amber from the
northern kind is that it passes from the colour of transparent or
opaque wax or honey through all possible shades of yellow to a
most beautiful hyacinthine red. We were shown urns, cups and
other things which had been carved from it, and it was clear that
remarkably large pieces must have been needed. These, some
incised shells from Trapani and some exquisite ivories were the
lady's special pride and joy, and she had some amusing stories to
tell about them. The Prince pointed out the more important
things, and in this manner we spent some entertaining and instructive hours.

When the Dowager Princess realized we were Germans, she
asked us for news of von Riedesel, Bartels and Münter, all of
whom she knew, and spoke of their characters and activities with
great discrimination and affection. We were sorry to have to

leave her, and she appeared sorry to see us go. There is something lonely about the life of these islanders which needs to be refreshed and nourished by chance meetings with sympathetic persons.

We then went with the Abbé to the Benedictine monastery. We entered a cell and he introduced us to a middle-aged monk whose melancholy and reserved features did not promise a very cheerful conversation. He was, however, a gifted musician, the only monk who could master the enormous organ in their chapel. When he divined our wishes – one can't say he heard them – without a word he led us into the vast chapel and began to play the admirable instrument, filling the remotest corners with sounds that ranged from the gentlest whisper to the most powerful trumpet blasts.

If one had not already seen this man, one would have thought that such power could only be exercised by a giant; now, knowing his personality, we could only wonder that he had not, long ago, succumbed in such a struggle.

4 May

Soon after dinner, the Abbé came with a carriage to show us the remoter quarters of the city. Just as I was getting into the carriage, a curious *contretemps* occurred. I had climbed in first, meaning to sit on his left, but when he got in, he positively ordered me to move and let him sit on my left. I begged him not to stand on ceremony. 'Excuse me', he said, 'for insisting that we sit this way. If I sit on your right, people will think I am driving with *you*, but when I sit on your left, it is understood that you are driving with *me*, that is to say, that, in the name of the Prince, I am showing you the city.' I had no answer to that, so I let the matter rest.

We drove up the streets, where the lava which destroyed most of the city in 1669 has remained visible to this day. The solidified stream of fire had been used like any other stone; streets had been marked out on it and some even built. Remembering what passions had been aroused before I left Germany by the dispute over the volcanic nature of basalt, I chipped off a piece; it is magma without any doubt. I did this in several other places so as to obtain a variety of specimens.

If the native inhabitants did not love their part of the country and take the trouble, from scientific interest or in hope of gain, to collect everything of note in their local neighbourhoods, the foreigner would long rack his brains to no purpose. The lava dealer in Naples had been of great help to me and now I found a much superior guide in the person of the Cavaliere Gioeni. In his extensive and elegantly displayed collection, I found the lavas of Etna, the basalt from its foot and various metamorphosed rocks, some of which I could recognize. I was received most kindly and shown everything. What I liked best were the zeolites from the stacks which rise out of the sea off the coast near Jaci.

When we asked the Cavaliere how we should go about climbing Etna, he refused even to discuss an enterprise which was so hazardous, especially at this time of year. He apologized for this and said : ' Most foreign visitors are too apt to consider the ascent a trifling affair. But we, who are near neighbours of the mountain, are content if we have reached the summit twice or thrice in a lifetime, for we never attempt it except under ideal conditions. Brydone, whose description first inspired people with a longing for the fiery summit, never reached it himself. Count Borch leaves the reader in doubt, but he too only reached a certain altitude, and the same can be said of many others. At the present moment the snow stretches too far down and presents insurmountable obstacles. If you will follow my advice, ride early tomorrow morning to the foot of Monte Rosso : you will enjoy the most magnificent view and at the same time see the place where the lava of 1669 poured down on our unfortunate city. If you are wise, you will let others tell you about the rest.'

5 *May*

We took the Cavaliere's good advice and set off early this morning on mules, turning our heads every so often to look at the view behind us. After some time we reached the lava zone. Unsoftened by time, jagged clumps and slabs stared us in the face, and the mules could only pick their way at random. On the first high

ridge we halted and Kniep made a sketch of what lay ahead of us
– masses of lava in the foreground, the twin summits of Monte
Rosso on the left, and directly above us the forests of Nicolosi,
out of which the snow-covered and faintly fuming peak emerges.
We retraced our steps a little in order to approach Monte Rosso,
which I climbed. It is nothing but a heap of red volcanic cinders,
ashes and stones. It would have been easy to walk all round the
rim of the crater if a blustering morning wind had not made
every step unsafe; to advance at all, I tried taking off my over-
coat, but then my hat was in danger of being blown into the
crater at any moment and myself after it. I sat down to pull
myself together and survey the landscape, but this did not help
much, as the gale was blowing directly from the east. A magnificent panorama was spread out far and wide below me. The whole
coast from Messina to Syracuse with its curves and bays lay
open to my view or only slightly hidden by coastal hills. I descended, half dazed, to find Kniep sitting in a sheltered place
where he had made good use of his time. With delicate strokes
he had fixed on paper what the fury of the wind had hardly
allowed me to see, let alone imprint on my memory.

On re-entering the jaws of the Golden Lion, we found the
waiter. We had had great difficulty in preventing him from
accompanying us. He now commended our decision to abandon
the ascent of the peak, but kept pressing us to hire a boat the
next day and visit the stacks of Jaci. No more delightful an
excursion could be made from Catania. We would take food and
drink and cooking utensils with us. His wife would be only too
glad to take care of everything. He recalled the happy occasion
when some English people hired a second boat to accompany
them and play music. They had a hilarious time.

To me, the stacks of Jaci were a great temptation, for I was
dying to chip off for myself some of those beautiful zeolites I had
seen in Gioeni's collection. After all, we could decline his wife's
offer and still make a brief visit. But the Englishman's ghostly
warning triumphed; I gave up the zeolites and felt inordinately
proud of my self-control.

6 May

Our clerical guide did not fail us, but took us to see some ancient architectural remains, water tanks, a *naumachia* and other ruins of a similar sort.

These, to be honest, demand of the spectator a considerable talent for imaginative reconstruction. Owing to the frequent destruction of the city by lava, earthquake and war, they are sunk in the ground or completely buried, so that only a professional expert can derive any pleasure or instruction from them.

The Abbé dissuaded us from paying the Prince a second visit, and we parted with cordial expressions of mutual gratitude and good will.

Taormina, 7 May

Thank goodness, everything we saw today has been sufficiently described already. Furthermore, Kniep has decided to spend the whole day up here sketching.

After climbing the steep cliffs near the sea, one reaches two summits connected by a half-circle. Whatever shape it may have had originally, Art has assisted Nature to build this semicircle which held the amphitheatre audience. Walls and other structures of brick were added to provide the necessary passages and halls. The proscenium was built in a diagonal at the foot of the tiered half-circle, stretching from cliff to cliff to complete a stupendous work of Art and Nature.

If one sits down where the topmost specatators sat, one has to admit that no audience in any other theatre ever beheld such a view. Citadels stand perched on higher cliffs to the right; down below lies the town. Though these buildings are of a much later date, similar ones probably stood in the same places in older days. Straight ahead one sees the long ridge of Etna, to the left the coast line as far as Catania or even Syracuse, and the whole panorama is capped by the huge, fuming, fiery mountain, the look of which, tempered by distance and atmosphere, is, however, more friendly than forbidding.

If one turns round, beyond the passages which ran behind the spectators' backs one sees the two cliffs and, between them, the road winding its way to Messina, the sea dotted with rocks and reefs, and in the far distance the coast of Calabria. I had to strain my eyes to distinguish it from a bank of gently rising clouds.

We descended into the theatre and stayed for a while among the ruins, which a talented architect should attempt to restore, at least on paper.

When we tried to beat a downhill path for ourselves through the gardens into the town, we discovered what an impenetrable barrier a hedge of closely planted cacti can be. You look through gaps in the tangle of leaves and think you can make your way through them, but the prickly spikes on their edges are a painful obstacle; you step on a colossal leaf, expecting it to support you, but it collapses and you fall into the arms of the next plant. But we extricated ourselves from this labyrinth at last and had a quick meal in the town. We could not tear ourselves away until after sunset. To watch this landscape, so remarkable in every aspect, slowly sinking into the darkness, was an incredibly beautiful sight.

On the seashore below Taormina, 8 May

I cannot praise Kniep enough or the good fortune which sent him to me. He has relieved me of a burden which would have been intolerable and set me free to follow my natural bent. He has just left to sketch all that we saw yesterday. He will have to sharpen his pencils again and again, and I cannot imagine how he is going to finish the job. I might have seen it all again too, and at first I was tempted to go with him, but in the end decided to stay where I was. Like a bird that wants to build its nest, I searched for a cranny and perched myself on the branches of an orange tree in a mean, abandoned peasant's garden. It may sound a bit strange to speak of sitting *on* the branch of an orange tree, but it is quite natural if you know that, when an orange tree is left to itself, it starts putting out branches above its roots which in time become real boughs.

There I was soon lost in fancy, thinking about a plot for my

*Nausicaa,** a dramatic condensation of the *Odyssey*. I think this can be done, provided one never loses sight of the difference between a drama and an epic.

Kniep has come back in high spirits with two enormous drawings which he is going to elaborate for me in everlasting memory of this wonderful day.

I must not forget to mention that we are looking down from a small terrace, looking over this beautiful seashore, seeing roses and hearing nightingales, which, we are told, sing for six months without stopping.

IN RETROSPECT

Thanks to the companionship and activity of a talented artist and to my own humble and sporadic efforts, I knew that, after this trip was over, I would possess permanent records of it in the form of sketches and finished drawings of all the most interesting landscapes. Consequently, I was all the more ready to yield to a desire of mine which had been growing ever stronger: namely, to take the magnificent scenery which surrounded me, the sea, the islands, the harbours, and bring it to life in noble poetic images, to compose in their presence and out of them a more homogenous and harmonious work than any I had written before.

The purity of the sky, the tang of the sea air, the haze which, as it were, dissolved mountains, sky and sea into one element – all these were food for my thoughts. As I wandered about in the beautiful Public Gardens of Palermo, between hedges and oleander, through orange trees and lemon trees heavy with fruit, and other trees and bushes unknown to me, I took this blessed strangeness to my heart. There could be no better commentary on the *Odyssey*, I felt, than just this setting. I bought a copy and read it with passionate interest. It fired me with the desire to produce a work of my own, and very soon I could think of nothing else: in other words, I became obsessed with the idea of treating the story of Nausicaa as a tragedy.

I cannot say now what I would have made of it, but I quickly

---

*One act and some fragments of *Nausicaa* were published in 1827.

had the plot clearly worked out in my mind. Its essence was this: to present Nausicaa as an admirable young woman with many suitors, but no inclination towards any one of them, so that she has refused them all. This indifference is overcome by a mysterious stranger whom she meets, and she compromises herself by a premature declaration of her love, a tragic situation in the highest sense.

A wealth of secondary motives was to have added interest to this simple fable, and there was to have been a sea-island quality about the imagery and atmosphere to give a pervading tone to the whole play.

The action, as I planned it, was to have gone as follows:

Act I. Nausicaa is playing with a ball with her maids. The unexpected encounter takes place. Her hesitation about accompanying the stranger personally into the city is the first sign that she feels drawn towards him.

Act II. The palace of Alcinous. The characters of the suitors are revealed. The act ends with the entrance of Ulysses.

Act III. The importance of the adventurer is brought out. I planned to produce an interesting artistic effect with a narration in dialogue of his adventures. Each listener responds to this with a different emotion. As the narration proceeds, passions run higher, and the strong attraction which Nausicaa feels for the stranger is at last revealed in action and counter-action.

Act IV. Off stage, Ulysses gives proof of his prowess, while on stage, the women give free expression to their sympathies, hopes and tender sentiments. Nausicaa cannot control her feelings and compromises herself irrevocably before her own people. Ulysses, the half guilty, half innocent cause of this, is finally forced to announce his determination to depart.

Act V. Nothing is left for the good girl but to kill herself.

There was nothing in this composition which I could not have drawn from life. I too was a wanderer; I too was in danger of arousing sympathies which, though not perhaps of the kind which end in tragedy, could still be painful and destructive; I too was far from my native land, in circumstances where one entertains an audience with glowing descriptions of distant objects, adventures while travelling, incidents in one's life;

where one is considered a demigod by the young and a braggart by the sedate; where one experiences many an undeserved favour, many an unexpected obstacle. It was facts like these which gave the plot its particular fascination for me. I spent all my days in Palermo and most of the time I was travelling through Sicily dreaming about it. On this classic soil I felt in such a poetic mood that I hardly suffered from all the discomforts, but could take in all I saw and experienced and enshrine it in my heart for ever.

As is my good or bad habit, I wrote down little or nothing but worked out most of it in detail in my head. Later a hundred distractions prevented me from going on with it, until, today, I can only recall it as a fleeting memory.

8 May. On the way to Messina

On our left we have high limestone cliffs. As we go on, they become more colourful and form beautiful coves. A type of rock appears which one might call a schist or a conglomerate. In the brooks we begin to find particles of granite. The river Nisi and the brooks further on carry mica. The yellow apples of solanum and the red blossoms of the oleander strike a cheerful note in the landscape.

9 May

Struggling against a strong east wind, we rode between the surging sea on our right and the cliffs from which we looked down yesterday on our left. All day we battled with water. We crossed numerous brooks, the largest of which, the Nisi, bears the honorary title of river; but all these were easier to deal with than the raging sea, which in many places swept across the road, dashed against the cliffs and doused us as it receded. But the magnificence of the spectacle made up for the discomfort.

There was no lack of geological interest. Weathering causes enormous rockfalls from the limestone cliffs. The softer parts of these are ground away by the action of the waves and only the more solid conglomerates are left on the beach, which is covered with colourful pebbles of iron pyrites. We picked up several specimens.

Messina, 10 May

We arrived in Messina and, since we did not know of any other place to stay, we agreed to pass the first night in the quarters of our *vetturino*, with the understanding that we would look for better accommodation in the morning. The immediate result of this decision was that we got a terrifying picture of a devastated city.* For a good quarter of an hour we rode on our mules through ruin after ruin till we came to our inn. This was the only house which had been rebuilt, and from its upper floor we looked out over a wasteland of jagged ruins. Outside the premises of this sort of farmstead, there was no sign of man or beast. The silence during the night was uncanny. The doors could neither be locked nor barred, and there was as little provision for human guests as in any other stable.

In spite of this, we slept peacefully on the innkeeper's mattress, which our *vetturino*, efficient as ever, had wheedled him into surrendering.

11 May

Today we bade farewell to our valiant *vetturino* and rewarded him for his conscientious services with a liberal gratuity. We parted in friendship, after he had found us a local factotum who was to take us at once to the best inn and show us the sights of Messina. Our host of last night was eager to get rid of us as quickly as possible and lent a helping hand with the transport of our baggage to a pleasant lodging nearer the living part of the city, that is to say, outside it. After the enormous disaster in which twelve thousand people were killed, there were no houses left in Messina for the remaining thirty thousand. Most of the buildings had collapsed and the cracked walls of the rest made them unsafe. So a barrack town was hastily erected in a large meadow north of the city. To get a picture of this, imagine

---

*Messina had been destroyed by an earthquake in 1783.

yourself walking across the *Römerberg* in Frankfurt or the market square in Leipzig during the Fair. All the booths and workshops are open to the street. Only a few of the larger buildings have entrances which can be closed, and even these rarely are, because those who live in them spend most of their time out of doors. They have been living under these conditions for three years now, and this life in shacks, huts and tents, even, has had a definite influence on their characters. The horror of that tremendous event, the fear of its repetition, drive them to take their delight in the pleasures of the moment. The dread of a new catastrophe was revived about three weeks ago, on April the twenty-first, when a noticeable tremor shook the grounds. We were shown a little church which was crowded with people at the time. A number of them, it is said, have not yet recovered from the shock.

A kindly consul volunteered to take care of us and acted as our guide; and, in a world of ruins, this was something to be grateful for. When he heard that we wished to sail soon, he introduced us to the captain of a French merchant vessel, who was about to sail for Naples – an opportunity which was doubly desirable, because the white flag would be a protection against pirates.

We had just been telling our guide that we would like to see the interior of one of the larger single-storey barracks, and get a picture of the furnishings and improvised way of life, when we were joined by a friendly man who introduced himself as a teacher of French. After we had finished our walk, the consul told him of our wish and asked him to show us his house and introduce us to his family.

We entered the hut, which was built and roofed with planks. It looked exactly like one of those booths at a fair, where wild animals and other curiosities are exhibited for money. The timberwork was visible and a green curtain separated off the front part, which had no flooring but seemed to have been beaten flat like a threshing floor. A few chairs and tables were the only furniture, and the only light came through chance chinks in the boards. We talked for a while and I was looking at the green curtain and the rafters above it when, all of a sudden, the heads of two pretty girls with black curls and inquisitive black eyes appeared from behind the curtain. When they saw they had been observed, they vanished in a flash, but, at the consul's request, they reappeared as soon as they had had time to get properly dressed. With their graceful figures and colourful dresses, they looked very elegant against the green curtain. From their questions it was easy to guess that they took us for legendary beings from another world, and our answers only confirmed them in their endearing delusion. The consul painted an amusing picture of our fabulous appearance in Messina. The conversation was very pleasant and we found it hard to leave. It wasn't till we had closed the door behind us that we realized we had never seen the inner rooms, for our interest in the construction of the hut had been driven out of our minds by the charm of its inhabitants.

12 *May*

The consul told me, among other things, that it would be expedient, if not absolutely necessary, for me to pay my respects to the Governor, because he was an odd old man who was capable of doing others a lot of good or a lot of harm, depending upon his mood or his prejudice. The consul would get into his good graces by introducing an eminent foreign visitor, and the visitor could never know when he might not need the support of such a personage in some way or other. So, to oblige my friend, I went.

When we came into the antechamber, we heard a tremendous racket going on in the room beyond. A runner, gesticulating like a Pulcinella, whispered in the consul's ear: 'An evil day! A dangerous moment!' Nevertheless, we entered and found the aged Governor sitting at a table near the window with his back to us. Before him was a pile of old letters and documents, from which he was cutting off the blank sheets with great deliberation, demonstrating thereby his love of economy. While engaged in this peaceful occupation he was bawling horrible insults and curses at a respectable-looking man who, to judge from his clothes, might have some connexion with the Knights of Malta. He defended himself quietly but firmly, though he was given little opportunity to speak.

The Governor apparently regarded him as a suspicious person, because he had entered and left the country several times without the necessary permit. In refutation of this, he produced his passports and spoke of his well-known position in Naples, but it did no good. The Governor went on cutting up his old letters, carefully putting the blank sheets on one side, and stormed away without stopping for breath. Besides the two of us, there were some twelve persons there, standing in a wide circle and witnessing this combat of beasts. They probably envied us our advantageous position near the door, for it looked as if at any moment, the irascible old man might raise his crooked stick and strike out. The consul's face fell; but I was comforted by the droll runner beside me, who, every time I looked round, pulled all kinds of faces to reassure me that matters were not very serious.

And indeed, the violent argument was finally settled quite mildly, with the Governor declaring that, though there was nothing to prevent him from arresting the accused and letting him cool his heels in prison, he had decided to let him go this time. He might stay in Messina for a certain number of days, but he was never to return. Without moving a muscle of his face, the accused took his leave, and bowed to all those present, and especially to us, who had to make way for him as he went out by the door. The Governor turned and was about to shout some more abuse after him, when he became aware of our presence. He controlled himself immediately, made a sign to the consul, and we both approached.

We saw a man of advanced years, who kept his head bent, but looked out with penetrating dark eyes from under his grey and bushy eyebrows. He now looked a very different person from what he had the moment before. He invited me to sit down beside him and, without interrupting his occupation, asked me a number of questions, which I did my best to answer. Finally he said that, as long as I stayed in Messina, I was invited to be a guest at his table. The consul was even more pleased than I was, since he knew better what danger we had escaped. He flew down the stairs, and I had lost all desire to venture a second time into this lion's den.

13 *May*

We woke on a clear sunny morning and in much pleasanter lodgings, but we still found ourselves in this accursed city.

There can be no more dreary sight in the world than the so-called Palazzata, a crescent of palazzi which encloses about a mile of the harbour waterfront. Originally they were all four-storey stone buildings. Several façades are still intact up to the coping; in other cases one, two or three floors have collapsed, so that this string of once splendid palazzi now looks revoltingly gap-toothed and pierced with holes, for the blue sky looks through nearly all the windows. The rooms inside are all in ruins.

There is a reason for this. The grandiose project was begun by the rich. The less well-to-do wished their houses to look as impressive from the street, so they concealed their old houses, which were built of rubble cemented with lime, behind new façades of quarried stone blocks. Such structures were unsafe in any case, and when there was an earthquake, they were bound to collapse. There are many stories of miraculous escapes which illustrate this. An inhabitant of one such building, for example, at the very moment of the catastrophe had just stepped into the deep enclosure of a window. The whole house collapsed behind him, but he was left safe and sound up there, waiting to be liberated from his airy prison.

That it was shoddy building, due to the lack of decent stone in the neighbourhood, which was the main reason for the almost total destruction of the city, is confirmed by the fact that the few buildings which were solidly constructed survived. The Jesuit college and church, which were built of quarried stone, are still intact. Be that as it may, Messina is a very disagreeable sight and reminded me of that primitive age when Sicels and Siculians quitted this unquiet soil to settle on the west coast of the island.

We spent the whole morning looking round, then went to our inn and ate a frugal meal. We were still sitting there together, feeling very content, when the consul's servant rushed in and breathlessly informed me that the Governor had sent people to hunt for me all over the city because he had invited me to dinner and I had failed to come. The consul, he said, implored me to go immediately, regardless of whether I had dined or not, or forgotten the hour or ignored it on purpose. Now I realized how incredibly reckless of me it had been, in my joy at escaping the first time, to dismiss from my mind the Cyclops' invitation.

The servant would brook no delay and his argument was urgent and convincing: the despot would take his fury out on the consul and any of his fellow countrymen who might be staying in Messina. I made myself tidy, plucked up my courage and followed my guide, secretly invoking Odysseus, my patron, and asking him to intercede for me with Pallas Athene. When I arrived at the lion's den, the comical runner I had seen the first time took me into a large banquet hall where about forty people were sitting at an oval table in absolute silence. He led me to an empty chair on the Governor's right. After bowing to my host and his guests, I gave as my excuse for failing to arrive on time the vast size of the city and the local method of counting the hours to which I was not yet accustomed and had been several times misled by. The Governor glared at me and said that in a foreign country one should learn its local customs and behave accordingly. I parried this by saying that I always tried to learn them, but it had been my experience that in a new place and unfamiliar circumstances one was apt, with the best will in the world, to make mistakes, for which one could only plead in excuse the fatigue of travelling, the distraction of seeing so many new things, and the preoccupation with finding decent lodging or making preparations for the next stage of one's journey. He asked me how long I intended to stay in Messina. 'I should like,' I replied, 'to stay a very long time, so that I might show my gratitude for your kindness by an exact observance of all your orders and regulations.' After a pause, he asked what I had actually seen in Messina. I gave him a brief account of this morning and added that what I had admired most of all was the tidiness and cleanliness of the streets. This was true. The rubble had been piled up within the areas enclosed by the ruined walls and a row of stone blocks set up against the houses to keep the middle of the streets free and open to traffic. Nor was it a lie when I flattered the worthy man by telling him that all the inhabitants of Messina gratefully admitted that they owed this benefit to him. 'Do they admit it?' he growled. 'They have yelled long enough about the severity of the measures we were forced to take for their own good.' Then I talked about the wise forethought of the government, of those higher purposes which are only recognized and appreciated later, and so forth. He asked if I had seen the Jesuit church and, when I said no, proposed to let me see it and everything it contained.

During our conversation, which went on with hardly a pause, I observed that the rest of the company were sitting in utter silence and without moving except to put food into their mouths. And so they remained. When dinner was over and coffee served, they stood along the walls like wax dolls. I went up to the chaplain who was to show me the church, and tried to thank him in advance for his kind offices; but he was evasive and said that he was only carrying out His Excellency's orders. Then I addressed a young foreigner standing next to him. Although he was a Frenchman, he too seemed ill at ease and was as petrified and speechless as all the others, among whom I recognized several who had anxiously looked on at yesterday's scene with the Maltese Knight.

The Governor left, and soon after the chaplain said it was time for us to go. I followed him while the others sneaked silently away. He brought me to the west door of the Jesuit church, which, in the familiar architectural style adopted by these fathers, soars into the air with impressive pomp. We were received by the verger, who invited us to enter, but the chaplain stopped me, saying we must wait for the Governor. Presently the latter arrived in his coach, which drew up in a neighbouring square. He beckoned to us and the three of us joined him at the door of the coach. He ordered the verger, not only to show me every part of the church, but also to give me a detailed history of the altars and other donations; further, he was to unlock the sacristies and show me everything of interest which they contained. I was a man, he said, whom he wished to honour, so that I might have good reason, when I got home, to speak of Messina in the highest

terms. Then, turning to me with a smile – in so far as those
features were capable of one – he said: 'Be sure to appear at
dinner at the proper hour, and you will be welcome so long as
you are here.' I hardly had time to thank him with proper respect before his coach rolled away.

From now on the chaplain became more cheerful and we
entered the church. The castellan, as one may be permitted to
call him in this deconsecrated, enchanted palace, had just begun
to carry out the orders he had been so peremptorily given,
when Kniep and the consul rushed into the empty shrine and
embraced me with loud exclamations of joy at seeing me again,
for they thought I must have been arrested. They had been waiting in mortal anxiety when the nimble runner, amply rewarded
no doubt by the consul, came to tell them of the happy ending to
my adventure. The antics and gestures with which he told the
story had cheered them up immensely. After hearing of the
Governor's courtesy with regard to the church, they had set off
at once to look for me.

By this time we were standing in front of the high altar, while
the ancient treasures were explained to us. Columns of lapis
lazuli, fluted, as it were, with gilded bronze bars; pilasters and
panels, inlaid after the Florentine manner; superb Sicilian agates
in profusion – everything combined again and again with bronze
and gilt.

Now a strange contrapuntal fugue began, with Kniep and the
consul reciting the complications caused by my adventure on the
one side, and the verger reciting the history of the treasures on
the other, each party engrossed in its subject and ignoring its
rival. For my part, I had the twofold pleasure of feeling how
lucky my escape had been, and of seeing the minerals of Sicily,
which I had so often examined in the mountains they came from,
employed for an architectural purpose.

My knowledge of the various substances out of which this
splendour was composed helped me to discover that the so-called
lapis lazuli of the columns was actually only calcara, but of a
beautiful colour I had never seen before, and assembled with
superb skill. A great quantity of this material must have been
needed in order to select pieces of uniform colour, not to men-

tion the highly important labour of cutting, grinding and polishing. But to the Jesuits, was anything impossible?

The consul continued to enlighten me about the danger with which I had been threatened: the Governor was annoyed with himself because, at my first visit, I had witnessed his violent behaviour towards the quasi-Maltese. He had therefore made up his mind to show me special honour, but, by failing to appear at dinnertime, I had upset his plan at the very outset. After waiting quite a time, the despot had sat down at his table without concealing his impatience and displeasure, so that his guests were in terror of having to assist at another scene, either when I appeared or after dinner.

Meanwhile the verger was trying to get a word in edgewise. He opened the secret repositories, which were well proportioned and tastefully, even ornately, decorated, where several portable sacred vessels were kept, shapely and polished like everything else. I could see no precious metal or any works of art from ancient or modern times that were authentic.

Our Italian–German fugue – the chaplain and verger psalmodizing in the first tongue, Kniep and the consul in the second – was drawing to a close, when we were joined by a member of the Governor's suite whom I had seen at the dinner table. This looked like more trouble, especially when he offered to accompany me to the port and show me some points of interest which were normally inaccessible to strangers.

My friends exchanged glances, but I was not going to let myself be deterred from going off alone with him. After some trivial conversation, I began to speak more confidentially. When I was sitting at the Governor's table. I told him, I had not failed to notice that several members of the silent guests were trying, with friendly signs, to assure me that I was not a stranger among strangers, but among friends, even perhaps among brothers,* and had nothing to worry about. 'I consider it my duty,' I said, 'to thank you and I beg you to convey my gratitude to the others.' He replied: 'We tried to reassure you because, knowing the temperament of our master, we were fairly certain you had nothing

---

* Brothers, i.e. Freemasons. Goethe was one.

to fear. An explosion like that with the Maltese is very rare. After one, the old man usually blames himself, watches his temper and is content to perform the duties of his office calmly and coolly, until some unexpected incident takes him by surprise, and he explodes again.'

My honest companion added that nothing would please him and his friends better than to make my closer acquaintance. I would therefore oblige them if I would reveal my identity, and this evening would be an excellent opportunity. I politely evaded this request by asking him to forgive what must seem to him a caprice, but, on my travels, I wished to be treated simply as a human being; if, as such, I could inspire confidence and gain sympathy, it would make me very happy, but many reasons forbade me from entering into other relations.

I did not try very hard to convince him, for I did not dare tell him my real reason. I was interested to learn, though, how under a despotic government men of innocence and good will had banded together for the protection of foreigners and themselves. I did not hide from him the fact that I knew much about their relations with other German travellers, and I spoke at length about the laudable goals at which they aimed. He grew more and more puzzled at this mixture of confidence and reserve and tried in every possible way to make me lift my incognito. He did not succeed, partly because, having escaped one danger, I had no intention of needlessly exposing myself to another, and partly because I knew very well that the ideas of these honest islanders were so different from mine that a closer acquaintance would afford them neither pleasure nor consolation.

This evening we spent several hours with the sympathetic consul who has helped me so much. He explained how the scene with the Maltese had come about. Though not actually an adventurer, this man was a rolling stone. The Governor came from a great family, and his ability and achievements were highly respected and appreciated; on the other hand, he had a reputation for unlimited caprice, violent temper and an adamant obstinacy. A despot by nature, and full of suspicions, as old men often are, he hated the sort of person who keeps moving from place to place, and believed they were all simply spies. The 'red-coat' had crossed his path just at a time when, after a considerable period of calm, he felt the need to lose his temper in order to relieve his liver.

Messina, and at sea, 13 May

We both woke with the same feeling: we were cross with ourselves for having let our first disagreeable impression of Messina make us so impatient to depart that we were now committed to the captain of the French merchant vessel. After the lucky outcome of my adventure with the Governor, my meeting with the upright man to whom I would only have had to make myself known, and a visit to my banker, who was living in the country in very pleasant surroundings, I had every reason to believe I would have enjoyed myself if I had arranged to stay longer. As for Kniep, he had made the acquaintance of some pretty girls, and was praying that the unfavourable wind, normally so odious, would go on blowing as long as possible.

Meanwhile we sat in discomfort; we could not unpack anything because we had to be ready to leave at any moment. Before noon the summons came and we hurried on board. Among the crowd gathered on the shore, we found our good consul and said goodbye to him with grateful hearts. The yellow-coated runner also pressed forward to get his *douceur*. I gave it him and instructed him to inform his master of our departure and apologize for my absence from his table. 'He who sails away is excused,' he cried, turned a somersault and disappeared.

As we moved slowly away from the shore, we were entranced by the wonderful view – the cresent-shaped Palazzata, the citadel, the mountains rising behind the city. On the other side of the straits we could see the shore of Calabria. While we were enjoying the unlimited vistas, we noticed a commotion on the water at some distance to our left and, somewhat nearer on our right, a rock rising out of the sea; one was Charybdis, the other Scylla. Because of the considerable distance in nature between these two objects which the poet has placed so close to one another, people have accused poets of fibbing. What they fail to take into account is that the human imagination always pictures the objects it considers significant as taller and narrower than they really are, for this gives them more character, importance and dignity. A thousand times I have heard people complain that some object they had known only from a description was disappointing when seen in reality, and the reason was always the same. Imagination is to reality what poetry is to prose : the former will always think of objects as massive and vertical, the latter will always try to extend them horizontally. The landscape painters of the sixteenth century, when contrasted with those of our own times, offer the most striking example of this. A drawing by Jodokus Momper set beside a sketch by Kniep would illustrate the difference perfectly. We spent the time talking about such matters, since, even for Kniep, the coastlines were not attractive enough to draw, though he had come prepared to do so.

Our boat was very different from the Neapolitan corvette. I was beginning to feel seasick and my condition was not relieved by a comfortable privacy as it had been on our previous passage. However, the common cabin was at least large enough to hold several people and there were plenty of good mattresses. As before, I assumed a horizontal position, while Kniep looked after me and fed me with red wine and good bread. In the condition I was in, our whole Sicilian trip did not present itself to me in a very rosy light. After all, what had we seen but the hopeless struggle of men with the violence of Nature, the malice and treachery of their times, and the rancours of their own rival factions. The Carthaginians, the Greeks, the Romans, and countless peoples after them built and destroyed. Selinunt was systematically laid waste. Two thousand years have not succeeded in demolishing the temples of Girgenti; Cantania and Messina were destroyed in a few hours, if not a few minutes.

But I did not allow myself to become too much obsessed with these seasick reflections of a person tossed about by the waves of life.

At sea, 13 May

My hopes that the voyage would be quicker this time and that I would recover from my seasickness sooner did not materialize.

At Kniep's suggestion, I tried several times to go on deck, but any enjoyment of the beautiful scenes was denied; only an occasional incident made me forget my dizziness. The sky was overcast with a haze of white clouds. Though we could not see the face of the sun, its light filtered through the haze and lit up the sea, which was an unimaginable blue. We were accompanied all the time by a school of dolphins, swimming and leaping. To them, evidently, from below and from a distance, our floating house appeared as a black point, which they took for prey or some other welcome food. The crew, at any rate, treated them as enemies, not escorts; they harpooned one, but did not haul it on board.

The wind remained unfavourable and our boat had constantly to change its course. The passengers were growing impatient, and some of the more knowledgeable declared that neither the captain nor the helmsman knew his job, that the former might do well as a merchant and the latter as a simple sailor, but neither was qualified to guarantee the safety of so many valuable lives and goods.

I begged these people, who no doubt meant well, to keep their misgivings a secret. The number of passengers was considerable and among them were women and children of various ages. Everybody had crowded aboard the French vessel with only one thought in their minds – the white flag would protect them against pirates. I warned the grumblers that their mistrust and alarm, if known, would cause great distress to those who had so far put their trust in a colourless piece of cloth without any insignia.

As a specific talisman, this white pennon between sky and sea is very curious. On occasions of departure, those who are leaving and those who are left behind wave to each other with white handkerchiefs, evoking by this sign mutual feelings of friendship and affection which are seldom felt so deeply as at the moment of separation. Here, in this simple flag, the basic idea behind this symbol is hallowed. It is as if someone should fix his handkerchief to the mast to proclaim to the whole world that a friend is coming across the sea.

From time to time I refreshed myself with bread and wine – to the annoyance of the captain, who demanded that I should eat what I had paid for. I was able at last to sit on deck and occasionally take part in the conversation. Kniep succeeded in cheering me up, not, as on the corvette, by boasting of the excellent meals, but by telling me how lucky I was to have lost my appetite.

14 May

The afternoon passed without our having entered the Gulf of Naples. On the contrary, we were steadily drawn in a westerly direction; the boat moved further and further away from Cape Minerva and nearer and nearer to Capri.

Everybody was glum and impatient, except Kniep and myself. Looking at the world with the eyes of painters, we were perfectly content to enjoy the sunset, which was the most magnificent spectacle we had seen during the whole voyage. Cape Minerva and its adjoining ranges lay before us in a display of brilliant colours. The cliffs stretching to the south had already taken on a bluish tint. From the Cape to Sorrento the whole coast was lit up. Above Vesuvius towered an enormous smoke cloud, from which a long streak trailed away to the east, suggesting that a violent eruption was in progress. Capri rose abruptly on our left and, through the haze, we could see the outlines of its precipices.

The wind had dropped completely, and the glittering sea, showing scarcely a ripple, lay before us like a limpid pond under the cloudless sky. Kniep said what a pity it was that no skill with colours, however great, could reproduce this harmony and that not even the finest English pencils, wielded by the most practised hand, could draw these contours. I was convinced, on the contrary, that even a much poorer memento than this able artist would produce would be very valuable in the future, and urged him to make an attempt at it. He followed my advice and produced a most accurate drawing which he later coloured, which shows that pictorial representation can achieve the impossible.

With equally rapt attention we watched the transition from evening to night. Ahead of us Capri was now in total darkness. The cloud above Vesuvius and its trail began to glow, and the longer we looked the brighter it grew, till a considerable part of the sky was lit up as if by summer lightning.

We had been so absorbed in enjoying these sights that we had not noticed that we were threatened with a serious disaster; but the commotion among the passengers did not leave us long in doubt. Those who had more experience of happenings at sea than we bitterly blamed the captain and his helmsman, saying that, thanks to their incompetence, they had not only missed the entrance to the straits but were now endangering the lives of the passengers, the cargo and everything else confided to their care. We asked why they were so anxious, for we did not see why there could be any cause to be afraid when the sea was so calm. But it was precisely the calm which worried them: they saw we had already entered the current which encircles Capri and by the peculiar wash of the waves draws everything slowly and irresistibly towards the sheer rock face, where there is no ledge to offer the slightest foothold and no bay to promise safety.

The news appalled us. Though the darkness prevented us from seeing the approaching danger, we could see that the boat, rolling and pitching, was moving nearer to the rocks, which loomed ever darker ahead. A faint afterglow was still spread over the sea. Not the least breath of wind was stirring. Everyone held up handkerchiefs and ribbons, but there was no sign of the longed-for breeze. The tumult among the passengers grew louder and louder. The women and children knelt on the deck or lay huddled together, not in order to pray, but because the deck space was too cramped to let them move about. The men, with their thoughts ever on help and rescue, raved, and stormed against the captain. They now attacked him for everything they had silently criticized during the whole voyage – the miserable accommodation, the outrageous charges, the wretched food and his behaviour. Actually, he had not been unkind, but very reserved; he had never explained his actions to anyone and even last night he had maintained a stubborn silence about his manoeuvres. Now they called him and his helmsman mercenary adventurers who knew nothing about navigation, but had got hold of a boat out of sheer greed, and were now by their incompetent bungling about to bring to grief the lives of all those in their care. The captain remained silent and still seemed to be preoccupied with saving the boat. But I, who all my life have hated anarchy worse than death, could keep silent no longer. I stepped forward and addressed the crowd, with almost the same equanimity I had shown in facing the 'Birds' of Malcesine. I pointed out to them that, at such a moment, their shouting would only confuse the ears and minds of those upon whom our safety depended, and make it impossible for them to think or communicate with one another. 'As for you,' I exclaimed, 'examine your hearts and then say your prayers to the Mother of God, for she alone can decide whether she will intercede with her Son, that He may do for you what He once did for His apostles on the storm-swept sea of Tiberias. Our Lord was sleeping, the waves were already breaking into the boat, but when the desperate and helpless men woke Him, He immediately commanded the wind to rest, and now, if it should be His will, He can command the wind to stir.'

These words had an excellent effect. One woman, with whom I had had some conversation about moral and spiritual matters, exclaimed : 'Ah, il Barlamè. Benedetto il Barlamè,' * and as they were all on their knees anyway, they actually began to say their litanies with more than usual fervour. They could do this with greater peace of mind, because the crew were now trying another expedient, which could at least be seen and understood by all. They lowered the pinnace, which could hold from six to eight men, fastened it to the ship by a long rope, and tried, by rowing hard, to tow the ship after them. But their very efforts seemed to increase the counter-pull of the current. For some reason or other, the pinnace was suddenly dragged backwards towards the ship and the long towing rope described a bow like a whiplash when the driver cracks it. So this hope vanished.

Prayers alternated with lamentations and the siuation grew more desperate, when some goatherds on the rocks above us whose fires we had seen for some time shouted with hollow voices that there was a ship below about to founder. Much that they cried was unintelligible, but some passengers, familiar with

---

*Il Barlamè. Probably St Barlaam, a figure in a Byzantine legend.

their dialect, took these cries to mean that they were gleefully looking forward to the booty they would fish out of the sea the next morning. Any consoling doubt as to whether our ship was really dangerously near the rocks was soon banished when we saw the sailors taking up long poles with which, if the worst came to the worst, they could keep fending the ship off the rocks. Of course, if the poles broke, all would be lost. The violence of the surf seemed to be increasing, the ship tossed and rolled more than ever; as a result, my seasickness returned and I had to retire to the cabin below. I lay down half dazed but with a certain feeling of contentment, due, perhaps, to the sea of Tiberias; for, in my mind's eye, I saw clearly before me the etching from the Merian Bible.* It gave me proof that all impressions of a sensory-moral nature are strongest when a man is thrown completely on his own resources.

How long I had been lying in this kind of half-sleep I could not tell, but I was roused out of it by a tremendous noise over my head. My ears told me that it came from dragging heavy ropes about the deck, and this gave me some hope that the sails were being hoisted. Shortly afterwards Kniep came down in a hurry to tell me we were safe. A very gentle breeze had sprung up; they had just been struggling to hoist the sails, and he himself had not neglected to lend a hand. We had, he said, visibly moved away from the cliff, and, though we were not yet completely out of the current, there was hope now of escaping from it. On deck everything was quiet again. Presently, several other passengers came to tell me about the lucky turn of events and to lie down themselves.

When I woke on the fourth day of our voyage, I felt refreshed and well, just as I had after the same period during the passage from Naples; so that even on a longer voyage I would probably have paid my tribute with an indisposition lasting three days.

From the upper deck I was pleased to see that the dangerous island was a considerable distance away, and that the course of our ship promised us an entrance into the Gulf, and this soon

---

* A folio Bible after Luther, illustrated by the Swiss engraver Matthaeus Merian (1627).

happened. After such a trying night, we could now admire the same objects in the morning light which had previously delighted us at sunset. Capri had been left behind and the right coast of the Gulf was close ahead of us. We could see the citadels, the town, with Posillipo to the left and the headlands which thrust out into the sea between Procida and Ischia. All the passengers had come on deck. In the foreground there stood a Greek priest, who must have been biased in favour of his native Orient, for when the Neapolitans, who had enthusiastically greeted their glorious homeland, asked him what he thought of Naples compared with Constantinople, he replied in a sad, homesick tone: 'Anche questa è una città! – This is a city, too.'

In due time we arrived in the harbour, which was buzzing with people as it was the liveliest time of the day. Our trunks and gear had just been unloaded and were standing on the shore, when two porters grabbed them. We had scarcely told them we would be staying at Moriconi's before they ran off with the load as if it were loot, and we had some difficulty keeping track of them through the crowded streets and across the square. Kniep carried his portfolio under his arm so that the drawings at least would be saved if the porters robbed us of all which the surging waves had spared.

NAPLES

17 *May*

HERE I am again, dear friends, safe and sound. My journey across Sicily was quick and easy, and when I get home, you shall judge for yourselves how well I have used my eyes. My old habit of sticking to the objective and concrete has given me an ability to read things at sight, so to speak, and I am happy to think that I now carry in my soul a picture of Sicily, that unique and beautiful island, which is clear, authentic and complete. There is nothing else I want to see in the south, especially since yesterday, when I revisited Paestum, the last vision I shall take with me on my way north, and perhaps the greatest. The central temple is, in my opinion, better than anything Sicily has left to show.

The sea and the islands gave me both joy and pain. I am satisfied with the results of my journey, but I must save the details for my return. Even in Naples, I find it impossible to collect my thoughts, though I hope I shall be able now to give you a better description of this city than I did in my earlier letters. On the first of June, unless a higher power prevents me, I shall go to Rome, and at the beginning of July, I plan to leave again. I must see you as soon as possible and am counting the days till we meet. I have accumulated a good deal of material and need the leisure to sort it out and work on it.

I am infinitely grateful to you for all your affection and kindness and all you have done for my writings. We may not see eye to eye on everything, but in all important matters our ways of thinking are as alike as it is possible for two people's to be. If you have made great self-discoveries during the past months, I too have acquired much, and look forward to a happy exchange of ideas.

The more I see of the world, the less hope I have that humanity as a whole will ever become wise and happy. Among the millions of worlds which exist, there may, perhaps, be one which can boast of such a state of affairs, but given the constitution of our world, I see as little hope for us as for the Sicilian in his.

A word about Homer. The scales have fallen from my eyes. His descriptions, his similes, etc., which to us seem merely poetic, are in fact utterly natural though drawn, of course, with an inner comprehension which takes one's breath away. Even when the events he narrates are fabulous and fictitious, they have a naturalness about them which I have never felt so strongly as in the presence of the settings he describes. Let me say briefly what I think about the ancient writers and us moderns. *They* represented things and persons as they are in themselves, *we* usually represent only their subjective effect; *they* depicted the horror, *we* depict horribly; *they* depicted the pleasing, *we* pleasantly, and so on. Hence all the exaggeration, the mannerisms, the false elegance and the bombast of our age. Since, if one aims at producing effects and only effects, one thinks that one cannot make them violent enough. If what I say is not new, I have had vivid occasion to feel its truth.

Now that my mind is stored with images of all these coasts and promontories, gulfs and bays, islands and headlands, rocky cliffs and sandy beaches, wooded hills and gentle pastures, fertile fields, flower gardens, tended trees, festooned vines, mountains wreathed in clouds, eternally serene plains and the all-encircling sea with its ever-changing colours and moods, for the first time the *Odyssey* has become a living truth to me.

I must also tell you confidentially that I am very close to the secret of the reproduction and organization of plants, and that it is the simplest thing imaginable. This climate offers the best possible conditions for making observations. To the main question – where the germ is hidden – I am quite certain I have found the answer; to the others I already see a general solution, and only a few points have still to be formulated more precisely. The Primal Plant is going to be the strangest creature in the world, which Nature herself shall envy me. With this model and the key to it, it will be possible to go on for ever inventing plants and know that their existence is logical; that is to say, if they do not actually exist, they could, for they are not the shadowy phantoms of a vain imagination, but possess an inner necessity and truth. The same law will be applicable to all other living organisms.

18 May

Tischbein has returned to Rome, but I find that he has been doing everything he can to ensure that I shall not feel his absence. He has evidently persuaded his friends that I am a person to be trusted, for they all prove to be friendly, kind and helpful. In my present situation this is especially welcome, because not a day passes without my having to turn to someone for some courtesy or assistance. I am just about to draw up a summary list of all the things I still would like to see; then the little time I have left will decide and dictate how much can really be retrieved.

22 May

Today I had a delightful adventure which set me thinking and deserves to be told.

A lady who had done me several favours during my first stay here invited me to come to her house on the stroke of five: an Englishman wished to meet me because he had something to say to me about my *Werther*.

Six months ago I would certainly have refused, even if I was twice as interested in her as I am: the fact that I accepted told me that the Sicilian journey had had a good influence: in short, I promised to be there.

Unfortunately, the city is so big and there are so many things to see that I was a quarter of an hour late when I climbed her stairs. I was just about to ring her bell when the door opened and out came a good-looking middle-aged man whom I immediately recognized as an Englishman. He had hardly spotted me before he said: 'You are the author of *Werther*.' I admitted this and apologized for being late. 'I couldn't wait another minute,' said the Englishman. 'What I have to say to you is very short and can just as well be said here, on this rush mat. I don't intend to repeat what you must have heard a thousand times. Indeed, your work has not made as violent an impression on me as it has on others. But every time I think what it must have taken to write it, I am amazed.'

I was about to say a few words of thanks when he cut me short by saying: 'I can't wait a moment longer. I wanted to tell you this personally. I have. Goodbye and good luck!' – and with that he rushed down the stairs. I stood there for a few moments reflecting on the honour of being so lectured, and then rang the bell. The lady was very pleased to hear of our encounter and told me many things about this extraordinary man which were greatly to his credit.

25 May

I am unlikely to see my frivolous little princess again. She has really gone to Sorrento, and, before she left, so her friends told me, she paid me the compliment of abusing me for having preferred the stony desert of Sicily to her company. They also told me more about this odd little person. Born of a noble but impecunious family and bred in a convent, she made up her mind to marry a wealthy old prince. She needed all the less persuasion because, though she was kind-hearted, she was by nature perfectly incapable of love. Finding herself, in spite of her wealth, imprisoned in a life entirely governed by family considerations, her intelligence became her only resource; being restricted in her company and her actions, she could give full rein, at least, to her loose tongue.

I was assured that her actual conduct was irreproachable, but that she seemed to have firmly made up her mind to fly in the face of all convention with her freedom of speech. It was said, jokingly, that no censorship could possibly pass her discourses if they were written down, for everything she uttered was an offence against religion, morals or the state. Many strange and amusing stories are told of her, one of which I shall tell here, though it is slightly improper.

Shortly before the earthquake devastated Calabria, she had retired to an estate there, owned by her husband. Not far from the big house there was a barrack, that is to say, a one-storey wooden house with no foundation, but otherwise papered, furnished and properly equipped.

At the first signs of the earthquake, she took refuge there. She was sitting on the sofa with a small sewing-table in front of her, tatting, and opposite her sat their old house chaplain. Suddenly the ground shook and the whole building tilted towards her, so that the sewing-table and the Abbé rose in the air. 'Fie!' she cried, leaning her head against the sinking wall. 'Is this proper for such a venerable old man? Why, you're behaving as if you wished to fall on top of me. This is against all morality and decorum.' In the meantime the house had resettled itself, but she could not stop laughing at the ridiculous and lustful figure which she said the good old man had made of himself. She showed no concern for the calamities and loss of life and property which had affected her family and thousands of others, as if this joke had made her forget everything else. Only an extraordinarily happy disposition could have enjoyed a joke at the very moment when the earth seemed about to swallow her up.

26 May

There is a good deal to be said for having many saints, for then each believer can choose his own and put his trust in the one who most appeals to him. Today was the feast day of my favourite saint, and, following his example and teaching, I celebrated it with devotion and joy.

Filippo Neri is held in high honour and at the same time remembered with gladness. One is edified and delighted when one hears about his reverent fear of God, and at the same time is told many stories about his good humour. From his earliest youth he was conscious of a fervent religious impulse and in the course of his life he developed the highest gifts for mystical experience – the gift of spontaneous prayer, of profound, wordless adoration, of tears, ecstasy, and even, as a crowning grace, the gift of levitation – all were his.

With these mysterious spiritual graces, he combined the clearest common sense, an absolute valuation or rather devaluation of earthly things, and an active charity, devoted to the bodily and

spiritual needs of his fellow men. He was strict in observing all the
duties which are demanded of a faithful member of the Church,
attendance at worship, prayers, fasting, and in the same spirit he
occupied himself with the education of the young, instructing
them in the study of music and rhetoric and arranging other
discussions and debates for the improvement of their minds as
well as their souls.

In all this, moreover, he acted of his own accord without any
direction from authority, and lived for many years without joining any religious order or even becoming ordained.

But the most interesting fact of all is that right in the middle
of Rome and at the very same time as Luther, a gifted, God-fearing
and energetic man should, like the Reformer, have thought of
combining the spiritual, even the sacred, with the secular and
relating the supernatural order to the natural, for this is the only
key which can unlock the prison of papalism and restore to the
free world its God.

In a short motto, Neri formulated his basic teaching 'Spernere
mundum, spernere te ipsum, spernere te sperni.' This expresses
everything. A hypochondriac may sometimes imagine he can fulfil
the first two of these demands, but, to submit to the third, a man
must be far on the way to saintliness.

                                                            27 May

Yesterday, through the kindness of Count Fries, all your dear
letters from the end of last month arrived from Rome. It gave me
such joy to read and reread them. The little box I had waited
for so anxiously also arrived, and I thank you a thousand times
for everything.

It is high time for me to escape from here. What with revisiting
various spots in Naples and its surroundings, in order to refresh
my memory, and winding up some of my affairs, the days have
been running away like water. Moreover, there were several very
nice people, both old and new acquaintances, whom I couldn't
possibly refuse to see. One of them was an amiable lady with
whom I passed some very agreeable days in Carlsbad last summer.
We spent many hours talking about one dear good friend after

the other, above all about our beloved, good-humoured Duke. She had kept the poem with which the girls of Engelhaus surprised him as he was riding away. The words brought back the occasion, the merry scene, their witty teasings and mystifications, their ingenious attempts to exercise the right of mutual retaliation. In no time we felt we were on German soil and in the best German society, surrounded on all sides by cliffs, united by the strangeness of the spot, but even more by respect and friendship. But then, as soon as we went to the window, the Neapolitan crowd went rushing by like a river and carried our peaceful memories away with it.

It was also impossible for me to get out of making the acquaintance of the Duke and Duchess von Ursel – an excellent couple with a genuine feeling for Nature and people, a real love of art and benevolent to everyone they meet. We had many long and fascinating conversations.

Sir William Hamilton and his Fair One continue to be very friendly. I dined at their house, and in the evening, Miss Hart gave a demonstration of her musical and melic talents.

At the suggestion of Hackert, who is kinder to me than ever and doesn't want me to miss anything worth seeing, Sir William showed us his secret treasure vault, which was crammed with works of art and junk, all in the greatest confusion. Oddments from every period, busts, torsos, vases, bronzes, decorative implements of all kinds made of Sicilian agate, carvings, paintings and chance bargains of every sort, lay about all higgledy-piggledy; there was even a small chapel. Out of curiosity I lifted the lid of a long case which lay on the floor and in it were two magnificent candelabra. I nudged Hackert and asked him in a whisper if they were not very like the candelabra in the Portici museum. He silenced me with a look. No doubt they somehow strayed here from the cellars of Pompeii. Perhaps these and other such lucky acquisitions are the reason why Sir William shows his hidden treasures only to his most intimate friends.

I was greatly intrigued by a chest which was standing upright. Its front had been taken off, the interior painted black and the whole set inside a splendid gilt frame. It was large enough to hold a standing human figure, and that, we were told, was exactly what it was meant for. Not content with seeing his image of beauty as a moving statue, this friend of art and girlhood wished also to enjoy her as an inimitable painting, and so, standing against this black background in dresses of various colours, she had sometimes imitated the antique paintings of Pompeii or even more recent masterpieces. This phase, it seems, is now over, because it was difficult to transport the apparatus and light it properly, and so we were not to share in this spectacle.

This reminds me that I have forgotten to tell you about another characteristic of the Neapolitans, their love of crèches, or *presepe*, which, at Christmas, can be seen in all their churches. These consist of groups of large, sumptuous figures representing the adoration of the shepherds, the angels and the three Magi. In this gay Naples the representation has climbed up on to the flat roof tops. A light framework, like a hut, is decorated with trees and evergreen shrubs. In it, the Mother of God, the Infant and all the others stand or float, dressed up most gorgeously in a wardrobe on which the family spends a large sum. The background – Vesuvius and all the surrounding countryside – gives the whole thing an incomparable majesty.

In depicting this sacred scene, it is possible that living figures were sometimes substituted for the dolls, and that in time this gave rise to one of the great diversions of noble and wealthy families, who pass many evenings in their palaces representing profane scenes from history or poetry.

If I may be permitted a comment, which a guest who has been so well treated ought really not to make, I must confess that our fair entertainer seems to me, frankly, a dull creature. Perhaps her figure makes up for it, but her voice is inexpressive and her speech without charm. Even her singing is neither full-throated nor agreeable. Perhaps, after all, this is the case with all soulless beauties. People with beautiful figures can be found everywhere, but sensitive ones with agreeable vocal organs are much rarer, and a combination of both is very rare indeed.

I am eagerly looking forward to reading the third part of Herder's book. Please keep it for me until I can tell you where to send it. I'm sure he will have set forth very well the beautiful dream-wish of mankind that things will be better some day.

Speaking for myself, I too believe that humanity will win in the long run; I am only afraid that at the same time the world will have turned into one huge hospital where everyone is everybody else's humane nurse.

28 May

Once in a while the good and ever-useful Volkmann forces me to dissent from his opinion. He asserts, for instance, that there are thirty to forty thousand lazy ne'er-do-wells in Naples, and who does not repeat his words? Now that I am better acquainted with the conditions in the south, I suspect that this was the biased view of a person from the north, where anyone who is not feverishly at work all day is regarded as a loafer. When I first arrived, I watched the common people both in motion and at rest, and though I saw a great many who were poorly dressed, I never saw one who was unoccupied. I asked friends where I could meet all these innumerable idlers, but they couldn't show me any either.

So, seeing that such an investigation would coincide with my sightseeing, I set off to hunt for them myself. I always began my observations very early in the morning, and though, now and then, I came upon people who were resting or standing around, they were always those whose occupation permitted it at that moment.

In order to get a just picture of this vast throng, I began by classifying by appearance, clothes, behaviour and occupation. This is much easier to do in Naples than anywhere else, because here the individual is left alone much more, so that his external appearance is a much better indication of his social status. Let me give some illustrations to back up my statements.

Porters. Each has his privileged standing place in some square or other, where he waits till someone needs his services.

Carriage Drivers. These with their ostlers and boys stand beside their one-horse chaises in the larger squares, grooming their horses, and at the beck and call of everyone who wants to take a drive.

Sailors and Fishermen. These are smoking pipes on the Molo or
lying in the sun because a contrary wind does not permit them to
leave port. In this area I saw several people wandering about, but
almost all of them carried something which indicated they were
busy.

Beggars. The only ones I saw were very old men, no longer
capable of work, and cripples. The longer and closer I looked, the
fewer real idlers I could observe, either of the lower classes or
the middle, either young or old, men or women, either in the
morning or during most of the rest of the day.

Small Children. These are occupied in many different ways. A
great number carry fish from Santa Lucia to sell in the city. Little
boys, ranging from five- or six-year-olds down to infants who can
only crawl on all fours, are frequently to be seen near the Arsenal
or any other place where carpenters work, collecting shavings, or
on the shore, gathering the sticks and small pieces of wood which
have been washed up and putting them into little baskets. When
these are full, they go to the centre of the city and sit down,
holding a market, so to speak, of their small stocks of wood.
Working men and people of modest means buy them to
use as kindling, as wood for their simple kitchen stoves,
or as potential charcoal for the braziers with which they warm
themselves.

Other children go round selling water from the sulphur springs,
which is drunk in large quantities, especially in the springtime.
Others again try to make a few pennies by buying fruit, spun
honey, sweets and pastries, which they offer for sale to other
children – possibly, only so as to get their share for nothing. It
is amusing to watch such a youngster, whose entire equipment
consists of one wooden board and one knife, carrying round a
watermelon or half a pumpkin. The children flock round him; he
puts down his board and starts cutting the fruit up into small
portions. The buyers are intensely in earnest and on tenterhooks,
wondering if they will get enough for their small copper coins,
and the little merchant takes the whole transaction just as
seriously and cautiously as his greedy customers, who are deter-

mined not to be cheated out of the smallest piece. I'm certain that if I could stay here longer, I would be able to collect many other examples of such child industry.

Garbage Collectors. A very large number of people, some middle-aged men, some boys, all very poorly dressed, are occupied in carrying the refuse out of the city on donkeys. The immediate area around Naples is simply one huge kitchen garden, and it is a delight to see, first, what incredible quantities of vegetables are brought into the city every market day, and, second, how human industry immediately returns the useless parts which the cooks reject to the fields so as to speed up the crop cycle. Indeed, the Neapolitans consume so many vegetables that the leaves of cauliflowers, broccoli, artichokes, cabbages, lettuce and garlic make up the greater part of the city's refuse. Two large, flexible panniers are slung over the back of a donkey : these are not only filled to the brim, but above them towers a huge mound of refuse, piled with peculiar cunning. No garden could exist without a donkey. A boy or a farm hand, sometimes even the farmer himself, hurry as often as possible during the day into the city, which for them is a real gold mine. You can imagine how intent these collectors are on the droppings of mules and horses. They are reluctant to leave the streets at nightfall, and the rich folk who leave the opera after midnight are probably unaware of the existence of the industrious men who, before daybreak, will have been carefully searching for the trail of their horses.

I have been assured that, not infrequently, such people have gone into partnership, leased a small piece of land, and, by working untiringly in this blessed climate, where the vegetation never stops growing, have been so successful that they were able to add considerably to their profits.

Pedlars, etc. Some go about with little barrels of ice water, lemon and glasses, so that, on request, they can immediately provide a drink of lemonade, a beverage which even the poorest cannot do without. Others carry trays, on which bottles of various liqueurs and tapering glasses are held safely in place by wooden rings. Others again carry baskets containing pastries of various kinds, lemons and other fruit. All of them, it seems, want nothing better than to contribute to the daily festival of joy.

There are other small traders who wander about with merchandise displayed on a plain board, or the lid of a box, or arranged in a square on the bare ground. They do not deal, like a shop, in any single line of goods, but they sell junk, in the proper sense of the word. There is no tiny scrap of iron, leather, cloth, linen, felt, etc., which does not turn up in this market for secondhand goods and cannot be bought from this vendor or that.

Finally, many persons of the lower class are employed by tradesmen and artisans as errand boys or general drudges.

True, one cannot take many steps before coming on some poorly clad, even ragged, individual, but it does not follow that he is a loafer or a good-for-nothing. On the contrary, I would say, though this may seem like a paradox, that in Naples it is the poorest class which works hardest.

What is meant here by working is not, of course, to be compared with what working means in the north, for there Nature compels people to make provision, not merely for the next day or the next hour, but for the distant future, to prepare in fair weather for foul, in summer for winter. With us the housewife has to smoke and cure the meat so that the kitchen will have supplies for the whole year; her husband must see to it that there are sufficient stores of wood, grain and cattle feed, etc. As a result, the finest days and best hours cannot be given over to play, because they are dedicated to work. For several months of the year we do not go out of doors unless we must, but take shelter in our houses from rain, snow and cold. The seasons follow each other in an inexorable round, and everyone must practise household management or come to grief. It is senseless to ask, Does he like it? He has to like it. He has no option, for he is compelled by Nature to work hard and show foresight. No doubt their national environment, which has remained unchanged for millennia, has conditioned the character of the northern nations, so admirable in many respects. But we must not judge the nations of the south, which Heaven has treated so benevolently, by our standards. What Cornelius von Pauw had the temerity to say, when speaking of the Cynic philosophers in his book, *Recherches philosophiques sur les Grecs*, fits in perfectly with my argument. It is false, he says, to think of these people as miserable; their principle of going without was favoured by a climate which gave them all the necessities of life. Here a poor man, whom, in our country, we think of as wretched, can satisfy his essential needs and at the same time enjoy the world to the full, and a so-called Neapolitan beggar might well refuse to become Viceroy of Norway or decline the honour of being nominated Governor of Siberia by the Empress of all the Russias.

A Cynic philosopher would, I am certain, consider life in our country intolerable; on the other hand, Nature invited him, so to speak, to live in the south. Here the ragged man is not naked, nor poor he who has no provision for the morrow.

He may have neither home nor lodging, spend summer nights under the projecting roof of a house, in the doorway of a palazzo, church or public building, and when the weather is bad, find a shelter where, for a trifling sum, he may sleep, but this does not make him a wretched outcast. When one considers the abundance of fish and sea food which the ocean provides (their prescribed diet on the fast days of every week), the abundance and variety of fruits and vegetables at every season of the year, when one remembers that the region around Naples is deservedly called *'Terra di Lavoro'* (which does not mean the land of *work* but the land of *cultivation*) and that the whole province has been honoured for centuries with the title *'Campagna Felice'* – the happy land – then one gets an idea of how easy life is in these parts.

Someone should try to write a really detailed description of Naples, though this would take years of observation and no small talent. Then we might realize two things: first, that the so-called *lazzarone* is not a whit less busy than any other class and, second, that all of them work not merely to *live* but to *enjoy* themselves: they wish even their work to be a recreation. This explains a good many things: it explains, for instance, why, in most kinds of skilled labour, their artisans are technically far behind those of the northern countries, why factories do not succeed, why, with the exception of lawyers and doctors, there is little learning or culture considering the size of the population, why no painter of the Neapolitan school has ever been profound or become great, why the clergy are happiest when they are doing nothing, and why most of the great prefer to spend their money on luxury, dissipation and sensual pleasures. I know, of course, that these generalizations are too glib and that the typical features of each class could only be established precisely after a much closer scrutiny and longer acquaintance, but I believe that, on the whole, they would still hold good.

To return to the common people again. They are like children who, when one gives them a job to do, treat it as a job but at the same time as an opportunity for having some fun. They are lively, open and sharply observant. I am told their speech is full of imagery and their wit trenchant. It was in the region around Naples that the ancient *Atellanae fabulae* were performed, and their beloved Pulcinella is a descendant from these farces.

Pliny, in Book III, Chapter V, of his *Historia naturalis*, considers Campania worth an extensive description.

In what terms to describe the coast of Campania taken by itself, with its blissful and heavenly loveliness, so as to manifest that there is one region, where Nature has been at work in her joyous mood! And then again all that invigorating healthfulness all the year round, the climate so temperate, the plains so fertile, the hills so sunny, the glades so secure, the groves so shady! Such wealth of various forests, the breezes from so many mountains, the great fertility of its corn and vines and olives, the glorious fleeces of its sheep, the sturdy necks of its bulls, the many lakes, the rich supply of rivers and springs, flowing over all its surface, its many seas and harbours, and the bosom of its lands offering on all sides a welcome to commerce, the country itself eagerly running out into the seas, as it were, to aid mankind. I do not speak of the character and customs of its people, its men, the nations that its language and its might have conquered. The Greeks themselves, a people most prone to gushing self-praise, have pronounced sentence on the land by conferring on but a very small part of it the name of Magna Graecia.*

---

* Transl. Loeb Classical Library. Book III, v, 40–42.

One of the greatest delights of Naples is the universal gaiety. The many-coloured flowers and fruits in which Nature adorns herself seem to invite the people to decorate themselves and their belongings with as vivid colours as possible. All who can in any way afford it wear silk scarves, ribbons and flowers in their hats. In the poorest homes the chairs and chests are painted with bright flowers on a gilt ground; even the one-horse carriages are painted a bright red, their carved woodwork gilded; and the horses decorated with artificial flowers, crimson tassels and tinsel. Some horses wear plumes on their heads, others little pennons which revolve as they trot.

We usually think of a passion for gaudy colours as barbaric or in bad taste, and often with reason, but under this blue sky nothing can be too colourful, for nothing can outshine the brightness of the sun and its reflection in the sea. The most brilliant colour is softened by the strong light, and the green of trees and plants, the yellow, brown and red of the soil are dominant enough to absorb the more highly coloured flowers and dresses into the general harmony. The scarlet skirts and bodices, trimmed with gold and silver braids, which the women of Nettuno wear, the painted boats, etc., everything seems to be competing for visual attention against the splendour of sea and sky.

As they live, so they bury their dead; no slow-moving black cortège disturbs the harmony of this merry world. I saw them carrying a child to its grave. The bier was hidden under an ample pall of red velvet embroidered with gold, and the little coffin was ornamented and gilded and covered with rose-coloured ribbons. At each of its four corners stood an angel, about two feet high, holding a large sheaf of flowers over the sleeping child, who lay dressed in white. Since these angels were only fastened in place with wires, they shook with every movement of the bier and wafted the fragrance of the flowers in all directions. One reason why they tottered so was that the procession was hurrying down the street at such a pace that the priest and candle-bearers at its head were running, rather than walking.

There is no season when one is not surrounded on all sides by victuals. The Neapolitan not only enjoys his food, but insists that it be attractively displayed for sale. In Santa Lucia the fish are placed on a layer of green leaves, and each category – rock lobsters, oysters, clams and small mussels – has a clean, pretty basket to itself. But nothing is more carefully planned than the display of meat, which, since their appetite is stimulated by a periodic fast day, is particularly coveted by the common people.

In the butchers' stalls, quarters of beef, veal or mutton are never hung up without having the unfatty parts of the flanks and legs heavily gilded.

Several days in the year and especially the Christmas holidays are famous for their orgies of gluttony. At such times a general *cocagna* is celebrated, in which five hundred thousand people vow to outdo each other. The Toledo and other streets and squares are decorated most appetizingly; vegetables, raisins, melons and figs are piled high in their stalls; huge paternosters of gilded sausages, tied with red ribbons, and capons with little red flags stuck in their rumps are suspended in festoons across the streets overhead. I was assured that, not counting those which people had fattened in their own homes, thirty thousand of them had been sold. Crowds of donkeys laden with vegetables, capons and young lambs are driven to market, and never in my life have I seen so many eggs in one pile as I have seen here in several places.

Not only is all this eaten, but every year a policeman, accompanied by a trumpeter, rides through the city and announces in every square and at every crossroad how many thousand oxen, calves, lambs, pigs, etc., the Neapolitans have consumed. The crowd show tremendous joy at the high figures, and each of them recalls with pleasure his share in this consumption.

So far as flour-and-milk dishes are concerned, which our cooks prepare so excellently and in so many different ways, though people here lack our well-equipped kitchens and like to make short work of their cooking, they are catered for in two ways. The macaroni, the dough of which is made from a very fine flour, kneaded into various shapes and then boiled, can be bought everywhere and in all the shops for very little money. As a rule, it is simply cooked in water and seasoned with grated cheese. Then, at

almost every corner of the main streets, there are pastrycooks
with their frying pans of sizzling oil, busy, especially on fast days,
preparing pastry and fish on the spot for anyone who wants it.
Their sales are fabulous, for thousands and thousands of people
carry their lunch and supper home, wrapped in a little piece of
paper.

30 May

Seen tonight from the Molo. The moon lighting up the edges of
the clouds, its reflection in the gently heaving sea, at its brightest
and most lively on the crest of the nearest waves, stars, the lamps
of the lighthouse, the fire of Vesuvius, its reflection in the water,
many isolated lights dotted among the boats. A scene with such
multiple aspects would be difficult to paint. I should like to see
van der Neer tackle it.

31 May

I am so firmly set on seeing the Feast of Corpus Christi in Rome,
and the tapestries woven after Raphael's designs, that no natural
beauty, however magnificent, can lure me away from my preparations for departure.

I ordered my passport. The custom here is the exact opposite
of ours; a *vetturino* gave me the earnest money as a guarantee
of my safety.

Kniep has been very busy moving into new lodgings which
are much better than his old ones. While the moving was going
on, he hinted more than once that it is considered strange, even
improper, to move into a house without bringing any furniture
with you. Even a bedstead would be enough to make the landlord
respect him. Today, as I was crossing the Largo del Castello, I
noticed, among countless secondhand household goods, a couple
of iron bed-frames painted a bronze colour. I bargained for these
and gave them to my friend as a future foundation for a quiet and
solid resting-place. One of the porters who are always hanging
about carried them, together with the requisite boards, to the new
lodgings. Kniep was so pleased with them that he decided to

leave me immediately and establish himself there, after quickly buying large drawing-boards, paper and other necessaries. According to our contract, I gave him a certain number of the sketches he had made in the Two Sicilies.

1 June

The Marchese Lucchesini* has arrived, and on his account I have postponed my departure for a few days. It was a real pleasure to make his acquaintance. He impressed me as being one of those people who have a sound moral digestion which allows them to enjoy themselves at the great world banquet, whereas a person like myself sometimes overeats like a ruminant, and then must chew and chew for a long time before he can take another bite. I also liked his wife very much; she is a good German soul.

I shall be glad to leave Naples; indeed, I must leave. During these last days I have done nothing but pay courtesy calls. Most of the people I met were interesting and I do not regret the hours I spent with them, but another two weeks and all my plans would be upset. Furthermore, the longer one stays here, the idler one gets. Apart from the treasures of Portici, I have seen very little since my return from Paestum. There is still a lot I ought to see, but I don't feel in the mood to stir a foot. The Portici museum is the alpha and omega of all collections of antiquities. It makes one realize how far superior to us the ancient world was in artistic instinct, even though it was far behind us in solid craftsmanship.

The servant I hired to bring me my passport said he was sorry to see me go, and told me that the great lava stream which has just issued from Vesuvius is moving towards the sea; it has already reached a point far down the steeper slopes and may well reach the shore in a few days. This news has put me in a dilemma. I have spent the whole day paying farewell visits which I owed to people; there have been many of them who have been kind and helpful to me, and I can guess what tomorrow will be like. When

---

*Marchese Lucchesini, Prussian Secretary of State, on a diplomatic mission in Italy.

travelling, it is impossible to avoid social life altogether, but the truth is, I can do nothing for these people, and they get in the way of the things which really matter to me. I am in a black mood.

1 June. Evening

My round of thank-you visits was not without pleasure and profit; I was shown several things which I had neglected. Cavaliere Venuti even let me see some hidden treasures. I took another reverent look at his priceless, though mutilated, Ulysses, and together we paid a farewell visit to the porcelain works, where I lingered over the Hercules and the beautiful Campanian vases.

He was most affectionate when we parted, and said that he only wished I did not have to leave him so soon. My banker, too, at whose house I arrived just at dinner-time, would not let me go. This would have been all very well if my thoughts had not been running on lava all the time. I was still settling bills, packing and doing this and that when night began to fall, and I hurried to the Molo to watch the lights and their trembling reflections in the agitated sea, the full moon in all its glory, the flying sparks of the volcano and, above all, the lava, which had not been there two nights ago, moving on its fiery, relentless way.

I thought of driving out to see it, but this would have been complicated to arrange and it would have been morning before I got there. Besides, I did not want impatience to spoil my present enjoyment, so I stayed where I was, sitting on the Molo, oblivious of the passing crowds, their explanations, stories, comparisons and senseless arguments about the direction the lava would take, until I could no longer keep my eyes open.

2 June

Another beautiful day, spent usefully and pleasantly, no doubt, with admirable people, but against my will and with a heavy heart. All the time I looked longingly at the cloud of smoke as it slowly moved towards the sea, indicating hour by hour the advance of the lava. Even my evening was not to be free. I had promised to visit the Duchess of Giovene, who is living in the royal palace. I climbed stairs and wandered along many corridors, the uppermost of which was obstructed by chests, closets and all the impedimenta of a court wardrobe, and was shown into a room which was large and lofty but not particularly spectacular. There I found an attractive young lady whose conversation revealed her to be a person of delicacy and refinement. Born in Germany, she is familiar with the development of our literature towards a more liberal and clear-sighted humanism. She especially admires everything Herder is doing and the lucid intellect of Garve. She has tried to keep up with the women writers of Germany, and it was obvious from what she said that she would like to become a famous writer herself and influence young ladies of noble birth – such a conversation is without beginning or end. No candles had been brought in, though it was already twilight and the window shutters were closed. We were walking up and down the room, when, all of a sudden, she flung open a shutter. If she meant to give me a surprise, she certainly succeeded, for the sight was such as one sees only once in a lifetime. The window at which we were standing was on the top floor, directly facing Vesuvius. The sun had set some time before, and the glow of the lava, which lit up its accompanying cloud of smoke, was clearly visible. The mountain roared, and at each eruption the enormous pillar of smoke above it was rent asunder as if by lightning, and in the glare, the separate clouds of vapour stood out in sculptured relief. From the summit to the sea ran a streak of molten lava and glowing vapour, but everywhere else sea, earth, rock and vegetation lay peaceful in the enchanting stillness of a fine evening, while the full moon rose from behind the mountain ridge. It was an overwhelming sight.

From the point where we were standing, though it was impossible to discern every detail of the picture, the whole could be taken in at a glance. For a time we watched in silence, and when we resumed our conversation, it took a more intimate turn. We had before our eyes a text to comment on, for which millennia would be too short. As the night advanced, every detail of the landscape stood out ever more clearly; the moon shone like a second sun; with the aid of a moderately strong lens, I even thought I could see the fragments of glowing rock as they were ejected from the abyss of the cone. My hostess, as I shall call her, since I have seldom eaten a more exquisite supper, had ordered the candles to be placed on the side of the room away from the window. Sitting in the foreground of this incredible picture with the moonlight falling on her face, she looked more beautiful than ever, and her loveliness was enhanced for me by the charming German idiom in which she spoke. I forgot completely how late it was till, at last, she had to ask me to leave because in a short while the doors would be locked as they are in a convent. And so to beauty, both near and distant, I bade a reluctant farewell, but blessing the Fates who, at its close, had so wonderfully rewarded me for a day unwillingly spent in being polite.

When I got outside, I thought to myself that, after all, a closer view of this great lava stream would only have been a repetition of the small one I did see, and that the evening I had spent was the only possible conclusion to my stay in Naples. Instead of going home at once, I started walking towards the Molo with the intention of seing the great spectacle with a different foreground. I don't know how it was – perhaps it was weariness after such a full day, perhaps a feeling that I ought not to spoil the beautiful picture I had just seen by any more looking – but I changed my mind and went back to Morconi's. There I found Kniep, who had come over from his new lodgings to pay me an evening visit, and we discussed our future relations over a bottle of wine. I promised him that as soon as I was able to exhibit some of his work in Germany, I would recommend him to the Duke of Gotha, who would probably give him commissions, and so, as close friends who look forward to a fruitful cooperation in the future, we said goodbye to each other.

3 June. Trinity Sunday

I drove away through the teeming crowds of this incomparable city which I shall probably never see again – half dazed but glad that I am leaving neither pain nor remorse behind me. I thought of my good friend Kniep and made a vow to do all I can for him when I am far away.

At the last police station on the outskirts of the suburbs, I

was startled for a moment by a waiter who smiled in my face
and then ran away. The customs inspectors had not yet finished
with my *vetturino* when the door of the coffee house opened and
out came Kniep, carrying on a tray a huge china cup of black
coffee. He walked slowly to the door of my coach with a serious
expression on his face, which, as his emotion was heartfelt, became
him very well. I was surprised and moved : one does not often
encounter such a visible sign of gratitude. He said to me : 'You
have been so kind and good to me that I shall remember you all my
life, and I want to offer you this as a symbol of my gratitude.'

I never know what to say on such occasions, so I only said very
laconically that the work he had done had already made me his
debtor, and that the use of our common treasure would put me
under still greater obligation to him.

We parted as two persons seldom do whom chance has thrown
together for a short time. Perhaps we should find more satisfaction
and gratitude in our lives if we always said quite frankly what we
expect from one another. If we did, both parties would be satisfied,
and we should find sympathy, which is the beginning and end of
everything, into the bargain.

On the road, 4, 5, 6 June

As I am travelling alone this time, I have leisure to think over
all I have seen and done during the past months, and I do so with
great pleasure. At the same time, I become aware of gaps in my
observations. When a journey is over, the traveller himself remembers it as an unbroken sequence of events, inseparable from each
other. But when he tries to describe this journey to someone else,
he finds it impossible to communicate this, for he can only present
the events one by one as separate facts.

This is why nothing has cheered me more than the assurances
in your last letters that you have been busy reading travel books
about Italy and Sicily and looking at engravings, and it is a great
comfort to learn that your studies have made my letters clearer,
as I knew they would.

Had you done this earlier, or told me so, I would have been
even more zealous in my efforts than I was. The knowledge that

men like Bartels, Münter and architects of various nationalities preceded me – men who, no doubt, pursued their investigations more carefully and objectively than I, who had only the inner significance of things in view – has often eased my mind when I was forced to recognize the inadequacy of my efforts.

If every human individual is to be considered only as a supplement to all the others, if he is never so useful or so lovable as when he is content to play this part, this must be particularly true for travellers and writers of travel books. Personality, purpose, the times, the chances of fortune and misfortune, are different in every case. If I know a traveller's predecessors, I find profit in reading him too, and shall welcome his successor with pleasure, even if, in the meantime, I have been so fortunate as to visit the same country myself.

FILIPPO NERI, THE HUMOROUS SAINT

Filippo Neri was born in Florence in 1515 and from childhood on seems to have been an obedient, well-mannered boy with great natural gifts. Luckily, a portrait of him from that time has been preserved and may be found in Fidanza's *Teste Scelte*, Volume V, plate 31. It would be difficult to imagine a more healthy-looking, sturdy and straight-faced boy. The son of a noble family, he was educated in all that was good and worth knowing, as the times understood it, and finally sent to Rome – it is not said at what age – to complete his studies. There he developed into a perfect youth, conspicuous for his good looks and abundant curls; at once attractive and reserved, grace and dignity accompanied his every action.

At a very sad time for Rome – she had been cruelly sacked* only a few years before – following the example of many other noblemen, he devoted himself to acts of piety, and the waxing strength of his fresh youth only intensified his enthusiasm. We hear of his constant attendance at church, especially at the seven principal churches, of his fervent prayers, his wrestling for Grace, his frequent confessions and communions.

At one such enthusiastic moment he threw himself down on

*Rome was sacked by German and Spanish mercenaries in 1527.

the steps of the altar and broke some ribs, which, healed badly, made him suffer all his life from palpitations of the heart and intensified his emotions.

A group of young men gathered round him and joined with him in pious good deeds; their zeal in caring for the poor and nursing the sick was unflagging, and they seem to have regarded their studies as of little importance. They probably spent their family allowances on charity; in short, they gave all their money and their time to help others and kept nothing for themselves. Later Neri expressly refused to take any assistance from his friends and commanded them to surrender to the needy any alms they were given and to live themselves in absolute poverty.

These young men who performed their deeds of piety with such sincerity and good cheer felt the need to meet together at times and discuss in a reverent manner what they felt about important matters. At first the little company had no meeting place of their own and gathered in any religious house where there happened to be an empty room at the moment. After a short, silent prayer, some passage from the Holy Scriptures was read; then one or another of them would give a short address on its meaning or application to the times. A discussion sometimes followed, but this was confined to what ought to be done here and now; dialectic and sophistry were strictly forbidden. The rest of the day was entirely devoted to caring for the sick, visiting hospitals and assisting the poor and needy.

Otherwise, there were no restrictions, and anyone was free to join the group or leave it as he liked. In consequence, their numbers multiplied rapidly, and they began to concern themselves at their meetings with a wider range of topics. Passages from the lives of the saints, from the Church Fathers and Church historians were also read, after which four of those present were expected to speak for half an hour each.

This pious, day-by-day, practical, even homely discussion of the highest concerns of the soul aroused more and more interest, not only among individuals, but also among whole communities. The meetings were transferred to the open cloisters of some church or other, and bigger crowds attended them. The Dominicans, especially, were drawn to this kind of devotion and many of them joined this group, which, under the energetic guidance of its leader and tested by various adversities, went forward united in spirit and purpose.

In obedience to the wisdom of their master, speculation was forbidden and all activities were directed towards life. But life is unthinkable without cheerfulness, and Neri also knew how to gratify the innocent desires of his companions. Early in spring he would take them to Sant'Onofrio, a pleasant spot at this season, for it lies on the heights and commands a wide view. There, where in spring everything should look young, they prayed in silence, then a handsome youth stepped forward and recited a poem he had learned by heart; this was followed by more prayers and finally by beautiful music, sung by a choir of specially selected singers. These meetings may have been the first occasions on which sacred music was sung out of doors.

So this congregation grew, both in number and influence. The Florentines practically forced their fellow citizen to move into the monastery of San Girolamo, which they controlled; the institution continued to grow until, finally, the Pope gave them a monastery near the Piazza Navona, which had just been completely rebuilt and could accommodate a large number of devout brethren. Here, too, their purpose remained what it had been from the beginning, to unite the Word of God with the thoughts and actions of everyday life.

They assembled as before, prayed, listened to the reading of some text, discussed it among themselves, prayed again, and finally enjoyed some music. What was then a frequent, even a daily occurrence, still happens today every Sunday, and any traveller who has learned something about the saintly founder will be greatly edified if he attends these innocent rites.

It must be remembered that most of the people involved in this movement were laymen. They had few priests among them, only enough to hear confessions and say Mass. Filippo Neri himself had reached the age of thirty-six without having felt the wish to be ordained, possibly because he felt he was freer and more independent as a layman than he would have been as a highly honoured but strictly controlled member of the great hierarchy of the Church.

But the authorities thought otherwise. His father confessor made it a point of conscience that he should be ordained a priest, and in the end he obeyed. The Church had cleverly drawn into her circle a man who hitherto had independently striven to lead a life in which the sacred and the profane, the noble and the commonplace were combined.

His ordination, however, does not seem to have had the slightest effect on his outward behaviour. He practised every kind of self-discipline even more rigorously than before and went on living in a miserable little monastery. At a time when food is very scarce, he gives the loaves reserved for him to another needy person, and he continues to serve the unfortunate.

But on his inner life, priesthood has a remarkable effect. The obligation to say Mass transports him into an ecstasy where the natural man completely disappears. He hardly knows where he is going and staggers on his way to the altar. At the Elevation of the Host it seems as though some invisible power is drawing him upward, and he is unable to lower his arms again. When he pours out the wine, he trembles, and when he has to partake of the transubstantiated elements, he behaves in an extraordinary and indescribably gluttonous way. He bites the chalice passionately as he sips the Blood of the Flesh which he has just greedily devoured. But once the ecstasy passes, he is himself again, a passionate, strange man certainly, but always practical and full of common sense.

A person with a lively and exceptionally energetic disposition like his was bound to appear eccentric, and his very virtues must sometimes have struck others as tiresome, even repellent. He had probably encountered hostility in the earlier part of his life, but when he continued, after his ordination, living meanly as the guest of a miserable monastery, his enemies came into the open and persecuted him reluctantly with gibes and sneers. He was, if I am not mistaken, one of those men who are conscious of their born superiority and their will to dominate, which they try to combat and conceal by leading a life of self-denial and poverty, and by inviting contempt.

His constant endeavour was to appear a fool in the eyes of the world so that he might devote himself all the more fervently

to the things of God, and he trained his pupils to do the same.
St Bernard's maxim :

> *Spernere mundum,*
> *spernere neminem,*
> *spernere se ipsum,*
> *spernere se sperni,*

seems to have taken possession of his whole being, or rather to
have been reinvented by him, for, when their intentions and
situations are similar, men build their lives on similar maxims.

Only superior and essentially proud men are capable of choosing on principle to taste the enmity of a world which is always
opposed to the good and the great, and empty the bitter cup of
experience to the dregs before it is offered them. The little stories
which have come down to us of the tests to which Neri was
always making his pupils submit are apt to make any life-loving
person who hears them lose patience, so one can imagine how
painful and almost intolerable must have been Neri's orders to the
person who was expected to obey them, and one is not surprised
that some were unable to endure these ordeals.

But before entering upon an account of these strange anecdotes,
which may not be to the taste of every reader, let us turn once
more to those great qualities which Neri's contemporaries ascribe
to him and praise highly.

His learning and culture, they say, were more a matter of in-
born gifts than of education; what others gain only through hard
study was, so to speak, in his blood. He is said to have possessed
extraordinary powers of insight both into other people, so that
he could immediately discern their characters and abilities, and
into worldly matters, so that he could foretell events to come. In
addition, he was endowed with great personal magnetism – what
the Italians mean by the beautiful word *attrattiva* – so that not
only human beings but also animals were irresistibly drawn to
him. For example, a dog belonging to one of his friends attached
himself to him and followed him everywhere. The owner tried to
woo him back with all sorts of baits, but the dog always ran back
to the attractive man and never left his side for a moment until,
some years later, he ended his life in the bedroom of the master of

his choice. This creature brings me back to the tests I spoke of, for he played a part in some of them.

We know that in most places during the Middle Ages, the leading and carrying of dogs was regarded as a menial and degrading duty, and Rome was no exception. Neri, therefore, used to lead his dog through the city on a chain and compel his pupils to carry it in the streets in their arms, exposing themselves to the mockery of the crowd.

This was not the only kind of undignified public appearance which he demanded of them. A young Roman prince who desired the honour of admission to the order was ordered to walk through the streets with a fox's brush tied to his back, and when he declined to do this, admission was refused. One, Neri sent into the city without a coat, another with his sleeves torn to pieces. A nobleman took pity on the latter and offered him a pair of new sleeves, which the young man refused, but he was then ordered to go back, accept them gratefully and wear them. When their new church was being built, Neri forced his followers to carry the building material to the masons as if they were day labourers.

If one of them showed signs of spiritual conceit, he would eradicate it in the same way. If a young man's sermon was having a success and the preacher seemed pleased with himself, Neri would interrupt him in the middle of a sentence, speak in his place or even order some less able pupil to continue the sermon at once. This unexpected stimulus often had the effect of making the extempore part of the sermon better than the prepared part which preceded it.

To understand how Neri could be so powerful and effective, one must bear in mind the chaotic conditions in Europe during the second half of the sixteenth century and the ferment Rome was in under various popes. By playing on its desires and fears, by training it in submission and obedience till it was able to renounce unconditionally even the reasonable and sensible, the customary and the seemly, he gave the human will the strength to overcome all obstacles. The following story of one of Neri's tests is well known, but it is so unusual and amusing that the reader will not mind hearing it again.

The Pope had been told there was a nun in a country convent who was performing miracles. This is always a matter of great importance to the Church, and Neri was commissioned to look into the case. He rides away on his mule but returns much sooner than expected and greets his surprised spiritual superior with these words: 'Most Holy Father, she does not perform miracles because she is lacking in the first Christian virtue, humility. I arrive at the convent, bespattered with mud and drenched by the rain. I hold out my boot to her and indicate that she is to pull it off. She recoils indignantly and angrily refuses my request. What do I take her for, she shouts. She is the handmaid of the Lord, not of anyone who comes to demand a menial service of her. I get up calmly, mount my mule and here I am, convinced that you will not find another test necessary.' The Pope smiled and let the matter drop. Probably the nun was forbidden any further miraculous performances.

If he claimed the right to submit others to tests, he also had to submit to them himself when bidden by men of kindred spirit who had chosen the same vow of self-denial.

One day in a very crowded street, he meets a mendicant friar who, like himself, stood in the odour of sanctity. The friar offers him a sip of wine from the flask he is carrying. Without hesitating for a second, Filippo Neri puts the narrow-necked wickered bottle to his mouth and bends his head back while the onlookers laugh and jeer at the sight of two pious monks drinking each other's health. Neri, who, for all his piety and humility, is rather cross at this, says to the friar: 'You have put me to the test; now it's my turn', and with these words presses his four-cornered biretta down on the friar's tonsured head, making him the laughing-stock of the crowd. But the friar goes on his way quite calmly, saying: 'Anyone who takes it off my head may keep it.' Neri takes it off him and the two part.

Only a man like Filippo Neri, whose acts were often regarded as miracles, could dare behave like this and still have a great moral influence.

As a father confessor he inspired fear and confidence; he would tell his penitents of sins which they had not confessed and faults which had escaped their notice. His fervent ecstatic prayer struck his followers as something supernatural and put them into that spiritual condition in which human beings believe that they are perceiving with their senses what their imagination, excited by passionate emotion, is suggesting to their minds. Moreover, stories of the miraculous and the impossible, if told often enough, eventually take the place of the real and the ordinary.

This explains why people declared that they had several times seen him levitated in front of the altar during Mass, and why others swore that once, when he was praying on his knees for the life of someone who was mortally sick, they had seen him lifted so high off the ground that his head almost touched the ceiling.

In such a mental atmosphere, devoted to feeling and imagination, it would be surprising if there was no intrusion of hostile demons. One day this pious man sees a revolting creature like a deformed monkey prancing about among the crumbling walls of the Baths of Antonius, but then, at his command, it vanishes into a crevice.

A more significant story concerns his attitude towards his followers when they start telling him about their delightful visions of the Mother of God and various other saints. Knowing only too well that such hallucinations are apt to breed spiritual pride, the worst and most obdurate of all the sins, he tells them that a diabolic darkness is undoubtedly hiding behind this heavenly beauty. To prove this, he orders them the next time they have a vision of the Blessed Virgin to spit in her face; they obey, and, instead of the vision, a devil's face is at once revealed.

In giving this command, the great man may have been conscious of what he was doing, but more probably he was prompted by a deep instinct: in any case, he knew that an image evoked by a fantastic love would be transferred into a caricature of itself when exposed to the counter-force of hatred or contempt.

He was entitled to employ such strange pedagogical tactics on the strength of his extraordinary intuitive gifts, which ranged from the extremely spiritual to the extremely physical. For example, he could sense the approach of people before they appeared, he was aware of distant happenings, he could read the thoughts of the person he was looking at.

It is not uncommon for a human being to possess one of such

powers, and many people have moments when they possess them, but that one individual should be endowed with all of them and be able to call on them at any time with amazing effect is very rare indeed and only conceivable, perhaps, in a century when spiritual and physical forces manifested themselves with astonishing energy.

St Francis Xavier's work among the idolatrous heathen had caused a great sensation in the Rome of that time, and Neri and some of his friends also felt attracted to the so-called Indies. They asked the permission of the Pope to go there too, but their father confessor – acting, no doubt, upon instructions from higher quarters – reminded them that godly men, dedicated to the betterment of their fellows and the propagation of the faith, could find enough of the Indies and a stage worthy of their activity in Rome itself. They were further told that Rome was threatened with a disaster, since for some time the Three Fountains near the Porta San Sebastiano had been running turbid and bloody, which was regarded as an infallible omen. So, willingly or not, Neri and his friends continued to work their wonders in Rome, and, year by year, Neri won more and more confidence and respect from both the great and the lowly, the old and the young.

Man is an extraordinarily complex being, in whose nature absolutely contradictory elements coexist, the physical and the spiritual, the possible and the impossible, the attractive and the repellent, the bounded and the unbounded – one could go on for ever with such a list. In Neri's case, all these opposites overtly manifested themselves, confusing the intellect by thrusting the incomprehensible upon it, unleashing imagination, outwinging faith, justifying superstition, juxtaposing and even uniting the most normal states with the most abnormal. It is not surprising, therefore, that such a man, working untiringly for nearly a century and on a vast stage, should have had the influence he did.

The high esteem in which he was held was so great that people not only derived benefit, grace and spiritual happiness from his life of healthy, vigorous action, but also from his illnesses, which were proof to them of his closeness to God. Even during his lifetime many honoured him as a saint, and his death only confirmed the feelings of his contemporaries about him.

Soon after his death, which was accompanied by even more miracles than his life, Pope Clement VIII was asked to give his permission to start the *process*, as it is called, which is a necessary prelude to beatification. In giving his assent, the Pope said: 'I have always regarded him as a saint, and so I can have no objections if the whole Church should declare and present him as such to the faithful.'

Neri lived to see fifteen popes, for he was born under Leo X and died under Clement VIII. This may partly explain his attitude of independence in his relation to the Papacy; though, as a loyal member of the Church, he always obeyed her general laws, he refused to be bound on points of detail, and even spoke up authoritatively to the Head of the Church. He firmly declined a cardinal's hat, for instance, and, sitting in his *chiesa nuova* like a rebellious knight in his old castle, dared to behave disrespectfully to his supreme liege lord.

But the best illustration of this is the memorandum which, shortly before his death, Neri addressed to the new Pope Clement VIII and the equally curious resolution which the latter appended to it. Though they date from the end of the sixteenth century, both are couched in the terms of earlier, cruder times. They reveal, better than anything else could, this relationship of a man, nearing eighty and about to be made a saint, with the Sovereign Head of the Roman Catholic Church, an able man, who was highly respected throughout his long reign.

MEMORANDUM OF FILIPPO NERI TO CLEMENT VIII

Holy Father! Well, what sort of a person am I that cardinals should come to visit me, as the Cardinals of Florence and Cusano did last night. Because I needed a leaf or two of manna-ash, the said Cardinal of Florence sent to San Spirito for two ounces, having already dispatched a large quantity to that hospital. He also stayed with me till the second hour of the night and said a great many good things about Your Holiness, many more, in my opinion, than were justified. Since you are the Pope, you ought to be humility in person. At the seventh hour of the night, Christ came to incorporate Himself in me, and Your Holiness might also visit our church once in a while. Christ is God and Man and He visits me quite often. Your Holiness is only a man, begotten of a holy and upright man, but He is begotten of God the Father. The mother of Your Holiness is Signora Agnesina, a most God-fearing lady, but His mother is the Virgin of all virgins. How much more could I say if I were to give vent to my spleen. I order Your Holiness to do my will respecting a girl whom I wish to send to Torre de' Specchi. She is the daughter of Claudio Neri, whose children Your Holiness promised him he would protect, and I would like to remind you that it is nice when a Pope keeps his word. So entrust the business to me but in such a way that, if necessary, I can use your name. I know the girl's mind and am certain that she is moved by divine inspiration. With all the humility I owe you, I kiss your holy feet.

THE POPE'S RESOLUTION, WRITTEN UNDER THE MEMORANDUM IN HIS OWN HAND

The Pope says the first part of this paper shows signs of the spirit of vanity, for We are meant to learn from it that the cardinals visit you so often, or else to be informed that these gentlemen are spiritually minded, a fact which is well known to Us. As to Our not coming to see you, We say that Your Reverence does not deserve it, because you would not accept the cardinal's hat which has been offered you so many times. As regards your command, We do not mind if, with your usual bossiness, you give those worthy mothers a good talking to when they don't do things your way. And now We command you to be good and not hear confessions without Our permission. But should our Lord visit you, pray for Us and for the urgent needs of Christendom.

PART THREE

SECOND ROMAN VISIT
JUNE 1787 – APRIL 1788

*Longa sit huic aetas, dominaeque
potentia terrae,
Sitque sub hac oriens occiduusque dies.**

*Ovid's *Fasti*, IV, v, 831–2.
The prayer of Romulus for Rome.

JUNE

CORRESPONDENCE

Rome, 8 June

I ARRIVED here safely two days ago, and yesterday the Feast of Corpus Christi rebaptized me as a Roman citizen. I hated to leave Naples because of the tremendous lava stream which was coursing from the summit to the sea and I would have liked to add to my experience by observing it from close quarters.

But today I feel I have been compensated for what I missed, not so much by the tumult of the feast itself, which, though impressive as a whole, occasionally offends one's feelings by details in bad taste, as by the sight of the tapestries after Raphael's designs, which are displayed at this time.

The best of them are undoubtedly his, and the others which are displayed with them, though probably designed by his pupils or his contemporaries, are not unworthy of the immense spaces they cover.

16 June

Just a few words, dear friends, to tell you that I am very well and more and more finding out who I am, learning to distinguish between what is really me and what is not. I am working hard and absorbing all I can which comes to me on all sides from without, so that I may develop all the better from within. During the last few days I have been in Tivoli. The whole complex of its landscape with its details, its views, its waterfalls, is one of those experiences which permanently enrich one's life.

I forgot to write by the last mail. After walking about Tivoli and sketching in the heat, I was very tired. I went out there with Hackert, who is a master at copying Nature and has such a sure hand that he never has to correct a drawing. He has praised, criticized and encouraged me, and in these few days I have learned a great deal from him. I now see clearly what and how I should study in order to throw off burdens which I should otherwise have to stagger under all my life.

One more observation. For the first time I can say that I am beginning to *love* trees and rocks, and, yes, Rome itself; till now I have always found them a little forbidding. Small objects, on the other hand, have always delighted me, because they reminded me of the things I saw as a child. But now I am beginning to feel at home here, though I shall never feel as intimate with these things as I did with the first objects in my life. This thought has led me to reflect on the subject of art and imitation.

During my absence, Tischbein discovered in the convent near the Porta del Popolo a painting by Daniele da Volterra. The monks were willing to sell it for one thousand *scudi*, a sum which Tischbein, being an artist, was unable to raise. Through the good offices of Meyer, he made a proposal to Signora Angelica, which she agreed to do. She paid the stipulated sum, took the painting into her house and later bought back from Tischbein, for a considerably higher figure, the fifty per cent commission due him. It is an excellent painting, depicting the Deposition. Meyer made a drawing of it which still exists.

20 June

Since my return I have been looking again at excellent works of art, and my judgement is, I think, becoming clearer and more sure of itself. To profit fully from Rome, I should need to spend at least another year, studying in my own way, and, as you well know, I cannot study in any other. If I were to leave now, I should only know how much I do not yet clearly understand. But let us drop this subject for the time being.

The Farnese Hercules has gone, but I have seen him on his original legs. One cannot understand why, for years and years, people found the substitute ones by Porta so good. Now it is one of the most perfect works of antiquity. The King plans to build a museum in Naples where all his art collections – the Herculaneum collection, the Pompeii murals, the paintings from Capodimonte, the whole Farnese legacy – will be housed and exhibited.

Our fellow countryman, Hackert, has been the prime mover in this magnificent project. Even the Farnese Toro will emigrate to Naples, to be erected on the Promenade. If they could detach the Gallery with the Carracci from the Palazzo Farnese and transport it, they would.

27 June

Hackert and I visited the Colonna Gallery, where paintings by Poussin, Claude Lorrain and Salvator Rosa are hung side by side. Hackert has copied several of them and studied the others thoroughly, and his comments were most illuminating. I was pleased to discover that my judgements of these pictures are still pretty much what they were when I paid my first visit. Nothing he said has compelled me to change my views; he has only confirmed and enlarged them. What one needs to do is to look at them and then immediately look at Nature to learn what they saw in her and in one way or another imitated; then the mind is cleared of misconceptions, and in the end one arrives at a true vision of the relation between Nature and Art. I shall never rest until I know that all my ideas are derived, not from hearsay or tradition, but from my real living contact with the things themselves. From my earliest youth this has been my ambition and my torment: now that I am grown up, I am determined at least to attain the attainable and do what can be done, after having so long – deservedly or undeservedly – suffered the fate of Sisyphus and Tantalus.

May you continue to love me and never lose faith in me. I now get along tolerably well with other people and I have learned the art of treating them with candour. I am well and enjoying myself all the time.

Tischbein is a very good fellow, but I'm afraid he will never reach a point where he can work with ease and freedom. I will tell you more about this remarkable man when I see you. My portrait is going to be very good; the likeness is striking and everyone is pleased with the general idea of the picture. Angelica is also painting me, but her picture is not going to come off. She is very disappointed that it is making no progress and is not like me. It remains the portrait of a handsome young fellow without any resemblance to me whatever.

30 June

The great feast of St Peter and St Paul has come at last. Yesterday we saw the illuminated dome and the fireworks of Castel Sant'Angelo. The illuminations are spectacular, like a scene from fairyland; one can hardly believe one's eyes. Now that I have learned to see objects just as they are and not, as formerly, to supply with imagination what is not there, a spectacle has to be really grand before I can enjoy it. On my journey I have seen, I count, about half a dozen, and this last one is certainly among the greatest. To see the colonnade, the church and, above all, the dome, first outlined in fire and, after an hour, become one glowing mass, is a unique and glorious experience. When one thinks that, at this moment, the whole enormous building is a mere scaffolding for the lights, one realizes that nothing like it could be seen anywhere else in the world. The sky was cloudless and the light of the risen moon softened the brightness of the lamps; but when the second lot of illuminations were set ablaze, the moonlight was eclipsed. Then the blaze was over, and again the full moon softened the lights and made everything a fairyland again.

The fireworks were beautiful because of their setting, but they did not compare with the illuminations of the church. We are going to see them both a second time.

End of June

The school in which I am enrolled as a pupil is far too great to let me leave it soon. I must cultivate my knowledge of the arts and my modest talents and reach some sort of maturity; otherwise, I shall bring you back but half a friend, and all my striving, toiling, crawling and creeping would have to begin all over again. If I were to tell all the pieces of good luck I have had, my letter would never come to an end. Why, everything I wished for has been handed to me on a platter. I have nice rooms, kept by nice people. As soon as Tischbein leaves for Naples, I shall move into his studio, which is spacious and cool. So, when you think of me, think of a lucky man. I shall keep on writing you letters and this way we shall always be together.

I am full of new thoughts. When I am left to myself and have time to reflect, I can recover the smallest details of my earliest youth and then, when I turn to the external world again, the splendour of the objects by which I am surrounded makes me forget myself and carries me as far and as high as my innermost being permits. My eye is becoming better trained than I would have believed possible and my hand should not altogether lag behind. There is only one Rome in the world. Here I feel like a fish in the water, or, rather, like the globule which floats on the surface of mercury, but would sink in any other fluid. Nothing clouds my thoughts except the fact that I cannot share my happiness with my dear friends. The sky is now wonderfully serene. Rome is slightly foggy in the morning and the evening, but on the hills of Albano, Castello and Frascati, where I spent three days last week, the air is always limpid and pure. *There* is a nature for you which is worth studying !

NOTE

While going through what I wrote at the time about my impressions and feelings, and starting to make extracts of general interest from my own letters which certainly convey the quality of the moment better than anything I may have written later, I came across some letters from friends which, perhaps, will serve my purpose still better. I have therefore decided to insert such epistolary documents here and there and shall begin now with a vivid description by Tischbein of his departure from Rome and arrival in Naples. His words will not only have the virtue of transporting the reader in an instant to these regions and of giving him a clear, close picture of their inhabitants; they will also illuminate the character of the artist himself who did such distinguished work and, if now and then he struck people as rather odd, deserves to be gratefully remembered as much for what he tried to do as for what he actually achieved.

TISCHBEIN TO GOETHE

Naples, 10 July 1787

Our journey from Rome to Capua was pleasant and without a hitch. Hackert joined us in Albano. In Velletri we dined with Cardinal Borgia and, to my especial delight, visited his museum, where I noticed several things I had overlooked the first time. At three in the afternoon we drove away across the Pontine Marshes. I liked them much better this time than last winter, for the green trees and hedges imparted a charming variety to these immense plains. Shortly before dusk we reached the centre of the marshes where one changes mail coaches. During the wait, while the postilions were bringing all their eloquence to bear on extorting money from us, a high-spirited white stallion took the opportunity to break loose and run away. He was a beautiful horse, white as snow and superbly built. He broke the rein by which he had been tethered, lashed out with his forefeet at anyone who tried to stop him, kicked with his hind legs and snorted and neighed so violently that everybody was afraid and kept out of his way. He jumped a ditch and galloped across a field, snorting and neighing all the time. Tail and mane waved high in the air, and his body was so beautiful in the freedom of its movements that everyone cried: '*O che bellezze! che bellezze!*' Then he ran up and down along another ditch, looking for a narrow place he could jump over and join several hundred foals and mares which were grazing on the other side. Finally he succeeded and went prancing up to the mares, who were scared by his raging and snorting and ran away across the plain in long files, with the stallion chasing after them and trying to mount them.

He then managed to head off one mare who ran away towards a large group of mares in another field. These, too, became frightened and ran to join the first herd. The field was now black with horses, a scene of panic and fury, as the white stallion went jumping among them. For a long time we watched with delight so many hundreds galloping over the field, now in long files, now in a cluster, and now dispersed, each running about by itself, while the air whistled and the ground shook beneath the thunder of their heavy hooves.

Nightfall finally deprived us of this unique spectacle, and when the moon rose from behind the mountains, the light of our coach lantern was eclipsed. After enjoying the gentle moonlight for a long time, I could no longer keep my eyes open and, despite my fear of the unhealthy air, I slept for over an hour and only woke up when we arrived in Terracina, where we again changed horses.

This time the postilions were very polite because the Marchese Lucchesini had put the fear of God into them. They provided us with the best horses and guides, for the road between the high cliffs and the sea is dangerous. It has been the scene of many accidents, especially at night when the horses shy easily. While ours were being harnessed and our passports inspected at the last Roman guard post, I took a walk between the cliff and the sea and observed a wonderful effect: the dark rocks stood out sharply in the light of the moon, which also cast a vividly flickering beam upon the blue sea, stretching from the horizon to the scintillating waves on the shore.

On the mountain top high above me in the dusky blue stood the ruins of Genseric's castle, which made me recall the days of long ago; I felt Conradin's ardent longing to escape and the anguish of Cicero and Marius, who also suffered in this region.

Later we drove in the moonlight along the foot of the mountain between the seashore and the huge rock boulders which had rolled down from above. Near Fondi, groves of olives, palms and pines stood out clearly in the light of the moon; only the lemon groves were at a disadvantage, for they can appear in their full splendour only when the sun shines upon the golden brilliance of their fruits. Then we crossed the mountain with its many olive and carob trees, and it was broad daylight when we reached an ancient city with many remains of sepulchral monuments. The largest of these is said to have been raised in honour of Cicero and to mark the very spot where he was murdered. The day was far advanced when we came to the lovely Gulf of Mola

di Gaeta. The fishermen had just returned with their catch and
the beach was a lively sight. Some were carrying fish and sea food
in baskets, others were busy preparing their nets for a second
haul. From there we proceeded to Garigliano, where excavations
are in progress by orders of Cavaliere Venuti. Here Hackert left
us, as he was in a hurry to get to Caserta, and we walked from
the road down to the seashore, where a breakfast was prepared
for us which might well have done for a dinner. The excavated
antiquities were on exhibition here, but they are deplorably
smashed. Among other beautiful things there is the leg of a
statue which is hardly inferior to the Apollo Belvedere. What a
piece of luck it would be if one could find the rest !

As we were very tired, we lay down to get a little sleep, and
when we woke, we found ourselves in the company of a charming
family that lives in the neighbourhood and had come to invite
us for dinner, an attention which we probably owed to Hackert.
Another table stood ready for us, but, in spite of the amiable
company, I could neither eat nor sit still, and took a walk
among the stones along the shore. Some of these were very odd,
especially those which had been perforated by marine insects
until they sometimes looked like sponges.

I also witnessed a delightful little scene. A goatherd came
down with his animals, who walked into the water to cool
themselves. Then a swineherd arrived with his beasts, who did
the same. The two of them settled down in the shade and made
music; the swineherd played a flute, the goatherd a bagpipe.
Finally a full-grown naked boy appeared on a horse and went
out so far into the sea that the horse had to swim. It was a
beautiful sight when the well-built lad emerged from the water,
came so close to the shore that I could see his whole figure and
then turned back towards the open sea until I could see nothing
but the head of the swimming horse and the shoulders of the
rider.

At three in the afternoon we set off again. Three miles beyond
Capua – by this time it was the first hour of the night – a rear
wheel of our coach broke. This caused a delay of several hours.
After it was replaced, we made a couple of miles more, then the
axle broke. This put us in a very bad temper; we were so close

to Naples, yet we could not communicate with our friends. We got there, at last, a few hours after midnight. There were still more people in the streets than one would be likely to find in any city at noon.

I found all our friends in good health and happy to hear the same of you. I am living in Hackert's house. The day before yesterday I visited Sir William Hamilton in his Posillipo villa. There is really no more glorious place in the whole world. After lunch a dozen boys went swimming in the sea. It was beautiful to watch the groups they made and the postures they took during their games. Sir William pays them to give him this pleasure every afternoon. Later we went for a row in a boat. I like him very much. We talked on many topics; I learned a great deal from him, and look forward to learning more in the future. Please send me the names of your other friends here so that I can make their acquaintance and give them your greetings. You shall hear from me again soon. Remember me to all our friends, especially to Angelica and Reiffenstein.

P.S. It is much hotter here than in Rome, but the air is more bracing because there is a fresh breeze all the time. Still the sun is stronger. The first days were almost unbearable. I lived on nothing but ice- and snow-water.

Later, undated

Yesterday, I wished you were here. Never in my life have I experienced such noise, such crowds of people, though all they were doing was buying food, and nowhere else have I ever seen such masses of food for sale. Yesterday and today I sat at table and was astonished at the way people gorged; the superfluity was almost sinful. Kniep was there and stuffed himself with delicacies till I was afraid he would burst. But this didn't deter him and he never stopped telling us about his appetite on the boat and in Sicily, when you, for all your good money, fasted and almost starved yourself, partly because you were indisposed and partly on principle. Naples is a city upon which God often bestows the blessing of pleasures for all the senses.

Later, undated

Enclosed is a drawing of the Turks who have been taken
prisoner. It was not, as was first reported, the Hercules* which
captured them but a vessel that was protecting the coral fishers.
The Turks sighted this Christian vessel and tried to capture it.
This was a mistake on their part, for the Christians proved
stronger, captured them and took them as prisoners to Naples.
There were thirty men on the Christian vessel and twenty-four
on the Turkish; six Turks were killed and one wounded. Not a
single Christian was killed; the Madonna protected them. The
captain has won a big prize for himself : he found much money,
silk, coffee and even valuable jewellery which belonged to a young
Moorish girl. It was curious to watch thousands of people
rowing out in boat after boat to see the prisoners, especially the
girl. Several fanciers wanted to buy her and offered large sums of
money, but the captain does not intend to sell her.

I also rowed out every day and once I met Sir William Hamilton and Miss Hart there. The latter was very moved and cried,
at which the girl also started crying. Miss Hart wanted to buy
her, but the captain was adamant and refused to sell her. Now
the prisoners have been taken away. My drawing will tell you
the rest.

SUPPLEMENT
THE PAPAL TAPESTRIES

I know nothing about the historical development of the art of
tapestry weaving. It is possible that in the twelfth century the
separate figures were each made in one piece by embroidery or
some other method and then joined together by other pieces of
worked material. Tapestries of this kind can still be seen above the
choir walls in old cathedrals. Such work bears a certain similarity
to stained-glass windowpanes of the early period, which were
also built up from very small pieces of stained glass; in the case

---

* *Hercules*, i.e., the ship which had brought the Farnese Hercules to
Naples.

of the tapestries needle and thread took the place of lead and strips of tin. All primitive artistic techniques are of this kind; I have seen Chinese rugs, worked in the same way.

But by the beginning of the sixteenth century, and probably under Oriental influence, the art of weaving with high warp, known as *haute lisse*, had already been raised to the pitch of perfection in the Netherlands, which were enjoying a splendid prosperity. Tapestries manufactured there had already found their way to the Orient and were undoubtedly also known in Rome, though probably from imperfect patterns in the Byzantine taste. Leo X, a great and in many respects a liberal spirit, particularly in aesthetic matters, wanted to have tapestries about him which would depict with equal ease the same great subjects as those he could see on frescoed walls, and at his request Raphael drew the cartoons, happily choosing subjects from the life of Christ with His Apostles, and the Acts of the Apostles after the death of their Master.

I only realized the proper destination of these tapestries on the Feast of Corpus Christi when colonnades and open spaces were transformed into magnificent halls and corridors, confronting the eye with the genius of a highly gifted man and providing a splendid example of how perfected art and perfected handicraft can unite to create a living work of the first order.

Raphael's cartoons, which have so far been preserved in England, will be eternally admired by the whole world. Most of them were undoubtedly executed by the hand of the master alone; others may have been completed after his drawings and sketches, and others even after his death, but they are all concordant with the same high artistic ideal, for artists of all nationalities flocked to Rome to find greater inspiration and develop their talents.

This gives me occasion for reflection on the tendency of the German artists of the period to be attracted in reverence and affection to Raphael's early works, the influence of which can be traced in theirs.

In any field of art, we feel a kinship with a talented, delicate-minded youth who dwells upon the gentle, graceful and natural, for, though we may not dare openly to compare ourselves with him, in secret we hope to emulate him and rival what he has done.

But with the mature artist, we feel less at our ease. We instinctively sense that the conditions under which even the most pronounced natural talent can attain the pinnacle of achievement are exceptional, and this frightens us. If we are not to despair, we have to turn back and compare ourselves with the inspiring artist in his formative stage.

That is why the German artists were drawn to Raphael's earlier, less consummate, works. Beside them, they could keep their self-confidence and even flatter themselves with the hope of accomplishing something which it had needed many successive centuries to make possible.

But let me return to Raphael's cartoons and say this: they are virilely conceived, dominated by a spirit of instinctive nobility and moral seriousness, and, though in places they are enigmatic, they are comprehensible to anyone who has read what Holy Scripture has to say about the miraculous gifts which the Redeemer bestowed on His disciples after His ascension.

Let me take just one example – the exposure and punishment of Ananias – and compare the small copperplate engraving after a drawing by Raphael, which has been attributed, not unjustly, to Marcantonio, with the reproduction by Dorigny of the cartoon.

In depicting an unusual and complex action in the clearest possible pictorial terms, there are few compositions which can bear comparison with it.

The Apostles stand waiting for the others to make a pious offering of their personal goods to the common chest. On one side the faithful are bringing their gifts, on the other the poor are receiving them and, in the centre, the fraudulent one is receiving his dreadful punishment. The symmetrical disposition of the figures is given by the situation, and their significance is not obscured but enlivened further by the demands of the subject, just as the necessarily symmetrical proportions of the human body derive their compelling interest only from the multifarious movements of life.

One could comment without end upon the many merits of

this work, but I shall confine myself to one. It is obvious that the two men who are approaching, bearing bundles of clothing, must be related to Ananias, but how are we to tell from them that a portion of his offering has been kept back and the common welfare cheated out of it? Then, however, we notice a pretty young woman who is cheerfully counting money from her right hand into her left, and we immediately recall the sacred words: 'Let not thy left hand know what thy right hand doeth.' From this and the cheerful, shrewd expression on her face, we know without any doubt that the woman is Sapphira, who is counting out the money which ought to be delivered to the Apostles in order to keep back some of it. The more one thinks about it, the more remarkable and terrifying this becomes. Before our eyes her husband is already being punished and writhing on the ground; only a few steps behind him, unaware of that is happening and without the slightest inkling of the fate which awaits her, his wife is maliciously plotting to cheat the men of God. The more one thinks of the eternal problem of the pictorial representation of action which this picture raises, the more one admires the way in which it solves it.

Marcantonio's engraving is the same size as Raphael's original drawing; Dorigny's copy is on a larger scale. A comparison of the two leads one to reflect upon the wisdom with which a man of Raphael's talent could take the same composition and, in a second treatment, modify and improve it. Studies of this kind, I am happy to admit, have been among the greatest joys of my whole life.

JULY

CORRESPONDENCE

Rome, 5 July

MY present life is exactly like a youthful dream; it remains to be seen whether Fate is going to allow me to enjoy it, or whether, like so many other dreams, it will turn out to be mere vanity.

Tischbein has left; his studio has been cleaned and tidied, so that I am enjoying living in it. At this season a pleasant refuge is an absolute necessity. The heat is terrific. I get up at dawn and walk to the Acqua Acetosa, a mineral spring about half an hour's walk from the Porta del Popolo, where I live. There I drink the water, which tastes like a weak *Schwalbacher*, but is very effective. I am home again by eight, and set to work in whatever way the spirit dictates. My health is excellent. The heat dispels all watery humours and drives any acidity in the body towards the skin, which is better than suffering from shooting and racking pains. In drawing, I continue educating my taste and my hand. I have started to concern myself more seriously with architecture, and everything comes surprisingly easy to me – the theoretical part, that is, not the practical, which requires a lifetime. My chief advantage has been that I arrived here without a conceited or presumptuous idea of myself and without preconceived expectations of what I should find. My one desire is that nothing shall remain a mere word to me; anything that is reportedly beautiful, great and venerable, I want to see and judge for myself. This cannot be done without copying, and I have now to sit down and use plaster heads for models. The artists are teaching me the proper method. I keep to myself as much as possible, though at the beginning of this week I couldn't refuse invitations to dine here and there. They want to take me along with them wherever they go, but I let them want and keep to my solitude. Moritz, several fellow countrymen who are living in the house and an honest Swiss are the people I see most of. I sometimes visit Angelica and Hofrat Reiffenstein, but I keep my distance and open my heart to nobody. Lucchesini has returned, a man who sees everyone and whom one sees everywhere. If I am not mistaken, he knows his *métier* well. I will write to you soon about various people I hope to meet in a short while.

I am working on *Egmont* and hope that it will turn out all right. At least, whenever I work on it, I have symptoms which hitherto have not deceived me. It is strange that, after having been so often interrupted in my work on it, it should be in Rome that the play is going to be finished. The first act is now ready in a fair copy, and there are other whole scenes which need no further revision.

I have had so many opportunities to think about every kind of art that my *Wilhelm Meister* is going to become very voluminous. But I intend to cut out all the old things in it; I have reached an age when, if I still want to produce something, I must not lose any time. As you can imagine, I have hundreds of new ideas in my head, but the main thing is making, not thinking; it is so damnably difficult to put things down in such a way that each is exactly where it ought to be, not somewhere else. I should like to talk long with you about art, but what can one say in the absence of the works themselves? I have many small difficulties, but I hope to overcome them. Therefore do not grudge me my time here, which for me is so strange and exciting, but give your loving approval to my stay in Rome.

I must now stop for the time being and, against my will, leave one page blank. The heat today was excessive and I fell asleep before sundown.

9 July

In future, I am going to write some lines every week, so that mailing days and unexpected events may not take me by surprise and prevent me from sending you a few sensible words.

Yesterday I saw and re-saw much; I visited about twelve of the churches which have the most beautiful altarpieces. Then, in company with Angelica, I went to see Moore, an English landscape painter, most of whose works are admirably thought out. Among his paintings he has one of the Flood which is unique. While other artists have painted the open sea, which conveys the idea of a vast watery expanse but cannot show that the waters are rising, he has depicted a secluded valley into which the waters are rushing and filling it up. The shapes of the rocks show that the water level has nearly risen to the summit, and since the valley is closed off diagonally in the background and all the cliffs are steep, the total effect is one of terror. All the tones in the picture are grey; the muddy, churning water and the pouring rain blend intimately; the water cascades and drips from the rocks as if their enormous masses were about to dissolve themselves into the universal element, and the sun, lacking all radiance, looks like a wan moon through the watery haze, although it is not yet night. In the centre of the foreground, some human beings have taken refuge on an isolated plateau, at the very moment when the rising flood threatens to overwhelm them. It is a huge picture, seven or eight feet long and five or six feet high. I saw two other excellent pictures of his, a Morning and a Night, but I have no space to describe them.

For three whole days there has been a festival on Ara Coeli in honour of two beatified members of the Franciscan Order. The church decorations, the music, the illuminations and the fireworks attracted large crowds. The Capitol nearby was also lit up and fireworks were let off in its square. All in all, the effect was beautiful but it was only a pale imitation of the festival of St Peter. Accompanied by their husbands or their friends, the ladies of Rome appeared for the occasion dressed in white with black sashes, which made them look very beautiful and elegant in the dark. The evening promenades and carriage drives on the Corso are now more numerous, because nobody leaves the house during the day. The heat is quite tolerable, and during the last few days we have always had a cool breeze. I stay quietly in my cool studio and am in a cheerful mood. I have been working hard and *Egmont* has made considerable progress. It is strange to think that in Brussels * at this moment they are enacting scenes which I wrote twelve years ago : now people will probably interpret some lines in them as topical lampoons.

---

* A revolt had broken out in Brussels against the reforms of Joseph II and the Regent, Maria Christine.

16 July

Yesterday I went with Angelica to the Farnesina, where the paintings of the Psyche legend are. You and I have so often looked at coloured reproductions of them in my rooms that I know them almost by heart, so that they made all the greater impression on me. This hall, or rather this gallery, has the most beautiful decorations I ever saw, despite the way they are now ruined by being restored.

Today there was beast-baiting in the Mausoleum of Augustus. For this, the great building, empty inside, open above and completely circular, has now been converted into an arena like an amphitheatre which is capable of holding four or five thousand persons. I found the spectacle itself far from edifying.

17 July

This evening I visited Albacini, the restorer of antique statues, to see the torso of a seated Apollo which has been found in the Farnese collection and is to go to Naples. It is of an unsurpassed beauty, one of the very best pieces which have come down to us from antiquity.

I dined with Count Fries. The Abbé Casti, who accompanies him on his travels, was there and recited one of his novellas, *The Archbishop of Prague*. It is slightly improper but extraordinarily well written in *ottava rima*. I knew Casti already as the author of *Re Teodoro in Venezia*, a great favourite of mine. Now he has written a *Re Teodoro in Corsica*, the first act of which I have read and found equally charming.

Count Fries is always adding to his collection; among other things, he has bought a Madonna by Andrea del Sarto for six hundred sequins. It is a lovely painting, but one cannot have any idea of it without having seen it. Last March Angelica made an offer of four hundred and fifty for it and would have paid the whole sum asked, but her cautious husband raised some objection. Now they are both sorry.

Every day something new comes to light for my delectation,

in addition to the old and permanent things. My eye is being well trained and in time I might become a connoisseur.

Tischbein complains in a letter about the terrible heat in Naples. Here too it is bad enough. A week ago today it was hotter, so some travellers told me, than it had been in Spain and Portugal.

Egmont has got as far as the fourth act; I do hope the play will please you. I expect to finish it in three weeks and will send it off to Herder at once.

20 July

I have had plenty of time here to discover two of my capital faults, which have pursued and tormented me all my life. One is that I could never be bothered to learn the mechanical part of anything I wanted to work on or should have worked on. That is why, though I have plenty of natural ability, I have accomplished so little. Either I tried to master it by sheer force of intellect, in which case my success or failure was a matter of chance, or, if I wanted to do something really well and with proper deliberation, I had misgivings and could not finish it. My other fault, which is closely related to the first, is that I have never been prepared to devote as much time to any piece of work as it required. I possess the fortunate gift of being able to think of many things and see their connexions in a short time, but, in consequence, the detailed execution of a work, step by step, irritates and bores me. Now it is high time for me to mend my ways. I am in the land of the Arts; let me study them really thoroughly, so that I may find peace and joy for the rest of my life and be able to go on to something else.

Rome is a marvellous place. One finds here not only objects of every kind, but also people of every kind who take their work seriously and know exactly what they are doing, and one makes rapid and easy progress in their company. I am beginning, thank God, to be able to learn from others and profit from their experience.

And so, I feel better than ever in body and soul. I hope you will remark this in my productions and approve of my absence. I am united with you by what I write and think; otherwise I am very much alone, and in company keep my thoughts to myself; but this is easier here than anywhere else because there are always enough interesting topics for conversation.

Mengs says somewhere, in reference to the Apollo Belvedere, that a statue which combined the grand style with a more realistic rendering of the flesh would be the greatest work humanly conceivable. The torso of Apollo (it may be Bacchus) which I mentioned earlier seems to me to meet his demands and fulfil his prophecy. Though my eye is not yet sufficiently trained to entitle me to judge in such a delicate matter, I am inclined to believe that this fragment is the most beautiful work I have ever seen. Unfortunately, besides being only a torso, the epidermis has been washed off in several places, probably from standing under the eaves of a roof.

22 July

I dined with Angelica – it has become a tradition that I am her guest every Sunday. In the morning we had driven to the Barberini palace to see the Leonardo da Vinci and Raphael's portrait of his mistress. It is a great pleasure to look at paintings with Angelica, for she has a trained eye and knows a great deal about the technical side of painting. Moreover, she is sensitive to all that is true and beautiful, and incredibly modest.

In the afternoon I visited the Chevalier d'Agincourt, a wealthy Frenchman who spends his time and money writing a history of art from its decline to its revival. If he ever finishes it, it will be a remarkable book. His collections are of the greatest interest, for they show one how, even in dark and troubled times, the spirit of man has always been active.

At the moment I am working on something which is teaching me a great deal. I have conceived and drawn a landscape which an able artist called Dies is colouring for me while I watch, so that I may learn more and more about colour and harmony. All in all, I am making good progress; the only trouble is that, as always, I will undertake too much. To my great joy, I find that, by training myself to study forms exactly, I am quickly acquiring a sense of figure and proportion, and at the same time my old feeling

for composition and unity has come back to me. Now everything
will depend upon practice.

23 July

In the evening I climbed the column of Trajan. Seen from that
height and at sunset, the Colosseum, with the Capitol close by,
the Palatine behind and the city all around, it was a superb sight.
It was getting late when I walked home slowly through the
streets. The Piazza di Monte Cavallo with its obelisk is a remarkable place.

24 July

I went to the Villa Patrizi to see the sunset and enjoy the fresh
air, and tonight I have seen the column of Antoninus and the
Chigi Palace by moonlight. The column stood on its gleaming
white pedestal, black with age against the lighter night sky. To
take in even a small part of everything there is to see here would
take a lifetime or, rather, the return of many human beings learning from each other in turn.

27 July

All the artists, both old and young, are helping me to prune
and improve my little talent. I have made some progress in perspective, architecture and landscape composition. But living
creatures stump me; there is a gulf there, yet maybe, if I seriously
apply myself, I may learn how to cross it.

My room is a very pleasant place to live in during the hot
weather. We have had one cloudy day, one day of rain, a thunderstorm and then a few clear days that were comparatively cool.

29 July

Went with Angelica to the Rondanini Palace. You will remember that, in one of my first letters from Rome, I spoke of a
Medusa which made a great impression on me. Now the mere

knowledge that such a work could be created and still exists in the world makes me feel twice the person I was. I would say something about it if everything one could say about such a work were not a waste of breath. Works of art exist to be seen, not talked about, except, perhaps, in their presence. I am thoroughly ashamed of all the babbling about art in which I used to join. If I can get hold of a good cast of this Medusa, I shall bring it back with me, but a new one will have to be made. There are some for sale, but, far from conveying any idea of it, they ruin it. The mouth, in particular, is inexpressibly noble.

30 July

I stayed at home all day and worked without stopping. *Egmont* is almost finished. The fourth act is as good as completed. As soon as I have made a copy, I shall send it off by the mounted courier. How happy I shall be if I hear that this production has met with your approval. I have felt very young again while writing it, and I hope that the reader will also get an impression of freshness.

In the evening I was invited to a little dance which was being given in the garden behind our house. Although it is not exactly the best season for dancing, I had a jolly time. Those little Italian minxes have a charm of their own. Ten years ago something might have happened, but that kind of fire is now cold, and I left before the festivities came to an end. The moonlit nights are incredibly beautiful; when the moon first rises and has not yet climbed above the haze, it is a warm yellow like *il sole d'Inghilterra*, and for the rest of the night it is bright and friendly. The moment there is a cool breeze, life starts up again. There are always groups of people in the streets until the small hours, who play music and sing. One sometimes hears duets which are as beautiful as anyone hears at the opera or a concert.

31 July

I tried to transfer some of these moonlight effects to paper, and then busied myself with various other artistic problems. In the evening I took a walk with a fellow countryman and we argued about the rival merits of Michelangelo and Raphael. I took the former's side, he the latter's, and we ended up in joint praise of Leonardo da Vinci.

At night I went to the Comic Opera. The new intermezzo *L'Impresario in Angustie* * is excellent and will run for many nights in spite of the theatre's being so hot. There is one very successful quintet in which the poet reads his play while on one side the impresario and the prima donna applaud him, and on the other the composer and the seconda donna find fault, until it ends with a general fracas. The *castrati*, dressed up as women, play their parts better and better and grow more and more popular. For a small scratch summer company, they are really very good. Of course, the poor devils suffer miserably from the heat.

SOME QUESTIONS ABOUT NATURE WHICH INTRIGUE AND PERPLEX ME

While walking in the Public Gardens of Palermo, it came to me in a flash that in the organ of the plant which we are accustomed to call the *leaf* lies the true Proteus who can hide or reveal himself in all vegetal forms. From first to last, the plant is nothing but leaf, which is so inseparable from the future germ that one cannot think of one without the other.

Anyone who has had the experience of being confronted by an idea, pregnant with possibilities, whether he thought of it for himself or caught it from others, will know that it creates a tumult and enthusiasm in the mind, which makes one intuitively anticipate its further developments and the conclusions towards which it points.

Knowing this, he will understand that my vision had become an obsessive passion with which I was to be occupied, if not exclusively perhaps, still for the rest of my life.

However, though this interest had seized me, body and soul, it was out of the question to pursue it methodically after my return to Rome. Poetry, art, antiquity, each claimed my whole

---

* *L'Impresario in Angustie.* Opera by Cimarosa.

attention and I have never spent more operose and exhausting days in my life. Professional botanists will no doubt think it very naïve of me when I say that day after day, from all the gardens, and on every walk and excursion, I carried away specimens of plants. I was particularly anxious to observe how, as the seeds begin to germinate, they appear when they first come into the daylight. For example, I watched the germination of *Cactus opuntia*, which has such a monstrous shape when full grown, and was delighted to see that it unfolded in two tender leaflets, like a dicotyledon, which on further growth would develop into its distorted form. I had also a curious experience with some dry seed pods of *Acanthus mollis* which I had taken home with me and was keeping in a lidless little box. One night I heard something crack and soon afterwards a noise as if small bodies were bouncing against the walls and the ceiling. At first I could not account for this, but later I discovered that my seed pods had burst open and scattered the seeds all over the room. The dryness of the room had completed the process of ripening in a few days. Pine kernels burst open in a peculiar manner. First they pushed up as if they were enclosed in an egg, but soon they threw off their hood and revealed the rudiments of their destined form, surrounded by a corolla of green needles.

Reproduction by bud is just as interesting as reproduction by seed. Hofrat Reiffenstein, who always broke off twigs during our walks, asserted, to the point of pedantry, that every one of them, if stuck into the ground, was bound to start growing immediately.

In proof, he took me into his garden and showed me some of these slips which had begun to strike roots. I wish he could have lived to see this method of reproduction universally adopted, and how important it has now become to horticulturists. The most startling sight of all was a carnation plant which had grown to the height of a bush. The vitality and reproductive powers of this plant are well known, how the stems are packed with buds, one above the other, and the nodes fitted into each other like a funnel. In this specimen the process had been continued, the buds forced out of their mysterious confinement to so high a degree of development that the completed flower itself had produced out of its calyx four more flowers. As there seemed no possibility of preserving this marvellous creation, I decided to make a drawing of it, from the study of which I hope to obtain a better insight into the fundamental principle of metamorphosis.

JULY

IN RETROSPECT

AFTER staying quietly at home for some time, keeping myself to myself and avoiding the distractions of high society, I made the mistake of attracting the attention, not only of our whole quarter, but also of society, which is always eager to hear of novel and unusual events. This is how it came about. Angelica never went to the theatre, and I never asked her the reason, but, being a passionate lover of the stage, I was always praising in her presence the grace and versatility of the singers and also the effectiveness of the music of my favourite composer, Cimarosa. What I wanted most of all, I told her was to share my delight with her. One thing led to another and some of the younger members of our group, in particular Bury, who is a close friend of the singers and musicians, got them to promise that some time they would come to our *salone* and perform for their enthusiastic admirers. This plan was often discussed and always postponed. What finally turned the scale was the unexpected arrival of Kranz, an excellent violinist in the service of the Duke of Weimar, who had given him leave to come to Italy for further study.

I now found myself in the happy position of being able to invite Angelica and her husband, Reiffenstein, Jenkins, Volpato, and everyone else to whom I owed a courtesy, to a respectable entertainment.

Some Jewish decorators fixed up the salone; the nearest coffee-house owner assumed responsibility for the refreshments, and on a lovely summer night we had a brilliant concert. A large crowd gathered in the street outside and rapturously applauded the songs as if they were in a theatre. But the great surprise was a large carriage load of orchestra players who were taking a nocturnal pleasure drive around the city. They stopped beneath our windows and applauded our efforts on the upper floor. Then a fine bass voice, accompanied by all the instruments, began singing one of the most popular arias from the same opera of which we were performing selections. We responded with loud applause, the crowd joined in the clapping, and everybody declared that they had taken part in many night entertainments, but never in one as perfect as this which had come about by chance.

Now, all at once, my quiet, respectable lodging opposite the Rondanini Palace became an object of curiosity to the Corso. It was rumoured that a rich Milord was living there, but nobody could discover his name or identify him with any of the well-known personalities in town. It is true that, if the performers had been hired for money, such an entertainment would have cost a great deal, but, in fact, since everything was done by artists to please other artists, the expenses were quite modest. I returned to my quiet way of life, but I could not shake off the rumour that I was rich and of noble birth.

Count Fries's arrival, however, gave me fresh incentive to lead a more social life. With him was the Abbé Casti, who gave me great pleasure by reading his unpublished *Novelle Galanti*. His clear and natural style of recitation brought his witty, if very risqué, stories vividly to life.

I felt sorry that an intelligent and wealthy art lover, like the Count, should sometimes deal with persons who were not very reliable. His acquisition of a fake carved gem gave rise to many arguments and caused him much annoyance. However, he could feel happy about having bought a beautiful statue of Paris or, as some think, Mithras. Its counterpart is now in the Museo Pio-Clementino: both were found in the same sand-pit. It was not only the art dealers who waylaid him; he had several other disagreeable experiences and, further, since he did not know how to take care of himself in the hot season, he naturally succumbed to various illnesses. All these embittered his last days in Rome. It was all the more painful for me because I was indebted to him for many favours, such as the opportunity of seeing Prince di Piombino's rare collection of gems.

At Count Fries's house I met, not only art dealers, but also the kind of *literati* who go about in *soutanes*. Conversations with them were wearisome. The moment one started talking about their national poetry, hoping for information on some point or other, one could count on being asked which poet one considered the greatest – Ariosto or Tasso. If one gave the sensible answer and said that we should be grateful to God and Nature for having granted to one nation two such great men who have both, in their different ways, given us such beautiful moments of comfort and delight, one satisfied nobody. Whichever of the two they had decided to prefer, they extolled to the skies and dismissed the other as being beneath contempt. At first I would try to defend the rejected one by pointing out his merits, but this had not the slightest effect. They had taken sides and therefore they stuck to their opinion. This happened again and again, and since I felt too seriously about the matter to enter into dialectical controversy, I avoided conversations of this kind, especially when I realized that they had no real interest in poetry and that their pronouncements were mere empty phrases.

It was even worse when Dante came up in the discussion. A young man of rank and intelligence, who genuinely admired that great poet, did not take kindly to my praise of him, declaring that no foreigner had the right to claim that he understood such a unique mind when even Italians could not always grasp what he meant. After some talking back and forth, I got rather cross and said that I must confess that I agreed with him, since I had never been able to understand how people could take the trouble to read these poems. I thought the *Inferno* absolutely horrible, the *Purgatorio* ambiguous, and the *Paradiso* a bore. The young man was delighted, for my words seemed a proof of his assertions. We parted as the best of friends and he even promised to write out some difficult passages for me, together with his interpretations, for it was only after long cogitations, he said, that their meaning had recently become quite clear to him.

Nor, alas, were conversations with artists and art lovers any more edifying. But in the end one has to forgive in others a fault which one finds in oneself. First it was Raphael I preferred, then it was Michelangelo. One can only conclude that man is such a limited creature that, though his soul may be open to greatness, he never acquires the capacity to recognize and appreciate equally, different kinds of greatness.

I missed Tischbein, but his lively letters did much to make up for his absence. Apart from his ingenious ideas and his witty accounts of curious incidents, he sent sketches and drawings of a painting which had made him famous in Naples. It depicted Orestes, in half-figure, at the moment when Iphigenia recognizes him at the sacrificial altar, and the pursuing Furies are about to disappear. Iphigenia was a striking portrait of Miss Hart, who later became Lady Hamilton. At that time she was at the height of her beauty and fame, and regarded as the proper model for all heroines and demi-goddesses. Even one of the Furies had been ennobled with her likeness. Any artist who was capable of such a work would have been more than welcome in Sir William Hamilton's distinguished circle.

AUGUST

CORRESPONDENCE

1 August

BECAUSE of the heat, I stayed quietly at home all day and worked. My greatest consolation during this heat wave is my conviction that you, too, must be having a fine summer in Germany. It is pleasant to watch the hay being brought in. At this time of the year it does not rain at all, so that the work in the fields can be done at any time they wish. It is only a pity that their methods of agriculture are so primitive.

In the evening I bathed in the Tiber from a well-appointed and safe bathing machine. Afterwards I walked to Trinità dei Monti, enjoying the fresh air and the moon. The moonlit nights here are like those in dreams or fairy tales.

The fourth act of *Egmont* is done; in my next letter I hope I shall be able to announce that I have finished the play.

11 August

I shall stay in Italy until next Easter. I cannot run away from school now. If I keep on with my studies I am certain that the progress I shall make will satisfy both my friends and me. I shall write regularly so that every time you get a letter, you will think of me as absent but alive, whom you so often used to mourn for as present but dead.

Egmont is nearly finished and I will send it off at the end of this month. After that I shall be anxiously waiting for your verdict.

Not a day goes by without my adding to my knowledge of art and improving my skill. Here, if one is willing and receptive, one can easily fill oneself to the brim like an open bottle plunged under water.

The sky is always cloudless and at noon the heat is ferocious, but I escape the worst of it by staying in my cool studio. I plan to spend September and October in the country, drawing from Nature. I may go to Naples again to profit from Hackert's teaching. During the two weeks I spent with him in the country, I made more progress than I could have made in years working by myself. I am not sending you anything now but shall wait till I can send you a dozen or so small sketches which I think good enough.

I have spent the past week working hard, and have learned much, especially in perspective. Verschaffelt, the son of the Director of the Mannheim Academy, who has studied this subject thoroughly, is teaching me his tricks. On my drawing-board I also have some moonscapes, and some other ideas which are really too crazy to tell you about.

I have written a long letter to the Dowager Duchess, advising her to put off the visit to Italy for another year. If she leaves in October she will arrive in this beautiful country just when the weather changes and she will not find it fun. But if she takes my advice on this matter and others, she should, with luck, have a good time. I am delighted, for her sake, about her proposed journey.

Everything has been so well arranged in Weimar that neither I nor the others need worry about the future. Nobody can change himself and nobody can escape his destiny, so now that I have told you what my plans are, I hope you will approve.

I shall write often and, throughout the winter, I shall always be with you in spirit.

Tasso will arrive soon after the New Year. *Faust* in his courier's cloak will announce my arrival. By that time I shall have lived through the most important period in my life and rounded it off neatly so that I can pick up my duties again. I feel much more at ease and can hardly recognize the person I was a year ago.

I am living on the spiritual riches of all that is especially precious to me. It is only during these last months that I have really come to enjoy myself. Now everything lies clear before me, and, as Minerva was born from the head of Jupiter, so art has become my second nature, born from the heads of great men. Later you will have to listen to me talking about all this for days, or rather years, on end.

I wish you all a fine September. At the end of August, when all our birthdays fall together, I shall be thinking of you constantly. As soon as it gets cooler, I am going into the country to draw; meanwhile I do what I can in my studio, but I am often forced to stop work. In the evenings one has to take great precautions not to catch cold.

18 August

This week I had to moderate my northern passion for activity; the first few days were really too hot. Therefore, I have not done as much as I should have liked. But for the last two days a pleasant tramontana has been blowing, and the air is perfectly fresh. September and October ought to be heavenly.

Yesterday I drove to Acqua Acetosa before sunrise; the variety, misty transparency and colouring of this landscape drove me wild with joy.

Moritz is now studying the works of antiquity with the intention of writing something unstuffy and free from the dust of the schools, which will make them accessible to the young and the average intelligent reader. He has a happy and sensible approach to such matters; I only hope he will take time enough to do a thorough job.

We take a walk together every evening: and he tells me what he has thought for himself during the day and what he has read in other authors. Through him, a gap in my knowledge is being filled, for other occupations have forced me to neglect these matters, and if I were left to myself, it would have taken me much time and effort to make up for my neglect. While we talk, I look at buildings, streets, landscapes, monuments, etc.; then, when we come home in the evening and sit chatting and joking, I draw some view which struck me particularly. I enclose one I made last night. It will give you a rough idea of how the Capitol looks as you climb the hill behind it.

Last Sunday I went with Angelica to see Prince Aldobrandini's pictures, particularly an admirable Leonardo da Vinci. Considering her great talent and her fortune, she is not as happy as she deserves to be. She is tired of commissions, but her old husband thinks it wonderful that so much money should roll in for what is often easy work. She would like to paint to please herself and have more leisure to study and take pains, and she could easily do this. They have no children and they cannot even spend the interest on her capital: indeed, they could live on the money she earns every day by working moderately hard. But she doesn't do anything about it and she won't. She talks to me very frankly; I have told her my opinion, given her advice and I try to cheer her up whenever we meet. What's the use of talking about misery and misfortune when people who have enough of everything do not know how to use it or enjoy it? For a woman, she has extraordinary talent. One must look for what she does, not what she fails to do. How many artists would stand the test if they were judged only by their failings?

To acquire an intimate knowledge of Rome, its atmosphere, its art, and to feel natural and at home, one must do as I am doing, live here and walk about the city day after day. The impressions of a mere tourist are bound to be false.

My chief problem is Roman society, which would like to draw me out of my solitary shell and interfere with my working habits; but I protect myself as well as I can. I promise, put off, promise again, and play the Italian among the Italians. The Secretary of State, Cardinal Buoncompagni, has been very pressing with his invitations, but I shall evade them until I go into the country in the middle of September. I avoid grand ladies and gentlemen like the plague: it upsets me even to see them driving past the house in their carriages.

23 August

The day before yesterday I received your dear letter, No. 24, just as I was leaving to pay another visit to the Sistine Chapel, and whenever I took a rest from looking and making notes, I read and reread it. I cannot tell you how much I wished you were here, for until you have seen the Sistine Chapel, you can have no adequate conception of what man is capable of accomplishing.

One hears and reads of so many great and worthy people, but here, above one's head and before one's eyes, is living evidence of what *one* man has done. I hold conversations with you constantly in my head; I only wish I could put them all down on this piece of paper. You say you want to hear about *me*. If I were really to tell you how I have been reborn, how renewed and fulfilled I feel, how fortified in all my faculties, it would take pages. Let me merely say that I shall hope to accomplish something. For some time, I have been seriously preoccupied with landscape and architecture and I now see what will come out of my efforts and how far I can go.

At long last the alpha and omega of all things known to us – the human figure – has come to grips with me and I with it, so that I say: Lord, I will not let Thee go except Thou bless me, even though I wrestle until I am lame. When I try to draw it, I get nowhere, so I have started to model it, and seem to be making some progress. At least I have arrived at an idea which makes many things easier for me. To tell you all the details would be too complicated, and in any case, it is better to do than to talk. It amounts briefly to this: my obstinate study of Nature and the careful attention I have paid to comparative anatomy have now brought me to the point where I have a vision of many things in Nature and sculpture as a whole which professional artists can arrive at only by a laborious study of details, and even if they at last succeed in getting there, their knowledge is something for themselves only, which they cannot communicate to others. I have started toying again with physiognomy – a game I chucked up out of pique with the Prophet * – and I find it quite useful. I have begun a head of Hercules; if it seems to be turning out well, I shall go on with it.

I am now so remote from the world that it gives me a curious feeling to read a newspaper. 'The fashion of this world passeth away' and my only desire is to follow Spinoza's teaching and concern myself with what is everlasting so as to win eternity for my soul.

Yesterday I was at the house of Sir Richard Worsley, who has travelled widely in Greece, Egypt, etc., and saw many of his drawings. The most interesting were of bas-reliefs from the

---

* J. K. Lavater (1741–1801), Swiss-German poet and physiognomist.

Acropolis in Athens, the work of Phidias. Nothing could conceivably be more beautiful than these few simple figures. Otherwise, there were very few things of interest; his architectural drawings are a little better than his landscapes, which are not felicitous.

Farewell for today. A bust is being made of me, and this has cost me three mornings this week.

TO HERDER

28 August

How wonderful it is to sow in order to reap! Here I have kept it a secret that today is my birthday, and when I got up this morning, I thought: 'I wonder if anything will arrive from home to celebrate it.' Then, lo and behold! To my inexpressible delight, your package arrived. I immediately sat down to read it and now that I have finished it, I want to thank you at once from the bottom of my heart. It is so comforting and refreshing to read your pure and beautiful words, so rich in noble thoughts about God, in this Babel, which is the mother of so much falsehood and error. Now is certainly the time when such sentiments and ideas can and should be disseminated. I shall often read and ponder over the book in my solitude, and make notes which may provide material for future discussions with you.

I wish we could see each other and have a long talk, so that you could elucidate some details and allusions. But enough. That will be granted us too. Meanwhile I thank you again with all my heart for having set up a pillar from which henceforth we can count our miles.

The French Academy is having an exhibition. There are some interesting things, a picture of Pindar, for example, who has prayed the gods to grant him a happy end, dying in the arms of a boy whom he dearly loves. An architect has had the ingenious idea of making two drawings: the first shows contemporary Rome, viewed from an angle where all its parts harmonize pleasantly with each other, the second ancient Rome as seen from the same standpoint.

The places where the old buildings stood and, in many cases, their actual shapes are well known, for a number of the ruins are still standing. He has taken out every new building and restored the old, to give a picture of Rome as it must have looked at about the time of Diocletian. This second drawing shows as much taste as learning and, in addition, is charmingly coloured.

Did I tell you that the Prince of Waldeck has commissioned Trippel to do a bust of me? It is almost finished and, as a whole, it is good and worked in a very sound style. After the clay model is finished, he is going to cast it in plaster, and then copy the cast in marble. I shall have to sit for him again when he puts the finishing touches to it, which cannot be done in any other material.

Angelica is painting a picture of the Mother of the Gracchi showing her most precious treasures, her children, to a friend who is displaying her jewellery. It promises to turn out very well.

After receiving your letter today, I thought everything over again, and I still remain convinced that it is essential for my study of art and my writing that I stay here longer. In art I have to reach the point where everything has become first-hand knowledge and nothing remains a mere name. This can be done only in Rome and in six more months I think I shall have reached it. As for my writings, I must at least finish my little pieces – I see them very much in the diminutive – with concentration and a happy heart.

When that is done, everything will draw me back to my native land. I may, when I get back, lead an isolated and private life, but I have so much to go over and fit together that I cannot see myself having any rest for the next ten years.

In the field of natural history, I shall have things to show and tell you which will surprise you. I believe I have come very close to the truth about the *how* of the organism. I hope you will rejoice when you hear about these manifestations – not fulgurations * – of our God, and you must tell me who, in ancient or more recent times, has made similar discoveries or thought along the same lines.

---

* *Fulgurations*, a term used by Leibniz.

AUGUST

IN RETROSPECT

It was at the beginning of this month that I definitely made up my mind to stay another winter. An instinctive feeling that, at this point, I was not nearly ready to leave and that I could not find anywhere else the proper peaceful atmosphere for finishing my works finally decided me, and once I had told my friends at home of my decision, a new era began.

The great heat, which grew steadily worse and set limits to any excessive activity, made one look for cool places to work in, and one of the most pleasant was the Sistine Chapel. At that time the artists had just rediscovered Michelangelo. In addition to all the other qualities they admired, they said that he surpassed all others in his sense of colour, and it became the fashion to dispute whether he or Raphael was the greater genius. The latter's *Transfiguration* was often severely criticized and the *Disputa* considered his best work. All this pointed towards the coming predilection for an earlier school of painting, a taste which a dispassionate observer could only regard as a symptom of mediocre and unoriginal talents.

It is so difficult to comprehend one great talent, let alone two at the same time. To make things easier for us, we take sides; that is why the reputation of artists and writers is always fluctuating. Now one rules the day, now another. Personally, I ignored these disputes and spent my time in direct observation of anything which seemed to me to be worth looking at. Soon the fashion for preferring the great Florentine spread from the artists to the art-loving public, which is why, just at this time, Count Fries commissioned Bury and Lipps to make watercolour copies of the frescoes in the Sistine Chapel. The custodian was handsomely tipped and let us enter by the back door next to the altar, and settle down there whenever we liked. We even used to have meals there, and I remember that one day I was overcome by the heat and snatched a noon nap on the papal throne.

Using white chalk on black gauze frames, Bury and Lipps first made careful tracings of the lower heads and figures of the altarpiece * which were in ladder's reach; these were then recopied in red chalk on large sheets of paper.

Another of the older masters who came into high favour at this time was Leonardo da Vinci, whose now famous painting *Christ among the Pharisees* I had seen with Angelica in Prince Aldobrandini's gallery. It had become a custom for Angelica, her husband and Hofrat Reiffenstein to call for me every Sunday at my house before noon; then we would drive, in as great comfort as was possible in the baking heat, to some gallery or other, stay there a few hours, then return to her home for an excellent dinner. I learned a great deal from seeing important works of art in the company of these fine friends, all of whom were specialists in their field, theoretical, technical or aesthetic. Hofrat Reiffenstein was also very helpful to me in another way. When people tried to make my acquaintance, I could always use his prestige as an excuse for sticking to my self-chosen privacy, and say that I could only be introduced by him.

The exhibition of the French Academy at the end of the month was an important artistic event. The *Horatii* by David converted everybody to the French School, and stimulated Tischbein to begin his life-size picture of Hector challenging Paris in the presence of Helen. The works of Drouais, Gagneraux, Desmarais, Gauffier and St Ours also created a sensation, and Boquet made a name for himself as a landscape painter in the style of Poussin.

Moritz was working hard at classical mythology. As he had done before, he came to Rome to secure the means to travel by offering to write a travel book. A bookseller gave him an advance, but after living in Rome for a short time, he realized that a travel diary, dashed off in a hurry, would not escape severe criticism. As a result of our daily conversations and seeing so many works of art, he got the idea of writing a history of classical mythology from a simple human point of view and illustrating it with drawings of carved gems.

I had some interesting talks with Trippel while he was model-

---

The Last Judgement by Michelangelo.

ling my bust, and found that his views coincided with my own. It gave me a unique opportunity for learning how far the human figure can be studied according to fixed canons of proportion and how much account should be taken of deviations caused by individual characteristics. Our meeting was doubly interesting for me because Trippel had got word of a head of Apollo in the Palazzo Giustiniani collection which had hitherto gone unnoticed. He considered it one of the noblest of works, and hoped to be able to buy it, but this was not to be. This antique relic later came into the possession of M. de Pourtalès, in Neuchâtel, and has become famous.

Verschaffelt gave a course of lectures in perspective which we all used to attend in the evenings, and try to put what we learned into practice right away. The best thing about them was that he did not try to teach us too much, only the essentials.

SEPTEMBER

CORRESPONDENCE

1 September

Egmont will be finished in a day or two. I kept finding places here and there which needed more working on. I shall send it by way of Zurich, because I want Kayser to compose the incidental music. When that is done, I want you to enjoy it.

Moritz has derived great benefit from Herder's ideas on God. Both his own nature and his talks with me had made him receptive to Herder's approach, and he immediately caught fire like a piece of dry wood: he will certainly regard the book as a milestone in his life.

Rome, 3 September

A year ago today I set out from Carlsbad. What a year it has been! And what a wonderful epoch began for me on the day which was both the birthday of our Duke and the birthday of my new life. At this moment I can give no account, either to myself or to others, of the use I have made of this year; I only hope the blessed hour will come when I shall be able to sum up everything with you and for myself.

I have taken up Egyptian things again and have several times lately gone to see the great obelisk of Sesostris,* which is still lying in a courtyard amidst dirt and rubble. It was erected in Rome in honour of Augustus and acted as the gnomon of a huge sundial marked out on the ground of the Campus Martius. This oldest and most marvellous of ancient monuments is now in fragments, and some sides have been damaged, probably by fire. Yet the parts which have not been destroyed look as fresh as if they had been made yesterday and show a beautiful workmanship of their own. I have ordered wax impressions of the sphinx near the top of the obelisk, and of other sphinxes, men and birds.

---

* Actually, the obelisk of Psammetichos II (594–89 B.C.).

Later these will be cast in plaster and be invaluable, because they say that the Pope intends to have the obelisk raised again, in which case it will be impossible to reach the hieroglyphs. I am making clay models of these figures so as to make them really my own, and I intend to do the same with the Etruscan objects.

5 September

I must write to you this morning because, for me, it is a morning to celebrate: *Egmont* is really and truly finished. I have written the title page, the list of characters, and filled up a few gaps which I had left open. Now I am looking forward eagerly to the hour when you receive and read it. I will enclose some drawings with it as well.

5 September

I had planned to write you a long letter in answer to your last, but I have been interrupted and tomorrow I am leaving for Frascati. This will have to be posted on Saturday, so I can only write a few words before I go. I am worried to hear that Herder is not well, and hope that I shall soon have better news.

I am in good health, both in body and soul, and dare to hope that I shall be radically cured. My work goes easily and well and sometimes even I feel the breath of youth. Yes, I can now say that I see the light and the point towards which all my powers are leading me. One has to reach a certain age before one can discover more or less who one is. It is not only Swabians who need the proverbial forty years to become wise.

Egmont goes off today too, but will arrive after this letter because I am sending it by mail coach. Perhaps it would be a good thing to start printing it soon. I should like the public to have the play while it is fresh, so please do what you can to arrange this. I shall not be behindhand with the rest of the volume.

The *God* is my constant and best companion. Moritz, too, has been really edified by it. He only needed a keystone to prevent his thoughts from falling apart, and this work had provided it, and now his own book is going to be very good. He has encouraged me to delve deeper into matters of natural history, and I have hit upon an ἓν καὶ πᾶν,* in botany especially, which amazes me. What its full implications will be, I cannot yet foresee.

The principle, by which I interpret works of art and unlock the secret which artists and art experts since the Renaissance have been laboriously trying to discover, seems to me sounder every time I apply it. It is verily the egg of Columbus. Without going so far as to claim I know how to use such a master key properly, I find myself competent to discuss with artists the details of their work, to see what point they have reached and what their difficulties have been. My own door stands open and I stand on the threshold, but alas, I have only time to peer into the temple before I must depart.

One thing is certain : all the artists of antiquity had as great a knowledge of Nature and as unerring a sense of *what* can be represented and *how*, as Homer. Unfortunately, the number of works of the first order still extant is much too small. But once one has seen them, one's only desire is to get to know them through and through and then depart in peace. These masterpieces of man were brought forth in obedience to the same laws as the masterpieces of Nature. Before them, all that is arbitrary and imaginary collapses : *there* is Necessity, *there* is God.

In a few days I am going to see the drawings of an able architect who has visited Palmyra. I hear they are done with great intelligence and good taste. As soon as I have seen them, I shall write you, for I am eager to hear your opinion of these remarkable ruins.

Rejoice with me that I am happy. Indeed, I can honestly say I have never been so happy in my life as now. If only I could communicate to the friends I love a small part of my joy.

I hope the dark clouds on the political horizon will soon be dispersed. Our modern wars make many miserable while they last, and none happy when they are over.

---

* ἓν καὶ πᾶν : one and all, i.e., one law is valid for all. A quotation from Xenophanes of Colophon.

I still seem to be a person who lives in order to work. During these last few days I have again worked more than I have amused myself. Now the week is coming to an end and you shall have a letter.

I am hurt that the aloe in Belvedere should have chosen to flower in the one year when I was away. In Sicily I was too early; here only one plant is in bloom this year, and, moreover, it is not very large and stands so high one cannot get near it. Besides, it is a plant from India and does not feel quite at home even here.

The Englishman's descriptions are not to my taste. The English clergy have to be very circumspect, but they hold the rod over the rest of the public, and the free Englishman proceeds with great discretion when he writes about morals.

Human beings with tails are no surprise to me; from the descriptions it seems quite natural. There are more miraculous things to be seen about us every day, but we do not notice them because they are not closely related to our concerns.

It is quite all right with me if B——, like so many others, after having had no genuine religious feelings all his life, should turn pious, as it is called, in his old age, provided he doesn't expect me to join in his devotions.

Frascati is a paradise. I spent some days there with Hofrat Reiffenstein, and on Sunday Angelica came to take us back to the city.

I have rewritten half of *Erwin und Elmire* in an attempt to give the little piece more interest and life. I have cut out all the extremely banal dialogue. It was the work of a schoolboy, or rather, it was slovenly written. All the pretty songs, around which everything turns, remain, of course.

My bust has turned out exceedingly well and everybody is satisfied with it. It is executed in a noble style, and I shall have no objection if posterity imagines I looked like that. If the problem of transportation were not so complicated, I would send you a cast at once. Perhaps, at some later date, I shall be able to ship one, for eventually I shall have to crate some of my belongings.

You don't say whether Kranz has arrived. I gave him a box to bring to the children.

In the Valle theatre they are playing a charming operetta. The last two were complete fiascos.

I shall soon be going to the country. It has rained several times, the weather is cooler and the landscape green again.

You have probably read in the newspaper, or soon will, about the great eruption of Etna.

15 September

I have now read the life of Trenck.* It is quite interesting and gives me food for reflection.

Cassas's drawings are unusually beautiful. I have stolen a lot of ideas from him which I shall bring back for you.

I am working hard as usual. I have just drawn the cast of a small head, as a test to see whether my principle holds good. I find that it does so perfectly and facilitates the execution amazingly. Nobody will believe I did it, though it really isn't anything yet. But I now see clearly how far I might come with steady application.

On Monday I shall go to Frascati again and after that probably to Albano to go on drawing from Nature. At present I am only really interested in producing something and training my senses. This is a malady I have suffered from since youth. Would to God I could get over it.

22 September

I have bought a collection of two hundred wax impressions of antique carved gems. They are among the most beautiful examples of antique craftsmanship and have been partly selected for the charm of their motifs. The impressions are unusually fine and distinct, and I could not come away from Rome with anything more precious.

---

*Freiherr Friedrich von der Trenck (1726–94), a favourite of Frederick the Great, later defamed and imprisoned for many years. In 1786 he wrote *The Strange Story of My Life*.

When I return in my little boat I shall bring many good things with me, and the best of all will be a happy heart and a greater capacity for enjoying the love and friendship which await me. Only, I must never again undertake anything outside the sphere of my talents, any task which exhausts me without bearing any fruit.

I must quickly send you another page by the courier. It has been a very memorable day for me – letters from many friends, from the Dowager Duchess, news about the celebration of my birthday and, last but not least, the arrival of my works.

It gives me a very strange feeling to think that these four slim volumes, the results of half my life, should find me in Rome, of all places. I can honestly say that there is not a word in them which I have not lived, felt, thought, enjoyed and suffered, and that makes them speak to me all the more vividly. I anxiously hope that the other four will not be inferior. Thank you for all you did for these pages and may they give you some pleasure. Please take care also of the ones which are to follow, like the loyal friend you are.

You tease me about the 'provinces'.* The expression was, I admit, very ill chosen. But you can see from this slip of the tongue how used one gets in Rome to thinking in grandiose terms. Really, I must be becoming a Roman, for the Romans are always accused of thinking and talking only about *cose grosse*.

The idea struck me the other day that in the wide circle of a great city even the poorest and the humblest person feels himself to be somebody, whereas in a small town even the best and the richest is not himself and cannot breathe.

Frascati, 28 September

I am very happy here. All day and far into the night we draw, paint, sketch in inks and practise the arts and crafts very much *ex professo*. Our host, Hofrat Reiffenstein, keeps us company and we are all in high spirits. In the evenings we visit

---

*In a letter to the Duke of Weimar, Goethe had used the term *provinces* instead of *territories*.

various villas by moonlight, and even when it was dark, we drew some striking subjects. We hunted out some which I should like to amplify further sometime.

Yesterday we drove to Albano and back and on the way we killed many birds with one stone. If only the day would come when I shall be able to send you something good instead of merely talking. I have a few little things which I am giving a fellow countryman to bring you.

I shall probably have the pleasure of seeing Kayser in Rome. So music will join the other arts and close the circle they have formed around me, as if they wished to make a wall between me and my friends. But that is a chapter I hardly dare think about, how very lonely I often feel, and how homesick for your company. My days are spent in a continual whirl, and I cannot and will not think beyond the present moment.

I have been spending very pleasant hours with Moritz explaining my botanical system to him. As we talk, I write down everything we say, so that I can see where I have got to. This is the only way in which I could get some of my ideas down on paper. But with my new pupil I have had the experience that even the most abstract ideas become intelligible to a receptive mind if they are presented properly. He enjoys our talks immensely and always anticipates my conclusions. My theory is difficult to describe in any case and, no matter how clearly and exactly it is written down, impossible to understand merely from reading.

So my life is happy because I am about my father's business. Remember me to all who do not grudge me my happiness and to all who, directly or indirectly, help, encourage and sustain me.

SEPTEMBER

IN RETROSPECT

THAT year I had several reasons for celebrating the third of September. It was the birthday of my Duke, who had always returned my loyal affection with so many acts of kindness, and it was the anniversary of my hegira from Carlsbad. I still did not dare to look back over a year which had been so important in my life and see what it had done for me and how I had developed. Besides, I had little time for serious reflection.

The French architect Cassas had returned from his journey to the Orient with drawings of the places he visited. Some showed them as they are at present, destroyed or in ruins; in others, tracing with ink or in water colour, he graphically reconstructed them as they must originally have looked. Here are some descriptions of them which I made at the time.

1. The seraglio of Constantinople, seen from the sea, with the mosque of St Sophia, and part of the city. One cannot imagine a more cheerful building than this residence of the Sultans on the most charming tip of Europe.

Between large, symmetrically placed groups of tall, well-tended trees, one sees, not high walls and palaces, but little houses, latticework, arcades, kiosks and hung carpets in a small-scale, friendly jumble which is a joy to behold. A beautiful stretch of sea washes the built-up shore. Asia is directly opposite and one can see part of the strait which leads into the Dardanelles. This pleasing coloured drawing is about seven feet long and three or four feet high.

2. General view of the ruins of Palmyra, drawn to the same scale. (Cassas had previously shown us a ground-plan of the original city as reconstructed by him.)

Originally a colonnade, the length of an Italian mile, stretched from the city to the Temple of the Sun, not in a perfectly straight line but with a slight knee-like bend in the middle. This consisted of four rows of columns, and the height of each was ten times its diameter. One cannot tell if the colonnade was roofed or not; Cassas thinks it was covered over with carpets. On the large drawing one part of the colonnade is still standing in the foreground. It was a happy idea to show a caravan passing through it. In the background rises the Temple of the Sun; to its right stretches a great plain over which janizaries are riding off at full gallop. The most peculiar feature of the picture is a blue line which closes it off like the horizon of the sea. Cassas explained to us that the horizon of the desert is normally blue in the distance and closes off the range of vision exactly as the sea does, and that in Nature the eye is as deceived as ours had been at first by the picture, although we knew Palmyra is some distance from the sea.

3. Tombs of Palmyra.

4. The Temple of the Sun in Baalbek, restored; also a landscape with the ruins as they stand.

5. The great mosque of Jerusalem, built on the foundations of the Temple of Solomon.

6. Ruins of a small temple in Phoenicia.

7. Landscape at the foot of Mount Lebanon. Very charming indeed. A pine grove, a stream bordered by willows which overhung tombs, the mountain in the distance.

8. Turkish tombs. Each tomb is crowned by the head-dress of the dead. Among the Turks, head-gear is a mark of distinction, so one can tell at once the rank of the person buried. On the graves of young girls, flowers are planted and tended with great care.

9. An Egyptian pyramid with the large head of a sphinx. Cassas told us that the head had been hewn out of a limestone cliff and then, because of the unevenness of the rock and the fissures in it, stuccoed and painted, traces of which can still be seen in the folds of the head-dress. Each side of the face is about ten feet high. Cassas could walk without difficulty along the lower lip.

10. A pyramid, tentatively restored after some documents. Along its four sides run projecting arcades with obelisks attached to them. These are approached by avenues lined with sphinxes,

similar to those which can still be seen in Upper Egypt. This drawing depicted the greatest architectural conception I ever saw in my life, and I do not believe it could be surpassed.

That same evening we went for a walk in the gardens on the Palatine which have reclaimed the waste spaces between the ruins of the Imperial palaces and made them attractive. There, on an open terrace beneath magnificent trees, with fragments of ornamental capitals, smooth and fluted columns, bas-reliefs, etc., strewn all around us in a wide circle in the same way that tables, chairs and benches are arranged for a merry party our of doors, we enjoyed the lovely hour to our heart's content, and when, at sunset, we surveyed the panorama with freshly washed eyes, we had to admit that, even after all we had seen that day, this picture was still worth looking at. Drawn and coloured by someone with Cassas's taste, it would arouse universal enthusiasm.

One consequence of our seeing these superb Egyptian monuments was that, on the following day, we visited a mean and lowly corner of the city where, fenced in by a hoarding, the broken pieces of the gigantic obelisk of Sesostris lay awaiting its resurrection by some adventurous architect. (It has now been reerected in the Piazza Monte Citorio, and once again, as in Roman times, serves as the gnomon of a sundial.)

The obelisk is made of the best Egyptian granite and covered all over with graceful, naïve carvings in the familiar style of the period. It felt strange to stand beside the point of the obelisk, which had once soared into the air, and see on its tapering faces sphinx after sphinx carved with exquisite skill, knowing that formerly these were visible, not to the human eye, but only to the rays of the sun. Here was a case of a sacred object which did not aim at making a visual effect upon the spectator.

The contrast between this noblest of monuments and the unattractive spot where it lay made us realize what a *quodlibet* Rome is. Yet, even as such, this city is unique in the advantages it offers. Here nothing was created by chance; chance only destroyed. Everything that is standing is magnificent. Her ruins are venerable, for, even in their wreck, one can still perceive their ancient symmetry; and the great forms of her modern churches and palaces have re-embodied it.

On September the twenty-first the memory of St Francis was celebrated, and his blood carried about the city, followed by a long procession. I watched the monks closely as they filed past. Their simple habit made one concentrate one's attention on the head, and it struck me that, in fact, it is the hair and the beard which are responsible for conveying to us the idea of masculinity. As the procession passed, I noticed, first with curiosity and surprise and then with delight, that their faces, framed by hair and beard, made quite a different impression from the beardless faces of the crowd. It made me understand the extraordinary fascination such faces have for us when we see them in paintings.

Hofrat Reiffenstein, who took his office of shepherding and entertaining foreign visitors very seriously, had long come to realize that people who arrive in Rome with no other idea than to see things and amuse themselves often suffer from the most awful boredom, because they are deprived of the ways in which they usually spend their free time. That connoisseur of humanity also knew how exhausting mere sightseeing can be, and how necessary it is to provide one's friends with some sort of self-occupation in which they can relax. He therefore picked on two activities with which he tried to keep them busy: encaustic painting and the imitation of antique jewellery in paste.

The art of using wax-soap as a colour-binding agent had only recently been revived, and become popular, for any new method of doing something stimulates interest and a desire to experiment in those who no longer feel inclined to employ the old one.

The bold project of making a copy of Raphael's *Loggias* for the Empress Catherine, of reproducing for the benefit of St Petersburg the whole of the architectural setting with all its ornamentation was facilitated by this new technique and, perhaps, would have been impossible without it. Exact copies of the panels, walls, socles, pilasters, capitals and cornices were manufactured from very thick boards and solid blocks of wood; everything was then covered with canvas and painted so as to provide a firm foundation for the encaustics. Under Reiffenstein's direction, a number of artists, Unterberger in particular, were busy on it for several years. When I arrived, most of it had already left for its destination, so I was able to see only the few parts of this great enterprise which remained.

This work made encaustic painting famous. Foreign visitors could acquire a working knowledge of the method if they had any talent; the colours, prepared beforehand, were inexpensive, and one could boil the wax-soap oneself; in short, there was always something to do in one's idle moments. Even mediocre artists found jobs as teachers or assistants, and, quite often, I saw visitors packing the encaustic works they had made in Rome and taking them home with the utmost self-satisfaction.

The other craft, the imitation of ancient gems in paste, was more suitable for men, and could conveniently be practised in a large vault of the old kitchen in Reiffenstein's villa, where there was more than enough space. The refractory mass which was heat-resistant was first ground to a very fine powder and sifted, and then kneaded into a paste. The gems were carefully dried and pressed on the paste, which was then enclosed in an iron ring and put in the fire. After that a molten glass paste was applied, and, in the end, a small work of art came out which was bound to delight anyone who could think that his fingers had done it all.

The great heat was only just over when Reiffenstein took me and some other artists to Frascati, where we found lodgings in a comfortably furnished private villa. We used to spend the whole day out of doors and then, in the evening, gather around a huge maple table and talk. Our conversations, though not uninstructive, sometimes took a malicious turn.

It was no secret that some of the younger artists had noticed in our good Reiffenstein certain idiosyncrasies, which are usually called weaknesses, and often used to talk about them and make fun of him behind his back.

One evening the Apollo Belvedere, that inexhaustible topic of artistic conversation, cropped up in our discussions. Somebody remarked that his ears were not really very well done, and this led us naturally to talk about the dignity and beauty of this organ, the difficulty of finding a beautiful one in Nature and of reproducing it adequately in Art.

Among our party was a native of Frankfurt, called Georg Schütz, who was famous for his shapely ears, particularly his right one. I asked him to sit close to the lamp so that I could draw it. It so happened that, when he took his rigid pose as my model, he found himself directly facing Hofrat Reiffenstein and could not – I would not let him move – take his eyes off him. The latter started reciting the lecture he was never tired of repeating, namely, that one should not begin by looking at the best; one should start with the Carracci in the Farnese Gallery, then move on to Raphael and only after that draw the Apollo Belvedere and go on drawing him till one knew him by heart, as the ultimate beauty beyond which there was nothing to desire or hope for.

Our good Schütz was seized with an uncontrollable fit of the giggles, and the more I tried to make him keep still in his pose, the more his agony increased.

This only shows how the teacher and the benefactor can always expect mockery and ingratitude if he lets his idiosyncrasies get out of hand.

Energetic, ambitious spirits cannot be satisfied by pleasure; they demand knowledge. This demand drives them to original activity, and whatever the results may be, such a person comes to feel that, in the end, he can judge nothing justly except what he has produced himself. But it is difficult for a human being to be clear about this, and one can easily be led into making misguided efforts which become all the more alarming the more sincere one's intention is. At that time, pleasant as the conditions of my life were, I was beset by doubts and suspicions that I would find it very difficult to fulfil my real desires and the true purpose for my being in Rome.

We returned from Frascati to Rome, where a new and charming opera, performed in a brightly lit and crowded house, was some compensation for the out-of-doors freedom we had lost.

The seats of the German artists, in one of the first rows of the *parterre*, were fully occupied as usual. We even managed to silence the chattering audience by crying 'Zitti!' – first softly and then in a voice of command, whenever the *ritornello* to a favourite aria or number began. Our friends on the stage rewarded us for this by addressing the most interesting parts of their performance directly to us.

OCTOBER

CORRESPONDENCE

Frascati, 2 October

I MUST start writing this letter now so that you may receive it in good time. I have both much and little to say. Drawing keeps me busy, but I think of my friends all the time. During these days I have been feeling very homesick for my country again, perhaps just because I have been having such a good time and yet felt that what was most precious to me was missing.

I am in a very strange state, but I shall pull myself together, make good use of every day, do what needs to be done, and keep working this way, I hope, all winter.

You can't imagine how profitable it has been for me, but at the same time how difficult, living for a whole year among absolute strangers, especially because Tischbein – this is between ourselves – has not turned out to be the person I hoped he was. At bottom he is a good fellow, but not as sincere or as frank as he sounds in his letters. I could give you a verbal description of his character which would not be unjust to him, but what are such descriptions worth? A man's character is his whole life. Now I am looking forward with the greatest pleasure to Kayser's visit. I hope to God nothing comes in the way to prevent it.

My primary concern is and will be to reach the point in my drawing when I do something with ease, not be forced to mark time and then have to start all over again, as happened to me so often, unfortunately, during the best years of my life. Still, I have this to say in my self-defence. To draw merely in order to draw is like talking merely in order to talk. So long as I had nothing to express, so long as nothing stimulated me, so long as I had to make a great effort searching for a worthy subject and, in spite of all my searching, seldom found one, where should I have found a genuine impulse to make pictures? But in this country, so much crowds in upon one and one absorbs so much that one cannot help becoming an artist and producing something. I know my disposition, I know the road to take and I am convinced that if I spent a few years here I would make considerable progress.

You have asked me, dear friends, to write about myself. Well, now you see I have. I have had occasion to ponder much about myself, others, the world and history, and, in my own way, I shall have many things to share with you, which are good, even if perhaps not new. Everything will in the end be condensed and summed up in *Wilhelm Meister*.

Moritz is, as ever, my favourite companion, though I was and still am afraid that my company may make him cleverer, but will not make him wiser, better or happier; and this always stops me from being completely open with him.

All in all, associating with more people agrees with me. I observe their various temperaments and the way each behaves. This one acts his part, that one does not; this one will make his way easily, that one with great difficulty; this one saves, that one wastes; this one is content with everything, that one with nothing; this one has talent but makes no use of it; that one has none but works hard. I see all this and myself in the middle; it amuses me and does not put me out of humour, because the lives of these people are no concern of mine and I am not responsible for them. It is only when each of them claims that the way he does things is the only way and then insists I agree with him that I feel I must either take to my heels or go crazy.

Albano, 5 October

I must try to get this letter to Rome in time for the mail tomorrow, so I can only write a thousandth part of what I should like to say.

Just as I was about to leave Frascati, I received in one bundle the Scattered* – or rather *Collected* – *Leaves*, the *Ideas*, and the four morocco-bound volumes of my works, so now I have a treasure of reading matter to last me all my *villeggiatura*. Last night I read *Persepolis*. I enjoyed it immensely. I have nothing to add because that sort of writing and thinking is still entirely

---

* All these works are by Herder.

unknown here. I shall look up in some library the books you recommend. Once again, many thanks. Please go on and on shedding your light on everything. Go on, because you must.

I have not touched the *Ideas* or the *Poems* yet. My own writings must now go out into the world, but I shall faithfully go on with my work. The copperplates for the last four volumes are going to be engraved here.

My relationship with the persons you mention* was nothing but a polite truce on both sides. I have always known that only those mature who can. The distance between us will steadily increase and will end, if things go as they should, in a silent break. One of them is a pretentious idiot. 'My mother has geese' may be more easily and naïvely sung than 'All glory be to God on high'. But, after all, he is a goose himself : 'They do not mind the hay and straw, the hay and straw', etc., etc. One must keep away from such people. Their first ingratitude is not so bad as their last. The other imagines he has come from a foreign land to find his disciples, but he comes to people who, without admitting it, admire no one but themselves. He is going to find himself an outsider and, probably, he will never know why.

But you, my dear brother, must go on meditating, discovering, relating, and writing poetry, without caring what other people say. One has to write as one lives, first for one's own sake, and then for the sake of a few congenial souls.

Plato wouldn't admit an ἀγεωμέτρητον † to his Academy. If I were to found mine, I wouldn't admit anyone who had not seriously and actively studied some field of natural science. The other day I came across, in a half apostolic, half friar-like pronouncement by the Prophet from Zurich, these nonsensical words: 'All that lives owes its life to something outside itself.' At least, that is what it sounded like. That's the sort of thing only such a missionary to the heathen could write down, and when he revised it, his genius did not pluck him by the sleeve.

---

*Goethe is referring to Matthias Claudius (1740–1815), poet and pietist, and F. H. Jacobi (1743–1817), philosopher, both of whom, together with Lavater, had attacked Herder's writings.

† ἀγεωμέτρητον : one ignorant of geometry.

These people haven't understood the first elementary truths of Nature, though, no doubt, they would dearly like to have reserved seats at the foot of the throne, which belong to others or to nobody at all. Don't worry about them any more than I do, though I admit it is easier for me.

Farewell, be happy, and when you feel sad, remember that all of you are together and can be what you are to each other, whereas I am a voluntary exile, a wanderer by design, unwise with a purpose, everywhere a stranger and everywhere at home, letting my life run its course where it will, rather than trying to guide it, since, in any case, I don't know where it will lead me.

Give my respectful regards to the Duchess. When we were in Frascati, Hofrat Reiffenstein and I made out a whole programme for her visit which, if everything works out right, will be a masterpiece of planning. We are at present negotiating for a country villa which, for some reason or other, has been sequestrated, and can therefore be rented. The others are either taken or would be made available by the great families only as an act of courtesy, which would involve one in obligations and unwanted intimacies. I shall write again as soon as I have something to report.

In Rome a beautiful house with a garden and standing in its own grounds is ready for her. I want her to find herself at home wherever she is; otherwise she will not enjoy anything – time flies, money goes, and before one knows it, happiness has slipped through one's fingers. I want to arrange everything for her so that she may not dash her foot against a stone.

There is still a little space left, but I can write no more now. Farewell, and excuse the haste of these lines.

Castel Gandolfo, 8 October (actually 12 October)

This week has gone by without my being able to write, so if you are to hear from me at all, I must scribble this little note and get it off to Rome.

I live here as one lives in a watering place, except that in the mornings I slip away to draw; for the rest of the day, one is expected to join the company and be social. I don't mind doing this for a little and, actually, for once I am seeing many people without wasting too much time. Angelica is living quite near; there are some lively young girls, some women, Mr v. Maron, Mengs's brother-in-law, and his family, who are either living in the house or in the neighbourhood. We are a merry company and there is always something to laugh about. In the evenings we go to see the Comedy, in which Pulcinella is the main character. The whole of the next day we amuse ourselves by recalling the *bons mots* of the night before. *Tout comme chez nous*, except for the wonderful clear sky. Today a strong wind kept me indoors. If anything could take me out of myself, these days would do it, but I always withdraw again into myself and my whole interest is concentrated on art.

Erwin und Elmire is nearly finished; I have the whole thing in my head and only need a few mornings when I feel in the mood to write.

Herder has asked me to supply Forster * with a list of questions and suggestions for his trip around the world. I should really like to do it, but I don't know when I shall find the time. We shall see.

The days in your part of the world are probably cold and gloomy by now; here we may look forward to another whole month in which it is pleasant to take walks. I can't tell you how delighted I am with Herder's *Ideas*. Since I expect no Messiah, this book is my favourite Gospel. Remember me to all. I am always with you in my thoughts.

TO HERDER

Castel Gandolfo, 12 October

Just a few hurried lines to thank you most warmly for your *Ideas*. To me they come as a lovable Gospel in which all the studies which have most interested me in my life are brought together. Everything I have toiled over for so long you present clearly and completely, and your book has revived in me a great

---

* Georg Forster travelled with James Cook and was planning a second voyage round the world, subsidized by Catherine the Great.

desire for all that is good. I have read only half of it so far. Please get somebody to copy out for me as soon as possible the whole passage of Camper * from which you quote on page 159, so that I can see what he has discovered about the rules which governed the ideals of Greek art. All I remember are the stages by which he demonstrates the profile from the engraving. Tell me more about it in your letter and make extracts from anything else which you think might be of use to me so that I may know the ultimate point at which these speculations have arrived, for in such matters I am still a newborn babe. Is there anything sensible about it in Lavater's *Physiognomy*?

I shall be glad to answer your cry for help on Forster's behalf, though as yet I don't see how it will be possible. I have no neat, isolated questions to put, but would have to expound my hypotheses fully, and you know what a trial it would be for me to do this in writing. But tell me the latest date by which it should be ready and where I should send it. At present I am sitting among the reeds cutting pipes, but I haven't got so far as being able to play them. If I undertake this task, I shall have to resort to dictation. I take your request as a sign that it is time I set my house in order and closed my books. The main difficulty is that I shall have to do absolutely everything from memory. I have literally nothing with me, not a page of my *collectanea*, not a drawing; and none of the latest books is available here.

I shall probably stay in Castel Gandolfo for another two weeks. In the morning I draw; after that, it is people all the time, but I don't mind because I see them all at the same time, not one by one, which would be a great nuisance. Angelica, too, helps me to stand it all.

The Pope is said to have already received information that the Prussians have taken Amsterdam. We shall know for certain when the next newspapers arrive. I call that a *sodezza*. This would be the first engagement in which our century shows itself in all its greatness. Without a sword being drawn, with just a cannon shot or two, the whole affair is over and nobody wants to prolong it.

---

* Petrus Camper (1722–89), Dutch anatomist, whose theory that man had no intermaxillary bone was disproved by Goethe.

Farewell. I am a child of peace and intend from henceforth to live in peace with the whole world, now that I have once and for all made peace with myself.

Rome, 23 October

By the last mail, dear friends, you received no letter. The hustle and bustle of life in Castel Gandolfo eventually became too much for me, and besides, I wanted to draw. I saw more Italians while I was there than I had seen in the whole year, and found it a pleasant experience.

I became interested in a young lady from Milan * who stayed for a week and distinguished herself from the ladies of Rome by her natural behaviour, common sense and good manners. Angelica was as helpful and considerate as she always is. One cannot know her without becoming her friend and one can learn a lot from her, especially how to work; it is incredible how much she accomplishes.

The weather has become much chillier during the last few days and I am very glad to be back in Rome. When I went to bed last night, I felt how good it was to be here. It seemed to me that I was lying on safe ground.

I should very much like to talk to Herder about his *God*. To me the most remarkable thing about it is this. People take it, in the way they take other books, as *food*, when in reality it is the *dish*. He who has nothing to put into it will find it empty. Let me explain myself a little further by an allegory which Herder will know best how to interpret.

By means of levers and rollers it is possible to transport loads of considerable weight; to move the pieces of the obelisk it was necessary to use winches, pulleys, etc. The heavier the load or the greater the precision required of a thing – take a clock, for example – the more complicated or ingenious the mechanism has to be and, at the same time, the more perfect the unity of its internal structure. The same is true of all hypotheses, or rather, all *general principles*. The person who has nothing much to move grasps the lever and scorns my pulley; what can the stonemason do with an endless screw? When Lavater uses all his

---

*Her name was Maddalena Ricci.

strength to make a fairy tale seem true, when Jacobi goes to enormous pains to make a god of the hollow fancy of a child's brain, when Claudius would like to turn himself from a peripatetic missionary * into an apostle, it is obvious they must abominate anything which reveals the depths of Nature. If this were not so, would the first dare to say: 'All that lives owes its life to something outside itself'? Wouldn't the second be ashamed of confusing knowledge with faith, tradition with experience? Wouldn't the third have to step down a peg or two? But no; they are so busy trying with might and main to arrange the chairs around the throne of the Lamb that they carefully avoid venturing upon the firm ground of Nature, where everyone is only what he is and we all have equal claims.

On the other hand, when one opens a book like the third part of the *Ideas*, sees what is in it and then asks: 'Could the author have written this without any real idea of God?' the answer is: 'Never.' Because the authenticity, greatness and spirituality which the book has, comes *in*, *from* and *through* a real idea of God in the world.

If anything is missing, the fault lies not with the merchandise but with the buyers, not with the machine but with those who don't know how to use it.

During our metaphysical discussions, I often noticed with silent amusement that 'they' did not take me seriously. Being an artist, I don't care. It might suit me much better if the principle upon which I work remains a secret. By all means, let them stick to their lever; I have been using my endless screw for a long time now and shall go on using it with ever greater ease and delight.

27 October

I have re-entered this magic circle and am immediately re-enchanted. I go on quietly with my work, oblivious of everything in the outside world, attended in my thoughts by the peaceful visits of my friends.

---

* A peripatetic missionary: Claudius used to sign his writings 'The Messenger from Wandsbeck'.

I spent the first days writing letters and looking through the drawings I made in the country; next week I shall start on something new. The hopes Angelica has given me of what I might do in landscape drawing, given favourable circumstances, are much too flattering to tell you. I shall probably never reach my goal, but at least I can go on trying to get nearer it.

Did I tell you that Kayser is coming? I expect him in a few days with the complete score of our 'scapineries'.* You can imagine what a day of celebration that will be. I shall start on a new operetta at once, and take advantage of his visit and advice to revise *Claudine* and *Erwin*.

I have now finished the *Ideas* and enjoyed the book enormously; the end is magnificent. Like the book itself, Herder will only gradually exert his good influence on mankind and then, perhaps, with the name of someone else. The more his attitude gains ground, the happier all thinking men will become.

While living this year among strangers, I have observed that all really intelligent people recognize, some in a refined, some in a gross way, that the moment is everything and that the sole privilege of a reasonable being is to behave in such a manner, in so far as the choice lies with him, that his life contains the greatest possible sum of reasonable and happy moments.

I should have to write a whole book to express all my thoughts about a single volume of Herder's. I have been rereading several passages at random and am delighted with every page. The section dealing with the Greek period is particularly beautiful. In the Roman period, if I may say so, I feel that something substantial is missing, but you will be able to guess the reason why for yourselves. It is natural that I should. At the moment I am preoccupied with the question of what, in all its complexity, the Roman State was, *per se*: to me it is an exclusive concept, like the fatherland. You would have to determine the value of this single entity in relation to the totality of the world, and in the process, much of course might shrink and go up in smoke.

I shall always find the Colosseum imposing, even when I re-

---

*Scapin and Scapine, commedia dell'arte figures in Goethe's Singspiel, *Jest, Cunning and Revenge* (*Scherz, List und Rache*), 1784.

member that, by the time it was built, the people who filled its enormous circle were no longer the ancient Roman people. A book on the paintings and sculptures of Rome has just reached us. It is a German product and, what is worse, by a German aristocrat. He seems to be a young man and full of energy, but he is also full of pretensions. He has taken great pains, running around, collecting information, listening and reading, and has shown skill in giving his book a semblance of completeness, but, side by side with much which is true and good, there are errors, nonsense, rehashed ideas, *longueurs* and digressions. One has only to skim through it to see what a monstrous hybrid between original thinking and mere compilation this voluminous opus has grown into.

I am delighted and relieved to hear that *Egmont* arrived. I am longing to hear a word from you about it, but perhaps it is already on its way. The morocco-bound copy has arrived and I gave it to Angelica as a present. Kayser and I are going to disregard all the advice we have been given about the operetta, and do something much more intelligent. Your suggestion is very good, and as soon as Kayser is here, you shall hear more about it.

The review is typical of the Old man's* style – too much and too little. My only concern now is to *produce*, for, as regards what has been produced, I see that, even though it is not perfect, it will go on being reviewed for a thousand years, as long as there is anything left to say about its existence.

A new era is beginning for me. My spiritual horizons have been so extended by all my looking and learning that now I have to knuckle down to some definite piece of work. Human individuality is a strange thing: it is only during the last year, when I have had to depend solely on myself and at the same time be in daily contact with complete strangers, that I have really come to know my own.

---

*C. M. Wieland (1733–1813), poet and editor of *The German Mercury* in which he had reviewed Goethe's works.

OCTOBER

IN RETROSPECT

THE weather at the beginning of this month was mild and fine. I went to Castel Gandolfo for the first time to enjoy a real *villeggiatura* and soon felt myself a native of that incomparable region. A wealthy English art dealer, called Mr Jenkins, was living there in an imposing house which had once been the home of the General of the Jesuits. It had plenty of accommodation for guests, salons for gay parties and covered walks where one could stroll in cheerful company.

Such an autumn resort is more like a watering place than anything else. Persons who have never met before are brought by chance into close contact. Meals, walks and excursions, serious and light conversation encourage rapid intimacy, and in a place like this where there is nothing to do – even the diversions of taking the cure and talking about one's ailments are lacking – it would be a miracle if marked elective affinities did not soon begin to develop among the visitors.

After I had been there for some days, a very handsome young lady and her mother arrived from Rome, where they had been my near neighbours on the Corso. Though I had often passed them in the evenings as they sat in front of their door, I had never spoken to them, for I stuck firmly to my resolve not to allow myself to be distracted from my pursuits by relations of that kind. I had noticed, though, that after my promotion to a 'Milord', they had returned my bow more warmly than before. Now here we were, brought together like old acquaintances, and it was easy to start a conversation by talking about the concert given in my house. The young lady expressed a lively interest in things that really matter, and her charms were enhanced by the melodious Roman dialect which she spoke rapidly but distinctly and with that noble accent which elevates even the middle classes above their station and imparts a certain dignity to the most ordinary and commonplace remarks.

The pair introduced me to a young lady from Milan who was with them. She was the sister of one of Mr Jenkins's clerks, a young man who, owing to his efficiency and honesty, was a great favourite with his employer. The three ladies seemed to be intimate friends.

The two young beauties – they really deserved the title – presented a marked but pleasing contrast. The Roman had dark-brown hair, a pale-brown complexion, brown eyes and was somewhat serious and reserved; the Milanese had light-brown hair, a clear delicate skin, blue eyes and was more outgoing, not so much forward as eager to know about things.

I was sitting one day between the pretty young pair, playing a kind of lotto, and had first pooled my stakes with the Roman one, but as the game went on, it came to pass that I also tried my luck by betting with the Milanese. In short, I was beginning to form a new partnership and, in my innocence, I was quite unaware that this divided interest was resented. But when the game ended, the mother took me aside and with the dignity of a Roman matron politely intimated to the 'respected foreigner' that, once he had shown interest in her daughter, it was not *comme il faut* to pay attentions to another, for, during a *villeggiatura*, it was an understood convention that persons who had formed a mild attachment should abide by it in public and carry on an innocent and graceful exchange of courtesies. I apologized as best I could, but defended myself by saying that, as a foreigner, I could not recognize obligations of this kind because in my country it was customary to be equally polite and attentive in society to all the ladies and that surely such behaviour was appropriate in the case of two ladies who were intimate friends.

But alas, as I tried to make my excuses, I felt oddly certain that, in an impetuous instant, my heart had already decided in favour of the Milanese, as can easily happen when one's affections are disengaged. One feels complacently sure of oneself, with nothing to fear or desire till, suddenly, one is confronted with a vision of all that is desirable and, at such a moment, is unconscious of the danger threatening one from behind its enchanting features.

The next morning the three of us found ourselves alone together, and the scales turned still more in favour of the Milanese. She had the great advantage over her friend that her eagerness for knowledge was obvious in everything she said. She did not say in so many words that her education had been neglected, but complained of its limitations.

'We aren't taught to write', she said, 'for fear we might use our pens to write love letters. We wouldn't even be taught to read if we didn't have to read our prayer books; but nobody would dream of teaching us foreign languages. I would give anything to know English. I often hear Mr Jenkins and my brother, Signora Angelica, Signor Zucchi, Signor Volpato and Signor Camuccini talking to each other in English, and I listen with envy. Then I see all those yard-long newspapers lying on that table, full of news from all over the world, and I don't know what they are saying.'

'It's a shame,' I said, 'especially since English is so easy to learn and you would very soon get a grasp of it. Why don't we have a try now?'

I picked up one of the immense English papers, glanced through it quickly and found an article about a woman who had fallen into the water but been fortunately rescued and returned to her family. There were certain interesting complications about the case : it was not clear whether she had meant to drown herself and which of her two admirers, the favoured or the rejected one, had risked his life to rescue her. I showed her this item and asked her to follow it carefully with her eyes while I read it.

First of all I translated all the nouns and tested her to see whether she remembered what they meant. In this way she soon got a general view of the key words in a sentence and the place they occupied. Next, I moved on to the causative, motivating and qualifying words, and pointed out to her, in as entertaining a fashion as I could, how they brought the whole to life. Again I catechized her for some time until, in the end, without any prompting from me, she read the whole passage aloud as easily as if it had been printed in Italian, accompanying her reading with the most graceful movements. I have seldom seen such an expression of joy on a face as on hers as she thanked me with the utmost warmth for having initiated her into this new world.

The visitors had increased in number. Angelica had also arrived and at dinner I was given the place on her right at the long common table. My pupil was standing on the other side, and while the others were bowing each other to their seats, without a moment's hesitation, she walked round and sat down next to me. Angelica looked surprised, for an intelligent woman like her could see at a glance that something had happened, and here was her friend, who till now had avoided the ladies even to the point of being curt and impolite, evidently tamed and captivated, much to his own surprise.

Outwardly I could still control myself fairly well, but possibly my emotions betrayed themselves by a certain awkwardness of manner as I divided my attention between my two neighbours. I tried to keep up a lively conversation with my older friend, who was rather silent that day, and to calm down the other with a quiet, almost passive interest, for she was still enraptured about the foreign language and like someone blinded by a sudden long-wished-for vision who does not know how to readjust herself to normal surroundings.

My state of excitement was very soon, however, to suffer a cruel surprise. Towards evening I went looking for my young friends and found the older ladies sitting in a pavilion with a glorious view. As I gazed at the picturesque landscape I felt a fascination which could not be attributed merely to the sunset and the evening air. The dazzling lights on the hilltops, the cool, blue shades in the valley looked more wonderful to me than any oil painting or water colour. I could not take my eyes off the scene, but at the same time I felt a longing to leave the spot and pay homage to the last rays of the sun in a smaller and more congenial company.

Unfortunately, I could not refuse when the Roman mother and her friends invited me to sit down, especially since they made room for me at the window which had the best view. They were talking about that inexhaustible subject, a trousseau. The precious time went by as I listened patiently to a discussion of what would be needed, the number and quality of the wedding presents, the essential things the family would be giving, the contributions of friends, male and female, some of which were still a secret, and God knows what else. What was more, the ladies had pinned me down to taking a walk with them later.

Then the conversation turned to the merits of the bridegroom. The description was in his favour, though no secret was made of his shortcomings; but they all seemed confident that the grace, intelligence and amiability of his bride would correct these once they were married.

I got more and more impatient and finally, just as the sun was sinking into the distant sea, I asked as discreetly as I could who the bride might be. They were all surprised that I didn't know what was a matter of common knowledge, and only then did they remember that I was not a friend of the family but a stranger.

I need hardly say how horrified I was to hear that the bride was none other than my pupil who had become so dear to me but a short while before. The sun had set and I succeeded under some pretext in disengaging myself from the company which, all unwittingly, had taught me so cruel a lesson. I returned to the house very late and, early next morning, I set off on a long ramble, after saying that I would not be back for dinner.

I was old and experienced enough to be able to pull myself together, but it hurt. 'It would be strange indeed,' I said to myself, 'if a fate like Werther's should pursue you to Rome and ruin the way of life you have so carefully maintained up till now.'

I returned without delay to Nature and the study of landscape, which I had been neglecting, and tried to copy it as faithfully as possible; but I was more successful at seeing than at doing. What little technical skill I possessed was barely sufficient for a humble sketch, but I found my perception of the objects in the landscape, rocks, trees, hills, lakes and brooks had become sharper and I felt reconciled to the pain which had thus heightened my sensibility.

From now on, I must cut my long story short. Our house and those in the neighbourhood were full of visitors, so that it was possible for us to avoid each other without affectation. An attraction of this kind is apt to make one friendly and polite to others and this is well received in society. My behaviour pleased, and I had no falling-out with anyone except with our host, Mr Jenkins. One day, after a lengthy excursion into the mountains and woods, I brought back a basketful of mushrooms and handed them over to the cook, who was delighted because this highly priced food was rare in those parts. He prepared a tasty dish of them, served it at dinner and everybody enjoyed it. But when someone, wishing me to get the credit for having brought them back from the wilderness, let out the secret, our English host was very angry that a stranger should have contributed a dish to the common table of which he knew nothing. He said nothing to me, but, behind my back, he complained that it was very rude to surprise a host at his own table with food which had been neither ordered nor chosen by him. Hofrat Reiffenstein had diplomatically to break all this to me after dinner. Suffering though I was inside from a very different kind of pain than that which can be caused by mushrooms, I kept my temper and replied that I had taken it for granted that the cook would report the gift to his master; but in future, if I came upon any such edibles during my walks, I would certainly show them first to our excellent host for his examination and approval.

To be just to him, the main reason for his indignation must have been the fact that mushrooms are a dubious food, and that they had been served without being properly examined first. Thinking over this culinary adventure, it struck me as funny that I, who had rashly infected myself with a very special poison, should, through another act of imprudence, have come under the suspicion of trying to poison a whole household.

It was not hard for me to behave as I had decided I should. I tried to avoid the English lessons by leaving the house very early in the morning, and I only approached my secretly beloved pupil when there were several other people present. My knowledge that she was a bride and the future wife of another man elevated her in my eyes above the trivial state of girlhood, and, though I still felt the same affection for her as before, I was soon able to meet her on terms of easy friendship as a person who, in any case, was no longer a lighthearted youth. In our personal contacts I showed my devotion – if one can call any natural attraction by that name – without any fuss but rather with a kind of reverence, and she, who certainly knew by then that her engagement was known to me, had no cause to complain of my behaviour. The others, who saw me talking freely with everybody, did not notice or suspect anything, and so the hours and days followed each other in their peaceful course.

Meanwhile, letters from home had revealed that my journey to Italy, so long planned, so often postponed, and eventually undertaken on the spur of the moment, had aroused restlessness and impatience among those I had left behind and even a wish to follow me and enjoy the same happiness of which my cheerful letters had painted such a favourable picture. In the intellectual and art-loving circle of our Duchess Amalia it had been a tradition, of course, to consider Italy as the New Jerusalem for all truly cultivated persons, and an acute longing, such as only Mignon could express, had long been alive in their hearts and minds. Now the dam had burst at last and it gradually became obvious that not only the Duchess, with her entourage, but also Herder and the younger Dalberg were making serious preparations to cross the Alps. I advised them to postpone their journey until after the winter was over, and then to enjoy by easy stages all the beauties which the surroundings of the capital of the world, southern Italy, etc., had to offer.

My advice was sincere and objective enough, but I also had my personal interest in mind. I had so far lived through this momentous period of my life among complete strangers and at long last, through accidental but natural contacts, had established a humane way of living which I was just beginning to enjoy. But the unchanging routine of life in a closed home circle among people to whom one is related or whom one knows inside out, now enduring, now accepting, now sharing, now going without, creates in the end a lukewarm state of resignation in which pain and joy, ill humour and pleasure obliterate each other, a mean average which abolishes all singularity.

Persuaded by these feelings and premonitions, I firmly made up my mind to leave Italy before my friends arrived. It was clear to me that my way of looking at things would not be theirs, at least not at first, for it had taken me a whole year of effort to rid myself of those Cimmerian ways of thinking which are native to the northern world, and accustom myself to observing and breathing more freely under a blue welkin. Almost without exception, I found German travellers very tiresome. Either they came to look for something which they should have forgotten, or they could not recognize what they had so long desired to see, even when it was before their eyes. The visitor from the north imagines that Rome will supplement his own existence and supply what he lacks: it only gradually dawns on him, to his great discomfort, that he has to alter his reactions completely and start from the very beginning. Strangers from Germany I could always avoid, but errors, superficialities and slow responses of people I loved and respected, yes, and even their attempts to enter into my way of thinking, would upset and frustrate me.

Though all this was clear to me, I wisely left everybody in the dark about the day of my departure and continued making good use of my time, thinking for myself, listening to the opinions of others, observing their efforts and making practical attempts of my own.

In all this I received much encouragement and profit from talking to Heinrich Meyer, a native of Zurich. He was a hard-working, self-disciplined artist who knew better how to use his time than the circle of younger ones who fondly believed that solid progress in theory and technique could be combined with fast living.

NOVEMBER

CORRESPONDENCE

3 November

OWING to Kayser's arrival, I have written no letters this week. He is still tuning the piano. When that is done, we shall go through the operetta page by page.

The reception of *Egmont* makes me very happy. I hope the play will lose nothing at a second reading. I know what I put into it and I know that it cannot all be taken in immediately.

What you found to praise is as I meant it to be, and if you say I have succeeded, I have achieved what I set out to do. It was an unspeakably difficult undertaking and I could never have done it if my soul and my life had not been free. Imagine what it means to take up a work, written twelve years earlier, and finish it without rewriting the whole thing. There are still two rocks in my path — *Faust* and *Tasso*. Since the merciful gods seem to have spared me the punishment they inflicted on Sisyphus, I hope I can shove these great lumps as well to the top of the hill. Once I get them there, I shall make a fresh start and do my very best to be worthy of the love and approval you give me, which, at present, I do not deserve.

I don't quite understand what you say about Klärchen: there is a nuance in the difference between the simple girl and the goddess which you have evidently missed. Perhaps you will see it on a second reading, and perhaps you will have more detailed comments to make in your next letter.

Angelica has designed the frontispiece for *Egmont* and Lipps has engraved it. Neither of these two jobs could or would have been done in Germany.

To my regret I am forced at present to neglect the visual arts because otherwise I could not finish my dramatic works, which demand extra concentration, peace and quiet if they are to amount to anything. I am now at work on *Claudine*. It will have

to be almost completely rewritten and all the chaff of my former
existence winnowed out of it.

Rome, 10 *November*

Since Kayser came, we are living *à trois*, with music as the third
partner. Kayser is a really fine fellow: we get on excellently together and are leading a life as close to Nature as is possible on
this earth. Tischbein is expected back from Naples, so we must
find new lodgings and make new arrangements, but since both
of us can take such upsets as they come, within a week everything should be running smoothly again.

I have proposed to the Dowager Duchess that she allow me to
spend on her account a sum of two hundred sequins for the
purchase of various small works of art. Please back me up in
this proposition, the details of which you will learn from my
letter to her. I don't need the money immediately nor in a lump
sum. You will guess how important the matter is without long
explanations on my part, though if you knew the conditions here
as I know them, you would understand still better how necessary
and practical my advice is. I shall have such small articles made
to order one by one, so that she may find them waiting for her
when she arrives. The pleasure they will give her will calm the
greed for possessions which is aroused in everyone when they
first arrive here, no matter who they are. Otherwise she would
either have to restrain it, which would be painful, or gratify it
at great loss and expense. I could go on for pages on this subject.

I was very pleased to hear that *Egmont* has met with approval.
I have never before felt so free in spirit while writing a play,
nor finished one with more scrupulous care; but the reader is
hard to satisfy. He likes what he is used to and always wants a
writer to go on turning out the same thing.

24 *November*

In your last letter, you asked me about the colour of the landscape in this neighbourhood. I can only say that on clear days,
especially in autumn, it is so full of colour that, in any reproduc-

tion, it must look like a confused motley. In a short while I shall be sending you, I hope, some drawings by a German who is now living in Naples. The watercolours fall short of the brilliant colours of nature, but, even so, you will think them impossible. The great beauty of these landscapes is that objects which are vividly coloured, even if they are only a little distance away, are softened by the atmosphere and that the contrasts of cold and warm tones, as they are called, are so pronounced. The clear blue shadows stand out delightfully against anything green, yellow, red or brown, and merge into the bluish haze of the distance. There is a brilliance and at the same time a subtly graded harmony which one can hardly conceive up in the north, where everything is either harsh or indistinct, either too bright or too drab. At least, I rarely remember having seen an effect which could have given me an inkling of what I see here every day. Perhaps now that my eyes are better trained, I might detect more beauty in the north as well.

As for the visual arts, I am already too old to do anything more than dabble in them. I can see what the others are doing, I can see that some are on the right track but that none of them has a long stride. The same, though, can be said of happiness and wisdom: their archetypes do but float before our eyes and at best we can touch the hem of their garments.

With Kayser's arrival, my work came to a standstill. But now our domestic problems have been largely solved, everything is moving again, and my operettas are nearly finished. Kayser is an excellent companion, orderly, sedate and, where his work is concerned, as firm and assured as anyone could be. At the same time, he is kindhearted and a good judge of character. He is one of those people in whose presence one becomes saner.

NOVEMBER

IN RETROSPECT

WHILE, in the silence of my thoughts, I was gradually detaching myself from others, an old friend from Frankfurt, Christopher Kayser, arrived, and a new tie was established. Years before, he had undertaken to compose the music for *Jest, Cunning and Revenge* and he had now begun to write the incidental music for *Egmont*. Instead of trying to collaborate by a lengthy correspondence, we decided it would be better if he came to Rome, which he did at once, and was well received in our circle.

We had difficulties to start with. It took days to procure a piano, try it out, tune it and find a place for it which would satisfy Kayser, who was very particular and always found something else that was wrong. But the effort and loss of time were more than made up for by the performances of this very talented musician, who played us with great ease the most difficult compositions of the period. So that a musicologist may know what I am talking about, I shall say that, in those days, Schubart * was thought to be without a rival, and that the test for a virtuoso pianist was to improvise a set of variations on a simple given theme.

The arrival of Kayser, who had brought with him his overture to *Egmont*, revived an old interest in music which now turned me, both from inclination and necessity, more and more towards the musical theatre.

In Germany they were waiting for *Erwin und Elmire* and *Claudine von Villa Bella*, but, as a result of my work on *Egmont*, I had become so much stricter in my standards that I could not bring myself to send them off in their original form. I was very fond of many of the songs which bore witness to so many foolish but happy hours, and to the pain and sorrow to which rash, impetuous youth will always be exposed. But the

---

* F. C. Schubart, Swabian poet and composer.

prose dialogue was too reminiscent of French operettas. Though I shall always remember the latter kindly, since they were the first to introduce cheerful melody into our theatre, they no longer satisfied me. Having become an Italian citizen, I wanted the arias to be linked by declamatory recitative. I revised both operettas along these lines and they have since enjoyed some popularity.

It is the fashion to find fault with Italian libretti for repeating phrases over and over again without thinking about what they mean. They are light and easy, one must admit, and make no more demands on the composer and the singer than either is willing to give. Without enlarging on the subject, I will only mention the libretto of *Il Matrimonio Segreto*. The name of the author is unknown,* but whoever he was, he was the most skilful of those who had worked in this field up to that time.

My intention was to make something similar, free but with a definite point, but I can't say how far I succeeded in doing so.

Kayser and I also spent some time on an undertaking which, unfortunately, appeared less and less workable as we went on. One must remember that the German opera stage of those days was very naïve and that a work like Pergolesi's *La Serve Padrona* was a huge success. A German *buffo* named Berger and his handsome, portly wife came on the scene, and the two of them used to tour the towns and villages of Germany, performing various light and amusing intermezzi in ordinary rooms with a modest wardrobe and a scratch orchestra; needless to say, every intermezzo ended with the deception and humiliation of an amorous old coxcomb.

I got the idea of adding a third part for a voice in the middle range, which would not have been hard to find, and so I wrote *Jest, Cunning and Revenge* and sent it to Kayser, who was living in Zurich. But that serious and conscientious composer treated it much too thoroughly and at too great a length. The libretto by itself had already exceeded the dimensions of an intermezzo, and trivial though my subject was, I had written so many arias that, even with little music between them, three singers would hardly have had the strength to get through a whole performance. But

---

* The libretto was by Giovanni Bertati.

on top of this, Kayser had treated the arias in the old careful style. There were many happy passages, and the whole thing was not without charm, but how and where should it be performed? In addition, because we had followed the old convention of being moderate in our musical demands, it suffered from a certain vocal thinness: we did not dare go further than writing a terzetto, though we would have dearly liked to make the Doctor's jars of theriac * come to life and turn into a chorus for the finale. But all our endeavours to limit ourselves to economy and simplicity were lost the moment Mozart appeared on the scene. *Die Entführung aus dem Serail* put an end to all our hopes, and the piece we had worked on so hard was never heard of again in the theatre.

My friend Kayser stimulated and broadened my love for music which had hitherto been limited to the opera. He followed with interest all the church festivals and induced me to listen with him to the solemn Masses which are sung on those days. To my ear they sounded rather worldly with their full orchestra. On St Cecilia's Day, I remember, I heard for the first time a bravura aria with chorus, which made an extraordinary impression on me, as it makes on the public to this day when it it heard on the opera stage.

Kayser had another virtue: since he was interested in old music and music history, he visited many libraries, the Minerva in particular. His bibliographical researches led him to draw my attention to the copperplate engravings of the early sixteenth century in such volumes as *Speculum romanae magnificentiae*, Lomazzo's *Architetture* and the later *Admiranda Romae*. These transported me back into those earlier times when antiquity was regarded with awe and reverence and its remains were skilfully reproduced.

Among the engravings of buildings I looked at, I remember the colossi which were still standing in their old place in the Colonna gardens, the half-ruined Septizonium of Severus (this has now vanished, but there was enough left standing at that time to give an idea of the building), St Peter's, before the façade

---

* The Doctor with his jars of theriac was the third character in *Jest, Cunning and Revenge*.

or the centre dome were added, and the old Vatican in the court of which tournaments could still be held.

From these one could get a good idea of the changes which had occurred during the last two hundred years and of the efforts which had been made, in the face of tremendous obstacles, to restore what had been ruined or neglected.

Heinrich Meyer, whom I have already mentioned on several occasions, though he lived a retired life and worked unceasingly, was never absent when there was anything important to see or learn, and his company was always welcome to our circle, because he was both modest and learned. He had followed faithfully in the footsteps of Winckelmann and Mengs, and, as an expert in sepia reproductions of antique busts after the style of Seydelmann, no one had more occasion than he to become familiar with the finer distinctions both in earlier and later periods of art.

Meyer was with us on the evening when we made a torchlight tour of the museum of the Vatican and the Capitol, an excursion which was popular among visitors, artists, connoisseurs and dilettantes alike, and I find among my papers an article of his referring to that memorable occasion which still floats before my mind's eye like a beautiful, gradually fading dream.

The custom of visiting the great Roman museums by torchlight seems to have still been fairly recent in the eighties of the last century, but I do not know when it first started.

There are several things to be said in favour of this kind of illumination: first, each work of art is seen by itself, isolated from all the others, so that the spectator's attention is exclusively focussed on it; second, in the bright light of a torch, the finer nuances of the work become more distinct, the confusing reflections (particularly annoying on highly polished statues) disappear, the shadows become more marked and the illuminated parts stand out clearer. But the greatest advantage of all is that only such illumination can do justice to statues which are unfavourably placed. Laocoön in his niche, for example, can only be seen properly by torchlight, for no direct light falls on him, only a reflected light from the small circular Cortile del Belvedere, which is surrounded by a colonnade.

The same applies to the Apollo, the so-called Antinous (Mercury), the Nile, the Meleager and, above all, to the so-called Phocion, because by torchlight the exquisitely carved body becomes visible through simple transparent drapery, something which cannot be seen at all by daylight.

Though the monuments in the Capitoline Museum are, on the whole, less remarkable than those in the Museo Pio Clementino, to form a just idea of their merits, it is also advisable to see them by torchlight. The so-called Pyrrhus, a piece of excellent workmanship, stands on the staircase and receives no daylight whatsoever. In the gallery in front of the columns, a splendid half-length figure, believed to be a draped Venus, receives only a faint light from three sides; the nude Venus, the most beautiful statue of its kind in Rome, does not show to advantage in daylight, because it is placed in a corner; the so-called 'well-dressed' Juno stands against a wall between windows, so that it receives only a little reflected light, and the famous head of Ariadne in the Hall of Miscellanies cannot be seen in all its splendour except by torchlight.

But, like so many things which become the fashion, this method of illumination can be misused. Provided that they are standing in a good light, works in the archaic style and even works in the high style have little to gain from it. The sculptors of those times did not yet know about light and shade, so how could they have counted upon their effects? The same is true of works from the decadent period, when the sculptors had become careless and taste had so far declined that attention was no longer given to light and shade, and the theory of masses was forgotten. What is the point of looking at monuments of that sort by torchlight?

Thinking about that festive occasion makes me remember Mr Hirt, who, in more ways than one, was of help to our circle. Born in Fürstenberg in 1759, he studied classical literature and, as a result, felt an irresistible urge to come to Rome. He had arrived there some years before I did, acquired a profound knowledge of architecture and sculpture, both ancient and modern, and assumed the role of a guide for such foreign visitors as were anxious to learn. Among those to whom he sacrificed much time was myself.

His main interest was architecture, and, as one might expect in a city so given to wrangling and taking sides, his theories on that art provoked stimulating debates and heated discussions. Hirt's thesis was that all Greek and Roman architecture was derived from the timber buildings of earlier times, and on this he based his judgements, favourable or unfavourable, skilfully backing up his contentions with historical examples. Those who disagreed with him argued that in architecture, as in any other art, artificialities could be found which were in good taste and that, indeed, given the many different conditions he has to face, the architect can never dispense with them and is always forced, in one way or another, to make an exception to the rule.

Though art consists in doing, not in talking, people will always rather talk than do; so it is not surprising that conversations of this kind were as endless in those days as they are now.

The divergence of opinion among the artists was responsible for many unpleasant scenes and even for broken friendships, but occasionally caused some amusing incident, such as the following.

A number of artists who had spent the afternoon at the Vatican left it at a late hour by the gate near the colonnade and walked home along the vineyards down by the Tiber so as to avoid a long walk across the city. On the way they started to quarrel, when they arrived at the river bank they were still quarrelling and they continued their heated discussion on the ferry. Had they disembarked in Ripetta, they would have had to separate, and the arguments they had not yet had time to produce would have been nipped in the bud. So they all decided to do the crossing a second time and give free rein to their dialectic on the rocking boat. But by now they had really got going, so the second crossing was insufficient, and they ordered the ferryman to repeat it a number of times. The latter had no objection, since he earned a *baiocco* a passenger for each crossing, a considerable profit which he could not expect to make in any other way at such a late hour. He complied with their wishes in complete silence until his little son asked him in amazement: 'What do they want to do this for?' when he said laconically: 'I don't know. They're crazy.'

About this time I received in a package from home the following letter:

Monsieur, je ne suis pas étonné que vous ayez de mauvais lecteurs; tant de gens aiment mieux parler que sentir, mais il faut les plaindre

*et se féliciter de ne pas leur ressembler. – Oui, Monsieur, je vous dois
la meilleure action de ma vie, par conséquent la racine de plusieurs
autres, et pour moi votre livre est bon. Si j'avais le bonheur d'habiter
le même pays que vous, j'irais vous embrasser et vous dire mon secret,
mais malheureusement j'en habite un, où personne ne croirait au
motif qui vient de me déterminer à cette démarche. Soyez satisfait,
Monsieur, d'avoir pu, à 300 lieues de votre demeure, ramener le coeur
d'un jeune homme à l'honnêteté et à la vertu; toute une famille va
être tranquille et mon coeur jouit d'une bonne action. Si j'avais des
talents, des lumières ou un rang qui me fit influer sur le sort des
hommes, je vous dirais mon nom, mais je ne suis rien et je sais ce
que je ne voudrais être. Je souhaite, Monsieur, que vous soyez jeune,
que vous ayez le goût d'écrire, que vous soyez l'époux d'une Charlotte
qui n'avait point vu de Werther, et vous serez le plus heureux des
hommes, car je crois que vous aimez la vertu.*

DECEMBER

CORRESPONDENCE

7 December

MY poetry came to a standstill, so I have spent the week drawing. One has to learn to take each period as it comes and make use of it. Our domestic Academy flourishes and we are trying to arouse old Anganthyr* from his sleep. In the evenings we study perspective.

Angelica is always kind and helpful, and I am indebted to her in more ways than one. We spend every Sunday together and I always visit her on one evening during the week. I simply don't understand how she can work as hard as she does, yet she always thinks she is doing nothing.

8 December

I can't tell you, you wouldn't believe it, how happy I am that you like my little song, that I have managed to strike a note which is in accordance with your mood.

I wish *Egmont*, of which you say so little, could have done the same. I suspect that you have been more pained than pleased by it. Oh I know well enough how difficult it is for a work on this scale to be in perfect tune throughout. After all, no one but the artist himself really knows how difficult art is. There is far more of a positive element in art, that is to say, something which can be taught and handed on from one generation to the next, than is usually believed. There are a great many mechanical devices by means of which one can produce the most soul-moving effects, provided, of course, one has a soul. When one knows these little tricks, much that seems out of this world turns out to be child's play and, for better or worse, Rome, I believe, is the place to learn them.

---

*Anganthyr: a Nordic hero who appears in Herder's *Collection of Folksongs of Various Countries*.

Rome, 15 December

It is very late at night, but I must at least write something for you. I have spent this week very pleasantly; during the previous week I could get nothing done, either in writing or drawing.

On Monday the weather turned fair and the signs I read in the sky seemed to promise more good days, so I set off with Kayser and my second Fritz * for the country. On Tuesday night we arrived at Frascati. On Wednesday we visited some beautiful villas; the best of all was the exquisite villa of Antinous in Mondragone. On Thursday we walked from Frascati to Monte Cavo via Rocca di Papa, of which I shall send you some drawings, for verbal descriptions are meaningless, and then down the hill to Albano. On Friday, Kayser was not feeling well and left us, and I walked with Fritz the Second to Ariccia and Genzano and along the lake of Nemi back to Albano. Today we went to Castel Gandolfo and Marino and from there returned to Rome. The weather was very kind to us, almost the finest Rome has had this year. Apart from the evergreen oaks, some trees are still in leaf, including the young chestnuts, though their leaves have turned yellow. There are tones in the landscape of very great beauty, and then, the wonderful, huge shapes in the darkness every night! I was very happy and felt very well.

21 December

I find that drawing and studying art is a help, not a hindrance, to my poetic faculty: while one ought to write only a little, one must draw a great deal. I only wish I could convey to you my conception of figurative art. The insight and consistency of the great masters is incredible. When I arrived in Italy I felt reborn; now I feel re-educated.

What I have sent so far were only rash attempts. I am giving Thurneisen a roll of things which you will like. The best are by other people.

---

*The first Fritz was a son of Charlotte von Stein, the second the painter Fritz Bury.

This year Christ was born amid thunder and lightning: just at midnight we had a tremendous storm.

The splendour of artistic masterpieces no longer dazzles me. In acquiring a discerning understanding, I owe more to Heinrich Meyer than I can express. He was the first to open my eyes to the details and the specific qualities of single figures and it was he who initiated me into the secrets of *making*. He is very modest and content with little. He actually enjoys works of art more than their noble owners, who do not understand them – more, too, than most other artists, who are too eager to imitate the inimitable. He has a heavenly lucidity of mind and an angelic kindness of heart. Whenever he talks with me, I wish I could write down everything he says, so precise and true are his words as he points out the one true path. As a teacher he will be irreplaceable. Compared to what I have learned from him, everything I learned in Germany is like the bark of the tree compared with the core of the fruit.

Some new foreigners have arrived, with whom I sometimes visit a gallery: they remind me of the wasps in my room which bang against the windows, thinking they are air, bounce back and then buzz about the walls.

I would not wish my worst enemy a silent, retired life, and to be regarded as sick and narrow-minded would suit me less than ever. Think of me, dear friend, and go on doing your best to keep me alive, for, otherwise, I shall be of no use to anyone. As a moral man, I must confess I have been very spoiled this year. For a while I was completely cut off from the world and alone. Now a new circle of friends has formed around me, all of them good and on the right track, the proof of which is that the more they think and act in the right way, the more they like me and enjoy my company. For I am merciless and intolerant with all those who slop about on their own or deviate from the right path while demanding to be regarded as experienced guides. I meet these people with sarcasm and gibes until they either mend their ways or go away. Of course, I am speaking only of

the nice ones. Idiots and cranks are dismissed without ceremony.
Already two or three have changed their lives and opinions under
my influence and will be grateful to me as long as they live. Perhaps this is because my ways of thinking have become much
broader and saner. But, like anyone else, when the shoe pinches,
my foot hurts, and I cannot see through a brick wall.

DECEMBER

DECEMBER opened with a period of almost uninterrupted fine weather and this prompted a scheme which was to give our happy company many pleasant days. Someone suggested we should pretend we had just arrived in Rome, impatient to become quickly acquainted with the most notable sights, and make a round tour. In this way we might get a fresh impression of things which we had come to take for granted.

We started to carry out this plan at once and stuck to it pretty faithfully. Unfortunately, I have little record of the many good things that were seen and said at this time. Letters, notes and sketches are completely lacking.

In a lower quarter of Rome, not far from the Tiber, stands a fairly large church on a site called Alle Tre Fontane. According to legend, these three fountains sprang up from the blood of St Paul when he was beheaded, and have been running ever since.

As the church stands on low ground, the water pipes inside increase the dampness of the atmosphere. The interior is scantily ornamented and almost deserted, and only cleaned and aired for an occasional service. Its greatest attraction are the life-size figures of Christ and the Apostles, painted on the pillars of the nave after drawings by Raphael. In other places he treated the Twelve as a group, all dressed alike, but here this extraordinary genius has depicted them separately and given each his distinctive attributes, not as if he were following the Master, but as though, after the Ascension, he had to stand on his own feet and work and suffer alone, according to the kind of person he was.

Here is an excerpt from an article of mine which appeared in *The German Mercury* in 1789.

In depicting the Apostles, Raphael has made the subtlest use of all that we know, from Scripture and tradition, about their characters, their social position, their occupations, their life and death, and has succeeded in creating a series of figures who, without resembling each other in appearance, have a common spiritual affinity.

Peter. A stocky, sturdy figure, presented in full face. As in some of the other figures, the extremities are slightly exaggerated to make the body look shorter. He has a short neck and his short hair is the curliest of them all. The main folds of his garment converge upon the centre of his body. He stands compactly before us like a pillar, capable of sustaining a weighty burden.

Paul. Like Peter, he stands upright, but is turning to one side like someone who is about to walk away but looks back for the last time. His raised cloak hangs over his arm and he is holding a book. His feet are set apart to show that nothing prevents him from setting forth. Hair and beard are like lambent flames, and his face glows with enthusiasm.

John. A noble youth, with beautiful, flowing locks, curled only at the tips. He seems quietly content to possess and display the testaments of Christianity – the Bible and the Chalice. With a happy stroke of inspiration, the Johannine eagle is spreading its wings and at the same time lifting up the mantle, so that its beautiful folds fall in exactly the right places.

Matthew. A well-to-do, agreeable man, content with his lot. His air of ease and composure is balanced by the grave, almost shy, look in his eyes. The folds of his garment, crossed over his body, and his money-bag give an indescribable impression of good nature and harmony.

Thomas. One of the most beautiful of the figures, impressive because of its extreme simplicity. He stands before us wrapped in a cloak, which hangs down on both sides in folds which are nearly symmetrical but, through slight modifications, are made to look quite dissimilar. One can hardly imagine a form that would give a stronger impression of stillness, peace and humility. The turn of the head, the grave, sad look, the exquisite mouth are in perfect harmony with the rest of the figure. Only his hair is in disarray, to indicate the impassioned soul behind the gentle exterior.

James the Great. The gentle figure of a pilgrim, walking past, wrapped in his cloak.

Philip. If one compares the drapery of this figure with those of the two preceding apostles, one sees that the folds are conspicuously richer and more ample. The assurance with which he stands, firmly holding the cross and fixing his gaze upon it, is in keeping with the richness of the robe he wears. The whole composition seems to intimate greatness of soul, composure and courage.

Andrew. He is embracing and caressing his cross rather than carrying it. The simple folds of his cloak are arranged with great skill.

Thaddeus. A youth who lifts up the skirt of his garment to prevent it from hampering his stride, as monks used to do on pilgrimages. This simple action creates very beautiful folds. In his hand he carries a long spear, the symbol of his martyrdom, like a pilgrim's staff.

Matthias. A jovial old man in a plain garment, enlivened by very skilful folds, he stands leaning upon a spear. His cloak hangs down his back.

Simon. He is turned three-quarters away from us. The folds of the cloak, the posture and the treatment of the hair make this figure one of the most beautiful of them all.

Bartholomew. He stands with his cloak wrapped wildly and carelessly about him, an effect which must have taken great skill to produce. From his hair, his posture and the way he holds his knife, one might almost think he was about to flay someone else, not to suffer this operation himself.

Christ. Anyone who comes expecting to see the miraculous image of a God-man will be disappointed. He is advancing simply and quietly, with His right hand raised to bless the people. One might reasonably object that His garment, which is raised off the ground in beautiful folds and exposing one knee, could not possibly stay there for a moment, but would be bound to fall down at once. What Raphael probably had in mind were two successive actions. The position of the folds indicates the preceding moment, when Christ was coming forward to bless – to do this He raised and held the garment with His right hand – and the upraised right hand indicates the subsequent moment of the blessing itself.

The stadium of Caracalla is largely in ruins but still conveys an idea of immense space. To draw it, a person should place himself at its left wing, where the charioteers used to start. To his right,

then, above the ruined seats of the spectators he will see the
tomb of Cecilia Metella in its new surroundings, then the line
where the seats once were, stretching on without end, and in the
far distance large villas and country houses. Turning back, he
will still be able to trace the ruins of the *spina* directly facing him,
and, if he has any architectonic imagination, he will have some
faint idea of the *hubris* of those ancient times. A skilful artist
could make a pleasant picture, but it would have to be twice as
long as it was high.

In the square in front of San Pietro in Montorio we paid our
respects to the powerful current of the Acqua Paolo, which flows
in five streams through the gates and openings of a triumphal
arch to fill an enormous basin. This great volume of water is
brought from beyond Lake Bracciano by an aqueduct twenty-
five miles long, which was restored by Pope Paul V. This takes a
peculiar zigzag course through the hills, satisfying the needs of
various mills and factories on the way, until it empties into a
wider channel in Trastevere.

The lovers of architecture among us extolled the happy
thought which had provided this water with a free, triumphal
entry open to all. The columns, arches, cornices and pediments
reminded us of those sumptuous arches through which, in times
past, returning conquerors used to enter in triumph. In this case,
it is the most peaceful of benefactors that enters with a like
power and is received with immediate gratitude and admiration
for its long and strenuous march. Inscriptions inform the visitor
that it is Providence and a beneficent pope of the Borghese
family who are making by proxy their stately and eternal
entry.

Someone who had recently arrived from the north objected
to the arch and said it would have been better to let the waters
emerge into the daylight in a natural manner over a pile of
rugged rocks, but we pointed out to him that they were not
natural but artificial, so that it was only fitting to hail their arrival
in an artificial manner.

But on this point there was as little agreement as there was
about Raphael's *Transfiguration*, which we had occasion, soon

afterwards, to admire in a neighbouring convent. There was a lot of talk, but the less loquacious of us were annoyed when the old objection to 'double action' came up again in the discussion. But such is a way of the world; a bad coin always is as acceptable on the market as the true currency. Nevertheless I was surprised that anyone should dare find fault with the unity of such a great conception as this.

In the absence of the Lord, the disconsolate parents have brought their possessed young son to the disciples after they had probably already tried to exorcize the evil spirit themselves. One of them has even opened a book to see whether a traditional spell could not be found which would be effective against this malady – but in vain. At this moment He who alone has power appears, transfigured in glory, and acknowledged by His two great forerunners, and all are looking up and pointing to the vision as the only source of salvation.

What is the point, then, of separating the upper action from the lower? Both are one. Below are those who are suffering and need help; above is the active power that gives succour: both are inseparably related in their interaction. And how would it be possible to express this in any other way?

Those who thought like me were only confirmed by this in our conviction that, like Nature, Raphael is always right, and most profoundly so when we understand him least.

Originally, we meant to make our tour of Rome all by ourselves, but this proved impossible. One member would fail to turn up, another would be unavoidably detained, outsiders who were going to visit the same places would attach themselves to our group. But there was a core of us who always stuck together and learned how to assimilate newcomers and how to get rid of them, when to lag behind and when to hurry on ahead. Now and then, of course, we had to listen to some very odd pronouncements. There was a certain sort of snap empirical judgement which had become current among travellers, particularly among the English and the French; they completely ignored the way in which any artist is conditioned by his talent, his forerunners, his masters, his time, his place, his patrons and clients, without which no just appreciation is possible. My good friend Volkmann, so observant and useful in other ways, seems to have swallowed these opinions of foreigners all too readily, so that his own judgements often sound very strange. For example, could one express oneself more infelicitously than he does when speaking of the Church of Maria della Pace?

In the first chapel Raphael has painted several sibyls, which have been much damaged. The drawing is correct but the composition is poor, which may be due to the cramped space.

This is nonsense. The space which the architecture gave him never worried Raphael in the least. Indeed, it is one of the greatest proofs of his genius that he could fill any given space in the most exquisite manner, as he showed in the Farnesina. *The Mass of Bolsena*, *St Peter Delivered from Prison* and the *Parnassus* would not be the masterpieces they are without the limitations of space. So, too, with the sibyls : the secret symmetry upon which everything depends in a composition carries all before it in the same masterly fashion. In art, as in the natural organism, it is precisely within the narrowest limits that life manifests itself most completely.

On me, the ultimate effect of this tour was to strengthen my sense of really standing on classic soil and convince my senses and my spirit that here greatness was, is and ever will be. It lies in the nature of time and the mutual interaction of physical and moral forces that greatness and splendour must perish, but my ultimate feeling was less of sadness at all that had been destroyed than of joy at so much which had been preserved and even reconstructed more splendidly and impressively than it had been before.

The Church of St Peter, for example, is a bolder and grander conception than any antique temple. Even the fluctuations in taste, now a striving for simple grandeur, now a return to a love for the multiple and the small, are signs of vitality, and in Rome the history of art and the history of mankind confront us simultaneously.

The observation that all greatness is transitory should not make us despair; on the contrary, the realization that the past was great should stimulate us to create something of consequence ourselves, which, even when, in its turn, it has fallen in ruins, may continue to inspire our descendants to a noble activity such as our ancestors never lacked.

All the time, however, my pleasure in beholding these instructive and elevating things was, I will not say spoiled, but interwoven with and accompanied by painful thoughts. I had learned that the fiancé of the nice young girl from Milan had broken off his engagement – under what pretext I did not know – and jilted her, and that she, poor child, from shock and despair had fallen victim to a violent fever and was in danger of her life. Though I had no cause for self-reproach – I had controlled my affection and stayed away from her, and had been explicitly assured that, whatever pretexts had been given, the *villeggiatura* was not among them – nevertheless. I was deeply moved to think that the dear face which I should always remember as so friendly and happy was now clouded and changed. I went every day to inquire how she was, twice daily at the beginning, and it was with pain that my imagination tried to evoke the impossible and picture those cheerful features, which deserved only sunshine and joy, now dimmed by tears and ravaged by sickness, their youthful bloom prematurely wasted and pale from mental and physical suffering.

In such a state of mind, the sheer presence of a succession of great works in their imperishable dignity was a welcome anodyne, but, understandably enough, I contemplated most of them with profound sadness.

I looked at the ancient monuments and saw only that, after many centuries, they had been reduced to shapeless masses; I looked at buildings of a later date, magnificent and intact, and they spoke to me only of the decline of many great families; I looked at things which were alive and blooming and, even there, I thought only of the secret worm within which would in time destroy them; I thought how vainly we put our trust in moral or religious support alone, for nothing on this earth can sustain itself if it lacks physical strength; and I brooded in a sad compassion. Just as a happy mind will invest even crumbling walls and scattered masonry with new life, like a fresh, perennial vegetation, so a melancholy mind robs a living creature of its most beautiful adornment and reduces it, in our eyes, to a bare skeleton.

I could not come to a decision about an excursion into the mountains, which I had planned to take before winter set in, until I knew for certain that she was better, and then I made arrangements, so that it was in the very place where I had first met her, so lively and amiable, during those beautiful days of autumn, that I received the news of her complete recovery.

The first letters from Weimar about *Egmont* had already brought me word that people had picked on this or that to criticize, and made me remember what I had often observed before. The unimaginative friend of the arts, smug in his bourgeois self-conceit, is always offended when a poet has tried to gloss over, conceal or solve a problem. Such a smug reader expects everything to take the conventional course. But the unconventional, too, can be true to nature, even though it may not seem so to people who cling to their set opinions. A letter exemplifying this arrived and I took it with me on a walk to the Villa Borghese; there I read that some scenes were considered much too long. I thought this over carefully, but could not see how they could be cut, since so many important themes had to be developed. But what the ladies seemed to find most objectionable was the laconic dying wish with which Egmont commends his Klärchen to Ferdinand's care.*

An excerpt from a letter of mine, in which I answered these points, will explain the position I took:

You know how much I would like to meet your wishes and be able to change Egmont's dying wish in some way or other, and to shorten some scenes. I have pondered over the action, characters and situations, and if I were to write down all my deliberations, pro and con, they would fill a book and this letter would become a dissertation on the economy of my play. On Sunday I went to see Angelica, who had

---

* Act V. EGMONT: 'And one thing more – I know a girl; you will not despise her, since she was mine. Now that I have entrusted her to your care, I die at peace. You are a noble-minded man; a woman who finds such a man is safe from harm.'

studied the play and had a copy of it, and put the question up to her. I wish you could have been there and heard with what feminine delicacy she went through everything, explaining it point by point. Her conclusion amounted to this: everything you want the hero to say in so many words is implicit in the vision. Since this is a manifestation of what is going on in the sleeping hero's mind, he could not have expressed in words how much he loves and values her more strongly than his dream does, in which his beloved is elevated, not merely to his own level, but high above it. Angelica felt it was absolutely right that the same Egmont who, one might say, has gone through life daydreaming, for in his living and loving he had considered only his own pleasure, should, at the last moment, awake, so to speak, in a dream and tell us without words how deep is his love and how lofty a place his beloved occupied in his heart.

She had other observations to make: that, for instance, in the scene between Egmont and Ferdinand any reference to Klärchen must be brief so as not to detract from the interest of his parting words to his young friend, who, in any case, would be incapable at that moment of hearing or understanding much.

MORITZ AS ETYMOLOGIST

Long ago a wise man said with truth that he whose powers are not up to the necessary and the useful likes to busy himself with the unnecessary and the useless. Some may think that this saying applies to what follows.

Even when surrounded by the masterpieces of Art and the wonders of Nature, my friend Moritz never stopped brooding upon the inner life of man, his instincts and his evolution, and he was obsessed by the problem of language in general. Following the theory stated by Herder in his prize essay *On the Origin of Language*, the prevailing view at that time, which was also in concordance with the way of thinking in other sciences, was that the human race had not propagated itself over the whole earth from *one* couple in the Orient but, at some unusually productive epoch and under specially favourable conditions, the human species had appeared simultaneously and perfectly developed in various places all over the globe, long after Nature had produced by degrees the animals in all their diversity. Man, it was thought, was born with a language which was intimately bound up with his organs and mental faculties, so that it was unnecessary to bring in supernatural guidance or traditional instruction. In this sense, a universal language does exist, which each autochthonic tribe attempted to speak. The affinity between all languages came from their conformity to the idea upon which the powers of creation had modelled the mind and body of the human species. This was why the vowels and consonants are so limited in number. It was natural and necessary, however, that the languages spoken by the various autochthons should have sometimes coincided and sometimes diverged, that one language should have deteriorated and another improved. This applied to the derivatives no less than to the root words. All this was to be accepted as being for the best, but a mystery which could never be completely explained.

But to return to Moritz. I find among my papers the following note :

I am so pleased that Moritz has come out of his black mood of brooding indolence, shaken off his doubts about himself, and taken up an activity which is very good for him, because it provides a firm basis for his whims and eccentricities and gives his fancies meaning and purpose. At present he is preoccupied with an idea which I have also fallen in with and which amuses both of us enormously. It is difficult to convey because at first it sounds crazy, but I will try.

He has invented an intellectual–emotional alphabet, by which he demonstrates that the letters are not arbitrary but are based upon human nature and that each when pronounced stands for some inner world to which it belongs. By this alphabet he claims he can judge all languages, for, though all peoples have tried to express this inner world exactly, all, wilfully or by chance, have deviated from the true way. So now we spend hours examining various languages, looking for those words which are most felicitously formed, now finding one in this language, now one in that. We then alter these words until they seem exactly right, form new ones, etc. And when we want to play this game really properly, we invent names for people, trying to find which name fits which person.

Already this etymological game is keeping a lot of people busy and entertained. Whenever we gather together, we take it up like chess and try out hundreds of combinations. Any stranger who overheard us would certainly think we were all mad, so it is not the kind of thing one should talk about except to one's closest friends. Still, it is the most ingenious game in the world and exercises one's feeling for language in an incredible way.

JANUARY

CORRESPONDENCE

10 January 1788

WITH this letter you will receive *Erwin und Elmire*. I hope this little piece will give you pleasure, though it is never enough just to read an operetta, however good : to get all that the poet intended, his words must be heard with the music. *Claudine* will soon follow. I have worked harder at these two plays than you would believe, for I had first to get Kayser to teach me about the structure of the *Singspiel*.

I am preparing myself for the hour of departure so that I may accept with good cheer what the Heavenly Powers have willed for Easter. Whatever happens is well.

If the publication of my writings is going to progress under the same lucky star, this year I shall have to fall in love with a princess so that I can write *Tasso*, and sell my soul to the Devil so that I can write *Faust*, though I feel no inclination to do either. So far my luck has never deserted me. When I needed something to renew my interest in *Egmont*, the Roman *Kaiser* obligingly picked a quarrel with the people of Brabant; when my operettas needed improving, the Swiss *Kayser* came to Rome. Am I not *a noble Roman!* as Herder would say, and it amuses me greatly that I should have become the *terminus* of actions and events which are no concern of mine. That is what I call good fortune. So, as regards the princess and the Devil, I shall wait and see.

When you read *Erwin und Elmire*, you will see at once that everything is calculated for the lyric stage, which I never had the opportunity to study before I came here. One has to watch out for a hundred things, see that all the characters are employed in a certain sequence, give them each their due weight, allow enough time for the singers to catch their breath, etc. To these considerations the Italians sacrifice any sense of the text, but I hope

I have succeeded in satisfying all these musical-theatrical demands without making my little play completely nonsensical. I had to bear in mind that both operettas might also be read, and must not disgrace their neighbour *Egmont*. No one reads an Italian opera libretto except on the night of the performance, and, in this country, to include one in the same volume with a tragedy would be as unthinkable as singing in German.

As regards *Erwin*, you will frequently come across, especially in the second act, verses written in trochaic metre, which is un-usual in German; they are not accidental but based on Italian models. This metre lends itself particularly well to music, and, by changing the rhythm and tempo, the composer can vary it, so that the listener no longer recognizes it. As a rule, Italians like only regular and simple metres.

Good luck with the fourth part of the *Ideas*. The third has become one of my sacred books which I keep under lock and key. Just recently I gave it to Moritz to read, and he now calls himself fortunate to be living in this epoch, which is doing so much for the education of mankind.

If only one day I could be your host on the Capitol and enter-tain you in return for all your kindnesses. There is nothing I would like more.

My old titanic ideas were only chimeras, the premature ghosts of a more serious period. I am now completely absorbed in the study of the human figure, which is the *non plus ultra* of all our knowing and doing. My assiduous preoccupations in the general nature of Nature, and in osteology especially, are helping me to take vigorous strides.

With Easter in mind, when a definite period of my life will come to an end, I am eagerly snatching up all I can, so that when I leave Rome it will not be with reluctance but with the hope of continuing my studies in Germany with thoroughness and in comfort, though at a slower pace. Here, as soon as I step into my little boat, the stream hurries me along.

JANUARY

IN RETROSPECT

Cupido, you wanton, obstinate boy, you begged me
To grant you merely an hour or two of shelter,
How many days and nights you have remained, becoming
Ever more demanding, the master of the household.

My ample couch I am expelled from; night-long
I huddle on the floorboards, self-tormented;
Fire upon fire enkindled by your mischief
Consumes my winter stores and scorches their poor owner.

My tools are missing or you have mislaid them,
And I, confused, am almost blind with searching:
You make such clumsy noises, I am fearful
The soul may escape from my cot to escape you.*

A reader need not take this little poem literally and think of
that daemon usually called Amor. Let him imagine instead a
crowd of busy spirits who compete for the interest of man's inner
self, drawing him this way and that and confusing him by the
variety of their divided appeals, through this symbol he will then
be able to enter into my frame of mind at the time, which my
letters and notes have already described, and realize what a great
effort it cost me to keep my balance amid so many forces, to
remain receptive to everything and not work myself to ex-
haustion.

MY ADMISSION INTO THE SOCIETY
OF THE ARCADIANS

At the end of 1786 I was besieged on all sides by people trying
to persuade me that I should allow myself to be admitted into
Arcadia as a distinguished shepherd. For a long time I held out
against this proposition, but in the end I had to yield to my
friends, who seemed to set great store by it. The general aims of

---

*This poem was introduced into the second act of the revised
version of *Claudine v. Villa Bella*.

the Arcadian Society are well known, but my readers may be interested to hear more about it.

During the course of the seventeenth century Italian poetry seems to have deteriorated in various ways, for, towards its end, men of culture and good sense began to attack the poetry of their time on two grounds.

They accused it, first, of completely ignoring content, which at that time was called inner beauty, and, second, of sacrificing grace and sweetness of form, or outer beauty, to barbaric diction, harsh-sounding verse, faulty images and tropes, and, worst of all, to a habitual use of incongruous metonymies and metaphors.

As always happens, the poets attacked did their best to suppress genuine and excellent work, so that their misuses of language might go unnoticed. Finally, feeling that this state of affairs could be tolerated no longer, in 1690 a number of far-sighted and determined men banded together to discuss the possibilities of a reform. In order not to draw attention to their meetings and provoke a counter-reaction, they used to assemble out of doors in those secluded gardens, of which so many can be found within the walls of Rome itself. There, close to Nature and breathing the fresh air, they could divine the primordial spirit of poetry. When they met in these chance places, they would lie down on the grass or sit on the fallen masonry of some ruined building – even if a cardinal was present, the only privilege he enjoyed was a softer cushion – to discuss their principles and plans and recite poems, in which they endeavoured to revive the spirit of Classical antiquity and of the noble school of Tuscany.

Perhaps one day one of them exclaimed in rapture : 'Here is our Arcadia', thus giving an apt name to a society of this idyllic character. They did not depend on the protection and patronage of some influential great personage, and they refused to have a president to rule them. A custodian was to open and close the gates of the Arcadian fields, and in emergencies he was to be assisted by a council of elected elders.

Among the early members of the society, Crescimbeni deserves a place of honour, for he may rightly be considered one of its founders, and, as its first custodian, for many years he

laboured faithfully and successfully, nursing a better and purer
taste and eliminating all that was barbaric. He propounded his
doctrines in a series of dialogues on *La Poesia volgare*. This term
cannot be translated as 'popular poetry', but means the poetry
which is true to the spirit of a nation, because it is written by
men of true talent and not distorted by the idiosyncrasies of
some muddle-headed minds. These dialogues are obviously the
fruit of Arcadian conversations and of the highest importance
because of their likeness to the aesthetic tendencies of our own
times. The poems of Arcadia which he published deserve careful
attention for the same reason.

One more observation. When human beings lie on the green-
sward in the open air and seek to come close to Nature, love and
passion have sometimes been known to insinuate themselves
into their hearts. But these worthy shepherds were ecclesiastics
and other men of dignity who were not allowed to be on intimate
terms with the Amor of the Roman Triumvirs. That god, therefore, was expressly dethroned. But love is indispensable to poetry,
so all they could do was to turn to super-terrestrial, more or less
platonic longings and, following in the footsteps of their great
forerunners, Dante and Petrarch, indulge themselves in allego-
rical delights, and it is this which gives their poems their peculiarly decorous character.

When I arrived in Rome, this society had existed for exactly
a century. It had often changed its places of meeting and its
artistic ideals, but it still maintained its outward form with great
respectability if not with an equal prestige. There were few
distinguished foreign residents in Rome who had not been in-
veigled into joining it, the more so because it was only their
contributions which provided the custodian of these poetic acres
with a modest income.

The function at which I was admitted took place as follows:
In the ante-room of a decently appointed building I was presented to a distinguished ecclesiastic, who was to act as my
sponsor and introduce me. We entered a large hall, which was
already rather crowded, and took our seats in the middle of the
front row, facing a high desk. More and more spectators kept
arriving. An imposing elderly man took the empty chair on my

right, who, to judge from his clothes and the respect with which he was treated, must have been a cardinal.

Speaking from the desk, the custodian made a few general introductory remarks and then called on several persons by name, who recited either in verse or in prose. After this had gone on for quite a time, the custodian delivered an address, which I shall omit because it was almost identical with the diploma I received and which I reproduce below. When this was over, I was formally declared a member, and everybody clapped loudly, while my sponsor and I rose to our feet and returned the applause with many bows. Then he too made a well-turned speech, which was not too long and to the point. This was again applauded and then I took the opportunity to thank various members individually and say some polite words. I also did my best to make the custodian feel highly satisfied with his new fellow shepherd.

The diploma, which I received the next day, follows here in the original Italian. I have not translated it because it would lose its distinctive flavour in any other language.

C.U.C.
Nivildo Amarinzio Custode Generale d'Arcadia

Trovandosi per avventura a beare le sponde del Tebbro uno di quei Genij di prim'Ordine, ch'oggi fioriscono nella Germania qual'è l'Inclito ed Erudito Signor de Goethe Consigliere attuale di Sua Altezza Serenissima il Duca di Sassonia Weimar, ed avendo celato fra noi con filosofica moderazione la chiarezza della sua Nascita, de suoi Ministerij, e della virtù sua, non ha potuto ascondere la luce, che hanno sparso le sue dottissime produzioni tanto in Prosa ch' in Poesia per cui si è reso celebre a tutto il Mondo Letterario. Quindi essendosi compiaciuto il suddetto rinomato Signor de Goethe d'intervenire in una delle pubbliche nostre Accademie, appena Egli comparve, come un nuovo astro di cielo straniero tra le nostre selve, ed in una delle nostre Geniali Adunanze, che gli Arcadi in gran numero convocati co' segni del più sincero giubilo ed applauso volle distinguerlo come Autore di tante celebrate opere, con annoverarlo a viva voce tra i più illustri membri della loro Pastoral Societa sotto il Nome di Megalio, e

*vollero altresì assegnare al Medesimo il possesso delle Campagne
Melpomenie sacre alla Tragica Musa dichiarandolo con ciò Pastore
Arcade di Numero. Nel tempo stesso il Ceto Universale commise al
Custode Generale di registrare l'Atto pubblico e solenne di sì
applaudita annoverazione tra i fasti d'Arcadia, e di presentare al
Chiarissimo Novello Compastore Megalio Melpomenio il presente
Diploma in segno dell'altissima stima, che fa la nostra Pastorale
Letteraria Repubblica de' chiari e nobili ingegni a perpetua memoria.
Dato dalla Capanna del Serbatojo dentro il Bosco Parrasio alla Neo-
menia di Posideone Olimpiade DCXLI Anno II. della Ristorazione
d'Arcadia Olimpiade XXIV. Anno IV. Giorno lieto per General
Chiamata.*

Nivildo Amarinzio
Custode Generale
Corimbo Melicronio, Florimonte Egireo
Sottocustodi

The seal shows a wreath, half laurel, half pines, in the centre
of which is a syrinx. Underneath, the words *Gli Arcadi.*

THE ROMAN CARNIVAL

In undertaking to write a description of the Roman Carnival,
I know I shall encounter the objection that a festivity of this
kind cannot really be described, that such a tumult of people,
things and movements can only be absorbed by each spectator
in his own way. The objection is not without point, for I must
admit that, on a foreigner who sees it for the first time, the
Roman Carnival cannot make an altogether agreeable impression : it will neither please his eye nor appeal to his emotions.
There is no point from which the whole of the long, narrow
street where it takes place can be overlooked; in the milling
crown within one's range of vision, it is hard to distinguish
details, the noise is deafening, and the end of each day unsatisfactory.

The Roman Carnival is not really a festival given *for* the
people but one the people give themselves. The state makes very
few preparations for it and contributes next to nothing. The
merry-go-round revolves automatically and the police regulate it
very leniently.

Unlike the religious festivals in Rome, the Carnival does not dazzle the eye: there are no fireworks, no illuminations, no brilliant processions. All that happens is that, at a given signal, everyone has leave to be as mad and foolish as he likes, and almost everything, except fisticuffs and stabbing, is permissible.

The difference between the social orders seems to be abolished for the time being; everyone accosts everyone else, all good-naturedly accept whatever happens to them, and the insolence and licence of the feast is balanced only by the universal good humour.

During this time, even to this day, the Roman rejoices because, though it postponed the festival of the Saturnalia with its liberties for a few weeks, the birth of Christ did not succeed in abolishing it.

I shall do my best to bring the tumult and revelling of these days before the imagination of my readers who live elsewhere, to revivify the memories of those who have seen it, and provide those who are planning to visit Rome with a general introduction to its overcrowded and torrential merriment.

The Corso

The Roman Carnival assembles in the Corso. Since it would be a different kind of feast if it took place anywhere else, I must begin by describing the street.

Like many other long streets in Italian towns, it takes its name from the horse races with which each evening of the Carnival concludes. Elsewhere similar races conclude the feast-day of a patron saint or the dedication of a church.

The Corso runs in a straight line from the Piazza del Popolo to the Piazza Venezia. It is approximately 3,500 paces long and lined with high and, for the most part, magnificent buildings. The width bears no proportion to its length or to the height of the buildings. The pavements on both sides take up from six to eight feet, leaving a space between which in most places is not more than twelve or fourteen paces wide, barely sufficient for three carriages to drive abreast.

During the Carnival the Corso is bounded at its lower end

by the obelisk in the Piazza del Popolo and at its upper by the Palazzo Venezia.

Driving in the Corso

Actually, there is nothing quite novel or unique about the Carnival. It is linked quite naturally to the Roman way of life, being only a continuation, or rather the climax, of the pleasure drives which take place on every Sunday and feast day.

All through the year on these days, the Corso is full of life. An hour or an hour and a half before sunset, the more eminent and wealthy Romans set out in their carriages in one long unbroken line and drive for an hour or more. The carriages start from the Palazzo Venezia, keeping to the left of the street, pass the obelisk and, in good weather, drive out of the Porta and along the Via Flaminia, sometimes even as far as the Ponte Molle.

The returning carriages keep to *their* left, so that the two-way traffic remains orderly. Ambassadors have the right to drive in either direction down the middle of the street between the two lines of carriages. This prerogative was also granted to the Young Pretender, who resided in Rome under the name of the Duke of Albany.

But as soon as the evening bells have rung, all semblance of order disappears. Looking for his quickest way home, each driver turns wherever he likes, frequently blocking the way and holding up other carriages.

The evening carriage drive, which is a brilliant sight in all large Italian cities, and is imitated in every small town that has any carriages at all, attracts many pedestrians to the Corso; everyone flocks there either to see or to be seen.

Climate and Clerical Dress

There is nothing unfamiliar about seeing figures in fancy dress or masks out on the streets under the clear sky. They can be seen every day of the year. No corpse is brought to the grave without being accompanied by hooded religious fraternities. The monks in their many kinds of costume accustom the eye to peculiar figures. There seems to be Carnival all the year round, and the black cassocks of the *abbati* seem the model for the more dignified kind of fancy dress, the *tabarro*.

Opening Days

The Carnival really starts with the opening of the theatres at the New Year. Now and then one sees one of the Fair Sex, sitting in a box, dressed up as an officer and displaying her epaulettes to the public with the utmost self-satisfaction; and already the number of carriages driving up and down the Corso is beginning to increase.

Preparations for the Final Days

Various preparations announce to the public the blissful hours to come.

The Corso, which is one of the few streets in Rome to be kept clean all the year round, is now swept and cleaned even more carefully. This street is beautifully paved with small pieces of basalt cut into almost equal squares; when these have worn unevenly, they are now removed and replaced by new ones.

Living presages of the future event begin to appear. As I said, every evening of the Carnival ends with a horse race. The horses which are specially trained for this purpose are mostly small ones, called *barberi*, because the best of them are of foreign breed.

Each horse is covered with a white linen sheet, bordered with brightly coloured ribbons at the seams and fitting closely around the head, neck and body, and led to the obelisk from which the races start. It is turned to face the Corso and trained to stand there for some time without moving. Then it is led very slowly up the length of the street to the Piazza Venezia, where it is given some oats so that, when it comes to the race, it will have an incentive to run fast to its goal.

Often fifteen or twenty are put through this exercise at the same time, and their promenade is always followed by a crowd of cheering boys.

In the old days the first families of Rome used to keep racing stables, and it was considered a high honour if one of their horses carried off the prize. Bets were laid and victory celebrated with a banquet. Recently, however, horse racing has lost favour with the nobility, and the passion has descended to the middle and even the lower classes of the population.

It is still the custom, which probably dates from earlier times, for a troop of horsemen, accompanied by trumpeters, to parade the streets of Rome, displaying the prizes, and enter the palazzi of the nobility, where, after a flourish of trumpets, they receive a gratuity.

The prize itself is a piece of gold or silver cloth, about three and a half yards long and a yard wide, with a picture of running horses woven diagonally across its lower border, and attached like a flag to a painted pole. It is called *palio*, and there are as many of these quasi-standards as there are days of Carnival.

Meanwhile the Corso is beginning to take on a different look. A many-tiered grandstand, looking directly up the street, is erected in front of the obelisk. In front of this are set up the lists from which the horses will start. The street is also extended into the piazza by stands abutting on to its first houses. On each side of the lists are small raised and covered boxes for the starters. At intervals all along the Corso you can see more stands, and the Piazza San Carlo and the Piazza Colonna are barricaded off by railings. Finally the street is strewn with *pozzolana* to prevent the horses from slipping on the smooth paving.

The Signal for Complete Licence

Shortly after noon the bell of the Capitol tolls, and from that moment on, the most serious-minded Roman, who has so carefully watched his step all year, throws dignity and prudence to the winds.

The workmen who have been banging on the paving stones up to the last minute pack up their tools and move off, cracking jokes. Carpets are hung out from one balcony and window after another; the stands are decorated with old embroidered tapestries. Chairs are placed all along the pavements, and the common people and the children pack the street, which has ceased to be a street and looks more like an enormous decorated gallery. The chairs accentuate the impression of a room, and the friendly sky makes one forget that it has no roof. When one leaves the house, it feels as if one were entering a salon full of acquaintances.

The Guard

The Corso grows livelier and livelier and now and then a Pulcinella appears among the crowd of people in ordinary dress. A troop of soldiers assemble in front of the Porta del Popolo, wearing brand-new uniforms. Led by their commander on horseback, they march along the Corso in good order to the stirring strains of a band, posting guards in the principal squares and occupying all the entrances to the street. Their task is to maintain law and order during the whole affair. Those who let the chairs and the seats on the stands now begin to importune the passers-by, crying out: '*Luoghi! Luoghi, padroni! Luoghi!*'

Masks and Fancy Dress

The number of people in fancy dress begins to increase. Young men disguised as women of the lower classes in low-necked dresses are usually the first to appear. They embrace the men, they take intimate liberties with the women, as being of their own sex, and indulge in any behaviour which their mood, wit or impertinence suggests.

One young man stands out in my memory. He played the part of a passionate, quarrelsome woman perfectly. 'She' went along the whole length of the Corso, picking quarrels with everyone and insulting them, while her companions pretended to be doing their best to calm her down.

Here a Pulcinella comes running along with a large horn dangling from coloured strings around his thighs. As he talks to women, he manages to imitate with a slight, impudent movement the figure of the ancient God of Gardens – and this in holy Rome! – but this frivolity excites more amusement than indignation. And here comes another of his kind, but more modest, accompanied by his better half.

Since the women take as much pleasure in dressing up as men as the men do in dressing up as women, many of them appear wearing the popular costume of Pulcinella, and I must confess that they often manage to look very charming in this ambiguous disguise.

Now an advocate elbows his way quickly through the crowd, declaiming as if he were addressing a court of justice. He shouts up at the windows, buttonholes the passers-by, whether in fancy dress or not, and threatens to prosecute every one of them. To one he reads out a long list of ridiculous crimes he is supposed to have committed, to another an exact tabulation of his debts. He accuses the women of having *cicisbei*, the girls of having lovers. He consults a book he carries with him, and produces documents – all this in a shrill voice and at great length. He tries to make everyone disconcerted and embarrassed. When you think he is going to stop, then he really gets going with a vengeance; when you think he is going away, he turns back; he walks straight up to one person and then does not speak to him, he grabs at another who has just passed; but should he come across a colleague, his madness rises to its highest pitch.

The *quaccheri** are another great sensation, though they are not as noisy as the advocates. The *quacchero* costume seems to have become universally popular, because of the ease with which old-fashioned dresses can be found in second-hand shops. The main requisites for a *quacchero* are clothes which, though old-fashioned, are made of rich material and still in good condition. Most of them are dressed in silk or velvet and wear brocaded or embroidered waistcoats; further, the wearer must be corpulent. The face mask is a full one with puffy cheeks and little eyes; the wig has an odd little pigtail; the hat is small and usually trimmed with braid.

One notices that this figure is very like the *buffo caricato* of Italian comic opera, and like him, the *quacchero* usually plays the part of a silly, infatuated and betrayed old fool; but some of them also play the vulgar fop. Hopping about on their toes with great agility, they carry mock lorgnettes, large black rings without glass in them, through which they peer into carriages and look up at windows. They make low stiff bows and express their

---

Quacchero: an imitation of the Quaker costume.

delight, especially when they meet each other, by leaping
straight up into the air several times and letting out high, pierc-
ing, inarticulate cries, joined together by the consonants *brr*.

Often they make this sound as a signal, which is taken up by
those nearest to them and passed on, so that in a few minutes
the shrill cry runs up and down the whole length of the Corso.

Meanwhile mischievous boys blow into large spiral shells and
offend the ear with intolerable sounds.

The space is so cramped and disguises are so alike – there are
at least several hundred Pulcinelle and about a hundred *quaccheri*
running up and down the Corso – that, unless they arrived early,
very few of the maskers can have come with the intention of
creating a sensation or drawing particular notice to themselves.
Almost everyone is simply out to amuse himself, have his fling
and enjoy the freedom of these days as much as he can.

The girls and married women, especially, try and manage to
have fun after their fashion. They all want to leave their houses
and disguise themselves in any way they can. Since few of them
have much money to spend, they show great ingenuity in inventing all sorts of disguises, though most of these conceal rather
than display their charms.

Beggar masks, male or female, are very easy to make. All that
is needed is beautiful hair, then a full white face mask, a little
earthenware receptacle, held by a coloured ribbon, a staff and a
hat carried in the hand. With a humble air they stop under a
window or in front of someone, and instead of alms, receive
sweets, nuts or whatever tasty thing one cares to give them.

Others take still fewer pains and wrap themselves in furs or
appear in a pretty house dress with only a face mask. Most of
them have no male escort but carry, both for defence and offence,
a little broom, made from the blossoms of reeds, with which
they ward off persons who become too importunate, and mischievously flourish in the faces of strangers and acquaintances
who are not wearing masks. Anyone marked down as a target
by four or five of these girls has no hope of escape. The tightly
packed crowd prevents him from getting away, and whichever
way he turns, he feels the little broom under his nose. To defend
himself effectively against teasing of this sort would be very

dangerous, for the maskers are considered inviolable, and every guard has orders to protect them.

The workaday clothes of all classes can also serve as fancy dress. Persons appear dressed up as stableboys with great brushes, with which they rub the back of anyone whom they care to pick on. *Vetturini* offer their services with their usual importunity. Others put on more handsome fancy dress and appear as peasant girls, women from Frascati, fishermen, Neapolitan boatmen and *sbirri*, or as Greeks. But the *tabarro* is considered the most dignified of all, because it is the least conspicuous. Occasionally a theatrical costume is copied. Some do no more than wrap themselves in sheets, tied over their heads, and hop out suddenly into your path in the hope of being taken for a ghost.

Humorous and satirical masks are very rare because they have a specific meaning, and those who wear them wish to be noticed. But I did see one Pulcinella who was playing the role of a cuckold. His horns were movable, so that he could protrude and retract them like a snail. He would stop under the window of some newly married couple and show just the tip of one horn, then under another and shoot out both horns to their full length. Little bells were attached to their tips, which tinkled merrily whenever he did this. Now and then the crowd would notice him for a moment and roar with laughter.

A conjuror mingles with the crowd and displays a book of numbers to remind them of their passion for lotteries.

Someone wearing a two-faced mask has got stuck in the crowd; nobody knows which is his back and which is his front or whether he is coming or going.

Strangers must also resign themselves to being made fun of. Northerners are taken by the Romans to be maskers on account of the strange round hats and long frock-coats with large buttons that they wear. The foreign painters, especially those who, because they are studying landscape and architecture, have to sit and draw in public and are therefore a familiar sight to the Romans, often encounter caricatures of themselves running about in the Carnival crowd in long frock-coats, carrying enormous portfolios and gigantic pencils.

The German baker-apprentices have a reputation in Rome

for often getting drunk, so figures may be seen, dressed up in their ordinary or slightly decorated costume, staggering about with flasks of wine. I can remember seeing only one obscene mask.

A proposal had been made to erect an obelisk in front of the Church of Trinità dei Monti, which was unpopular with the people because the piazza was too small, and to raise it to the proper height, the little obelisk would have to be set on a very high pedestal. This had given someone the idea of wearing a cap shaped like a huge white pedestal with a tiny red obelisk on top. The pedestal bore an inscription written in large letters, but probably only a few people could guess what it meant.

Carriages

All the pavements are blocked by stands or chairs which are already occupied by spectators. Carriages are moving up one side of the street and down the other, so that the pedestrians are squeezed into the space between them, which is at most eight feet wide, pushing their way through as best as they can, while another packed crowd looks down from windows and balconies upon the crush below.

During the first days the carriages one sees are mostly ordinary ones, for those who have any more elegant and sumptuous vehicles to display are reserving them for the days to follow. But presently open carriages begin to appear, some of which can seat six; two ladies facing each other on raised seats, so that one can see their whole figure, and four gentlemen in the corner seats. Coachmen and footmen are always masked and the horses decorated with gauze and flowers. Often one sees a beautiful white poodle, decorated with rose-coloured ribbons, sitting between the feet of the coachman while bells tinkle on the harness of the horses, and attracting momentary attention from the crowd.

As one might expect, only beautiful women have the courage to expose themselves so conspicuously to the gaze of the whole population, and only a great beauty dares to appear without a mask. Her carriage moves very slowly, all eyes are riveted on her, and she has the satisfaction of hearing on all sides: '*O quanto è bella!*'

It seems that in earlier times these gala coaches were more numerous, more costly and more interesting, because they represented subjects drawn from myth and allegory. But lately, for some reason or other, persons of rank have come to prefer the pleasure of losing themselves in the crowd during this festival to that of distinguishing themselves from others.

With each succeeding day of Carnival, the merrier the carriages look. Even the most sedate, who sit in their carriages without a mask, allow their coachmen and footmen to wear fancy dress. Most of the coachmen choose to dress up as women, so that, in the final days, the job of driving horses seems to be reserved for women only. Often their costumes are very proper and even alluring; now and then, however, there comes a squat ugly fellow, dressed up in the latest fashion with a high coiffure and feathers, who looks like a crude caricature. Just as the beautiful lady has to listen to eulogies, he has to put up with people shoving their faces into his and shouting: '*O fratello mio, che brutta puttana sei!*'

When a coachman spots women in the crowd whom he knows, it is customary for him to lift them up on to his box. They are usually dressed up as men, and there they sit beside him, dangling their pretty Pulcinella legs with small feet and high heels over the heads of the passers-by. The footmen follow suit and haul up their friends, male and female, on to the back of the carriage. A few more and they climb on to the roof as people do on English stagecoaches. Yet their masters seem pleased to see their coaches so thoroughly loaded up; anything is allowed and proper during these days.

The Crush

As I said, two lines of carriages are moving up and down both sides of the street, and the space between them is packed with pedestrians who do not walk but shuffle along. So long as it is possible, the carriages keep some distance between each other so as to avoid a collision every time the crawling line is brought to a halt. To slip out of the crush or at least get a breath of fresh air, many pedestrians take the risk of walking between the wheels of one carriage and the horses of another, and the more dangerous this becomes, the greater their audacity.

Since the majority, who stick to the middle of the street in their anxiety to protect their limbs and their clothing from being caught by a wheel, leave more space between themselves and the carriages than is necessary, any pedestrian who dares to use this space can cover a considerable distance before some new obstacle halts him.

The Procession of the Governor and the Senator

Now and then a member of the Papal Guard comes riding through the crowd to deal with a traffic block, and one has no sooner got out of the way of a coach horse before one feels a saddle horse breathing down one's neck. But there are worse discomforts in store.

In his large state coach and followed by a cortège of other coaches, the Governor comes driving down the middle of the Corso, preceded by footmen and Papal Guards, who clear the pedestrians out of the way while the procession passes.

But like water which, at the passage of a ship, divides for a moment and then immediately flows together again behind the rudder, the crowd immediately re-forms into one solid mass behind the procession.

But soon it is broken up by another commotion. This time it is the Senator who is advancing with a similar cortège. The coaches look as if they are swimming above the heads of the crowd they have squeezed aside, and, though the hearts of Romans and foreigners alike have been captivated by the charm of the present Senator, Prince Rezzonico, the Carnival is the only occasion, perhaps, on which everybody is happy to see his back.

These two, one the Chief Justice, the other the Chief of Police, drive through the Corso only on the first day to inaugurate the Carnival with due solemnity. But the Duke of Albany made this drive every day, to the great inconvenience of the crowd, reminding Rome, the ancient ruler of kings, throughout these days of universal mummery, of the Carnival comedy of his kingly pretensions. The ambassadors, who enjoy the same privilege, made use of it sparingly and with a humane discretion.

The Fashionable World at the Palazzo Ruspoli

In the neighbourhood of the Palazzo Ruspoli, the street is no wider than elsewhere, but the pavements are higher. Here fashionable society congregates, and the stands and chairs are soon occupied or reserved. The most beautiful women of the middle class, in charming fancy dress and surrounded by their friends, expose themselves to the inquisitive looks of the passers-by. Everyone who finds himself in their vicinity lingers to look up and down the pleasing rows; everyone is curious to see if, among the many male figures who seem to be sitting there, he can pick out which ones are ladies, and discover, maybe, in a handsome officer the object of his longing.

It is here that the general movement first comes to a standstill, because here the carriages linger as long as they can, and if one must stop at all, one would rather do so where the company is so pleasant.

Confetti

Now and then, a masked fair lady mischievously flings some sugar-coated almonds at her passing friend to attract his attention and, naturally enough, he turns round to see who has thrown the missile. But real sugared confetti is expensive, so a cheaper substitute must be provided for this kind of petty warfare, and there are traders who specialize in plaster bonbons, made by means of a funnel, which they carry in large baskets and offer for sale to the crowd. No one is safe from attack, everyone is on the defensive, so now and then, from high spirits or necessity, a duel, a skirmish or a battle ensues. Pedestrians, coachmen, spectators alternately attack others and defend themselves.

The ladies carry little gilded or silvered baskets filled with these confetti, and their escorts are very adroit in defending their fair companions. The windows of the coaches are lowered in anticipation of attack, and their occupants exchange pleasantries with their friends or defend themselves stoutly against strangers.

The great place for these mock battles is around the Palazzo Ruspoli. The maskers sit there with baskets, bags and handkerchiefs tied together by their four corners. They take the initiative in attacking others: no carriage passes without being molested by at least some of them, no pedestrian is safe, and when an *abbate* in his black cassock comes into range, he is attacked from all sides, and, since gypsum and lime leave marks, he is soon covered all over with grey and white spots. But sometimes these mock battles turn serious, and, to one's amazement, one sees personal jealousy and hatred being vented in public.

A masked individual sneaks up and flings a handful of confetti at one of the ladies in the front row with such force and success of aim that her mask rattles and her neck is injured. Her escorts, sitting on each side of her, become furious and pelt the assailant with the contents of their bags and baskets; but he is too well padded and armoured to feel their missiles and increases the violence of his attack, while the lady's defenders protect her with their *tabarros*. Presently, in the heat of battle, the aggressor manages to injure several of her neighbours, and they join in. Some have a heavier kind of ammunition in reserve, almost as big as sugar-coated almonds, with which the assailant is now pelted from all sides until, when his own ammunition is exhausted, he is forced to retire.

A person who sets out on such an adventure usually has a companion hand him fresh ammunition, and, during the fight, the dealers in plaster confetti run from one combatant to another, weighing out as many pounds as he asks for.

I witnessed one such battle at close quarters. When the combatants ran out of ammunition, they started throwing their little gilded baskets at each other's heads, without heeding the warnings of the guards, who were getting hit themselves as well.

There is no doubt that many of these fights would end with knives being drawn if that famous instrument of torture of the Italian police, the *corde*, was not hung up at various corners to remind everyone, in the midst of their revelry, that it would be very dangerous to use a dangerous weapon at this moment.

An open carriage full of Pulcinelle comes driving towards the Palazzo Ruspoli, intending to pelt one spectator after another as they pass; but the crowd is too thick and they come to a dead stop. With one mind all the spectators turn on them, and a hailstorm descends on the carriage. The Pulcinelle have soon exhausted their ammunition and for some time are exposed to a crossfire from all sides, until the carriage looks as if it were completely covered with snow and hailstones. It slowly moves off, amid shouts of laughter and cries of disapprobation.

Meanwhile, at the upper end of the Corso, another kind of public is enjoying another kind of entertainment. Not far from the French Academy, the so-called *Capitano* of the Italian theatre, in Spanish dress, with feathered hat and large gloves, steps forward from a crowd of maskers on a stand and begins telling the story of his great deeds by land and sea in stentorian tones. Before long he is challenged by a Pulcinella who, after pretending to accept everything in good faith, casts doubts and aspersions on the hero's tale, and interrupts his rodomontade with puns and mock platitudes. Here again, everyone who passes stops to listen to the lively exchange of words.

The King of the Pulcinelle

Often a new procession increases the general crush. A dozen Pulcinelle, for example, assemble, elect a king, crown him, put a sceptre in his hand, seat him in a decorated carriage and accompany him along the Corso with music and loud cheers.

Now one perceives that each of them is wearing his own individual variation of this commonest kind of fancy dress. One wears a wig, another a bonnet, and another has a birdcage on his head instead of a cap, in which a pair of birds, dressed up as an *abbate* and as a lady, are hopping about on their perches.

Side Streets

The terrible crush naturally forces many of the maskers off the Corso into the side streets. There, loving couples can find more peace and privacy, and merry young blades the space to put on all kinds of grotesque performances, especially in the Via del Babuino and the Piazza di Spagna.

Here, for example, comes a group of men, wearing short jackets over gold-laced waistcoats, the Sunday clothes of the common people, and with their hair gathered up in nets which hang down their backs. With them are other young fellows dressed up as women, one of whom seems to be far advanced in pregnancy. They are all strolling up and down peacefully until, suddenly, the men start to quarrel. A lively altercation ensues, the women get mixed up in it, and the brawl grows more and more violent, until both sides draw huge knives of silver cardboard and attack each other. The women cry murder and try to part them, pulling them this way and that. The bystanders intervene, just as if they believed the affair were in earnest, and try to calm both parties down.

Meanwhile, as if from shock, the pregnant woman is taken ill. A chair is brought, and the other women give her aid. She moans like a woman in labour, and the next thing you know, she has brought some misshapen creature into the world, to the great amusement of the onlookers. The play is over, and the troupe moves on to repeat the performance, or some farce like it, elsewhere.

It seems that the Roman, who is constantly hearing stories of murder, is glad of any opportunity to toy with the idea of assassination. Even the children play a game they call *Chiesa*, which is somewhat like our Prisoner's Base. The *he* is an assassin who has taken sanctuary on the steps of a church; the other children pretend to be the *sbirri*, who must try to catch him somehow without entering his sanctuary.

A crowd of *quaccheri* are performing a manouevre which makes everyone laugh. They come, twelve abreast, marching straight ahead on tiptoe with quick, tiny steps. They preserve an unbroken front until, on arriving in a square, all of a sudden half of them wheel right, half left, and they trip off in single file until they come to another street, when they make a sudden right turn and march down it abreast again, then, quick as lightning, another left turn; the column is shoved, like on a spit, into the doorway of a house, and the madcaps have vanished.

Evening

A S evening draws near, more and more people press into the
Corso. The carriages have come to a standstill long ago. It can
happen that, when night falls, they haven't been able to budge
for two hours.

The Papal Guard and the Watch are now busy seeing to it that
all the carriages are lined up in straight rows along the sides of
the street, a procedure which is the cause of much disorder and
irritation among the crowd. There is a lot of backing and pushing
and lifting. When one coachman backs, all those behind him
have to back too. At last one of them gets into such straits that he
has to lead his horses out into the middle of the street. The
guards start cursing and threatening him, ordering him to get
back in line, while the unfortunate coachman pleads in vain that
this is obviously impossible and that it is not his fault. Either he
must get back into line or drive into a side street, but these are
usually already full of standing carriages, which came too late
to get into the Corso, because the vehicles there had already
ceased to circulate.

Preparations for the Race

It is nearing the time for the horse race, the moment when the
excitement of the thousands of spectators reaches its peak.

The chair vendors grow more insistent than ever with their
shouts of 'Luoghi! Luoghi avanti! Luoghi nobili! Luoghi,
padroni!' and, to make sure that all their seats are sold, offer
them in these last moments at a reduced charge. One is lucky if
one can still find a seat. Now the General comes riding down the
Corso, preceded by some of the guard, who chase the pedestrians
away from the only space that was still left to them. Everyone
tries to find a place somewhere, on a coach, between two carriages
or at some friend's window.

In the meantime the space in front of the obelisk has been
completely cleared of people and presents one of the finest sights
that can be seen anywhere in the world today. Against the three

carpeted façades of the grandstand, thousands and thousands of heads, in row upon row, recall the picture of an ancient amphitheatre or circus. Above the centre stand, which hides only its pedestal, the obelisk soars into the air, and it is only now, when measured against the immense mass of people, that one realizes its stupendous height.

Everyone is looking at the empty lists which are still roped off. The Corso has now been cleared, the General is coming, and the guard behind him sees to it that no one steps out into the street again. The General arrives and takes his place in one of the boxes.

The Start

In an order decided by lot, the horses are led into the lists behind the ropes by grooms in splendid livery. The horses wear no harness of any kind. Now spurs, in the shape of spiked balls, are attached by cords to their bodies, but the places they touch are protected until the last moment by pieces of leather. Large sheets of tinsel are also stuck on them.

Most of them are already frisky and impatient; the presence of so many people makes them nervous, and the grooms need all their strength and skill to manage them. They kick against the partition or try to jump over the rope, and all this commotion increases the excitement of the onlookers.

The grooms, too, are overexcited, because, in deciding the outcome of the race, much depends upon the skill with which the horse is released at the start.

At last the rope falls, and they're off.

So long as they are still in the square, each one strives to gain the lead, but once they enter the Corso, the space between the two lines of carriages is so narrow that overtaking is almost impossible.

A few horses are usually out in front, straining every muscle. In spite of the scattered *pozzolana*, their hooves strike sparks from the pavement, their manes are flying, the sheets of tinsel crackle, and they are gone in the twinkling of an eye. The ones behind jostle and chase each other; a lonely late straggler comes galloping along; pieces of torn tinsel flutter over the empty track. Soon the horses are far out of sight, the crowds flock together from all sides, and the racecourse is again full of people.

In the Piazza Venezia other grooms have been waiting for the horses. When they arrive, they are skilfully caught and tied up in an enclosure. The prize is awarded to the winner.

And so the festivity for which thousands have been waiting for hours is over in a flash; perhaps only a very few could explain why they had waited for this moment or why they had enjoyed it so much.

It will be evident from my description that this sport can be dangerous both for animals and men. For instance, the space between the two lines of carriages is so narrow that a rear wheel has only to project a little into the street to create a hazard. A horse, jammed in a row with others and fighting for room, may easily collide with it. I myself saw one horse trip and fall in this way. The three horses following stumbled over it and fell too. The ones behind cleared them with a jump and continued their race.

Often a falling horse is killed on the spot, and several times spectators have also lost their lives. A similar disaster can occur if the horse turns around. Malevolent and envious persons have been known, on seeing a horse out far in front, to flap their cloaks in front of its eyes, forcing it to turn aside or around. It is still worse if the grooms in the Piazza Venezia fail to catch their horses, for then there is nothing to stop them from turning back, and, since the racecourse by this time is again crowded with people, accidents must often occur which one does not hear about or of which no notice is taken.

Order is Suspended

The race usually starts just before dark. As soon as the horses have reached the Piazza Venezia, little mortars are discharged, and this signal is repeated, first halfway down the Corso and then nearer the obelisk.

Immediately, some carriages turn round into the middle of the Corso, causing confusion, and should one driver take it into his head to drive up the street and another to drive down it, neither is able to move an inch, and the more reasonable drivers who have stayed in line are also prevented from making any progress. Should a runaway horse now run into such a tangle, more trouble will ensue.

Night

The muddle is finally straightened out, thought not without delays and mishaps. Night has fallen and everyone is hoping for some peace and quiet.

The Theatres

From this moment on, all masks are taken off, and a large section of the public hurries to the theatre. In the boxes one may still see some *tabarros* or some ladies in fancy dress, but the whole of the parterre are in their ordinary clothes. The Aliberti and the Argentina give *opera seria* with ballets between the acts; the Valle and the Capranica comedies and tragedies with comic operas as intermezzi. The Pace does the same, though its standards are lower, and there are many other minor kinds of performance, down to puppet shows and tightrope dancers.

The great Teatro di Tordinona, which burned down and then collapsed the moment it was rebuilt, is no longer there, unfortunately, to amuse the people with its historical melodramas and other spectacular shows.

The Romans have a passion for the stage, and in the old days were all the more ardent theatre-goers during Carnival because this was the only season at which they could satisfy it. Nowadays, at least one playhouse is also open during the summer and autumn.

The Festine

I must say a few words about the *festine*, as they are called, the great fancy-dress balls which are given on several nights in the splendidly illuminated Teatro Aliberti. On these occasions, also, the *tabarro* is considered the most elegant costume both for men and for women, and the whole ballroom is filled with black figures, with only a sprinkling of more colourful ones. The curiosity is all the greater, therefore, when an imposing figure appears dressed up as one or another of the statues in Rome. One sees Egyptian deities, priestesses, Bacchus and Ariadne, the Tragic Muse, the Muse of History, a City, Vestal Virgins or a Consul.

The Dances

The dances at these balls are usually danced after the English fashion, in long rows, the only difference being that their few steps usually pantomime some typical action; for example, the falling-out and reconciliation of two lovers, who part and meet again.

Their ballets have accustomed the Romans to an emphatic style of gesture, and, even in their social dancing, they love expressive movements, which to us would seem exaggerated and affected. No one dares to dance unless he has studied it as an art. The minuet, in particular, is treated as a work of art, and it is only performed by a few couples. The other dancers stand in a circle round such a couple, watching them with admiration and applauding when their dance is over.

The Morning

While the fashionable world is amusing itself in this manner into the small hours, workmen are already busy at dawn, cleaning and tidying up the Corso. Particular care is taken to distribute the *pozzolana* evenly over the middle of the street.

Presently grooms come leading back to the obelisk the horse which came in last yesterday. A little boy is seated on its back, while another rider urges it with a whip to strain every muscle to run the course as swiftly as possible.

The Last Day

Stands and chairs are occupied earlier than on previous days, although the seats are now more expensive, and the horse race is expected with greater impatience than ever.

When they have flashed by, and the signals announce that the race is over, neither the carriages nor the maskers nor the spectators make the slightest motion to leave, while the dusk slowly deepens. All is silent, all is still.

Moccoli

The darkness has scarcely descended into the narrow, high-walled street before lights are seen moving in the windows and on the stands; in next to no time the fire has circulated far and wide, and the whole street is lit up by burning candles.

The balconies are decorated with transparent paper lanterns, everyone holds his candle, all the windows, all the stands are illuminated, and it is a pleasure to look into the interiors of the carriages, which often have small crystal chandeliers hanging from the ceiling, while in others the ladies sit with coloured candles in their hands as if inviting one to admire their beauty.

The footmen stick little candles round the edges of the carriage roofs; open carriages have paper lanterns, some pedestrians carry lanterns on their heads shaped like tall pyramids, other stick their candles on reed poles which often are two or three stories high. It becomes everyone's duty to carry a lighted candle in his hand, and the favourite imprecation of the Romans, '*Sia ammazzato*', is heard repeatedly on all sides.

'*Sia ammazzato chi non porta moccolo* – Death to anyone who is not carrying a candle.' This is what you say to others, while at the same time you try to blow out their candles. No matter who it belongs to, a friend or a stranger, you try to blow out the nearest candle, or light your own from it first and then blow it out. The louder the cries of *Sia ammazzato*, the more these words lose their sinister meaning, and you forget that you are in Rome, where at any other time but Carnival, and for a trifling reason, the wish expressed by these words might be literally fulfilled.

Just as in other languages curses and obscene words are often used as expressions of joy or admiration, so, on this evening, the true meaning of *Sia ammazzato* is completely forgotten, and it becomes a password, a cry of joy, a refrain added to all jokes and compliments. Someone jeers: '*Sia ammazzato il Signore Abbate che fa l'amore*'; another greets a good friend with: '*Sia ammazzato il Signore Filippo*'; another combines flattery and compliment: '*Sia ammazzata la bella Principessa! Sia ammazzata la Signora Angelica, la prima pittrice del secolo.*'

All these phrases are shouted loudly and rapidly with a sustained note on the penultimate or antepenultimate syllable. Meanwhile, the business of blowing out candles and relighting them goes on without stopping. Wherever you meet someone, in the house, on the stairs, in a room with visitors or leaning out of the window next to yours you try to get the better of him and blow out his candle.

All ages and all classes contend furiously with each other. Carriage steps are climbed; no chandelier and scarcely a paper lantern is safe. A boy blows out his father's candle, shouting: '*Sia ammazzato il Signore Padre!*' In vain the old man scolds him for this outrageous behaviour; the boy claims the freedom of the evening and curses his father all the more vehemently. The tumult subsides at both ends of the Corso, for everyone is gathering at its centre till the crush is beyond conception and even the liveliest imagination cannot recall it later.

No one can move from the spot where he is standing or sitting; the heat of so many human beings and so many lights, the smoke from so many candles as they are blown out and lit again, the roar of so many people, yelling all the louder because they cannot move a limb, make the sanest head swim. It seems impossible that the evening can end without some serious injury, that the carriage horses will not get out of hand, that many will not get bruised and crushed.

Still, in time, everyone begins to feel the need to get out of the throng, to reach the nearest side street or square and catch a breath of fresh air; the mass of people begins to melt away and this festival of universal freedom and licence, this modern Saturnalia, ends on a note of general stupefaction.

The common people are leaving in a great hurry to feast with relish on the meat which will be forbidden them after midnight, while the fashionable world goes to the various playhouses to bid farewell to the plays, which are cut very short this evening, for to these pleasures, too, the approaching hour of midnight will put an end.

Ash Wednesday

And so the exuberant revelry has passed like a dream or a fairy tale, leaving fewer traces, perhaps, on the soul of the author, who took part in it, than on the souls of his readers, to whom he has attempted to present it with a certain coherence.

In the course of all these follies our attention is drawn to the most important stages of human life: a vulgar Pulcinella recalls to us the pleasures of love to which we owe our existence; a Baubo * profanes in a public place the mysteries of birth and motherhood, and the many lighted candles remind us of the ultimate ceremony.

The long, narrow Corso, packed with people, recalls to us no less the road of our earthly life. There, too, a man is both actor and spectator; there, too, in disguise or out of it, he has very little room to himself and, whether in a carriage or on foot, can only advance by inches, moved forward or halted by external forces rather than by his own free will; there, too, he struggles to reach a better and more pleasant place from which, caught again in the crowd, he is again squeezed out.

If I may continue to speak more seriously than my subject may seem to warrant, let me remark that the most lively and exquisite delights are like horses racing past, the experience of an instant only, which leaves scarcely a trace on our soul; that liberty and equality can be enjoyed only in the intoxication of madness, and desire reaches its highest pitch of excitement only

---

* Baubo: Demeter's nurse who tried to cheer her up when she lost Persephone by telling her bawdy stories.

in the presence of danger and the voluptuous half sweet, half
uneasy sensations which it arouses.

In so concluding my Ash Wednesday meditation, I trust that I
have not saddened my readers. Such was very far from my intention. On the contrary, knowing that life, taken as a whole,
is like the Roman Carnival, unpredictable, unsatisfactory and
problematic, I hope that this carefree crowd of maskers will make
them remember how valuable is every moment of joy, however
fleeting and trivial it may seem to be.

FEBRUARY

Rome, 1 February

HOW happy I shall be when Tuesday is over and the fools are silenced. Nothing is more boring than to watch others go mad when one has not caught the infection oneself.

So far as it has been possible during these days, I have continued with my studies. *Claudine* has made some progress, and, unless all the genii deny me their aid, the third act will soon go off to Herder, and I shall have the fifth volume over and done with. But then I shall have fresh trouble in which no one can give me advice or help. *Tasso* must be completely rewritten; what I have written so far won't do at all – I can neither finish it nor throw it away. Such is the toil which God ordains for Man! The sixth volume will probably contain *Tasso*, *Lila*, *Jery und Bätely*** – all so revised that nobody will recognize them.

I have been looking over my short poems for the eighth volume, which I may publish before the seventh. It's a strange business, drawing up a *summa summarum* of one's life like this. How slight are the traces left by a whole existence!

People have been pestering me with translations of *Werther*, asking me which is the best one and if the story is really true. This is a plague which would pursue me to India.

6 February

Here is the third act of *Claudine*. I hope it will give you half the pleasure it has given me to be finished with it. Now that I know more about the needs of the lyric stage, I have sacrificed a good deal to humour the composer and the actor. Any fabric which is designed to be embroidered upon must be wide-meshed, and, for a comic opera, as coarsely woven as canvas. But I have also tried, as

---

* *Lila*, *Jery und Bätely* : two *Singspiele*, 1780.

I did with Erwin, to make it something which can be read. In short, I have done what I could.

I am feeling calm and contented and, as I told you before, ready and prepared for any call. For the visual arts I am too old, so what difference does it make if I bungle a little more or a little less. I have slaked my thirst, I am on the right road to contemplation and study, and my pleasures are peaceful and modest. Please give all this your blessing. I now have little more to do than finish off my last three sections. After that: *Wilhelm Meister*, etc.

9 February

On Monday and Tuesday the fools were still making a tremendous racket, especially on Tuesday, when the frenzied business of the *moccoli* was in full swing. On Wednesday I thanked God and the Church for Lent. I did not go to any of the *festine*, as the masked balls are called here. I am working hard and learning as much as my head will hold. I have just been reading Leonardo da Vinci's treatise on painting and understand why, when I first tried it, I couldn't make head or tail of it.

Mere onlookers are lucky fellows! They fancy themselves as being so clever and believe they are always right. The dilettantes and connoisseurs are just as bad. You can't imagine what a self-contented crew they are. All a good artist can do in their company is keep his mouth shut. I have recently developed a violent aversion to hearing anyone pass judgement who has not worked himself. Such talk is as offensive to me as the stink of tobacco.

Angelica has treated herself to the pleasure of buying two paintings, one by Titian, the other by Paris Bordone. They both cost her a lot of money, but since she is so rich that she can't even spend the interest on her capital, and earns more every year into the bargain, it is a good thing that she should buy what not only gives her pleasure but also stimulates her painting. As soon as she got the paintings hung in her house, she began to paint in a new style, and tried to make certain devices of these masters her own. She is a tireless worker, both at painting and at studying, and I greatly enjoy looking at works of art with her.

Kayser, too, has set to work like the serious artist he is. His music to *Egmont* is making good progress. I have not heard all of it yet, but what I have heard seems to me very appropriate. He is just about to set 'Cupido, you wanton obstinate boy'. I shall send it you the moment it is finished and hope it will often be sung in my memory. Among my little songs, it is one of my favourites.

My head is in a whirl from so much visiting, working and thinking. I have grown no wiser. I still make too many demands on myself and undertake too much.

22 *February*

Something happened this week which has greatly distressed our artistic colony. A young Frenchman called Drouais has died of smallpox. He was only twenty-five, the only son of a doting mother, rich, cultured and considered the most promising of all the artists studying here. In his deserted studio I saw a life-size painting of Philoctetes, who was depicted soothing the pain of his wound by fanning it with the wing of a bird of prey he had just killed. A well-conceived picture and showing much merit in its execution, but left unfinished.

I am cheerful and working hard, while I wait to see what the future will bring. I realize more clearly every day that I was really born to be a poet, and that in the next ten years, which are all, at most, which I shall be allowed to work in, I must cultivate this talent and produce something good. The time when the fire of youth enabled me to accomplish things without much study is now over; I shall have the benefits of my long sojourn in Rome to look back upon, even though I shall have to give up practising the visual arts.

Angelica has paid me the compliment of saying that she knows very few people in Rome who *see* better in art than I do. I know quite well where and what I don't see at all yet, but I feel I am improving and I know what I must do to see still better. But enough of this. My wish that I should no longer blindly grope my way in a matter which attracts me passionately has been fulfilled.

I shall send you soon a new poem, 'Amor as a landscape painter', which I hope you will like. I have been trying to arrange my short poems in some kind of order. They look rather strange to me. The poems on 'Hans Sachs' and 'Mieding's Death' will conclude the eighth volume and hence all my writings for the time being. Should I be laid to rest beside the Pyramid of Cestius, these two poems will serve as my dying confession and my funeral oration.

Tomorrow morning the papal choir will start singing the famous old musical offices which will be the high points of interest when Holy Week comes. From now on I shall go every Sunday morning in order to make myself familiar with their style. Kayser, who specializes in these matters, will probably be able to explain them to me. We are expecting by every mail a printed score of the music for Maundy Thursday which Kayser left behind in Zurich. We shall first hear it on the piano and then in the Sistine Chapel.

FEBRUARY

THE article I wrote about the Roman Carnival which I have reprinted here was based on notes I took at the time. I asked a member of our household, Georg Schütz, to make quick sketches of individual costumes and masks and colour them, which he did with his usual kindness. These drawings were later engraved in quarto and coloured by Melchior Kraus of Frankfurt, now director of the Free Institute for Drawing in Weimar, as illustrations to the first edition, which was published by Unger and has become quite a rarity. All this meant that I mingled more with the masked crowd than I would otherwise have done, for, even when looked at from an artistic point of view, it frequently struck me as repulsive and uncanny. After having spent a whole year in Rome, preoccupied with noble works of art, my spirit felt out of tune with the spirit of Carnival.

But for my inner and better life a most comforting experience was being prepared. In the Piazza Venezia, where some coaches stop before rejoining the moving string of the others so as to let the occupants look at the maskers going by, I caught sight of Madame Angelica's coach and went up to the carriage door to greet her. She had barely leaned out to give me a friendly nod before she drew her head in again to let me see sitting beside her, the young Milanese, now completely recovered. I did not find her at all changed, but then, why should a healthy young person not recover quickly? Her eyes seemed even more animated and brilliant than ever and they looked into mine with a joy that went to my heart. We looked at each other for some time without speaking, until Madame Angelica broke the silence. 'I am only acting as interpreter,' she said, while her companion leaned forward to hear what she was saying, 'because my young friend cannot find words to express what she has wished and meant to say to you and has repeatedly said to me, how grateful she has been for your interest when she was ill. Her main consolation,

which contributed greatly to her recovery and has enabled her to
face life again, has been the sympathy shown by her friends and,
in particular, by you. After those dark days of utter solitude
she has found herself surrounded again by a friendly circle of
good and kind people.'

'That is the truth !' exclaimed the girl, leaning across her friend
and holding out her hand, which I could touch with mine, but
not with my lips. I felt calm and happy as I stepped back into
the throng of fools, and tenderly grateful to Angelica for comforting and taking care of the girl after her misfortune. She had
drawn her into her most intimate circle – something which rarely
happens in Rome – an action which moved me all the more
because I could flatter myself that my interest in the beautiful
girl had been in no small manner responsible for it.

The Senator of Rome, Count Rezzonico, had paid me a visit
after his return from Germany and brought me greetings from
two dear friends and benefactors of mine, Mr and Mrs von
Diede, with whom he had become intimate. Though, as usual, I
kept my distance, I was to be drawn inevitably into his circle.

The Von Diedes came to Rome to visit the Count in return,
and I could not decline a number of invitations, especially as Mrs
von Diede was a famous pianist, who had consented to perform
at a concert given in the Senator's residence on the Capitol, and
my friend Kayser, whose competence was well known, had also
received an invitation to play. The sun was setting and the view
of the Colosseum and its surroundings from the Senator's windows was magnificent, but I could not give myself up to it without seeming to show a lack of manners and respect for the
society which had assembled there. Mrs von Diede played an
interesting concerto with great skill. Soon after, my friend was
asked to play, which he did, and, judging by the applause, proved
himself worthy of the occasion. Various other musicians performed, including a lady who sang a popular aria, and the concert
concluded with Kayser again improvising a number of variations
on a charming theme.

Everything went off very well. I had an amiable conversation
with the Senator, who, however, could not resist telling me, half
apologetically, in his soft Venetian accent, that he did not really

care for variations of this kind, but was delighted every time with the adagios of 'his' lady. I cannot go so far as to say that I actually dislike those languishing sounds which are so often dragged out in an adagio or a largo, but I have always preferred the more stirring kind of music, since my own emotions and reflections on loss and misfortune are only too apt to overcome and depress me. But I could not grudge our Senator his delight in listening to these sounds which assured him that, in the most beautiful place in the world, he was the host of a friend he loved and admired so much.

For the rest of the audience, especially for those of us who were German, it was a great treat to hear a distinguished lady whom we had known and admired for so long elicit from the piano the most ravishing sounds and, at the same time, to look down from the windows over a region unique in this world. I had only to turn my head slightly to survey a vast panorama, lit by the glow of the setting sun and extending on my left from the arch of Septimius Severus, along the Campo Vaccino to the Temple of Minerva and the Temple of Peace. In the background stood the Colosseum, and I let my glance wander beyond it past the arch of Titus, until it was lost in the labyrinth of the ruins on the Palatine and the wilderness around them, embellished with wild flowers and cultivated gardens.

(I would recommend to my readers very highly a panorama of the north-western part of Rome, as seen from the tower of the Capitol, which was drawn and engraved in 1824 by Fries and Thürmer. Their viewpoint is several stories higher than the Senator's window, and their picture shows the recent excavations, but the lights and shades of the sunset are the same as those I saw that evening. They will have, of course, to imagine for themselves the blazing colours with their shadowy blue contrasts and all the magic which the scene derived from them.)

On this occasion I also had the good fortune to see at my leisure the best picture, perhaps, which Mengs ever painted – his portrait of Clement XIII Rezzonico, to whom his nephew, our host, owed his senatorship.

MARCH

CORRESPONDENCE

Rome, 1 March

LAST Sunday we went to the Sistine Chapel, where the Pope and Cardinals were celebrating Mass. For me it was a novel spectacle, since, during Lent, the cardinals are robed in violet instead of red. A few days before I had seen some paintings by Albrecht Dürer and therefore enjoyed all the more seeing something similar in real life. The whole ceremony was of a unique grandeur and yet quite simple, so that I don't wonder that the foreigners who flock here during Holy Week are overwhelmed. I knew the chapel very well (last summer I ate my midday meal there and took a siesta on the papal throne), and the frescoes almost by heart, but when these form the surroundings to the function for which the chapel was intended, they look quite different, and I hardly recognized the place.

They sang an old motet by the Spanish composer Morales, which gave us a foretaste of what is still to come. Kayser says that it is only here that one can hear and should hear this kind of music, first, because nowhere else can singers be found who are sufficiently accomplished to sing unaccompanied by organ or instruments and, secondly, because this way of singing is in perfect accord with the function of the papal chapel and the ensemble of Michelangelo's works, the Last Judgement, the Prophets and the stories from the Bible. Kayser is a fervent admirer of ancient music and is making a serious study of it.

We now have in the house a collection of Psalms, translated into Italian verse and set to music by a Venetian nobleman, Benedetto Marcello, at the beginning of this century. For many of them he has taken the chants of German and Spanish Jews for the main tune; others he has based upon ancient Greek melodies and elaborated them with great skill and good taste. They are composed for a solo voice, or for two voices or for chorus, and are extraordinarily original, though one has to acquire a taste for them. Kayser admires them very much and is going to copy out some. One day perhaps it will be possible to acquire the whole work, which was printed in Venice in 1724 and contains the first fifty Psalms. I wish Herder would try to track down this interesting work; he might find it in some catalogue.

I have had the temerity to plan out my last three volumes simultaneously and now know exactly what I am going to do. May Heaven grant me the inspiration and good luck to do it.

It has been a fruitful week which, in retrospect, seems more like a month.

First I worked out a plan for *Faust*, and hope this scheme will work. To finish the piece now will be a different matter than it would have been fifteen years ago, but I do not think it will lose by the delay, for I believe I have found the thread again. I am also confident about its general tone. I have already written one more scene, which, if I were to scorch the page a little, would be indistinguishable from the others.

A long period of peace and solitude has given me back myself and I am surprised to find how much I resemble my old self and how little my newer self has been touched by all that has happened to me during the years.

It gives me an odd feeling sometimes when I see the old manuscript lying before me. It is still the untouched first version in which I flung off the principal scenes without making any preliminary draft, so that it really looks like the fragment of some old codex. Instead of transporting myself by thought and intuition into a remote past, as I did then, I must now transport myself into a past in which I once lived myself.

My plan for *Tasso* is also worked out now and most of the miscellaneous poems for the last volume have been written out in fair copy. *Des Künstlers Erdenwallen* must be rewritten and the *Apotheosis* added. This is the first time I have seriously looked over these juvenilia and they have become very alive to me in every detail. I have the greatest hopes for the last three volumes, and already I see them standing before me all complete. All I need is the leisure and peace of mind to realize my intentions step by step.

For the arrangement of the shorter poems, I have taken your *Scattered Leaves* as a model and hope I have found the right way to combine so much disparate material and make the over-personal and occasional pieces more palatable.

As I was thinking about all this, the new edition of Mengs's writings reached me, a work which I now find extremely interesting since I have acquired the sensory understanding without which not a word of it is comprehensible. It is excellent in every respect and one cannot read a page without profit. I have been much enlightened as well by his *Fragments on Beauty*, which many find obscure.

I have also been making all sorts of speculations on the subject of colour, a matter which is close to my heart, since it is the aspect of art about which till now I understood least. I see that, with practice and reflection, I shall learn to enjoy fully this pleasure of the external world.

7 March

Another peaceful, productive week has passed. On Sunday I did not go to the Sistine Chapel; instead, I went with Angelica to see a beautiful painting which can certainly be attributed to Correggio. I also saw the collection in the Accademia di San Luca where the skull of Raphael is preserved. This relic seems to me authentic. An exquisite bone structure in which a beautiful soul could walk about in comfort. The Duke wants to have a cast of it, which I can probably procure.

I have visited Cavacceppi's house, which I had hitherto neglected. Among many excellent things there, I was particularly delighted with the casts of the heads of the Colossi on Monte Cavallo; unfortunately, the finer of the two, as a result of time and weathering, has lost about a tenth of an inch from the smooth surface of its face, so that, from close up, it looks as if it were pitted by smallpox.

Today a Requiem Mass for Cardinal Visconti was held in the Church of San Carlo. Since the papal chorus was singing, we went there to purify our ears for tomorrow. The Requiem was for two sopranos and the strangest music I ever heard. On this occasion, too, there was neither an organ nor any other instrument.

What a disagreeable instrument the organ is! This struck me especially last night in St Peter's, when it accompanied the choir at vespers. It does not blend with the human voice and it is much too loud. What a joy, on the other hand, to hear the choir in the Sistine Chapel, singing unaccompanied.

For the past few days, the weather has been cloudy and warm. The almond tree has lost most of its blossoms, except for a few at the top, and is now green. It is the peach tree's turn to ornament the gardens with its lovely colour. On all the ruins *Viburnum tinus* is in bloom; the elder bushes and other shrubs which I don't know are coming into leaf. Walls and roofs are becoming green, and on some of them flowers are beginning to appear. Since I am expecting Tischbein back from Naples, I have changed lodgings, and from my new room I have an entertaining view of numerous little gardens and back balconies.

I have started modelling a little. When it is a matter of theory, I can proceed correctly and with assurance, though I am still slightly confused when it comes to the practical application. But this happens with all my fellow students.

14 March

Next week it will be impossible to think or to do anything; one will have to float with the current of religious ceremonies. After Easter, I shall see to various matters I still have to do, loosen all ties, pay my bills, pack up my bags and set off with Kayser. If everything goes as I plan and wish, I shall be in Florence by the end of April. In the meantime you will still be hearing from me.

It is strange that a suggestion * from outside should have forced me to take several measures which resulted in new relationships and have made my stay in Rome more pleasant than ever.

Indeed, I can say that, during these last eight weeks, I have felt more content than ever before in my life and that now I know

---

* The Duke had asked Goethe to stay longer in Rome and make preparations for the visit of his mother, the Dowager Duchess.

the highest temperature from which in future to calibrate the thermometer of my existence.

In spite of the bad weather, life this week has continued to be pleasant. On Monday we heard a motet by Palestrina in the Sistine Chapel. On Tuesday, as luck would have it, several sections of his music for Holy Week were sung in a private house in honour of a foreign lady, so that we could listen to it in comfort and begin to get an idea of it after we had already gone through it several times at the piano.

The motet is an incredibly great and simple work of art which can probably only be preserved by its recurrent performance in this chapel. A comparison of the performance with the edition Kayser had shows that various vocal elaborations have crept in and become a tradition for which there is no authority. But in spite of them, it is something extraordinary, a revelation. Kayser will be able to give a full account of it later. He is obtaining special permission to attend a rehearsal in the chapel, to which, as a rule, nobody is admitted.

This week I have been modelling a foot, after having previously studied the bones and muscles, and my teacher made complimentary remarks. If I had studied the whole human body in this manner, I would now be a good deal wiser – provided, of course, I had done it in Rome, with all its facilities and plentiful expert advice. I have in my possession the foot of a skeleton, a beautiful anatomy, cast from Nature, half a dozen casts of the most beautiful antique feet, some good, some bad, the former for imitation, the latter as a warning. I also consult Nature, and whenever I enter a villa, I look at the pictures to see how painters have treated the foot. Three or four artists pay me daily visits and I make use of their comments and advice, but actually it is only from Heinrich Meyer that I benefit much. If with such a wind and such a sea, a ship should make no progress, it would be one with no sails or with a mad helmsman.

I continue wandering around, looking at things I had neglected. Yesterday I went for the first time to Raphael's villa, where he preferred life at the side of his beloved to all art and glory. Prince Doria has bought it and apparently intends to treat it, as it deserves to be treated, as a sacred monument. Raphael has painted his beloved twenty-eight times on the walls, in every kind of costume: even the women in his historical compositions resemble her.

From there I went to the Villa Albani, but had only a cursory look around. It was a beautiful day. Last night it rained heavily, but now the sun is shining and from my window I can see a paradise. The almond tree is fully green, the peach is already beginning to shed its blossoms, while those of the lemon are bursting open in the top branches.

Three people are really going to miss me when I leave here. They will never find again what I have given them and it hurts me to say good-bye. In Rome I have found myself for the first time. For the first time I have been in harmony with myself, happy and reasonable, and it is as such that these three, each differently and to a different degree, have known me and made me their friend.

22 *March*

I am not going to St Peter's today, so shall write a little note instead. Holy Week with its miracles and penances is over, to-morrow I am going once more to receive a benediction, and after that, my thoughts will turn to a completely new life.

Thanks to the good offices of dear friends, I have seen and heard everything, but it took a lot of pushing and squeezing to see the Washing of the Feet and the Feeding of the Pilgrims.

The music in the Sistine Chapel is unimaginably beautiful, especially the *Miserere** and the so-called *Improperi,** that is, the Crucified's reproaches to His people, which are sung on Good Friday. The moment when the Pope is stripped of his pontifical pomp and steps down from his throne to adore the cross, while all the others stay where they are in silence, until the choir begins – *Populus meus, quid feci tibi?* – is one of the most beautiful of all these remarkable rites. You shall hear more about it all in detail when I get back, and such of the music as is transportable Kayser is going to bring with him. I have had my wish, enjoyed

---

* *Miserere for nine voices* by Vittorio Allegri (1584–1652); *Improperi* by Palestrina (1514–94).

everything on these occasions which was enjoyable, and kept my
thoughts to myself about the rest.

What most people call effect had none on me: I cannot say
that I was personally much moved, but I had to admire everything and admit that the Christian traditions have been carried
out to perfection. At services in which the Pope takes part,
particularly those in the Sistine Chapel, everything in the
Catholic ritual which is usually offensive is done with perfect
taste and great dignity. But this, of course, is possible only in a
place where for centuries all the arts have been at the disposal of
the Church.

If I had not obeyed the suggestion to prolong my stay and
believed I would have to stay still longer, I could have been
leaving next week. But this delay has been all for the good. I have
spent the extra time studying, and the epoch on which I had set
such hopes is now rounded off. It is always a strange feeling
suddenly to abandon a road along which one has been advancing
with great strides, but one must reconcile oneself to the necessity
and not make a great fuss about it. In every parting there is a
latent germ of madness, and one must beware not to tend it and
let it ripen in one's mind.

Kniep, the painter who accompanied me to Sicily, has sent me
some beautiful drawings of Naples. A few of them are really
delightful on account of their colour tones, and you will hardly
believe how beautiful that world is. They are lovely fruits of
my travels and will be most pleasant to you. The safest gift is
something one can let another see with his own eyes.

It is sad that I must leave Rome at the very point in my progress when I most deserve to stay, but I must be grateful that I
have been able to stay long enough to get as far as I have.

As I write these words, Christ has risen amid a terrific noise.
The cannons of the Castello are being fired off, all the bells are
ringing and from every part of the city one hears the explosions
of petards, rockets and powder trains. It is eleven o'clock in the
morning.

MARCH

FILIPPO NERI considered it his duty to give manifest proof of his pious fervour by frequent visits to the seven major churches of Rome, that is to say: San Pietro, Santa Maria Maggiore, San Lorenzo fuori le Mura, San Sebastiano, San Giovanni Laterano, Santa Croce di Gerusalemme, and San Paolo fuori le Mura. This visitation is now required of every pilgrim who comes to Rome for the Jubilee; it must be accomplished in a single day, and, considering how far apart these churches are, this amounts to another long pilgrimage in itself.

Some of the faithful who live in Rome also make this pilgrimage during Holy Week, most of them on Good Friday. Besides the spiritual benefit of the Indulgence which the faithful win thereby, a material advantage is now offered which makes that pilgrimage still more attractive. After completing the round and receiving a certificate to that effect, each pilgrim returns by the Porta San Paolo, where he is given a ticket which entitles him to participate on certain days in a public festival in the Villa Mattei. Those who are admitted receive a collation of bread, wine and cheese or eggs; they are allowed to picnic in various parts of the garden, and the favourite spot is its small amphitheatre. Facing this stands the Casino of the Villa, where high society – cardinals, bishops, princes and noblemen – gathers to enjoy the spectacle, which owes its existence to a charitable bequest by the Mattei family.

I saw a procession of some forty ten- to twelve-year-old boys, all of them modest and well behaved, advancing in double file and piously reciting their litanies. They were not dressed as seminarians; the uniforms they wore made them look more like apprentices on a Sunday. Their leader was an elderly man, who looked like a robust artisan and was walking beside them, keeping an eye on the group.

I was rather surprised to see that the rear of this procession of well-dressed boys was brought up by half a dozen beggarly-looking children in rags, who walked along, however, with the same good discipline and decorum. In response to my inquiries, I was told the following story. The man was a shoemaker by profession and without children of his own. Some time ago he had felt called by his conscience to take a boy into his house as an apprentice, clothe him with the help of charitable offerings from others, and set him up in life. Other masters had been inspired by his example to take in children whom he supported and assisted in various ways and, in this way, he had gathered about him a little band of children. To protect them against the dangers of idleness on Sundays and feast-days, he kept them continuously busy with godly works and even required them to visit the seven major churches in one day. This pious institution had steadily grown, and since there were now always more children applying to join it than could be accepted, as a stimulus to the charitable feelings of the public, he had hit upon the expedient of adding to his procession those children who were still in need of care and clothing, and he always managed to raise enough money for at least one of them.

While I was listening to this story, one of the older, well-dressed boys came up to me with a plate and asked in a modest, well-spoken manner for a contribution in aid of the naked and unshod. The foreigners who were present were touched and gave liberally, and even the Romans, who are stingy people, gave something and did not fail to add to their scanty donation the pious weight of their blessings and many words of commendation.

I was told, furthermore, that after the procession is over, the pious foster-father always gives his pupils a share of what they have collected, which shows that the takings for this worthy purpose must be quite considerable.

APRIL

CORRESPONDENCE

10 April

I AM still in Rome in the flesh but not in the spirit. As soon as I had made up my mind to leave, I lost all interest. I would rather have left two weeks ago, and have stayed on only for Kayser's and Bury's sake. Kayser has still to complete some research which he can only make in Rome, and collect some music. Bury has to finish the drawing for a painting; this was my idea and he needs my advice. But I have now fixed the day of my departure for April twenty-first or twenty-second.

11 April

The days go by and I can't do anything any more. I can hardly bring myself even to look at anything. My faithful friend Meyer is still at my side, so that I can enjoy the pleasure of his company up to the last moment. If it were not for Kayser, I would have taken him with me. If I could have him as a teacher for even one year, I should make considerable progress. He would be especially useful in helping me to overcome the difficulties I have in drawing heads.*

14 April

My state of confusion could hardly be greater. While I have never stopped working away at modelling the foot, it occurred to me that I must tackle *Tasso* forthwith, and all my thoughts are now turned in that direction. He will be a welcome companion on my imminent journey. In the meantime I have started packing. I had no conception, till I did, of how much stuff I have managed to accumulate.

---

*Goethe got his wish. Meyer settled in Weimar in 1792.

APRIL

MY correspondence during the last weeks of my stay contained little of consequence. I felt too torn between art and friendship, possession and aspiration, a familiar present and a future to which I would have to get used, to write much, and in the letters I did write, my joy at the prospect of seeing old friends again was expressed with moderation, while no secret was made of my grief at the thought of parting with new ones. What follows, therefore, is a scanty record, confined to what I can remember and what I can find preserved in notes and journals.

Tischbein was still in Naples, although he had repeatedly announced that he was coming back to Rome in the spring. In most respects he was easy to live with, but a certain habit of his made things difficult in the long run. Whenever he had to make plans, he would leave everything vague and so, without meaning to, he often caused others inconvenience and annoyance. In my case, since I was expecting his return and wanted us all to be comfortable, I had moved out of his rooms. The upper floor had just been vacated, so I rented it and moved in, in order that he should find everything downstairs just as it was when he left.

The upper rooms were like the lower ones, except that they enjoyed a delightful view of our garden and of neighbouring gardens in all directions, for our house stood on a corner. From my windows I looked down on many gardens of different sizes, separated by walls of equal height, and displaying an infinite variety of trees and flowers. From this paradise architectural forms of a noble simplicity emerged everywhere – garden pavilions, balconies, terraces and, on the higher houses in the background, loggias.

In our garden, an old secular priest looked after a number of lemon trees of medium height, planted in ornamental terracotta vases. In summer these enjoyed the fresh air, but in winter they were kept in a greenhouse. When the lemons were ripe, they were picked with care, wrapped singly in soft paper, packed and sent off. They were particularly choice specimens and much in demand on the market. Such an orangery was regarded by middle-class families as a captital investment which would pay a certain interest every year.

The same windows from which I could look out on so much beauty also provided me with a perfect light for looking at pictures. In accordance with our agreement, Kniep had just sent me a number of watercolours, executed after the sketches he drew on our journey across Sicily. Perhaps no one has been more successful in conveying the lucidity of the atmosphere than this artist, who made it his speciality. These water colours of his looked really enchanting; when I put them up, they made me believe I was back in Sicily again, seeing with my own eyes the ocean, the blue shadows of the rocks, the orange tones of the mountains and the horizon fading into the luminous sky. But it was not only water colours that benefited from the lighting in my room; any painting placed on an easel in the same place looked more striking than it did elsewhere. Several times when I entered the room and caught sight of one, I was spellbound.

At that time, the secret of proper lighting had not yet been discovered. People realized that lighting could be favourable or unfavourable, but this was regarded as accidental and inexplicable.

My new rooms made it possible for me to set up the plaster casts I had been steadily collecting in a pleasant order and to enjoy them by a good light.

The presence of works of art, like those of Nature, makes us restless. We wish to express our feelings and judgements in words, but before we can do that, we must first recognize, by intuition and understanding, what we are looking at; so we begin to identify, classify, differentiate. But then we find that this, too, if not impossible, is very difficult, so in the end we return to a wordless beholding.

The most decisive effect of all works of art is that they carry us back to the conditions of the period and of the individuals who created them. Standing amid antique statues, one feels as if all the forces of Nature were in motion around one. One is made aware of the multiplicity and diversity of human forms and brought back to man at his most authentic, so that the beholder himself is made more human and authentic. Even their drapery, which is true to Nature and brings out the figure in stronger relief, is agreeable as a rule. In Rome, where one is surrounded by such statues day after day, one becomes covetous and wishes to make them part of one's permanent surroundings, and the best way to do this is to acquire good plaster casts. Then, every morning, when one opens one's eyes, one is greeted by perfection; one's whole thinking becomes permeated by their presence, until it becomes impossible ever again to relapse into barbarism.

The first place in my rooms was occupied by Juno Ludovisi, which I valued all the more highly because the original was only rarely on view. Next to her stood some smaller Junos for comparison, several Jupiters, the Medusa Rondanini – a marvellous, mysterious and fascinating work, which represents a state between death and life, pain and pleasure – a Hercules Anax and a Mercury. The originals of these last two are now both in England.

Also, arranged in good order about my rooms, were half-reliefs, casts of terracotta works, Egyptian casts taken from the top of the obelisk, and sundry other fragments.

At the time I am speaking of, these treasures had stood there for only a few weeks, and I felt, as I looked at them, moved but calm, like someone making his will. The complications and expense of shipment and a certain lack of practicality on my part deterred me from sending the best of them back to Germany at once. My friend Angelica was to have the Juno Ludovisi, and a few other things were intended for my closest friends among the artists; several objects belonged to Tischbein and others were to be left behind for Bury, who was going to move in when I left.

As I write, my thoughts wander back to my youth and I recall the occasions when I first became acquainted with works of this kind which, immature as I was, yet filled me with such enthusiasm and an unbounded yearning for Italy.

When I was a boy, I did not see a single work of plastic art in my native town. The first I ever saw in my life was the Faun in Leipzig, who seemed to me to be dancing for joy as he clashed his cymbals, and I can vividly recall every detail of the cast to this day. Then for a long time I saw nothing until I suddenly discovered the Mannheim collection – I remember that the hall was well lit from above – and was completely overwhelmed.

Several years later some craftsmen arrived in Frankfurt with a number of original plaster casts which they had brought with them from Italy. They made copies of these which they sold at modest prices. In this way I was able to acquire a fairly good head of Laocoön, the daughters of Niobe, a small head, later identified as a Sappho, and a few other things. These noble forms acted as a kind of secret antidote at a time when I was in danger of falling a victim to the mediocre, the spurious and the mannered. During all those years, in fact, I was tormented by an unsatisfied longing for the unknown, which I never succeeded in suppressing, though I often tried. So, when I had to leave Rome, I suffered greatly at parting with all these possessions, which I had so longed for and at last acquired.

The laws governing plant organization of which I had become aware in Sicily continued to occupy my mind, as any interest is apt to do when it is suited to one's capacities. Though it is now neglected and uninteresting, the Botanical Garden in Trastevere was a beneficial influence, for much that I saw there was new and unexpected, and I was prompted by it to collect many rare plants and to observe the later development of those I grew from seed and kernels.

When I left Rome, several friends were anxious to divide these growing plants between them. I planted a promising pine shoot, the small model of a future tree, in Angelica's garden. After many years this grew to a considerable height, as I was happy to learn from more than one traveller, while in return I was able to tell them what I remembered about the spot. Alas, after the death of my dear, dear friend,* the new owner must have thought

---

* Angelica had died in 1807.

that it looked incongruous to have pine trees growing in the middle of his flowerbeds, for, later, when some kindly travellers investigated for me, they found the spot empty and that memorial to an amiable existence obliterated.

I had better luck with some date palms I had grown from kernels. From time to time I had sacrificed specimens in order to observe the stages of their peculiar growth. I gave the rest, which were in healthy condition, to a Roman friend, who planted them in a garden on the Via Sistina, where, as a distinguished visitor has graciously informed me, they are still alive and have grown to a man's height. May they never become inconvenient to their owners but continue to grow there and keep my memory green.

On my list of things to be visited before leaving Rome were two very disparate monuments, the Cloaca Maxima and the Catacombs of St Sebastian. The former was even more colossal than Piranesi's designs had led me to expect. My visit to the Catacombs, however, was not much of a success. I had hardly taken a step into that airless place before I began to feel uncomfortable, and I immediately returned to the light of day and the fresh air and waited, in that unknown and remote quarter of the city, for the return of the other visitors who were more daring and less sensitive than I was.

Later I learned all about what I had seen, or rather failed to see, from Antonio Bosio's great work *Roma sotterranea*, which made up sufficiently for what I had missed.

I made another pilgrimage, however, with more profit. I visited the Accademia di San Luca to pay homage to the skull of Raphael,* which has been preserved there ever since his tomb was opened in the course of some building operations. It was wonderful to look at – a brain-pan of beautiful proportions and perfectly smooth, without any of those protuberances and bumps which have been observed on other skulls and to which Gall's phrenological theories attach such importance. I could hardly tear myself away, and as I left, I thought how all lovers of Nature and of Art would value a cast of this skull, if it were in any way pos-

---

* Raphael: the skull was not authentic.

sible to get one made. My influential friend, Hofrat Reiffenstein, gave me hopes that he might be able to arrange this, which, after some time, he did and sent a cast to Germany for me, which I often look at and reflect upon.

I was also delighted by Raphael's picture of the Madonna appearing to St Luke, so that he may paint her in all her divine grace and beauty.* At some distance from the painting evangelist stands Raphael himself, still in his youth. It would be impossible to express more charmingly the way in which a man finds himself drawn to a particular vocation. The painting was originally owned by Pietro di Cortona, who left it to the Academy in his will. Though it has been damaged and restored in certain places, it is still a most important work.

During these days I was beset by a temptation which took me by surprise and threatened to prevent my departure and fetter me to Rome anew. A certain Signor Antonio Rega, who was both an artist and an art dealer, arrived from Naples, and went to see my friend Meyer, whom he invited to accompany him to a boat moored alongside the Ripa Grande, where, he told Meyer in confidence, he had on board an important antique statue, that very dancer or Muse which from time immemorial had occupied a niche in the courtyard of the Palazzo Carafa Colombrano in Naples and had always been considered an excellent work. Rega wished to sell it, but secretly, and wanted to know if Meyer himself, perhaps, or some friends of his whom he could trust would be interested in such a transaction. For this rare work of art he was asking the extremely modest sum of three hundred sequins, a figure which would certainly have been much higher if for the seller as well as for the buyer there had not been some reason for caution and secrecy.

I was told about the matter and the three of us hurried off at once to the landing place, which was at some distance from our home. A crate was lying on deck; Rega prised up a board and there we saw a charming little head, which looked as if it had never been separated from its torso, gazing up at us from out of

*The painting was not by Raphael but by Timoteo della Vite.

its ringlets, and, little by little, the whole graceful, slender, decorously clothed figure was uncovered. The figure itself was very little damaged and one hand was in a perfect state of preservation.

Immediately I had a vivid recollection of the place and the circumstances when I first saw her, little thinking that one day I would see her at such close quarters.

The thought now struck us, as it could hardly have failed to do, that someone who had been excavating for a whole year and at great expense would have thought himself extremely fortunate if, in the end, he had come upon such a treasure. We could not take our eyes off her; we had rarely seen such a perfect work of antiquity and one, moreover, which it would be easy to restore. But we tore ourselves away at last and left, having promised to give Rega an answer soon.

Both our minds were in a state of conflict; from many points of view it seemed inadvisable to make this purchase. We decided therefore to lay our problem before Angelica, who was not only well-off and therefore in a position to buy the statue, but was also a competent and qualified judge in such matters as restoration. Meyer, who acted as an intermediary before in the case of the picture by Daniele da Volterra, again undertook to do this, and we entertained high hopes of success. However, the prudent Angelica and, even more firmly, her thrifty husband would have nothing to do with it. Though they spent considerable sums on paintings, they refused to consider buying any sculpture.

After receiving this negative answer, we thought over this whole matter again and grew more and more excited; such a chance seemed far too good to miss. Meyer examined the statue again carefully and was satisfied that all the evidence pointed to its being a Greek work, dating from long before the Augustan age, perhaps from the time of Hieron II.* I had enough credit to buy it, and Rega even seemed willing to be paid in instalments, and there came a moment when I saw myself as its proud owner and imagined it standing in a good light in our *sala*.

Just as many sober reflections must intrude between a pas-

---

* Hieron II, tyrant of Syracuse (270–216 B.C.).

sionate affection and a binding marriage contract, so I could not go further without taking the advice of the Zucchis; for, in an ideal, Pygmalion-like sense, the thought of possessing the creature had struck deep roots in my heart. Indeed, to show how much I flattered myself in this matter, I have to confess that I took this incident as a sign that higher spirits meant to keep me in Rome and squash all the practical reasons which had made me decide to leave.

Fortunately I had already reached an age when reason usually comes to the rescue of the mind in such cases, and my passionate eagerness to possess this work, my sophistry and superstition finally yielded to Angelica's wisdom and common sense. Listening to her objections, I realized all the difficulties and risks which told against a venture of this kind. Till then I had quietly dedicated myself to the study of art and antiquity; if I were now suddenly to involve myself in the art trade, I would arouse the jealousy of the professional dealers. Then there were many difficulties about restoring the statue, and it was doubtful whether I could get this done honestly and at a reasonable cost. Even when all the arrangements had been made for shipping, it was not at all certain that a hitch might not occur at the last moment over the export permit required for works of art of this kind, not to mention all the possibilities of an accident during the voyage, the unloading, and the getting it home. The professional dealer, she pointed out, can disregard such considerations because of the volume of his trade, but a single venture like this would always be very risky.

Such arguments gradually weakened my desire though they never completely extinguished it, especially when in the end the statue achieved a place of great honour, for it now stands in a small room adjoining the Museo Pio Clementino, the floor of which is inlaid with beautiful mosaics of masks and festoons. Visconti has described this statue and interpreted it in his own fashion in his third volume, which is dedicated to this museum, and he gives a reproduction of it on Plate xxx, so that every lover of art can share my regret that I did not succeed in bringing it to Germany to give to one of our country's great collections.

My readers will hardly be surprised to hear that I did not forget to pay a farewell visit to the fair young lady from Milan. I had in the meantime often had pleasant news about her, how she had become more and more intimate with Angelica, and how well she behaved in the high society to which my friend had introduced her. I had also good reason to suppose that a well-to-do young man, a friend of the Zucchis, was not insensitive to her charms, and to hope that his intentions were serious and that he meant to declare them.

I found her in a becoming morning gown, like the one in which I had seen her for the first time in Castel Gandolfo. She was openly glad to see me and again expressed her gratitude for the interest I had taken in her. 'I shall never forget', she said, 'that when I was recovering from my fever, I heard you mentioned as being one of those dear and kind persons who had inquired after my health. I asked many times if this was really true, and was told that you continued to make inquiries for several weeks, until at last my brother could visit you and thank you on behalf of us both. I do not know if he delivered my message exactly as I gave it him; if it had been proper I would have come with him.' She asked me about the route I was going to take, and when I had told her my itinerary, she said: 'You are lucky to be so rich that you can afford all this; we others have to resign ourselves to the station in life which God and the Saints have allotted to us. For a long time I have been watching the little boats loading and unloading; it is very amusing but I often think: where do they come from and where do they go to?' Her windows looked out directly on the stairs of the Ripetta, and the traffic at this time was very busy.

She spoke with tenderness of her brother and told me how happy she was to keep house for him and enable him to save something out of his modest salary to invest in a profitable business; in short, she made me quite familiar with her domestic situation. Her conversation gave me great pleasure. To tell the truth, I cut a rather strange figure, since I was compelled to relive so quickly all the details of our affectionate relationship from the first moment to the last. But then her brother entered and our farewell ended in sober prose.

When I left the house I found my carriage but no driver and sent a boy to look for him. She looked out of a window on the mezzanine floor of their handsome house – the window was not very high up and we could easily have shaken hands. 'You see', I called up to her, 'the Fates don't want me to go away. They seem to know that I leave you against my will.'

What she said then and what I said in return – the course of this delightful conversation, free from all restraint, in which the inner feelings of two people who were half in love with each other were revealed – I shall not profane by repeating. Occasioned by chance, extorted by an inner need, it was a strange, laconic, final confession of an innocent and tender mutual affection, which has never faded from my soul.

My farewell to Rome was heralded in a particularly solemn manner: for three consecutive nights a full moon stood in a cloudless sky, diffusing its magic over the immense city, and more than ever before, I felt myself transported into another simpler and greater world.

At the end of each day, spent in distractions mingled with sadness, I took a walk with a few friends, and on one evening I went out quite alone. After having wandered along the Corso – perhaps for the last time – I walked up to the Capitol, which rose like an enchanted palace in a desert. The statue of Marcus Aurelius reminded me of the Commendatore in *Don Giovanni*, for it seemed to be intimating to the wanderer that he was venturing upon something unusual. Nevertheless, I walked down by the stairs at the back. There I was suddenly confronted by the dark triumphal arch of Septimius Severus, which cast a still darker shadow. In the solitude of the Via Sacra the well-known objects seemed alien and ghost-like. But when I approached the grand ruins of the Colosseum and looked through the gate into the interior, I must frankly confess that a shudder ran through me, and I quickly returned home.

Any gigantic mass has a peculiar effect on me; it has something about it which is at once fascinating and awe-inspiring. I drew up a *summa summarum* of my whole stay in Italy, and this aroused in my agitated soul a mood I might call heroic-elegiac, for it tried to embody itself in the poetic form of an elegy.

At such a moment, how could I fail to remember the elegy of Ovid,* the poet who also was exiled and forced to leave Rome on a moonlit night? *Cum repeto noctem.* I could not get him out of my head, with his homesick memories, his sadness and misery far away on the shores of the Black Sea. I tried to recite his poem to myself and parts of it came back word for word, but the only effect of this was to confuse and frustrate my own composition, and when, later, I tried to take it up again, I could get nowhere with it.

> *Cum subit illius tristissima noctis imago,*
> *Quae mihi supremum tempus in Urbe fuit;*
> *Cum repeto noctem, qua tot mihi cara reliqui;*
> *Labitur ex oculis nunc quoque gutta meis.*
> *Iamque quiescebant voces hominumque canumque:*
> *Lunaque nocturnos alta regebat equos.*
> *Hanc ego suspiciens, et ab hac Capitolia cernens,*
> *Quae nostro frustra iuncta fuere Lari.*

* Ovid's *Tristia*, Book III.

INDEX

Academy of the Olympians (Vicenza), meeting, 67
Accademia di San Luca, 492
Acqua Acetosa, 358, 375
Acqua Paola, 432
Agincourt, Chevalier d', 363
Albacini, C., 361
Albani, Cardinal, 160
Albano, 349, 387, 389, 398, 426
Albany, Duke of (the Young Pretender), 448, 457
Alcamo, 260, 261
Aldobrandini, Prince, 375, 381
Allegri, Vittorio, 483n
amphitheatre (Verona), 52
Andreas, F. (restorer of old paintings), 206
Angelica, see Kauffmann
Antoninus, column, 364
Apollo, the Giustiniani, 382
Apollo Belvedere, 11, 136, 148, 152, 352, 363, 394
aqueduct (Spoleto) 124
Arcadian Society, 442–6
Archenholz, J. W., 146
Ariosto, 92, 105, 371
art, collections, 196, 315, 491 picture galleries
Art and Nature, see Nature
art dealers, 370
Assisi, 120–2
Atellanae fabulae, 322

Balsamo family, see Cagliostro
Bartels, J. H., 282, 331
Baudelaire, C., 12
beast baiting, 361

Beccaria, C. B., 192
Bembo, Cardinal, 70
Benediktbeuren, monastery, 29
Berio, Marchese, 221
Biscari, Dowager Princess, 282
Biscari, Prince, 281–2
boatmen, singing of Venetian, 91–3
Bodmer, J. J., 134
Boehme, Jacob, 95
Bologna, 107–15
Bolzano, 37–8
Borch, Count, 245, 284
Bordone, Paris, 472
Borgia, Cavaliere, 179
Bosio, Antonio, 492
botanical gardens, 65, 71, 147, 491
botanical speculations 17, 71, 147, 174, 204, 258–9, 262–3, 310–11, 366–8, 379, 386, 389, 491
Buoncompagni, Cardinal, 376
Bury, F., 15, 369, 380, 381, 426n, 487, 490
Byron, 16

Cagliostro, 8, 18
Caltabellotta, 264
Caltanissetta, 273
Camper, P., 402
Capitol, 163, 360, 364, 375, 441, 476, 497
Capua, 207
Caracalla stadium, 137, 431–2
Carlsbad, 14, 23, 31, 314
Carracci, 110, 395
Caserta, 207–9

Cassas, L. F., 387, 390–2
Castel Gandolfo, 400–3, 406, 426, 496
Castelvetrano, 263–4
Casti Abbé, 361, 370
castrati, 366
Castrogiovanni, 275–6
catacombs, 492
Catania, 278–81
Catherine, Empress, 393, 401n
Cento, 106–7
Chigi, Prince, 179
Chigi Palace, 364
Cimarosa, D., 366n, 369
Claudius, Matthias, 399n, 404
Clerisseau, C. L., 169
Cloaca Maxima, 492
coins, collections, 196, 242, 281
Colosseum, 137, 168, 364, 405, 497
copperplate engravings, 16th c., 420
Corneille, 11
Correggio, 216, 480
Corso (Rome), 447–8
Cortona, Pietro di, 493
Crébillon, P., 90
crèches, Neapolitan, 316
Crescimbeni, 316
Cupido, you wanton, obstinate boy ... (poem), 442, 473

Dalberg, 413
Dante, 371, 444
David, J. L., 381
Diede, Mr and Mrs von, 476
Dies, 363
Domenichino, 110, 139
Doria, Prince, 482
Dorigny, 356, 357
Dow, Gerard, 213

Drouais, 473
Dürer, Albrecht, 108, 478

earthquakes, 193, 291, 312
Egyptian art, 391, 392
encaustic painting, 146, 393–4
English in Italy, 70, 96, 102, 159, 315–16
Enna, 277
Etna, 271, 279, 286, 387

Etruscan vases, 196–7

Feast: of St Anthony, 162; of St Joseph, 213; of Corpus Christi, 325, 345, 355; of St Peter and St Paul, 348
Ferrara, 105–6
Filangieri, Cavaliere, 190–2, 197, 202, 203
Florence, 117
Foligno, 121
food, 50, 202–3, 213, 247, 266, 324–5, 353
Forster, G., 401, 402
Francia, Francesco, 108
Francis, St, 393
Frascati, 138, 349, 384, 387, 388–9, 394–5, 426
Frederick II, 274
Freemasons, 299n
French Academy, exhibition, 378, 381
Fries, Count, 314, 361, 370, 380, 477

Garda, Lake, 41–8, 51
Garve C., 328
gems, carved, 370, 379; wax impressions of, 387; paste imitations of, 393, 394; geological comments, 23, 23–4,

25, 27–8, 31, 125, 126–7,
230, 243, 260, 261, 262–3,
264, 267, 270, 271, 273, 274,
275, 276, 284–5, 290–1. 298;
see also mineralogical
comments
Gioeni, Cavaliere, 284
Giordano, Luca, 191
Giotto, 10
Giovene, Duchess of, 327
Girgenti, 264–73
Goethe:
  as poet and writer, xiii–xiv,
    7–10, 11, 12, 16–17
  on his literary work, 17, 35,
    155, 156, 157–8, 169–70,
    207–8, 216, 224, 287–90, 359,
    365, 373, 374, 383, 384, 386,
    398, 399, 401, 405, 415–16,
    418–19, 425, 440–1, 471–2,
    473, 474, 479
  publication of his works, 35,
    169, 207, 388, 398, 406, 474,
    479–80
  views on describing things,
    8–10, 125
  life crises, 11
  at Weimar, 12–13
  interest in historical
    development, 9–10
  scientific studies, 13; *see also*
    botanical speculations,
    geological, meteorological,
    mineralogical comments
  interest in anatomy, 163
  appreciation of art, 10–11, 346,
    347, 362, 363, 365, 379, 380,
    381, 385, 425, 426, 472, 473
  learning to draw, 15, 172, 206,
    345, 358, 363, 365, 373–4,
    375, 387, 395, 400, 411, 487

  modelling, 481, 482, 487
  and visual arts, 417, 473
  portraits of, 153–4, 174
  bust of, 378, 379, 381, 386
  appreciation of music, 82–3,
    416, 418–20, 480–1; musical
    party given by, 369–70
  longing for Italy, 13, 103–4,
    128–9, 491
  memories of his father, 74, 129,
    186
  dream of a boat, 112, 222
  hopes for humanity, 309–10,
    316–17
  relationships, 15, 16, 144, 154,
    166, 186–7, 204, 210, 314–15,
    326–7, 358, 370–1, 380, 397,
    398, 399, 400–1, 402, 403,
    427–8, 475–6, 483; with
    Maddalena Ricci, 403, 407–13,
    435, 475–6, 495–7; *see also*
    Bury, Kauffmann, Kayser,
    Kniep, Tischbein *et. al.*
  comments: on himself, 38,
    136–7, 148, 151, 152, 167, 209,
    210, 216, 220, 221, 246, 258,
    269, 345, 346, 347, 348–9,
    374, 377, 380, 383, 386, 387,
    388, 389, 397–8, 400, 406,
    413, 427–8, 441, 442, 472, 473,
    481, 482, 483, 484, 487, 488,
    490; on political events,
    36n, 385, 402
  works referred to:
    *The Accomplices (Die
      Mitschuldigen)*, 30n
    The Birds (Die Vögel), 35n,
      44, 247n
    Claudine von Villa Bella,
      405, 415–16, 418, 440,
      442n, 471

Goethe—*continued*
  works referred to—*continued*
    Egmont, 16, 17, 359, 360, 362,
      365, 373, 383, 384, 406,
      415, 416, 418, 425, 436–7,
      440, 441, 473
    Erwin und Elmire, 386, 401,
      405, 418, 440–1, 472
    Faust, 7, 17, 374, 415, 440, 479
    Götz von Berlichingen, 158n
    Iphigenie auf Tauris, 16, 17,
      35, 111–12, 155–6, 157–8,
      164, 169–70, 175, 187, 204,
      207
    Italian Journey, compilation
      and publication of, 18
    *Das Jahrmarktsfest zu
      Plundersweilern*, 173n
    Jery und Bätely, 471n
    *Jest, Cunning and Revenge
      (Scherz, List und Rache)*,
      405n, 418, 419, 420n
    Lila, 471n
    Nausicaa, 258, 288 and n,
      289–90
    Tasso, 17, 170, 175, 208, 224,
      225, 226, 374, 415, 440,
      471, 479, 487
    Werther, 11 221, 237, 311–12,
      424, 471
    Wilhelm Meister, 216, 359,
      398, 472
Goldoni, C., 100–1
Gotha, Duke of, 329
Greek art, 161–2
Guercino, 106–7, 111, 131
Guido [Reni], 110–11, 131

Hackert, Philipp, 138, 139, 186,
  205, 206, 268, 273, 315, 345,
  347, 350, 374

Hamilton, Sir William, 208, 216,
  315, 353, 354, 372
Hannibal, 229n
harp player's daughter, 28
Harrach, Countess, 143
Hart, Miss (later Lady Hamilton),
  8, 208, 315, 316, 354, 372
Herculaneum, 211
Hercules, the Farnese, 161, 346
Herder, J. G., 13, 14, 35, 104, 151,
  153, 157, 173, 204, 220, 316,
  328, 362, 383, 384, 398n, 401,
  403, 405, 413, 437, 440, 471,
  479; letters to, 309–11, 378–9,
  401–3
Hirt, A. L., 422–3
Holy Week, 481, 482, 483–4
Homer, 236, 310, 385

Innsbruck, 30
Italians, comments on, 50–1,
  68–9, 118–19, 129, 144, 145,
  199

Jaci, the stacks of, 285
Jacobi, F. H., 399n, 404
Jacquier, Father, 166
Jenkins, T., 369, 407, 408, 412
Jesuits, 24–5, 39–40, 297
Joseph II, 192, 360n

Kauffmann, Angelica: her
  appreciation of Goethe's
  poetry, 15, 165, 169, 405,
  436–7; as painter, 204, 346,
  375–6, 379, 415, 472; as
  companion for looking at
  pictures, 359, 361, 363, 375,
  381, 480; as friend, 401, 402,
  425, 491–2; befriends
  Maddalena Ricci, 475–6,

495–6; other references, 15, 165n, 346, 361, 369, 386, 401, 405, 409, 410, 472, 494, 495

Kayser, Christopher, 15, 383, 389, 397, 405, 406, 415, 416, 417, 418, 419, 426, 440, 473, 474, 476, 478, 479, 481, 482, 483, 487

Kierkegaard, 12

Kniep, C. H.: relations with Goethe, 217–18, 219, 221, 241, 247, 285, 325–6, 329, 330; travelling companion on Sicilian journey, 223, 224, 225, 226, 227, 228, 229, 236, 259, 267, 268, 272, 285, 286, 287, 298, 299, 301, 302, 303, 304, 307, 308, 353; as artist, 212, 217–18, 225, 227, 241, 280, 302, 304, 484, 489; his sweetheart, 219–20

Kranz, J. F., 369, 387

Kraus, Melchior, 475

Lavater, J. K., 377n, 399n, 402, 403

Lawrence, D. H., 9

legal trial at the Palazzo Ducale, Venice, 84–6

Leibniz, 379n

Leonardo da Vinci, 166, 363, 366, 375, 381, 472

Lido, 96–7

Liechtenstein, Prince, 143, 144

Linnaeus, 33

Lipps, J. H., 15, 380, 381, 415

literati, 370

Lorrain, Claude, 174, 347

Lucchesini, Marchese, 326, 351, 359

Malcesine, 8

Malta, 272

Mantegna, A., 72

Maratti, Carlo, 131

Marcantonio, 356, 357

Marcello, Benedetto, 478

Marlborough, 60

Medusa, the Rondanini, 152, 364–5, 490

Mengs, A., 140, 363, 421, 477, 480

Merian, Matthaeus, 307n

Messina, 291–301; Governor, 8, 293–4, 296–7, 209, 300, 301

meteorological comments, 23, 25, 26 27, 29, 49, 125, 272

Meyer, Heinrich, 15, 132, 346, 414, 421, 427, 482, 487, 493, 494

Michelangelo, 141, 147, 366, 371, 380, 478

Mignon, 182, 413

mineralogical comments, 25, 27–8, 49–50, 114–15, 140, 181, 188–9, 194, 204, 214–15, 230, 245–6, 261, 262, 256, 267, 270, 283–4, 298, 327, 328; see also geological comments

Molimenti, 278

Momper, Jodokus, 302

Monreale, 242, 259

Montesquieu, 192

Monti, Abbate, 143, 161

Moor, J., 359–60

Morales, C., 478

Moritz, K. P., 15, 19, 145, 149, 157, 158, 173, 358, 375, 381, 383, 389, 398, 437, 438, 441

mosaic, 94

Mozart, 420

Munich, 25

Münter, F., 151, 282, 331
museums, 54, 179–80, 204, 211–12,
    242, 326, 346–7; seen by
    torchlight, 421–2

Naples, 184–222, 309–41;
    characteristics, 185, 207, 210,
    215, 323–4; beauty of, 186,
    191, 219; compared with
    Rome, 189, 208; art treasures,
    195; *see also* crèches,
    painting
Naples, the King of (Ferdinand
    IV), 185, 186, 192, 206, 209,
    346
Nature, 147, 157, 171, 173, 188,
    196, 279, 320, 377, 400, 404,
    411, 433, 443, 482; a work
    of art and, 286; relation
    between Art and, 347, 385
Neapolitan Princess (Princess
    Ravaschieri di Satriano), 8,
    200, 201–3, 312–13
Neapolitans: happiness of,
    184–5; 199–200; naturalness
    of, 213; laziness of, confuted,
    317
Neer, A. van der, 325
Neri, Filippo, 313–14, 331–41, 485

Odyssey, 258, 288, 310
opera, 65, 83, 370, 395–6
operettas, 418–20
Orbetto, 57
Ossian, 11
Ovid, 342, 498

Padua, 69–73
Paestum, 11, 217–18, 309
painting, Neapolitan school, 191
Palatine, 137, 364, 392

Palermo, 226–59; filth of, 232–3;
    Public Gardens, 235, 258, 288,
    366, 236, 237
Palestrina, 482, 483n
Palladio, 11, 63–4, 66, 68, 70,
    80–2, 95, 96, 103, 120, 121
Pallagonia, Prince of, and his
    villa, 11, 237–42, 245
Pantheon, 136, 148
Pauw, Cornelius von, 320
Pergolesi, G. B., 419
Perugia, 119
Perugia, Pietro di, 108
Petrarch, 444
Piazzetta, G. B., 72
picture galleries, 25–6, 57–8,
    347, 381; *see also* art,
    collections of
Plant, the Primal, *see* botanical
    speculations
plant life, 32–3, 37, 71, 96–7,
    117–18, 147, 170, 181, 182,
    207, 209, 238, 262, 264, 265,
    266, 267, 274, 275, 276, 277,
    278, 287, 481
Plato, 399
Pliny 322
Pompeii, 198–9, 203–4
Pontine Marshes, drainage, 180
Pope, 130, 157
Pordenone, 132
Porta, Guglielmo della, 162, 346
Pourtalès, M. de, 382
Poussin, 347
presepe, 316
Propaganda, 160
Psammetichos II, obelisk, 383n
Pulcinella, 212, 213, 239, 401,
    451, 469

Racine, 11

Raphael, 108, 111, 135, 139, 147, 325, 345, 356–7, 363, 366, 371, 380, 393, 395, 429–31, 432–3, 434, 482–3; the skull of, 480, 492–3

Ravaschieri di Satriano, Princess, 197n; *see* Neapolitan Princess

Rega, Signor Antonio, 493, 494

Regensburg, 24–5

Reiffenstein, Hofrat J. F., 136, 138, 146, 165, 169, 358, 369, 381, 386, 393, 394, 395, 400, 412, 492

Rezzonico, Count, 457, 476, 477

Ricci, Maddalena, 403; *see* Goethe: relationships

Riedesel, J. H. von, 269, 282

Roman Carnival, 174–5, 446–7, 476

Roman State, 405

Rome, 128–76, 345–498; first impressions, 132–3; as an education, 148–9, 151, 154, 164, 171, 175, 374, 392–3; history 165–6, 167; moonlight walk through, 168; German travellers to, 414; a tour of, 429–36

Rosa, Salvator, 347

Rosalie, Santa, shrine, 233–5

Rosso, Monte, 284, 285

Rousseau, J. J., 92, 210

Rubens, 26

St Cecilia, church, 142

St Peter, church, 136, 141–2, 157, 434, 481

Sakuntala, 187 and n

Salerno, 216

San Martino, monastery, 242–3

Sant'Agata, 182–4

Sarto, Andrea del, 361

Scamozzi, V., 66

Schiller, 15

Schlosser, Georg, 202

Schubart, F. C., 418

Schütz, Georg, 15, 395, 475

Schwendimann, 145

sculpture, 26, 94–6, 152, 159, 161–2, 195, 231, 243, 265, 363, 364–5, 489–91, 493–5

Scylla and Charybdis, 301–2

sea, comments, 96, 97, 98, 99–100, 173, 181, 196, 204, 227, 288, 310

Segesta, 261–3

Sesostris, obelisk, 383–4, 392

Seydelmann, 421

Shakespeare, 7, 11

Sicily: thoughts of voyage to, 190, 207, 209, 220–1; voyage to, 223–6; visit, 226–308; return voyage from, 8, 301–8; 'the clue to everything', 246; 'the Granary of Italy', 273

Sistine Chapel, 141, 146, 148, 171, 376, 380, 474, 478, 480, 482, 483, 484

Spinoza, 104, 187n, 377

Spoleto, aqueduct, 124

Stein, Charlotte von, 12, 13

Sturm und Drang, 11

Sulzer, J. G., 139, 206

Syracuse, 272

Tacitus, 125

Taormina, 286–8

Tapestries, Papal, 354–5

Tasso, 92, 105, 170; *see also* Goethe: works: *Tasso*

Temples: Minerva (Assisi),
120–1; Segesta, 261–2;
Girgenti, 265, 267–8, 269
theatres, 86, 88, 89, 90, 100–2,
103, 157, 196, 387, 401, 465
Theron, tomb, 268
Thürmer, 477
Thurneisen, 426
Tiber, bathing, 373
time measurements, Italian and
German, 61
Tintoretto, 58
Tischbein, J. H. W.: relations
with Goethe, 134–5, 138–9,
140, 141, 153, 175, 176, 192,
194, 195, 209, 212, 311, 347,
371–2, 397, 488; as a painter,
134–5, 153, 174, 208, 349, 358,
416, 481
other references, 15, 132, 141,
158, 186, 187, 188, 205, 346,
362, 490; letter from, 350–7
Titian 57, 72, 94, 131, 472
Tivoli, 345
Torremuzza, Prince, 244
Trajan Column, 364
Trenck, F. von der, 387
Trento, 38–40
Trippel, A., 379, 381–2
Turra, A., 65
Tuscany, 117–18

Unterberger, 394
Ursel, Duke and Duchess von,
315

Velletri, 180
Venice, 74–104
Venuti, Cavaliere, 327

Verona, 52–63
Veronese, 58, 93, 94
Verschaffelt, M. von, 374, 382
Vesuvius, 8, 145, 174, 183, 184,
186, 192, 196, 214, 219, 304,
325, 326, 328–9; ascents of,
188–9, 192–5, 214–15
Vicenza, 63–9
Vico, Giambattista, 192
Virgil, 42
Visconti, Cardinal, 480
Vite, Timoteo della, 493n
Vitruvius, P., 103, 120
Volkmann, J. J., 42, 107, 120, 172,
317, 434
Volpato, G., 371, 409
Voltaire, 166
Volterra, Daniele da, 346, 494

Waldeck, Prince, 187, 196, 222,
379
Waldsassen, monastery, 23
water-colour painting, 228
Weimar, Dowager Duchess of,
374, 388, 400, 413, 416, 481n
Weimar, Grand Duke of, 12, 14,
315, 369, 390, 481n
Wieland, C. M., 406 and n
Winckelmann, J. J., 145, 148,
159, 167, 195, 269, 282, 421
Winterkasten 124 and n
Worsley, Sir Richard, 377

Xenophanes of Colophon, 385n

Yeats, W. B., 13

Zucchi, A., 165n, 169, 363, 369,
409, 491 and n, 494, 495

MORE ABOUT PENGUINS

Penguinews, which appears every month, contains details of all the new books issued by Penguins as they are published. From time to time it is supplemented by *Penguins in Print*, which is a complete list of all books published by Penguins which are in print. (There are well over three thousand of these.)

A specimen copy of *Penguinews* will be sent to you free on request, and you can become a subscriber for the price of the postage. For a year's issues (including the complete lists) please send 4s. if you live in the United Kingdom, or 8s. if you live elsewhere. Just write to Dept EP, Penguin Books Ltd, Harmondsworth, Middlesex, enclosing a cheque or postal order, and your name will be added to the mailing list.

Some other Penguin Classics are described on the following pages.

Note: *Penguinews* and *Penguins in Print* are not available in the U.S.A. or Canada

ALSO BY GOETHE

FAUST

PARTS ONE AND TWO

Translated by Philip Wayne

Goethe's activities as poet, statesman, theatre director, critic, and scientist show him to be a genius of amazing versatility. This quality is reflected in his *Faust*, which ranks with the achievements of Homer, Dante and Shakespeare. The mood of the play shifts constantly, displaying in turn the poet's controlled energy, his wit, his irony, his compassion, and above all his gift for lyrical expression. *Faust*, which Goethe began in his youth and worked on during the greater part of his lifetime, takes for its theme the universal experience of the troubled human soul, but its spiritual values far transcend mere satanism and its consequences.

In *Part 1* Goethe gives the world the famous myth that embodies love and devilment and human aspiration. In *Part 2* he brings the constantly striving Faust through the utmost reaches of human speculation to a salvation evoking the most profound poetic compassion. Together they form an integrated whole which, in Goethe's words, 'permanently preserves the period of development of a human soul'. *Faust* is universal and relevant to every age – a myth in which each man may discover his own meaning.

THE PENGUIN CLASSICS

The Most Recent Volumes

LA BRUYÈRE
Characters *Jean Stewart*

PLATO
The Laws *T. J. Saunders*

GREEK POLITICAL ORATORY
A. N. W. Saunders

TURGENEV
Home of the Gentry *Richard Freeborn*

SCHOPENHAUER
Essays and Aphorisms *R. J. Hollingdale*

MENCIUS
D. C. Lau

BEROUL
The Romance of Tristan *Alan S. Fedrick*

XENOPHON
Memoirs of Socrates *and* The Symposium *Hugh Tredennick*

ZOLA
L'Assommoir *L. W. Tancock*

BALZAC
A Harlot High and Low *Rayner Heppenstall*